Ambiguities of Empire

This book comprises essays offered by friends, colleagues, and former students in tribute to Andrew Porter, on the occasion of his retirement from the Rhodes Chair in Imperial History at the University of London. The contributors, including many distinguished historians, explore through a variety of case studies 'ambiguities of empire' and of imperial and quasi-imperial relationships, reflecting important themes in Professor Porter's own writing.

Whilst the range of articles reflects the breadth of Andrew Porter's scholarly collaborations and interests, the chapters focus in particular on two aspects of imperial history which have been the subject of his particular attention: religion and empire, and the end of empire. This book contains original pieces on the history of British imperialism currently the subject of considerable scholarly attention. This book will be invaluable to students and scholars of empire, religion and colonialism.

This book was published as a special issue of the *Journal of Imperial and Commonwealth History*.

Robert Holland is Professor of Imperial and Commonwealth History at the School of Advanced Study, University of London. Amongst his chief publications are *Britain and the Commonwealth Alliance, 1918-39* (1981); *European Decolonization, 1918-91: An introductory survey*; *The Pursuit of Greatness: Britain and the World Role, 1900-1970*; and most recently *Britain and the Revolt in Cyprus, 1954-59*.

Sarah Stockwell is Senior Lecturer in Imperial and Commonwealth History in the History Department, King's College, London. Her previous publications include *The Business of Decolonisation: British Business Strategies in the Gold Coast*; *Imperial Policy and Colonial Practice, 1925-1945* (co-edited with S.R. Ashton); and her recent edited volume, *The British Empire. Themes and Perspectives*.

Ambiguities of Empire

Essays in Honour of Andrew Porter

Edited by Robert Holland and Sarah Stockwell

LONDON AND NEW YORK

First published 2009 by Routledge
2 Park Square, Milton Park, Abingdon, Oxon, OX14 4RN

Simultaneously published in the USA and Canada
by Routledge
711 Third Avenue, New York, NY 10017

Routledge is an imprint of the Taylor & Francis Group, an informa business

© 2009 Edited by Robert Holland and Sarah Stockwell
First issued in paperback 2013

Typeset in Times by Value Chain, India

All rights reserved. No part of this book may be reprinted or reproduced or utilised in any form or by any electronic, mechanical, or other means, now known or hereafter invented, including photocopying and recording, or in any information storage or retrieval system, without permission in writing from the publishers.

British Library Cataloguing in Publication Data
A catalogue record for this book is available from the British Library

ISBN13: 978-0-415-46658-5 (hbk)
ISBN13: 978-0-415-85260-9 (pbk)

Contents

Notes on Contributors   vi

Professor Andrew Porter   viii

Introduction
Andrew Porter   **Robert Holland and Sarah Stockwell**   1

1. Transatlantic Protestantism and American Independence   **P. J. Marshall**   5

2. 'A Good West Indian, a Good African, and, in Short, a Good Britisher': Black and British in a Colour-Conscious Empire, 1760–1950   **David Killingray**   23

3. Patterns of Anglo-Hellenism: A 'Colonial' Connection?   **Robert Holland**   42

4. Missionary Manhood: Professionalism, Belief and Masculinity in the Nineteenth-Century British Imperial Field   **Rhonda A. Semple**   56

5. The Ambiguous Amir: Britain, Afghanistan and the 1897 North-West Frontier Uprising   **Keith Surridge**   75

6. The Church of the Three Selves: A Perspective from the World Missionary Conference, Edinburgh, 1910   **Brian Stanley**   93

7. Distance and Proximity in Service to the Empire: Ulster and New Zealand between the Wars   **Keith Jeffery**   110

8. Law, Politics and Analogy in Akan Historiography   **Richard Rathbone**   130

9. Leaders, Dissidents and the Disappointed: Colonial Students in Britain as Empire Ended   **A. J. Stockwell**   144

10. The Central African Federation and Britain's Post-War Nuclear Programme: Reconsidering the Connections   **L. J. Butler**   165

11. Overseas Mission, Voluntary Service and Aid to Africa: Max Warren, the Church Missionary Society and Kenya, 1945–63   **John Stuart**   182

12. 'Splendidly Leading the Way'? Archbishop Fisher and Decolonisation in British Colonial Africa   **Sarah Stockwell**   199

Index   219

Notes on Contributors

L. J. Butler is senior lecturer in contemporary British history at the University of East Anglia. After doctoral research at King's College London supervised by Andrew Porter, he held lectureships at Queen Mary (University of London) and the University of Luton. His publications include *Industrialisation and the British Colonial State: West Africa 1939–1951*, *Britain and Empire: Adjusting to a Post-Imperial World* and *Copper Empire: Mining and the Colonial State in Northern Rhodesia, c.1930–64*.

Robert Holland is professor of imperial and Commonwealth history in the Institute of Commonwealth Studies, University of London. He has written extensively on British and European decolonisation, and in recent years has been principally interested in eastern Mediterranean history during the nineteenth and twentieth centuries. His most recent book (with Diana Markides) is *The British and the Hellenes: Struggles for Mastery in the Eastern Mediterranean, 1850–1960* (Oxford University Press, 2006).

Keith Jeffery is professor of British history at Queen's University Belfast. He is the author or editor of thirteen books including *Field Marshal Sir Henry Wilson: A Political Soldier* (Oxford University Press, 2006), which was awarded the Society for Army Historical Research's Templer Medal Book Prize in 2007; *The GPO and the Easter Rising* (Irish Academic Press, 2006); *Ireland and the Great War* (Cambridge University Press, 2000); and *A Military History of Ireland*, edited with Thomas Bartlett (Cambridge, 1996). In 2005 he was appointed to write the *Official History of the British Secret Intelligence Service, 1909–49*, which is scheduled for publication in 2010.

David Killingray is emeritus professor of history, Goldsmiths College, and a senior research fellow at the Institute of Commonwealth Studies, the University of London. He has written books and articles on aspects of African, Caribbean, imperial and English local history.

P. J. Marshall was Rhodes professor of imperial history at King's College, University of London, from 1981 to 1995. He was editor of *The Cambridge Illustrated History of the British Empire* (Cambridge, 1996) and of *The Oxford History of the British Empire*, vol. 2, *The Eighteenth Century* (Oxford, 1998). His books include *East India Fortunes: The British in Bengal in the Eighteenth Century* (Oxford, 1976) and *The Making and Unmaking of Empires: Britain, India and America c. 1750–1783* (Oxford, 2005).

Richard Rathbone is professor emeritus of modern African history at the School of Oriental and African Studies, University of London, and honorary professor in history and Welsh history at Aberystwyth University. His books include *Ghana* (London, 1992), *Murder and Politics in Colonial Ghana* (New Haven, 1993), *Nkrumah and the Chiefs* (Oxford, 2000) and, with John Parker, *African History: A Very Short Introduction* (Oxford, 2007).

Rhonda A. Semple completed her PhD training under the guidance of Andrew Porter in 2000. That work examined British Protestant women in missions with a focus on missions to India and China, and it has subsequently been published as *Missionary Women* (Boydell & Brewer, 2003). She is currently working on a project that addresses gender in Methodist missions, and the secular impact of mission institutions on communities both in south Asia and in diaspora. Rhonda Semple is Assistant Professor in History at St Francis Xavier University in Antigonish, Nova Scotia, Canada.

Brian Stanley is director of the Henry Martyn Centre for the Study of Mission and World Christianity and a fellow of St Edmund's College, Cambridge. He has written or edited a number of books on the history of the Protestant missionary movement. With Sheridan Gilley he was co-editor of volume 8 of *The Cambridge History of Christianity* (2006). From January 2009 he will be Professor of World Christianity in the University of Edinburgh.

A. J. Stockwell is emeritus professor of modern history at Royal Holloway, University of London and President of the Royal Asiatic Society. His publications include *Malaya* (British Documents on the End of Empire, Series B, Volume 3, 1995) and *Malaysia* (British Documents on End of Empire, Series B, Volume 8, 2004). With Andrew Porter he published *British Imperial Policy and Decolonization, 1938–1964* (2 vols, 1989). He co-edited the *Journal of Imperial and Commonwealth History* for many years.

Sarah Stockwell is senior lecturer in imperial and Commonwealth history at King's College London. Her publications include *The Business of Decolonization: British Business Strategies in the Gold Coast* (2000), co-edited with S. R. Ashton, *Imperial Policy and Colonial Practice, 1925–1945* (British Documents on the End of Empire, Series A, Vol. 1, 1996) and her recent edited collection *The British Empire: Themes and Perspectives* (2008).

John Stuart is senior lecturer in history at Kingston University, London. He is a former PhD student of Andrew Porter. His research focuses primarily on the activities of British Protestant missionaries in twentieth-century colonial Africa. He is currently writing a history of missionaries and the 'end of empire'.

Keith Surridge's PhD thesis was supervised by Andrew Porter and published as *Managing the South African War, 1899–1902: Politicians vrs Generals* (1998). He has also published (with Dennis Judd) *The Boer War* (2002) as well as articles on that conflict and on Lord Kitchener. He teaches in various American university programmes in London.

Professor Andrew Porter

INTRODUCTION

Andrew Porter

Robert Holland and Sarah Stockwell

Few historians have shown such dedication to their subject as Andrew Porter. After undergraduate and graduate years spent at St John's College, Cambridge, he took up his first academic post as a temporary lecturer in the History Department in the University of Manchester in 1970, and the following year moved to what soon became a permanent lectureship at King's College London. He has remained there ever since, becoming professor in 1990 and then three years later succeeding P. J. Marshall as Rhodes Professor in Imperial History, the post from which he retires this summer. In 2005 he was made a Fellow of King's in recognition of his long and distinguished service to the college as well as his standing in the profession. Porter swiftly emerged as a prolific historian of empire, but one whose contribution to the profession in a great variety of other ways has been quite extraordinary. This commitment went beyond research and writing in specialised areas, though we return to such matters below. However vast the field, and however ideologically diverse its exponents might be, Porter has conceived of the practice of imperial history, and history in general, as a collective intellectual enterprise.

He was instrumental and often indispensable to virtually all the main editorial and collaborative endeavours relating to 'Britain overseas' during his career. He was joint editor of the *Journal of Imperial and Commonwealth History* between 1979 and 1990, as well as involved from the start in the planning of the *British Documents on the End of Empire* series, chairing its steering committee as it went on to produce a stream of volumes especially valuable for scholars unable to make their own forays to Kew. Porter also played a critical role in the evolution of *The Oxford History of the British Empire*, for which he edited Volume 3 on *The Nineteenth Century* (1998). With such extensive responsibilities, some colleagues and friends were somewhat taken aback when Porter also assumed editorial responsibility for the *Bibliography of Imperial, Colonial and Commonwealth History since 1600* (2002) for the Royal Historical Society Bibliography series. They need not have worried, since he carried this massive and painstaking task through to successful conclusion, and still managed to serve as an associate editor for the *Oxford Dictionary of National Biography*, contributing himself, principally on missionaries and other church figures. Meanwhile he found time to edit the *Atlas of Overseas British Expansion* (1991) and participate in the North Atlantic Missiology project as a member of its international steering committee and national project committee; one of the fruits of this was the volume Porter edited on *The Imperial Horizons of British Protestant Missions, 1880–1914* (2003).

Not all his endeavours in support of the field have left such an obvious publication trail. For over thirty-five years he headed each Monday in term for the imperial history seminar at the Institute of Historical Research, in which, after his appointment as Rhodes Professor, he took the lead role. Here the scholarly community of historians of empire has benefited in equal measure from exposure to his sharp critical faculties and from his genuine enthusiasm for fostering interesting and rigorous projects in his field. If in seminars and committee meetings, as in published academic exchanges, Porter could be naturally combative on matters he regarded as vital, his collegiality – both professional and private – was always warm and supportive, usually with a vein of understated humour running through it.

It was symptomatic of Andrew Porter's remarkable commitment to – one might say belief in – his chosen profession that he slid naturally into a leadership role in history beyond his own subject area. He was head of the history department in King's College for many years, and led from the front, expecting a lot of his colleagues, but no more than he demanded of himself. He also chaired the board of management of the Institute of Commonwealth Studies in London, his tact and deftness helping to steer that institution through some particularly stormy times. Porter was an active member of the History at the Universities Defence Group at a time when history in the universities itself was seemingly under grave threat. Given his track record, he could perhaps hardly have escaped an involvement with the Royal Historical Society, of which he was honorary secretary 1986–90. Given all this, to say that a debt of gratitude is owed to Andrew Porter by fellow historians, both those who shared his special enthusiasms and many who did not, is truistic.

Nevertheless, the reputations of historians, and lasting perceptions of them, are defined essentially by the characteristics and influence of their own writing. To a perhaps unusual degree, especially in an era of increasingly tight subject specialisation, Porter's scholarship defies easy categorisation. His work has ranged extraordinarily widely in time and theme, extending from at least the late eighteenth century to the 1960s, and from empire building, through the high imperialism of the late nineteenth century, to the end of empire. It is equally grounded in analysis both of the state and of non-state organisations, business and financial, and, more recently, religious. He has reflected on both the individual and collective experience of empire. This range is most obviously on display in various works of synthesis, not least his own contributions and introduction to the *Oxford History of the British Empire* and also in his chapter in P. J. Marshall's edited *Cambridge Illustrated History of the British Empire* (1996). That this breadth has been attained without any loss of authority or feel is evident from the award in 2006 of the Trevor Reese Prize in Imperial and

Commonwealth History for his major publication *Religion versus Empire? British Protestant Missionaries and Overseas Expansion, 1700–1914* (2004). At the other end of the chronological span of empire, his collection of documents co-edited with A. J. Stockwell, *British Imperial Policy and Decolonization, 1938–64* (1987), remains widely used in many undergraduate courses, as does his short book *European Imperialism, 1860–1914* (1994). The many and diverse post-doctoral projects that Porter has supervised are further testimony to the variety and scope of his interests and expertise. His students include the late Martin Lynn, while several others (Butler, Semple, Stuart and Surridge) have contributed to this volume.

One answer then to the question of how best to define Porter's approach is as a refusal to become trapped into a set period or a sharply compartmentalised approach. The rigorous and fiercely logical reading of widely sourced evidence is certainly another characteristic. The second trait came out very strongly in his first book, *The Origins of the South African War: Joseph Chamberlain and the Diplomacy of Imperialism, 1895–99* (1980). His nuanced evocation of British 'opinion' and its relationship to events 'on the ground' displayed early on a conviction that the historian of empire has to take the metropolitan and the local equally seriously, since to do otherwise would be to mistake the very nature of the beast. In the debate which afterwards took shape around the role of gold-mining and the origins of the war, he was consistently sceptical as to whether the sources available pointed to any sustained and causal linkage between 'goldbugs' and the decisions taken by British ministers. '"Contexts" which may be little other than a description of more or less coincidental phenomena', he wrote ('Context and Motive Reconsidered', *Historical Journal* 21, 1990), 'are too rapidly used in the absence of particular evidence to attribute motive and decisive influence to individuals or "interests".' Such a refusal to jump from contextual generalisation, with all its inevitable simplifications, to precise conclusions reflected not only a self-denying impulse embedded in Porter's personality as an historian, but an unremitting intellectual honesty. His refusal to be moved from such a position might entail friction with those who saw evidential patterns in a different way, but he was always courteously insistent on his own values and *modus operandi* as a historian.

Equally crucial in shaping Porter's practice as an historian was a conviction that empire could not be seen as a hermetically sealed or integrated universe, and that imperial experience was played upon by an infinite variety of other forces, motivations and beliefs. Explanations and theories which held up only by excluding from view much more complicated and often contradictory realities were particularly vulnerable to the cutting logic and expanded frame of reference to which Porter was instinctively drawn. To study missions and missionaries, therefore, required a focus not only on imperial themes and developments but also on their theological counterparts, because to leave the theology out – to consider that it was somehow a purely surface element in the narrative – was to elide from view a dynamic and driving force. This was a critical theme in what will surely stand as his most influential and wide-ranging book, *Religion versus Empire? British Protestant Missionaries and Overseas Expansion, 1700–1914*. As he states early on in that work, 'issues of theology, belief and ideas about the nature of the church are to be taken seriously.... Missionaries viewed their world first of all through the eyes of faith and then through theological lenses' (2004, 13). Taking seriously what individuals in history said about themselves, and accepting the constraints – be they mental, moral or political – within which colonial lives were lived, has been central to Porter's methodology. Others might be surprised, for example, that members of colonised societies fought bitterly for their place in a hierarchy which latter-day historians are sometimes apt to parody, but to Porter it was entirely logical that they did so. It was, after all, the only world they had open to them.

Thematically, too, he was voraciously catholic. For him the economics could not be drained out of empire, any more than theology could be drained out of missions. His 1986 biography of Donald Currie (*Victorian Shipping, Business and Imperial Policy: Donald Currie, the Castle Line and Southern Africa*), just like his more lasting fascination with Cecil Rhodes, showed a tenacious determination to take on board commercial and technological 'drivers', but not without closely calibrating them with the complex ambitions and personalities of the figures themselves. It was consequently wholly natural that Porter should emerge as a leading protagonist in the argument surrounding 'Gentlemanly Capitalism' following the publication of a seminal work by A. G. Hopkins and Peter Cain in 1993. Indeed, it was perhaps the most bruising academic controversy of Porter's career, and brought out his own capacity for fierce refutation. But the very force of his own views in this case was grounded not only in a continuing and indeed intensified scepticism regarding over-generalised theory, but in a reaction against 'reading across' supposed tendencies from one part of empire (in this case, the British metropole) to the messy realities of the so-called 'periphery'.

The core outcome of Porter's ceaseless professional labours was a belief in the value not so much of imperial history, but of imperial histories. In exploring these histories, he did not expect to find rigid and finite 'answers', and frankly suspected those who did. More important than fixed and neatly ordered conclusions was the exactitude and integrity with which masses of evidence were scrutinised. Perhaps infuriatingly, he himself did not only question the evidence; he questioned the very questions that others were asking of the evidence. Since wry self-criticism was very much a Porter hallmark, he was conscious himself of having an irresistible proclivity for inconclusive conclusions, on show in his *European Imperialism*, with its incisive and crisp summary of hugely intractable issues. Yet this was fundamentally a measure of his sense of the elusiveness of truth in history, and the shifting quality of meanings at all levels. It is this defining aspect of Andrew Porter's craft that led friends, colleagues and former students, in co-operating in this collection of essays in his honour, to take as their theme 'Ambiguities of Empire'.

Transatlantic Protestantism and American Independence

P. J. Marshall

I

This essay tries to bring together two of the major themes to which Andrew Porter has devoted much scholarly attention: the history of Protestantism within the framework of the British empire and the winding up of that empire. With some notable exceptions, such as the Irish Free State after 1922, which became a Catholic 'confessional state' to a degree that it had certainly not been under the Union,[1] the position of the Protestant denominations did not change greatly after former colonies became independent. Well before independence they had become rooted in local communities and had generally ceased to be regarded as agents of metropolitan authority. In the thirteen colonies of North America most Protestant denominations had become distinctly American in personnel and outlook by the middle of the eighteenth century. Even so, independence was a significant disruption for many of them, bringing changes above all in relations with Christians in Britain.

Protestant denominations that had been transplanted from the British Isles to North America maintained links throughout the colonial period with their fellow Protestants in Britain. As was the case with so many other transatlantic connections, these links were generally strengthening and getting more close-knit rather than weakening in the years before the Revolution. Some denominations recognised the spiritual authority of parent churches in Britain; others saw themselves as autonomous. All, however, maintained close contacts across the Atlantic and looked for support in various ways. The eighteenth-century colonial clergy was for the most part American, but ministers, evangelists and college teachers still came out from Britain. Devotional and scholarly books were sent across the Atlantic in great quantities. Virtually all denominations in America sought money from their connections in Britain, above all for founding and sustaining the new colleges launched in the mid-eighteenth century. Denominational rivalry was often intense. All denominations looked to British supporters to use their influence on their behalf with the British government and, if need be, with parliament, to win advantages over their opponents and to protect their interests in dealing with local colonial authorities.

The Church of England was formally, if not necessarily in practice, the least autonomous of the denominations and the most dependent on Britain. Without its own bishops, it was subject to the Bishop of London. Its clergy had to go to England for ordination. It received powerful aid from the Society for the Propagation of the Gospel. The society was supported by voluntary contributions and by legacies, often considerable ones, from an extensive clerical and lay membership and by special national collections from the public at large. On the eve of the Revolution the society was maintaining seventy-seven missionary clergy in North America at the cost of more than £5000 a year.[2] Nearly all the society's missionaries ministered to the colonial population, but it was also committed to missions to the Native Americans, above all to the Six Nations. Although it was established in six colonies and its support was growing considerably, the Church of England in America was in essence no more than a denomination in competition with other denominations. Its clergy looked to the bishops and to the SPG in London to exert influence on their behalf with the British government. They were, however, well aware of the limitations on what they could achieve. Archbishop Secker explained to his colonial correspondents in 1763 that, although he hoped that 'the civil power in America will have directions to help us. Yet I speak not too confidently of these things'. On the most contentious issue, the appointment of a colonial bishop, he doubted with good reason whether ministers had 'zeal enough to undertake what will certainly meet with opposition'.[3]

Opposition to favours to the Anglicans could be expected from the three Dissenting denominations, the Congregationalists, or Independents, the Presbyterians and the Baptists. The Congregationalists, descendants of the New England Puritans, had the status of an established church in Massachusetts, Connecticut and New Hampshire. Relatively secure in their privileges and with long-established colleges, they had less need of British support. New England Congregationalists, however, kept in close touch with sympathetic English radicals, such as Thomas Hollis, a great benefactor of Harvard, about supposed threats to them from across the ocean. By contrast Presbyterians, fuelled by large-scale immigration from Ulster, were a new and rapidly expanding denomination in eighteenth-century America, especially in the middle colonies where they spread into frontier areas. They formed themselves into presbyteries and synods, which sent appeals to Britain for money, ministers and support. In 1753–54 over £3,000 was raised in Scotland for the College of New Jersey at Princeton. In 1760 the General Synod of Ulster sponsored a collection for Presbyterian ministers who had suffered in the war that had ravaged the frontier of Pennsylvania.[4] In 1768 the New Jersey College recruited from Scotland as its president the Presbyterian minister John Witherspoon, described by John Adams as 'as high a son of liberty as any man in America' and to be a member of Congress and signatory of the Declaration of Independence. The synods of New York and Philadelphia told the General Assembly in 1772 that they looked on their 'connection with the Church of Scotland' as 'the means of securing our constitutional privileges especially our religious liberties'.[5] American Baptists were slower to organise, but in the 1760s the New England Baptists formed their Warren Association, opened Rhode Island College (the future Brown University) and began correspondence with British Baptists, asking them to raise money and to lobby the Board of Trade against a Massachusetts act requiring a Baptist community to pay tithes to the local Congregational church.[6]

The boundaries between Dissenting denominations were not rigid. A group in Britain, including notable luminaries such as Joseph Priestley and Richard Price, have come to be known as Rational Dissenters.[7] They had liberal views on what they saw as the insubstantial basis for many orthodox doctrines, above all that of the Trinity. They drew support principally from English Presbyterians but included men who had left the Anglican Church. They enjoyed the esteem of like-minded Americans, usually free-thinking, politically radical laymen rather than clerics. The Church of Scotland's Society for the Propagation of Christian Knowledge was another example of inter-denominational cooperation. It channelled money raised in Britain for Indian missions through boards of Presbyterians and Congregationalists in America.[8] In England the denominations worked together easily through the organisation of prominent laymen called the Dissenting Deputies.[9] Archbishop Secker feared the close connection between the Dissenters in America and England and their capacity to make trouble in the House of Commons.[10] On the eve of the Revolution, John Witherspoon saw the Dissenting Deputies as important allies in 'the grand struggle' for 'religious liberty', which 'we or posterity may be called upon to make in the glorious cause in which the happiness of thousands yet unborn may be deeply interested'.[11]

The revivals of the Great Awakening in America of the 1730s and 1740s profoundly affected Congregationalists, Presbyterians, Baptists and some Anglicans and caused deep divisions, although within rather than between denominations. Revivals created new and vibrant links across the Atlantic. There were similar phenomena in the British Isles, most notably at Cambuslang in Scotland. George Whitefield exercised his charismatic powers on both sides of the Atlantic. News of providential happenings was eagerly passed to and fro across the ocean. Ministers and congregations were linked in 'Concerts of Prayer'.[12] On the eve of the Revolution, the Methodist revival within the Anglican Church was beginning to gain a foothold in the middle colonies and John Wesley was dispatching itinerant preachers to America.[13] Revivals powerfully stimulated missionary endeavours, above all to Native Americans after the Seven Years War. An American Congregationalist in Britain believed that 'America lies near the heart of the children of God in England when they address the Divine footstool ... and particularly importunate for the spread and success of the Gospel among the natives'.[14] Large sums for missions were collected for the SPG, the Scottish Society and for Eleazar Wheelock's school for Indians in Connecticut, for which Samson Occom, an Indian pastor, raised £12,000 in Britain in the 1760s. On both sides of the Atlantic there were millennial expectations of when the task of Indian conversion should come to its fruition.[15]

Quakers stood entirely outside the Dissenting denominations. They were highly organised on both sides of the Atlantic. Yearly Meetings in the colonies and in Britain exchanged detailed 'Epistles'. In London there was a structure of committees to keep a close watch on matters of concern to Quakers in America as well as Britain.[16] The British Quaker elite of merchants and professional men was rich and respectful of authority and the Quakers were said to be 'a body of people of great weight and much esteemed here'.[17]

Behind the willingness of British Christians to commit their money on a very large scale, £24,000 on colonial colleges alone between 1749 and 1775,[18] and such influence as they could wield in respect of American causes clearly lay a strong sense of a transatlantic Protestant community, albeit one often seen as divided along denominational lines. The sense of commitment to this community seems to have ranged from the exalted fellow feeling of those who found themselves caught up in revivals which they knew were also sweeping through the colonies to the preoccupations of leading figures such as Archbishop Thomas Secker, to whom, in the words of his contemporary biographer:

> The advancement of true piety and learning, the conversion of the Indians and the Negroes, as far as it was practicable, the establishment of proper schools, the distribution of useful books, the good conduct of the missionaries, the preservation of peace and harmony amongst the different religious communities in those parts of the British empire had a very large share in his thoughts.[19]

The biographer of John Erskine, prominent in the Popular Party of the Church of Scotland and therefore a man of an entirely different outlook from Secker, wrote of Erskine's wide network of American correspondents and that 'his connections with America had a strong hold on his mind .... His solicitude for her prosperity, and especially for her progress in literature and religion was always expressed with eagerness and affection'.[20]

Many Americans had come to believe that their country had a unique destiny in God's providential designs for the world.[21] So too did some people in Britain. Thomas Randall, a radical within the Church of Scotland, wrote in 1767 that he had 'long thought that the intentions of Providence (after the abuse of our great mercies and our dreadful degeneracy) [were] to fix the great seat of truth and righteousness in America'.[22] The Anglican polemicist George Horne hoped to see 'the clouds of infidelity disperse before the sun of righteousness, rising to the American, perhaps as he sets in the European world'.[23] For the many British people who saw themselves as in varying degrees part of a transatlantic Protestant community, revolution and war were catastrophic events which sundered cherished links and shattered expectations. Many saw these happenings as divine chastisement for national dereliction. Sermon after sermon from all denominations called for national repentance and reform of manners. Beyond that they blamed human agency. Some attributed the disaster to the rebellious ambitions of the Americans, others to the high-handed and oppressive intransigence of government and parliament.

II

All Protestant denominations on both sides of the Atlantic, even the Quakers who had great difficulty in defining the neutrality to which they wished to adhere,[24] were divided by the Revolution. This was certainly the case with Anglicans, although many saw the Revolution as aimed against them. From the outset it was denounced as a plot to overthrow both church and state. This view was summed up in a newspaper paragraph in 1776, which identified New England as the cradle of revolt. 'They are republicans in politics – puritans in religion – and of consequence disaffected to the established government in Britain in church and state.'[25] Another correspondent in another paper saw many examples of 'the national hatred that the people of the twelve ancient provinces bear to our government in general, our religion in particular'.[26] Presbyterians soon came to be joined with Congregationalists as fomenters of rebellion. That Anglican clergy were the most conspicuous early victims of the Revolution heightened the impression that it was a war against the church. A group consisting largely of SPG missionaries, who had been trying to sustain Anglicanism in adverse conditions in New England or in the middle colonies, fled to Britain. Their sufferings were publicised by the SPG: 'Numerous indeed and truly pitiable are the accounts received by the Society.'[27] Preaching at Oxford, the exiled Myles Cooper assured his audience that he 'could unfold such scenes of persecution and cruelty as would excite the indignation and horror of every soul in this assembly'.[28] The view that religious Dissent was at the heart of the rebellion was shared in some degree in official circles. Lord George Germain believed that the other colonies had been 'gradually seduced into rebellion' by the Massachusetts 'Independants' (Congregationalists).[29] In England Anglican preachers frequently called into question the loyalty of the Dissenters in their midst. The role that British Dissenters were assumed to have had in inciting revolt in America later became a stock weapon in Anglican polemics against them over the Test and Corporation Acts.

Any simple view of Anglicans as the victims of revolution and of Dissenters as its propagators would, however, be highly misleading. A large segment of the revolutionary leadership was Anglican. Throughout the colonies as a whole only about a quarter of the clergy emigrated. Anglicans became most embattled with the Revolution in northern colonies where they were in a minority and where there was a previous history of conflict. In Virginia and Maryland, where the church was established, and further south a large majority of the Anglican laity and many of the clergy seem to have sided with the Revolution or at least to have accepted it. The ardent patriot William Lee explained to an Anglican parson in his native Virginia that he saw 'most clearly the work of providence in this American business' and then asked: 'Do I not talk like a true Church of England man, not a High Church man?'[30] By High Church men, he meant in particular the New England Anglicans. In England the bishops and church hierarchy almost without exception opposed the Revolution, as did most of lower clergy. It has, however, been suggested that members of the Anglican laity constituted the majority of those who petitioned against the war in 1775.[31]

Propositions equating Dissenters with supporters of the Revolution must be severely qualified. Such propositions would apply to all except a small minority of Congregationalists in America and to most exponents of Rational Dissent in England. The same would probably be the case for most Presbyterians of Irish origin in America and for many Presbyterians in Ireland itself.[32] In 1784 the 'Independent parsons' from 'almost every parish in Down and Antrim' were said to 'preach up the principles of Republicanism and doctrines that can only lead to sedition and rebellion in the most bare-faced manner'.[33] Scottish Presbyterians in America, however, were by no means united behind the Revolution. Many, especially in New York and the Carolinas, fought for the Crown and then emigrated to Canada or Nova Scotia. The official institutions of the Church of Scotland were firmly loyalist and this probably reflected the views of a majority of the political nation in Scotland. There was, however, a strong Popular Party within the Kirk who opposed the war and may have had quite wide support.[34]

The allegiance of English Dissenters, that is, of Congregationalists, Presbyterians and Baptists who were not members of the Rational Dissenting congregations that strongly opposed the war, is contentious.[35] James Bradley's conclusion based, on very impressive research, is that in the petitioning movement against the war of 1775 'the great majority of Dissenters gave strong support to conciliatory measures'.[36] Dismay and revulsion at the prospect of civil war and at the policies of the government that seemed to be bringing it on was not, however, necessarily the same as being 'pro-American', often as that elision is made. As the war ground on year after year and it became clear that Americans would accept nothing short of independence (an eventuality which even Rational Dissenters deplored)[37] and would go so far as to ally with France and Spain, Britain's hereditary Catholic enemies to get it, their cause seemed less attractive to many. The government seemed also to be trying to restore good relations with Dissent by its 1779 Act relieving ministers and teachers of the obligation to subscribe to the 39 Articles.[38] The views of John Rogers, Congregationalist minister of Long Lane Chapel, Southwark, and perhaps significantly a 'strict Calvinist', may be characteristic. He was 'a Whig as to the American quarrel but against the Americans on the point of separation'. He 'much faulted the Americans for their severities to the friends of Great Britain and most of all for joining the interests of the chief Popish powers' and he regretted that so much money had been sent to them in the past.[39] When William Gordon, an Independent, returned to England, having served as chaplain to the Massachusetts Congress, he commented on 'the coolness with which I have been treated by several, even of my brethren in the ministry' and he knew of London Dissenting ministers 'who would have rejoiced to have had the promoters or encouragers of revolution, whether in civil or sacred orders, hanged as rebels'.[40] He was 'abused and insulted by one of his brethren in a coffe[e] house where the Dissenting ministers meet every Tuesday'.[41]

III

Andrew Porter has described the relations between British and American Protestants involved in missionary activity overseas by the nineteenth century as taking 'many, often overlapping, forms ... personal friendships, professional contacts, exchanges of information and literature, political cooperation and the transfer of revivalist impulses'.[42] This is a fair summing up of the whole range of relations between Protestants on both sides of the Atlantic. This pattern of multifarious contacts between individuals and groups that developed in the nineteenth century was, however, rather different from the close-knit transatlantic Protestant community, underpinned by institutionalised bonds between denominations, which had existed before the Revolution.

The old order had been shattered by war and independence and by the bitterness and alienation which they generated. Most American Protestants not surprisingly saw the hand of divine providence in their victory. It was widely believed that the new republic had a God-given destiny to redeem the world. The Warren Baptist Association of New England believed that the Revolution was 'one important step towards bringing in the glory of the latter day .... Nor is it at all improbable that America is reserved in the mind of Jehovah to be the grand theatre on which the divine redeemer will accomplish glorious things'.[43] The British Unitarian Newcome Cappe in a sermon at York in 1781 was inclined to agree. 'It may be the purpose of providence, beyond that friendly ocean to prepare an asylum for the calamities which are coming on a land that will not be reformed.'[44] Most British Protestants were, however, more reserved. Early reports of the newly independent republics were often far from encouraging. It was to take time for a new order of close transatlantic contacts to be established.

The main features of what that new order would be quickly became apparent, however. It was above all to be a new order based on a rough equality. The British churches would no longer exercise spiritual authority or the kind of patronage over a dependent church that Thomas Secker had conscientiously tried to dispense. Deference would no longer be paid to them, but in return the British would no longer render services. The tendency for the American denominations to develop institutions to manage their own affairs free of outside influence accelerated rapidly after 1783. With independence the capacity of the British denominations to lobby ministers and parliament on behalf of American interests immediately lost all relevance, but the supply of British money and ministers also quickly dwindled to a trickle.

American Anglicans experienced the most complete relinquishment of authority and drying up of support. The Church of England in America had come out of the war badly damaged. The 286 clergymen in 1774 had shrunk to 155 by the peace.[45] Many churches had been closed and their congregations dispersed. The financial support accorded to the church in the six ex-colonies where it had been established was taken away as disestablishment was enforced in the new states. In spite of the entreaties by the Connecticut clergy that 'to their former calamities this insupportable one may not be added, – the being discarded by the Society',[46] discarded they were. The SPG interpreted its charter, which directed its attention to the spiritual needs of 'our plantations, colonies and factories beyond the seas' as precluding activities outside the dominions of the Crown. In April 1785 it decided that it would no longer pay stipends to missionaries in the United States, but that it would do its best to provide for those who were willing to go to the surviving British colonies.[47]

The war also disrupted the society's missions to Native Americans. The territory of the Six Nations was bitterly fought over and in 1783 was ceded to the United States. The SPG, however, accepted responsibility for the Mohawk communities, believed to be under the authority of the Anglican military hero, Joseph Brant, who had relocated north of Lake Ontario in Canada. There the Mohawks built a new church, which Brant wished to have 'decently ornamented', including the royal arms, as 'vastly pleasing to the congregation, as well as striking their visiting Indian neighbours with awe and respect'.[48] The Scottish Society continued after the war to make payments to missions to the Six Nations through their agents at Harvard. The Revd Samuel Kirkland, who as Congress's emissary to the Oneida had tried to rally Indians against the British during the war, received a Scottish salary until 1796.[49] By then, however, public zeal in Britain for Native American conversion had largely evaporated. Missionary enthusiasm was increasingly directed towards enslaved Africans and the new Indian subjects of the East India Company.

With the ending of the war, those American Anglicans who did not feel compelled to emigrate hoped to re-build their church under the relatively benign regime of religious freedom promised in the state constitutions. Once they were seen to have been loosed from their subordination to England, American secular authority, at least at its higher levels, was sympathetic to their designs. Nevertheless, they still needed acts of English authority to enable them to stand on their own. Candidates for ordination still had to go to Britain and to swear allegiance to the Crown. In 1784 a bill was passed in the British parliament, put forward by the Bishop of London, enabling foreign subjects to be ordained by English bishops without swearing the oath of allegiance.[50] The question of an American bishop, which had proved so contentious in the past, still remained to be resolved. In the view of the Republican elite, it now presented no problems. A bishop without any claim to temporal authority would be entirely acceptable.

The English bishops and the British government, however, moved slowly and cautiously. The bishops were lobbied by two conflicting elements among the American Anglicans. First in the field were the High Church clergy of New England. They were alarmed by the plans of the rest of the clergy for an episcopacy under lay authority. In 1783 they dispatched Samuel Seabury to London to seek consecration from the English bishops. He made little progress, being told that the bishops would not act without the approval of the British government and that the government was wary of giving offence in the United States. After a year he decided to bypass the English bishops and seek consecration from bishops who felt no obligation to obey British secular authority. These were the bishops of the episcopal church of Scotland, suspected in England to be rank Jacobites. Seabury was consecrated by them as Bishop of Connecticut at Aberdeen in November 1784. This was an outcome that had been foreseen even before Seabury left America and it was one that appealed strongly to the High Church clergy in Connecticut. In Seabury's view, the connection between the Church of England and the British state was far too 'intimate', whereas from the Scots 'a free, valid and purely ecclesiastical episcopacy may ... pass into the western world'.[51]

The majority of American Anglicans, including those who had sided with the Revolution, proceeded very differently. They hoped to rebuild the Anglican Church from the parish level upwards. State associations of clergy and laity came together and elected delegates to represent them at national conventions.[52] The similarities with Republican secular constitution-making were obvious. To those who sought to defend their view of the Anglican tradition, this was 'a motley mixture of episcopacy, presbytery and ecclesiastical Republicanism'; the English bishops must be expected to reject 'a scheme formed with such a design to degrade the episcopal order' when the Philadelphia Convention submitted it to them in 1785 together with their revised liturgy and the names of candidates to be consecrated as their first bishops.[53] The English bishops were concerned at trends in the liturgy, particularly about alterations to the creeds which seemed to them to show Socinian tendencies,[54] and asked for clarification, but otherwise they had no inclination to object. They were wary about sanctioning something that 'will be called a branch of the Church of England, but afterwards may appear to have departed from it essentially, either in doctrine or discipline',[55] but they had little scope for effective intervention. They agreed to consecrate the three candidates to be sent over, even though two of them had played active roles in the Revolution and the third, Dr Provoost of New York, certainly had suspect views about the Trinity. The Archbishop of Canterbury was reported to have told an American episcopal clergyman that the bishops 'from the bottom of their hearts wished our prosperity, and would do all in their power to promote it', that the government had no objections and that the King had 'expressed great satisfaction' in it.[56] An act of parliament was duly passed authorising the consecration of American bishops 'without taking the oaths of allegiance and supremacy and the oath of due obedience to the archbishop of the time'.[57]

The English bishops cannot have had much enthusiasm for what they had done and were to show very little interest in the new Episcopal Church of the United

States with its quasi-republican institutions. They had got out of a difficult situation as well as they could. The alternatives were even worse. If they did not consecrate bishops for the Philadelphia Convention, future conventions might assume the power of licensing clergy for themselves, others might resort to the Scottish 'Jacobites', and the bishops were warned that Wesley had sanctioned superintendents in America who were calling themselves bishops and ordaining their own Methodist clergy.[58] They chose to cut their losses in the United States and to focus their attention elsewhere, above all on the remaining British North American colonies, Nova Scotia and Canada.

Here the SPG acted in close co-operation with the British government which helped them to construct what were essentially state-supported Anglican churches directly financed by parliamentary grants, a radical departure in British colonial policy. This strategy was based on somewhat debatable assumptions: that Dissenters had inspired the Revolution, that the great bulk of Anglicans had been loyal and, most debatable of all, that a large majority of those who were emigrating to Canada and Nova Scotia were Anglicans.[59] The Church of England was therefore to be built up as a bulwark against sedition and a check on American expansion. Government grants supplemented the society's salaries for missionaries in Nova Scotia, New Brunswick, Cape Breton Island and Quebec and paid for church and parsonage house building in New Brunswick and Cape Breton Island. In 1787 the New York loyalist Charles Inglis was appointed the first bishop of Nova Scotia. An Anglican college and schools were to be opened in Nova Scotia. The Church of England sought to entrench itself with the aid of the secular power in the face of a majority drawn from very diverse sects in Nova Scotia, 'infected', so a shocked governor reported, 'by the cursed enthusiastick spirit of religion'. He encountered 'Anabaptists . . . Sandimonians, Swedenburgers' as well as Presbyterians, Congregationalists and numerous Methodists.[60] In Quebec Anglicans were swamped by a huge Catholic majority. In numerical terms in Nova Scotia, New Brunswick and what was to be Upper Canada the church became what it had been in thirteen colonies, a Protestant denomination competing with other Protestant denominations.

By the end of the Revolutionary War, Methodists in America had moved far out of the fold of the Church of England and were effectively placing themselves beyond any control that Wesley might hope to exert over them. Identified with collaboration with Britain, Methodists had suffered severely during the Revolution, but they made a most remarkable recovery. By 1788 they were claiming 1,000 preachers and over 30,000 adherents and numbers were growing with astonishing speed. Methodism was also spreading very rapidly in Nova Scotia. Francis Asbury, who had emerged as the leading American superintendent, later styling himself bishop, was prepared to accept 'union but no subordination, connexion but no subjection' with Methodism in Britain.[61] The charter that enabled him to assert his independent leadership was the instructions sent by Wesley in 1784, recognising that the Americans were now 'totally disentangled both from the state and from the English hierarchy' and that, while he would not ordain ministers in England, he saw no alternative to empowering his superintendents to ordain them in America.[62] This they proceeded to do to good effect, setting up their own church structure, the Methodist Episcopal Church, at Baltimore in 1784. Wesley clearly regretted the ensuing separation. When later asked why he had conceded so much in 1784 he was reported to have said that:

> As soon as we had made peace with America, and allowed them their independence, all religious connexion, between this country and the independent colonies was at an end; in consequence of which the sectaries fell to work to increase their several parties, and the Anabaptists in particular were carrying all before them. Something had to be done, without loss of time, for his poor people as he called them in America; he had therefore taken the steps in question, with the hope of preventing further disorders.[63]

Whatever Wesley's motives may have been, the American Methodists were able to seize the chance of going their own way, leaving Wesley with only a nominal authority over them.[64]

The Revolution may have been a defeat for the Church of England in America, albeit one to which many American Anglicans and Methodists responded in creative ways. For Dissenters, a category often stretched to include Scottish Presbyterians, somewhat inappropriately in view of the established status of the Church of Scotland, it is generally assumed to have been a victory. Many are presumed to have found the new order in church and state across the Atlantic much preferable to that in Britain. Robert Southey wrote of British nonconformists after 1783 that 'New England was more the country of their hearts than the England wherein they had been born and bred'.[65] This might have been true when Southey wrote it in the early nineteenth century, but in the immediate aftermath of the war, which a number of them had ultimately come to support, many British Dissenters seem to have been doubtful about the new America.

Rational Dissenters were an obvious exception. They had uniformly opposed the war and they enthusiastically welcomed the new state constitutions. In his *Observations on the Importance of the American Revolution and of the Means of Making it a Benefit to the World* of 1784 Richard Price hailed 'a new aera in the history of mankind'. He particularly commended the total separation of church and state. The United States were now happily free of 'tyrannical laws against heresy and schism, and . . . slavish hierarchies and religious establishments'.[66] Rational Dissenting ministers happily consorted with John Adams, the first American ambassador in London. The Adams family regularly attended Price's meeting house. The rise of liberal unitarian and universalist doctrines among the New England clergy, particularly in Boston, enabled the Rational Dissenters to establish new links across the Atlantic and to extend their influence. The London Unitarian Theophilus Lindsey was delighted to record that a 'loyalist high churchman' had been driven out of the Anglican King's Chapel in Boston and that the service there had been 'altered from Trinitarian to Unitarian'.[67] In 1791 an outraged Philadelphia Presbyterian wrote of the Boston ministers that '[s]ome are Calvinists, some Universalist, some Arminians, some Arians and at least one a Socinian'. Yet 'they will meet and shake hands, and talk of politics and science, and laugh and eat raisins and almonds, and apples and cakes, and drink wine and tea, and then go about their business when they please'.[68] Such people were natural soul mates for British Rational Dissenters.

Quakers were another group who quickly re-established connections after the war. The long-standing practices of transatlantic visits and of exchanging epistles, which were spasmodically transmitted during the war, were restored. Thirteen American ministers immediately came over to Britain and asserted themselves in urging stricter discipline and greater activity on their British colleagues, above all in goading them into launching a campaign against the slave trade.[69] Friends from England were welcomed at American meetings in 1785 and 1786 and the Philadelphia Meeting wrote of 'the bands of Christian fellowship ... long experienced and often lovingly felt'.[70]

Beyond the Rational Dissenters and the Quakers, it proved more difficult to re-establish transatlantic Dissenting connections. Indeed John Adams, in reporting on the general public aversion to the United States experienced by so many of the first wave of Americans in post-war London, concluded: 'I had almost said the friends of America are reduced to Dr Price and Dr Jebb.'[71] The vicissitudes of John Witherspoon in England and Scotland in 1784 exemplified these difficulties. The College of New Jersey had suffered severely in the war and Witherspoon hoped to revive the practice of fund-raising for American colleges in Britain. He did not get a good reception and collected virtually no money. John Wesley commented that, since he had been 'the grand instrument of tearing away children from their parents to whom they were united by the most sacred ties', he could hardly be surprised.[72] In the view of John Erskine, who wished him well, and of all Witherspoon's Scottish friends whom Erskine had consulted, the venture was 'utterly imprudent'.[73] Initially alarmed at his appearing in Britain, the government was gratified by his failure. The Lord Justice Clerk of Scotland thought him 'a designing, turbulent and bad tempered man', who had been 'unnoticed' in Edinburgh, 'except by a few religious bigots'. He was 'a fool to expect any support for his plan for promoting education and literature in America'.[74] Other attempts to raise money, such as that by Benjamin Rush on behalf the new Dickinson College in Pennsylvania or by the New England Baptists for their Rhode Island College, like Princeton, ravaged by war, produced little except books. Richard Price warned a Rhode Island supplicant that it was too soon after the war and that 'the Dissenting interest' was too impoverished to sustain a collection. 'The time has come', he told Ezra Stiles, 'when the Dissenters of England have more reason to look to America, than America has to look to them.'[75] This was a realistic assessment of the shift of power within dominations, as with the Methodists or the Quakers, from one of American dependence to one of at least equality. Abigail Adams found the English Dissenting clergy 'a very different set of men' from those in the United States. 'They are cramped, contemned, degraded', lacking an air of independence or of 'consciousness of their own worth'.[76]

Immediately after the ending of the war, there was concern in the press and government circles, amounting to something like panic, that emigration to America was resuming on a large scale, especially from Ireland and Scotland. This does not seem to have happened for some years, although groups and individuals left. These may have included one or two who professed a desire to live in a land of religious freedom. John Price, a Welsh Anglican clergyman told John Jay that he and 'many more of the principality of Wales, intend, if God willing, to cross the Atlantic to a land of freedom and liberty'.[77] It seems unlikely that Price ever went, but Charles Nisbet of the Popular Party of the Church of Scotland certainly crossed the Atlantic. He was induced to become the first president of Dickinson College by Benjamin Rush, who had been instrumental in bringing Witherspoon to New Jersey twenty years before. Nisbet was a close friend and admirer of Witherspoon, of very similar views in Scotland, where he had strongly opposed the war. His reactions to the new America were, however, to be entirely different. He served Dickinson College for twenty years, but detested his sojourn at Carlisle in Pennsylvania, where he lived 'like a pelican in the wilderness'. Far from seeing America as God's chosen land, he believed that 'the Divine Providence has a controversy with the United States'. 'We have no men of learning or taste and of religious people fewest of all.' 'We are a weak, foolish and divided people.'[78] On their own, Witherspoon and Nisbet can hardly be regarded as exemplars of different phases of British-American relations. Nisbet's case does, however, seem to show that people who might have been disposed to be favourable to America would, in fact, have great difficulty in adjusting to the new order of independence.

In time, however, contacts, less through institutionalised denominational links than by the coming together of like-minded individuals and groups, such as those with a common interest in foreign missions, were to multiply. On the one hand, the growing stability of its political life associated with the enacting of the federal constitution and the recovery of its economy from post-war dislocation, made the United States an increasingly attractive proposition for British opinion by the 1790s, while, on the other, the rising intolerance of religious heterodoxy in Britain associated with the war with France and fear of Jacobinism set off what has been called the British 'radical diaspora' across the Atlantic.[79] Joseph Priestley, who left in 1794, was the most distinguished of a number of Rational Dissenters to go. Such men could be disconcerted by the vibrancy of popular evangelicalism which they encountered at the end of the century in the United States. The revivals, especially among the Methodists and the Baptists, of what has been called the Second Great Awakening spread across the Atlantic creating religious links between Britain and America of a very different kind. These were symbolised by the appearance in Britain of the exotic Lorenzo ('Crazy') Dow with his flowing locks. He was an exponent of mass outdoor camp meetings, which appealed not only to a transformed popular Methodism splitting away from its established leadership but also to many of the rank and file of the old Dissenting denominations.[80]

The Second Great Awakening of the beginning of the nineteenth century restored the transatlantic revivalist links of the 1730s and 1740s, but in a very different Anglo-American world. The old world of close denominational links and eager millennial expectations had been shattered by the fratricidal war. On the British side there was to be a phase of retreat and disillusion before a different pattern of links could be established. Attempts to answer the question of who in Britain cared about the colonies usually focus on calculations of profit and power and tend to come to the conclusion that Britain reconciled herself relatively easily to the loss of empire. Many British Protestants, however, cared deeply about the colonies and were not easily reconciled to what Wesley called the 'tearing away children from their parents to whom they were united by the most sacred ties'.

Notes

[1] Foster, *Modern Ireland*, 534.
[2] Pascoe, *Two Hundred Years of the S.P.G*, I, 79; II, 830–31.
[3] Letters to H. Caner, 30 March 1763, and J. Duchè, 16 Sept. 1763, Perry, ed., *Historical Collections*, III, 390; II, 495.
[4] *Records of the General Synod of Ulster*, II, 436–37, 467–68.
[5] Hook, *Scotland and America*, 32.
[6] McLoughlin, *New England Dissent*, I, 496–535.
[7] See the essays on them in Haakonssen, ed., *Enlightenment and Religion*.
[8] *State of the Society in Scotland for Propagating Christian Knowledge*, 16–19.
[9] Olson, *Making the Empire Work*, 100. Professor Olson's work is an invaluable guide to transatlantic religious connections.
[10] Letter to W. Johnson, 27 Sept. 1763, Lambeth Palace Library, MS 1123, no. 121.
[11] Letter entered in minutes of meeting of 19 Oct. 1774, Guildhall Library, Dissenting Deputies Minute Book, 2, p. 180.
[12] O'Brien, 'Transatlantic Community of Saints'; Crawford, *Seasons of Grace*.
[13] Andrews, *Methodists and Revolutionary America*.
[14] D. De Berdt to E. Wheelock, 24 March 1759, 'Letters of Dennys De Berdt', 413.
[15] Bloch, *Visionary Republic*, 47–48.
[16] Olson, *Making the Empire Work*, 99.
[17] T. Penn to W. Peters, 7 July 1756, Historical Society of Pennsylvania, Thomas Penn Letter Books, 6, f. 316.
[18] McAnear, 'The Raising of Funds', 606.
[19] Porteus, *A Review of the Life of Thomas Secker*, 67–68.
[20] Wellwood, *Account of the Life of John Erskine*, 163.
[21] Hatch, *Sacred Cause of Liberty*; Bloch, *Visionary Republic*.
[22] Letter to J. Witherspoon, [4 March 1767], in Butterfield, *Witherspoon Comes to America*, 29.
[23] Horne, *An Apology*, 26–27.
[24] Olson, *Making the Empire Work*, 168–69, 180–81.
[25] 'Pacificus', *Morning Chronicle*, 8 Aug. 1776.
[26] 'D. T.', *Public Advertiser*, 19 Aug. 1776.
[27] *An Abstract of the Proceedings of the Society for the Propagation of the Gospel in Foreign Parts for 1776*, 37.
[28] Cooper, *National Humiliation and Repentance*, 19.
[29] Letter to W. Howe, 18 Oct. 1776, *HMC Stopford Sackville MSS*, II. 43.
[30] Letter to Rev. Mr Hurt, 15 March 1775, Virginia Historical Society, MS L 51, f. 415.
[31] Bradley, *Popular Politics*, 192.
[32] McBride, *Scripture Politics*.
[33] Hillsborough to Rutland, 15 July 1784, *HMC Rutland MSS*, III. 124.
[34] Donovan, 'The Popular Party of the Church of Scotland'.
[35] See discussion in Clark, *Language of Liberty*, 329–35; Olson, *Making the Empire Work*, 152.
[36] Bradley, *Religion, Revolution and English Radicalism*, 398.

[37] A point well made in Bonwick, 'English Dissenters', 104.
[38] Langford, 'English Clergy and the American Revolution', 301–03.
[39] Upton, ed., *Diary of William Smith*, I, 41.
[40] Letter to J. Manning, 13 Sept. 1786, in Guild, *Early History of Brown University*, 441.
[41] Abigail to J. Q. Adams, 27 July 1786, in Hogan et al., eds, *Adams Family Correspondence*, VII, 284.
[42] *Religion versus Empire?*, 117.
[43] McLoughlin, *New England Dissent*, II, 741–42.
[44] Cappe, *Sermon*, 17.
[45] Mills, *Bishops by Ballot*, 156.
[46] Letter of 6 May 1783, Rhodes House Library, Society for the Propagation of the Gospel (SPG) Journals, 23, p. 142.
[47] SPG Journals, 24, pp. 81–82.
[48] D. Claus to E. Nepean, 24 April 1787, The National Archives (TNA), CO 42/19, f. 127.
[49] Taylor, *Divided Ground*, 209, 370–71, 374.
[50] 24 Geo. III, c. 35.
[51] Letter to Connecticut Clergy, 26 July 1784, in Beardsley, *Life of Seabury*, 137.
[52] Mills, *Bishops by Ballot*.
[53] T. Chandler to W. Johnson, 28 Dec. 1785, in Beardsley, *Life of Johnson*, 370.
[54] G. Sharp to B. Franklin, 19 Aug. 1786, Lambeth Palace Library, SPG Papers, 8, f. 195.
[55] Letter of English Bishops, 24 Feb. 1786, in White, *Memoirs of the Protestant Episcopal Church*, 298.
[56] R. Peters to W. White etc., 4 March 1786, ibid., 330–31.
[57] 26 Geo. III, c. 84.
[58] A. Beach to SPG, 8 Feb. 1785, Rhodes House Library, SPG Journals, 24, p. 102; G. Sharp to Archbishop, 15 Sept. 1785, Lambeth Palace Library, SPG Papers, 8, f. 190.
[59] For an exposition of these views, see Guy Carleton to North, 26 Aug. 1783, TNA, CO 5/110, f. 257.
[60] J. Parr to Lansdowne, 3 Sept. 1787, British Library, Bowood MSS, B 41, f. 131.
[61] Letter to J. Winscon, 15 Aug. 1788, Clark, et al, eds, *Journal and Letters of Asbury*, III, 63.
[62] Letter of 10 Sept. 1784, in Telford, ed., *Letters of Wesley*, VII, 238–39.
[63] Jones, *Memoirs of Horne*, 155–56.
[64] See the account in Andrews, *Methodists and Revolutionary America*.
[65] Cited in Lincoln, *Political and Social Ideas*, 26.
[66] Price, *Observations*, 3, 19.
[67] Letter to W. Tayleur, 7 Sept. 1785, in Ditchfield, ed., *Letters of Lindsey*, 472.
[68] Wright, *The Unitarian Controversy*, 52.
[69] Brown, *Moral Capital*, 414–22.
[70] Friends House MSS, Epistles Received, 5, p. 262.
[71] Letter to J. Jay, 30 Aug. 1785, in Adams, ed., *Works of Adams*, VIII, 313.
[72] Letter to B. Collins, 11 March 1784, in Telford, ed., *Letters of Wesley*, VII, 214.
[73] Letter of 5 Feb. 1784, in Green, *Life of Witherspoon*, 200. Other letters conveyed the same message, ibid., 192–231.
[74] T. Miller to Sydney, 1 Aug. 1784, TNA, HO 100/3, ff. 143–44.
[75] Price to H. Merchant 6 Oct. 1783, to E. Stiles, 15 Oct. 1784, in Thomas and Peach, eds., *Correspondence of Price*, II, 199, 236.
[76] Letter to E. Smith, 29 Aug. 1785, in Ryerson, ed., *Adams Family Correspondence*, VI, 315.
[77] Letter of 29 Oct. 1783, in Johnston, ed., *Correspondence of Jay*, III, 92.
[78] Morgan, *Dickinson College*, 63–66.
[79] Durey, *Transatlantic Radicals*, 9.
[80] Ward, *Religion and Society*, ch. 2; Carwardine, *Trans-Atlantic Revivalism*.

References

An Abstract of the Proceedings of the Society for the Propagation of the Gospel in Foreign Parts for 1776. London, 1776.

Adams, Charles F.,ed. *The Works of John Adams.* 10 vols. Boston, MA: Little Brown, 1856.

Andrews, Dee E. *The Methodists and Revolutionary America 1760–1800: The Shaping of an Evangelical Culture.* Princeton, NJ: Princeton University Press, 2000.

Beardsley, E. Edwards. *The Life and Correspondence of the Right Reverend Samuel Seabury.* Boston, MA: Houghton Mifflin, 1881.

Beardsley, E. Edwards *The Life and Correspondence of Samuel Johnson, DD.* 3rd edn. Boston, MA: Houghton Mifflin, 1887.

Bloch, Ruth H. *Visionary Republic: Millennial Themes in American Thought, 1756–1800.* Cambridge: Cambridge University Press, 1988.

Bonwick, Colin 'English Dissenters and the American Revolution'. In *Contrast and Connection: Bicentennial Essays in Anglo-American History*, edited by H. C. Allen and Roger Thompson. London: G. Bell, 1976. 88–112.

Bradley, James E. *Popular Politics and the American Revolution in England: Petitions, the Crown and Public Opinion.* Macon, GA: Mercer University Press, 1986.

———. *Religion, Revolution, and English Radicalism: Nonconformity and Society in Eighteenth-Century Politics and Society.* Cambridge: Cambridge University Press, 1990.

Brown, Christopher L. *Moral Capital: Foundations of British Abolitionism.* Chapel Hill, NC: University of North Carolina Press, 2006.

Butterfield, L. H. *John Witherspoon Comes to America: A Documentary Account.* Princeton, NJ: Princeton University Press, 1953.

Cappe, Newcome. *A Sermon Preached on Wednesday 21st of February 1781, the Late Day of National Humiliation to a Congregation of Protestant Dissenters.* London, 1781.

Carwardine, Richard. *Trans-Atlantic Revivalism: Popular Evangelicalism in Britain and America 1790–1865.* Westport, CT: Greenwood, 1978.

Clark, Elmer T. J., J. Manning Potts and Jacob S. Payton, eds. *The Journals and Letters of Francis Asbury*, 3 vols. London: Epworth Press; Nashville, TN: Abingdon Press, 1958.

Clark, J. C. D. *The Language of Liberty 1660–1832: Political Discourse and Social Dynamics in the Anglo-American World.* Cambridge: Cambridge University Press, 1994.

Cooper, Myles. *National Humiliation and Repentance and the Causes of the Present Rebellion in America.* Oxford, 1777.

Crawford, Michael J. *Seasons of Grace: Colonial New England's Revivalist Tradition in its British Context.* Oxford and New York: Oxford University Press, 1991.

Ditchfield, G. M., ed. *The Letters of Theophilus Lindsey (1723–1808).* Woodbridge: Boydell & Brewer, 2007.

Donovan, R. K. 'The Popular Party of the Church of Scotland and the American Revolution'. In *Scotland and America in the Age of Enlightenment*, edited by Richard B. Sher and J. L. Smitten. Edinburgh: Edinburgh University Press, 1990, 81–99.

Durey, Michael. *Transatlantic Radicals in the Early American Republic.* Lawrence, KS: University of Kansas Press, 1997.

Foster, R. E. *Modern Ireland 1600–1972.* London: Penguin, 1989.

Green, Ashbel. *The Life of the Revd John Witherspoon*, edited by H. L. Savage. Princeton, NJ: Princeton University Press, 1973.

Guild, Reuben Aldridge. *Early History of Brown University.* New York: Arno Press, 1980. Originally published Providence, RI, 1897.

Haakonssen, Knud,ed. *Enlightenment and Religion: Rational Dissent in Eighteenth-Century Britain.* Cambridge: Cambridge University Press, 1996.

Hatch, Nathan O. *The Sacred Cause of Liberty: Republican Thought and the Millennium in Revolutionary New England.* New Haven, CT: Yale University Press, 1977.

Historical Manuscripts Commission: Rutland MSS. 4 vols. London: HM Stationery Office, 1888–1905.
Historical Manuscripts Commission: Stopford Sackville MSS. 2 vols. London: HM Stationery Office, 1904–10.
Hogan, Margaret A, C. James Taylor, Celeste Walker, Anne Decker Cecere, Gregg L. Lint, Hobson Woodward and Mary T. Claffeyeds, eds. *Adams Family Correspondence.* Vol. 7. Cambridge, MA: Harvard University Press, 2005.
Hook, Andrew. *Scotland and America: A Study of Cultural Relations 1750–1835.* Glasgow: Blackie, 1975.
Horne, George. *An Apology for Certain Gentlemen in the University of Oxford.* Oxford, 1756.
Johnstone, Henry P. *The Correspondence of Jay.* 4 vols. New York: G. P. Putnam, 1890–93.
Jones, William. *Memoirs of the Life, Studies and Writings of George Horne, Late Bishop of Norwich.* London, 1795.
Langford, Paul. 'The English Clergy and the American Revolution'. In *The Transformation of Political Culture: England and Germany in the late Eighteenth Century,* edited by E. Hellmuth. Oxford: Oxford University Press, 1989, 275–307.
'Letters of Dennys De Berdt 1757–1770'. *Publications of the Colonial Society of Massachusetts* 13 (1910–11).
Lincoln, Anthony. *Some Political and Social Ideas of English Dissent 1763–1800.* Cambridge: Cambridge University Press, 1938.
McAnear, Beverly. 'The Raising of Funds by Colonial Colleges'. *Mississippi Historical Review* 38 (1952).
McBride, Ian R. *Scripture Politics: Ulster Presbyterians and Irish Radicalism in the Late Eighteenth Century.* Oxford: Oxford University Press, 1998.
McLoughlin, William G. *New England Dissent, 1660–1833: The Baptists and the Separation of Church and State.* 2 vols. Cambridge, MA: Harvard University Press, 1971.
Mills, Frederick V. *Bishops by Ballot: An Eighteenth-century Ecclesiastical Revolution.* New York: Oxford University Press, 1978.
Morgan, James Henry.*Dickinson College: The History of One Hundred and Fifty Years.* Carlisle, PA, 1933.
O'Brien, Susan. 'A Transatlantic Community of Saints: The Great Awakening and the First Evangelical Network, 1735–55'. *American Historical Review* 91, no. 4 (1986): 811–32.
Olson, Alison Gilbert. *Making the Empire Work: London and the American Interest Groups 1690–1790.* Cambridge, MA: Harvard University Press, 1992.
Pascoe, C. F. *Two Hundred Years of the S. P. G.: An Historical Account of the Society for the Propagation of the Gospel in Foreign Parts 1701–1900.* 2 vols. London, 1901.
Perry, William Stevens,ed. *Historical Collections Relating to the American Colonial Church.* 5 vols. Hartford, CT.
Porter, Andrew. *Religion versus Empire? British Protestant Missionaries and Overseas Expansion, 1700–1914.* Manchester: Manchester University Press, 2004.
Porteus, Beilby. *A Review of the Life and Character of the Right Rev. Dr Thomas Secker.* 5th edn. London, 1797.
Price, Richard. *Observations on the Importance of the American Revolution and of the Means of Making it a Benefit to the World.* London, 1784.
Recordsof the General Synod of Ulster from 1691 to 1820. 3 vols. Belfast, 1890–98.
Ryerson, R. A.,ed. *The Adams Family Correspondence.* Vol 6. Cambridge, MA: Harvard University Press, 1993.
Stateof the Society in Scotland for Propagating Christian Knowledge. London, 1771.
Taylor, Alan. *The Divided Ground: Indians, Settlers and the Northern Borderland of the American Revolution.* New York: Knopf, 2006.
Telford, John,ed. *The Letters of the Rev. John Wesley.* 8 vols. London: Epworth Press, 1931.

Thomas, D. O. and W. Bernard Peach, eds. *The Correspondence of Richard Price*. 3 vols. Cardiff: University of Wales Press, Durham, NC: Duke University Press, 1983–94.
Upton, L. F. S., ed. *The Diary and Selected Papers of Chief Justice William Smith, 1784–93*. 2 vols. Toronto: Champlain Society, 1963–65.
Ward, W. R. *Religion and Society in England 1790–1850*. London: Batsford, 1972.
Wellwood, Scott Moncrieff. *An Account of the Life and Writings of John Erskine*. Edinburgh, 1818.
White, William. *Memoirs of the Protestant Episcopal Church in the United States of America*. 2nd edn. New York, 1836.
Wright, Conrad. *The Unitarian Controversy: Essays on American Unitarian History*. Boston, MA: Skinner House Books, 1994.

'A Good West Indian, a Good African, and, in Short, a Good Britisher':[1] Black and British in a Colour-Conscious Empire, 1760–1950

David Killingray

Racial difference lay at the heart of the British empire, more so after 1763 when the majority of imperial subjects were black or brown. Most people throughout the empire, irrespective of race, colour or religion, legally were 'subjects' of the Crown. Being black was a distinctive identity which, for peoples in the diaspora of the imperial 'black Atlantic' world and for African educated elites, overlapped with a sense of being

'British'. This British identity was shaped by crown service, imperial institutions and ideologies which created empire loyalties. However, few whites anywhere in the empire could conceive of Britons other than as white. In contesting this blacks had to bear the bitter burden of slavery, the power of a racially ordered empire and the persistent white prejudice which refused to recognise black achievement as 'civilised', well educated, Christian and respectable. Blacks attempted to claim equal rights with whites, often by recourse to law, although in the colonies this invariably proved a blunt instrument.

A number of scholars have pursued questions of imperial identity, mainly of white perceptions of identity in an imperial context.[2] This essay looks at how people of African origin and descent perceived their British identity within a racially constructed empire.[3] Being 'British' meant different things to different people all over the world, and was shaped by origin, place of residence, social class and accent, culture, as well as law.[4] Attempting to examine what imagining 'Britishness' meant in an imperial context is thus fraught with difficulties. While a modern sociologist might conduct surveys to determine how people perceived their identity, the historian has to rely on relatively few voices scattered through place and time, and those mostly of literate people and, in the case of this paper, drawn from the Americas, Africa and also Britain and spread over a span of 200 years.

Black colonial subjects in the Atlantic world laid claim to British identity for a variety of reasons. Perhaps one important idea, increasingly in circulation after the 1770s, was that English law as administered in England, and unlike the forms of law framed by American colonial legislatures, spelt freedom and a measure of racial equality before the courts. Such an idea did not have to be true, only to be believed to be so. In North America, knowledge of the Mansfield judgment of 1772, and offers of liberty given to runaway slaves by British military commanders during the Revolutionary War, helped foster the idea of English liberties, a view that accompanied black settlers from Nova Scotia to Freetown. Among the creole population of Freetown and in the other west African coastal towns where small Christian elites emerged from the 1840s, the claim to Britishness was invoked not only for legal purposes and self-interest but because it offered to a new class of people a formal identity that was implicit in being a subject of the British Crown. British identity meant association with and protection provided by the most powerful state in the world. Black people in the British Caribbean colonies, slave and free, with few exceptions, had always been 'British' even if that had meant being owned by white Britons. Emancipation in the 1830s helped to promote the idea of a beneficent queen, the liberator of the slaves, the guardian of their future freedoms, who merited allegiance. For Caribbean black subjects the obvious political allegiance was in being British, and for the small but growing middle class this identity was often shaped by the practice of Christianity and a life of moral respectability. Across the Atlantic and in the liberal political climate of the mid-nineteenth century Cape constitution, the new African elites, urged by Christian missionaries to embrace 'civilisation' and thus modernity, had every expectation of becoming equal members of the colony. Their cultural adaptation was accompanied by a growing sense of being part of a British system. Embracing Protestant Christianity, learning to read and write English, dressing and marrying well, using the plough, having access to a colour-blind franchise, living in a rectangular building, in short leaving the world of the 'savage' and the 'native' for the 'civilised' world, was a transition that included allegiance to a modern polity and being 'British'. Claiming Britishness also had another purpose, in that Africans could invoke the protection of the law against white settlers who refused them a place in the new 'civilised' order. In the southern African colonies the very success of African cultural adaptation and commercial advance stirred white hostility and resulted in measures to deny them access to equality. This in turn strengthened African appeals to the law to uphold their Britishness.

I

The British empire became increasingly concerned with race following the Seven Years' War when Britain acquired new territories in the Americas and India containing several million non-European peoples. Many were slaves who had experienced uprooting, displacement and forced movement. Being black was thus a badge of inferiority. Individual freedom from slavery and eventual total emancipation brought little change to their status and role, and white rulers and settlers regarded themselves as culturally and morally superior. As Morgan and Hawkins argue, 'many whites in the Empire devoted much effort to fixing blacks in place and denying them cultural resources'.[5]

Despite this, some metropolitan observers saw the empire as potentially inclusive. Burke described Indians as 'fellow citizens'; Macaulay's Education Minute of 1835 looked forward to a British India with 'a class of persons, Indian in blood and colour, but English in taste, in opinions, in morals, and in intellect'.[6] Certain Victorian humanitarians argued that the soundest policy for subject peoples was 'to assimilate them perfectly with ourselves', a view fiercely opposed by white settlers and officials in many colonies.[7] In Jamaica, the Franchise Act of 1859, Eyre's brutal suppression of the Morant Bay rising in 1865 and subsequent Crown Colony government graphically illustrated that there were two classes of British subjects who could expect different standards of colonial law and justice.[8] In the small west African colonies after 1870, educated blacks, who were fashioning new identities, were steadily denied access to positions of authority in state and church.[9] In the southern African white-ruled settler colonies, non-Europeans had consistently been excluded on the grounds of race. A few whites spoke of Christian civilisation and social progress but very few argued for an inclusive empire in which educated non-Europeans would take a place of social and political equality alongside whites. The 'Greater Britain' ideas of Seeley and of Dilke were essentially about white English-speaking peoples, although Fox-Bourne, the secretary of the Aborigines' Protection Society, suggested, in 1900, that all Africans who chose to give up their 'tribal' life permanently should be entitled to full rights of British citizenship, political and social.[10]

The free-trade nineteenth-century empire also meant the free movement of people, although several colonies imposed restraints on non-Europeans. Black imperial subjects were entitled to unimpeded entry and right of abode in Britain. 'Britishness' was defined not by geography but by 'allegiance to the Crown', a status reaffirmed in 1914, modified in 1948 and enduring until 1962.[11] Colonial subjects travelled with a British passport, a confirmation of Britishness. Black Britons who got into tight corners or straitened circumstances in odd corners of the globe were often grateful for the 'watchful eye and the strong arm of England'.[12] James Aggrey, the Gold Coast educator and a member of the Phelps-Stokes Commission, was delighted at the ease with which foreign doors were opened by a British passport, writing in 1920 to his wife Rose that 'it is great to be a British Subject'.[13] In Britain black colonial subjects possessed legal rights of movement, association, residence and also, if qualified, the vote, often denied them by constitution or ordinance in their home colony.[14] It was not uncommon for colonial subjects in Britain to be referred to as 'English' or 'British'.[15] As Westlake neatly put it in 1910, 'English law ... admits to the character of subjects all who are born within the king's allegiance; that is, speaking generally, within the British dominions'.[16] Ironically when he was writing there were white communities within the empire – Irish and Boer – eager to disclaim British identity, while many black people were keen to be fully acknowledged as British. During the Second World War, a Nigerian air-raid warden in a London shelter, faced with angry European refugees 'of many nations' intent on imposing segregation, told them bluntly that:

> The British Empire, which is also known as the Commonwealth of Nations, is made up of peoples of many races. I said that though I am an air-raid warden, I am still an African. I also said that I am one of many peoples of other countries that make up the Empire. Then I spoke of the three classes in the shelter – namely, His Majesty's subjects, protected persons, and guests.[17]

II

Most eighteenth-century American colonial legal codes endorsed black slavery. English and Scottish law on the matter was ambiguous. Slave status in England and Wales was dented, but not formally ended when Chief Justice Mansfield ruled in 1772 that black slaves could not forcibly be removed from the country to the colonies. In Scotland slavery was ruled to be illegal in 1778. Granville Sharp's legal case for black liberty in England, in 1769, was on the basis 'that Negroes, and all other Aliens are the *King's Subjects*, when resident in this kingdom; and that they are entitled to the Protection of the English Laws in general, and of the Habeas Corpus Act in particular'.[18] Black people in Britain were sometimes described as 'aliens', and occasionally in the colonies a private Act might enable the joint off-spring of a white man and a free mulatto woman to enjoy 'the same rights and privileges with English subjects born of white parents under certain restrictions'.[19]

This idea of a 'British' common identity was taken further in 1772 by Maurice Morgann who argued that slavery was incompatible with natural law. He imagined that over time free blacks would intermarry with whites and come to form, in the southern colonies of North America, a society where people 'will talk the same language, read the same books, profess the same religion, and be fashioned by the same laws: they will all depend on the same mother country'. His speculations were transatlantic, embracing the metropole, and possibly new west African colonies, where English as a 'universal language' would be spoken by 'an united people of various habits and complexion, [who] shall with one tongue gratefully commemorate the auspicious era of universal freedom'.[20] Some black slaves brought to Britain in the eighteenth century falsely believed that their presence on English soil endowed them with freedom. News of Mansfield's judgment of 1772 swiftly crossed the Atlantic to the American colonies and escaped slaves were eager to catch a ship for England in order to assert their freedom.[21] In his deposition for liberty to a Scottish court in 1778, Black Tom/David Spens claimed that his enslavement and return to the West Indies 'would deprive our Sovereign Lord the King, of a good subject'.[22]

In the late eighteenth century some black people spoke of Britain as 'home'. Towers Bell, describing himself as 'a true Brittain' (*sic*), wrote to the military authorities at the end of the revolutionary war stating that he had been removed from Britain against his will and sold as a slave, suffering 'the Greatest Barbarity in this Rebellious Country', and that now he wished to return 'home to England'.[23] George Liele, writing from Freetown in 1793, referred to Britain as 'home', resulting in a clarificatory note by his fellow Baptist John Rippon that by this 'he means England ... that is speaking of this country he generally called it *home*; and being asked why he did so, he replied, Almost all our people in different parts call it so'.[24] The African-British writers of the late eighteenth century claimed a dual identity. The frontispiece of Equiano's autobiography, published in 1789, proclaimed that he was 'The African', which he may have been by birth. However, his authorial name 'Gustavus Vassa' was a slave name, and by life, adoption and acculturation he had become 'almost an Englishman'.[25] Cugoano, or John Stewart, who described himself as 'a Native of Africa', had a dual identity, while Sancho, a property owner and an elector in Westminster, described himself in a letter to a friend as 'only a lodger [in England] – and hardly that'.[26] The former slave John Jea, when imprisoned in France in the early nineteenth century, denied that he was American, asserted his British Protestant identity and refused to fight against the English.[27]

Black slaves who identified themselves with the British cause during the American war of revolution, often on the basis of promised liberty, were widely known as 'loyalists'. Removed to Nova Scotia by the retiring British at the end of the war, they described themselves as 'a down-trodden race under a British flag', and named their church the British African American Methodist. They stated categorically: 'We are Britishers and we have the law and constitution of our glorious Empire to support us, and our rights we claim and our rights we will demand'.[28] As self-emancipated people they regarded themselves as 'free British subjects and entitled to all privileges as such'.[29] When black Nova Scotians emigrated to Sierra Leone in 1791, Wilberforce told John Clarkson that he should refer to them as 'Africans', arguing that this was 'a more respectable way of speaking of them'. However, this was not how the black settlers perceived themselves, arguing that they were free British subjects and Christians.[30]

The final emancipation of slaves in the West Indies in 1838 was marked by celebrations that emphasised their Britishness. At Falmouth, 'orchestrated by the British Baptist missionary William Knibb and his black deacons', a great procession was held, the coffin 'of slavery' solemnly buried and 'a flag reading FREEDOM together with the Union Jack was then raised and a tree of liberty planted'. In Lucea the celebrations included a great cheer for '"Britons never will be slaves". Black men and women could think of themselves and be thought of as Black Britons (a term almost forgotten until one hundred and fifty years later), part of the great nation, part of the empire.'[31] Christian conviction and English law met in an attempt to confirm that black people, now free from the constraints of slavery and apprenticeship, could hold to a British identity in order to protect themselves against the discriminatory acts of local legislatures. Protesting at police actions in 1865, Paul Bogle called on the governor of Jamaica to protect the 'petitioners of St Thomas in the East', who 'are Her Majesty's loyal subjects'. In order to identify themselves as 'civilised', equal to white people, African colonial subjects sometimes referred to themselves as 'a born British subject', as did James Davies writing to Henry Venn in 1861. Colonial administrators used similar terminology, Governor Hay of Sierra Leone in 1888 describing the black administrator Thomas George Lawson as a servant 'of unimpeachable loyalty and devotion to his Queen and Country'.[32]

III

Service in the British army and the Royal Navy fostered a sense of Britishness. During the American revolutionary war, slaves were encouraged to flee their masters with the promise of freedom if they joined the British forces.[33] Certain ex-slaves referred to themselves as 'the King of England's soldiers'.[34] The close quarters of a warship, with sailors receiving the same pay, benefits and health care, did not privilege one colour over another. The Admiralty viewed a naval vessel as 'a little piece of British territory in which slavery was improper'. A British captain refused to surrender the escaping Briton Hammon to the Spanish in Havana, saying 'he could not answer it, to deliver up any *Englishman* under *English* Colours'.[35] In 1823 an Act of Parliament legitimised the position of black seamen to be 'as much British seamen as a white man would be', while Indians and other non-whites were to be paid less and accorded treatment inferior to either black or white.[36] The recently discovered portrait of Mary Seacole (voted in 2004 the 'Greatest Black Briton'), now in the National Portrait Gallery, shows her proudly wearing her British medals from the Crimean War, a statement of her sense of patriotism and British identity.

At the end of the Great War, many black and Asian soldiers and sailors confidently laid claim to what they believed to be their earned rights as imperial citizens rather than as mere colonial 'subjects'. In South Africa, writes Bill Nasson, black and coloured servicemen saw their war effort as a 'buoyant opportunity' to promote 'political claims of full citizenship on the segregationist state'.[37] During the war, the *Educational Journal* of the Teachers' League, a coloured association in South Africa, proclaimed that 'we look forward with calm confidence to the triumph of British might and British right. We are prouder than ever of being subjects of the glorious British Empire.'[38] Certain Jamaican soldiers returning home from Britain in 1919 carried with them the slogan 'I am a British soldier'. Some, who had had experience of white British mob violence in the race riots of 1919, argued in terms of *Civis Romanus sum*.[39]

A message from Ndebele leaders to the British high commissioner in South Africa in 1918 stated that, 'when the King called upon us for help, we sent our young men, who fought and died beside the English, and we claim that our blood and that of the English are one'.[40]

In British ports and on British ships colonial subjects who had served in the Great War had the confident expectation that their loyal service would be recognised. They were sadly disillusioned immediately at the end of the war and through the 1920s as a combination of ship-owners, the seamen's union and the government sought to deny them their rights of citizenship and access to employment. The struggle to secure equal treatment on ships ran throughout the inter-war years to the disadvantage of both black Britons and colonial subjects.[41] In southern Africa, chiefs in the High Commission Territories, desperate that Britain should not abandon them to South Africa, played the political card of wartime loyalty and Britishness. Chief Montshiwa of the Baralong wrote to his men in 1943:

> War service is the means by which we are requesting through the Head of our administration, to the members of the forthcoming peace conference, that we may be considered and declared as citizens of the British Nation, and as such entitled to receive all rights of citizenship, politically, industrially and socially.[42]

IV

The steam ship, the telegraph and the postal system (the sovereign's head on every stamp) strengthened colonial ties with the metropole. The symbol of the Crown, the governor, the Union Jack, celebrations of monarchical rituals and holidays, naval and army uniforms, the churches, the educational system and organisations such as the Boys' Brigades, Scouts and Guides, all helped to promote an imperial ideology and to fashion a collective sense of British identity.[43] Formal education, largely in Christian mission schools, promoted the use of English using an English modelled curriculum based on school books published in Britain. And, for many black students in the Atlantic world, a modern education in English allied to 'progress', 'improvement' and 'respectability' – in dress, manners and hygiene – meant entry into 'civilised' society and expectation of equal rights without distinction of race.[44] In Cape Colony the English language was not only international, unlike Dutch/Afrikaans, but 'the language which inspires the noblest thoughts of freedom and liberty'.[45] In the West Indies and the African colonies, the small but growing numbers of students in schools were very conscious of their place within an empire that was British. Lessons in schools in Kingston, Jamaica, were similar to those in Kingston upon Thames thousands of miles away.

Large crowds turned out to celebrate royal occasions, and especially to greet royal visitors at the Cape in August 1901, and also when the royal family toured South Africa in 1947.[46] The novelist Richard Rive recalled the decade after the end of the Second World War as 'those red-white-and-blue days'.[47] On these and other occasions 'loyal addresses' were produced by the small political organisations that were founded in the early years of the twentieth century in all parts of the black Atlantic world. The Union Jack could also be used as a political symbol by black colonial subjects. F. Z. S. Peregrino, in a pamphlet addressed to coloured voters in Cape Province in 1915, wrote that the British flag 'knows no colour, race or creed'.[48] Louisa Mvemve, an Xhosa woman of relatively little formal education, described herself in letters that she wrote in the 1920s and 1930s, as 'a civilised person, native healer, public benefactor and loyal subject of the Crown', stating that 'I was born under the British flag'.[49] Johana Kunyiha, a founder of the Kikuyu Independent School Association in Kenya, argued for the use of English in the curriculum rather than the prescribed vernacular: 'I am one of the subjects of [the King] and I am bound to teach his tongue in our schools.'[50] In most colonies the increase in the number of schools led to a growth of literacy and a wider readership for books and newspapers in English. Protestant Christianity underpinned much of this. Sports were also 'English' and ideas of 'fair play' were supposedly shaped on the cricket field and football pitch; also a vaguely defined set of 'British values' imparted by many teachers, black and white, influenced student thinking. While education and Christianity stirred new radical political ideas they also encouraged imperial loyalties.

V

In the mid- and late nineteenth century the vast majority of black people who had received a 'modern' education thought of themselves as being British, a loyalty primarily focused on the person of the monarch. Within different colonies there were different views of monarchy. In the British West Indies the British monarch was the sole hereditary ruler; in African colonies there were local monarchs, although this did not prevent people thinking in terms of dual loyalties, for example to the Zulu king and also to Queen Victoria. Most politically articulate black subjects aimed for inclusion and racial equality within a colony, not separation from empire. Thus embracing British identity and British institutions was a way of promoting and supporting claims to equality. Being British did not mean that Africans could not also embrace and value other identities. Tiyo Soga, educated in Scotland, married to a white Scot, in 1864 could write of himself as 'the loyal subject of the best government for the aborigines that ever existed under heaven', yet at the same time, as an Xhosa patriot, could believe that the interests of his own people were best served by remaining under the British Crown.[51]

This was argued with greater energy by black elites as the tide of pseudo-scientific racism gained ground from the mid-nineteenth century onwards and influenced the affairs of state and church. Colonial 'nationalisms' in the late nineteenth century argued for equality and integration within a colour-blind empire, not for separation. Robert Love, the Jamaican 'nationalist', argued: 'We desire to be English, in spite of some faults which we see and feel there is much that is good and sound in the great heart of England, and we have confidence in Her great intentions.'[52] This was a touching optimism given the widespread racial discrimination practised in the Crown colony at the time. Similar ideas were expressed by African radicals in the imperial capital. In the first issue of Dusé Mohamed Ali's *African Times and Orient Review*, published in 1912, he proclaimed that '[w]e, as native and loyal subjects of the British Empire, hold too high an opinion of Anglo-Saxon chivalry to believe other than that African and Oriental wrongs have but to be made manifest in order that they may be righted'.[53] At the end of the Great War, in which the west African elite had demonstrated their loyalty, the National Congress of British West Africa was 'founded on the loyalty and faith of a people under British Rule' with the aim of achieving 'universal liberties', and, as J. E. Casely Hayford reminded his fellow political activists in early 1923, 'the policy of the NCBWA "is to maintain strictly and inviolate the connection of the British West African Dependencies with the British Empire"'.[54] In west Africa, the West Indies and also in South Africa, educated Africans hoped and expected that their loyal and active support in wartime would be rewarded by political reforms and constitutional changes that promoted their role in local government. In fact, few rewards were given.

Empire loyalism was common, there being few other perceived political prospects for Caribbean and African colonies than association with Britain and the extension of metropolitan norms to the colonies. A prime aim of the African Association, formed by Henry Sylvester Williams in London in September 1897, was 'to promote and protect the interests of all British subjects claiming African descent, by circulating accurate information on all questions affecting their rights and privileges, and by direct appeal to the Imperial and local governments'. Five year later Williams, in a brief booklet pointedly entitled *The British Negro*, argued that the inhabitants of British territories 'are made British' but are generally denied those full privileges because of 'colour prejudice'.[55] Addressing the Pan-African Conference in London in 1900, C. W. French, from St Kitts, clearly stated the demands of black Britons: 'The coloured people claimed from the British Government just that recognition which they were entitled to as men – namely that under the Queen's rule men of colour should have equal place and position with the white race.'[56] Even in the exceptional circumstances of white settler rule in the two South African colonies, non-Europeans continued vainly to hope for metropolitan intervention long after the Act of Union in 1910 and further imposition of racially discriminatory legislation. Among Africans and coloured people there was a strong sense that rule by the British meant a degree of 'fairness'. Samuel Mqhayi, the Xhosa praise poet, distinguished between white settlers and a distant government when he wrote: 'You occupied this land by force,/You settled on this land like a pest./You will leave this land like a still-born./As always we still say we are British.'[57] During the South African war, most African and coloured peoples in Cape Colony and Natal supported the British not out of mindless patriotism, argues Nasson, but because they believed that they could turn rhetoric into reality.[58] A contemporary song in Afrikaans sung by coloured people in Cape Town contained the line 'Come Britannia, the civilizing one'.[59] Conscious of coloured 'loyalist' sentiment, at the election of 1898 Rhodes changed the slogan of his pro-British South African League from 'equal rights for all whites' to 'equal rights for all civilized men south of the Zambezi'. Such changes helped spur optimism that change was possible, even in a white-settler-dominated colony.

When hopes were dashed by the Treaty of Vereeniging, rebuff to appeals and deputations, and later by the Act of Union, the coloured paper *APO*, urged its readers to improve themselves as 'we shall be required to prove that we are worthy of these and other rights which we claim as loyal British citizens'.[60] An appeal to King Edward VII from the Native United Political Associations of the Transvaal in April 1905, began by stating '[t]hat your petitioners are loyal subjects of Your Most Excellent Majesty, residing in the Transvaal Colony', and went on to state their right of 'enjoying the liberty, freedom and equality to which as British subjects they claim to be entitled'. The following year a petition to the House of Commons, from 'J. Tengo-Jabavu and thirteen other signatories', began: 'The petition of the undersigned British subjects ... native residents in the Cape Colony, are loyal British subjects'.[61]

The educational system and the institutions of the British West Indies helped to forge in many people a strong sense of British empire loyalism. Harold Moody, founder of the League of Coloured Peoples in London in 1931, came to study in London early in the century with a very strong sense of being British and coming 'home' to the 'motherland'. As he told a meeting at Friends House in October 1932: 'I am proud of my British citizenship. I am still more proud of my colour. I do not want to feel that my colour is robbing me of the privileges to which I am entitled as a British citizen.'[62] Even C. L. R. James confessed to being imbued with similar ideas and feelings when he first came to Britain in 1932. So did many West Indians who served in the armed forces during the 1940s. Connie Macdonald, a Jamaican who joined the Auxiliary Territorial Service, stated:

> We were British! England was our mother country. We were brought up to respect the Royal family. I used to collect pictures of Margaret and Elizabeth, you know. I adored them. It was the British influence. We didn't grow up with any Jamaican thing – we grew up as British.[63]

VI

Imperial subjects made frequent reference to English law and the rights conferred on British subjects. Cato Perkins and Isaac Anderson, carrying a Sierra Leone petition to London in 1793, complained that within the new colony, to which they had gone voluntarily as British subjects, 'we are certainly not protected by the laws of Great Britain'.[64] What was sought then, and later, was *entitlement*, access to equal rights enjoyed under law by white British subjects. In the self-governing settler colonies of the Cape and Natal, non-Europeans suffered the constant indignities of discrimination. A spokesman for the *amakholwa* – 'civilised' Africans – at the Edendale community, outside Pietermaritzburg, told his fellow farmers in 1863:

> We have left the race of our forefathers; we have left the black race and have clung to the white. We imitate them in every way we can ... Look round you. You have an English house, English tables, chairs.... [E]verything round us is English but one, and that is the law. The law by which our cases are decided is only fit to be eaten by vultures.[65]

The feisty Charlotte Manye, touring with the African Choir, told British audiences in 1891: 'Let us be in Africa as we are in England. Here we are treated as men and women. Yonder we are but as cattle. But in Africa, as in England, we are human. Can you not make your people at the Cape as kind and just as your people here?'[66] A few years later Magema Fuze, who had accompanied the Zulu king Dinuzulu into exile on St Helena as a translator, protested to the governor that his mail was opened by officials 'the first time I have received this bad treatment. The English government is Christian one with justice. And is always expected to treat everyone with justice. And I thought this was forbidden by English laws.'[67] M. K. Gandhi's early political years, from 1893 to 1914, were spent in South Africa. He was a patriotic member of the British empire and remained so for many years despite the constant discriminatory abuse which he met from white colonial settlers.[68] As a lawyer he was very conscious of the power of law and also how the courts could be used to challenge inequities, his appeals to London being 'consistently to a "British" discourse of rights'.[69]

Conditions in southern Africa became more difficult in the years of Reconstruction as steps were taken to create a unified British dominion. Settler interests rejected ideas of legal racial equality or a non-European franchise, while African elites hoped that appeals to London to redress their wrongs might result in rights being enshrined in law rather than denied by law. A petition signed by 15,000 Cape coloured British subjects, carried to London in 1906, argued that they were 'fully civilized British coloured subjects mostly registered voters at municipal, divisional and parliamentary elections' who wished 'to retain their full independent rights as British subjects in any South African British Colony'.[70] Writing of South Africa in 1908, Bandele Omoniyi, a Nigerian medical student in Edinburgh, stated:

> the African Native has political rights as a British citizen and subject ... I believe and I claim that the natives from the day they came under British dominion became British subjects, possessing all the rights which British subjects possess, and that therefore they are no [sic] foreigners or aliens.[71]

When black and coloured delegates came to London in 1909 to protest the imposition of the Union on South Africa's peoples, again in 1914 to campaign against the recent Land Act and yet again in 1919–21 to ask that London support their interests, the consistent demand was for equality of rights as British subjects. Sol Plaatje's *Native Life in South Africa*, published in London in 1916, was a direct appeal to British public opinion 'on behalf of five million loyal British subjects who shoulder "the black man's burden"'.[72] The ambiguity of the African position, wanting to blame Britain for betraying black loyalists and yet claiming the protecting arms of the imperial system, was caught by Modiri Molema, writing in Glasgow where he was completing his medical studies, when he urged Britain to resume its responsibilities for South Africa.[73] Plaatje was more outspoken, telling the Pan-African Congress in Paris in 1921, that 'when we see how men of another race and colour, who hate the British flag, are accorded British protection and allowed to revel in plenty at the expense of the loyal black millions, we sometimes wonder whether our loyalty has not been the means of our undoing'.[74]

The law and claims to be 'British' subjects of the Crown were two vital weapons used in the political battle for non-European civil rights. In the British West Indies, black people struggled in the late nineteenth century to secure equal treatment in the affairs of state and church. Robert Gordon, a Jamaican who became a Garveyite activist, complained that black people were 'restricted by the "system" and ... denied their rightful inheritance'. Robert Love's People's Convention, formed in Jamaica in 1901, urged that Emancipation Day 'should be *utilized to the end* that the Negro subjects of the British Crown will eventually rise to the full dignity of their national privileges, and *enjoy without any distinction* the full political manhood embraced in British citizenship'.[75]

English law and practice in Britain were ambiguous on matters involving race and colour. While the British Nationality and Status of Aliens Act of 1914 declared that 'any person born within His Majesty's dominions and allegiance [was] ... a British subject', the *Manual of Military Law* stated that 'any negro or person of colour' was an alien, and that all officers had to be of 'pure European descent'.[76] Racial discrimination, overt and covert, led Theophilus Scholes, the Jamaican missionary turned political writer, to remark in despair:

> You may give [the black man] the rights of citizenship by law; you can never make him the real equal, the real fellow, or citizens of European descent ... The Negro may be a man and a brother in some secondary sense; he is not a man and a brother in the same full sense in which every western Aryan is a man and a brother ... He cannot be assimilated; the laws of Nature forbid it.[77]

Ten years later, in 1919, F. E. M. Hercules, the Trinidad-born general secretary of the Society of Peoples of African Origin, wrote to *The Times* protesting at colour prejudice: 'We are taking our stand on this fundamental principle of the British Constitution that for every British subject there shall be equality before the law regardless of the colour of a man's skin.'[78]

The vain hope that a distant Britain would address the discriminatory ills of South Africa's segregationist regime lingered long in African minds. Addressing the Natal Native Congress, of which he had just been elected president, J. T. Gumede in 1924 said 'that the South African legal system had failed and final resort would be to "England['s] judges"'.[79] The prophet Nontetha Nkwenkwe claimed in the 1930s to be in communication with Queen Victoria and employed the queen's image as an 'icon of liberty, justice and support for suppressed colonial peoples'.[80] Davidson D. T. Jabavu, touring Britain in 1931 to counter Hertzog's policies that denied civil rights to blacks and laid claim to the High Commission Territories, told audiences that 'we Blacks much prefer direct rule under the Imperial Government, for we still look to Great Britain as our fountain of justice and regard her as our paramount protector'.[81] As late as the royal tour of South Africa in 1947, there were black South Africans who had a touching belief that London would intervene in South Africa's domestic affairs and bring about a more egalitarian society.[82] In west Africa opponents of empire used their 'Britishness' in order to contest colonial laws. Wallace Johnson successfully appealed to London against his conviction in the Gold Coast in 1936, his attorney arguing that his words were 'an expression of opinion made by him under his right, as a British subject of African descent, to discuss public affairs fully and freely'.[83] In the post-Second World War years, when both the British and the French governments, in Fred Cooper's words, 'were trying to construct some kind of junior citizenship through which colonized peoples could partake of some, but not all, of the qualities of a metropolitan citizen',[84] they opened themselves further to claims for rights from colonial subjects aspiring to full citizenship. Even Gikuyu detainees during the Mau Mau emergency addressed petitions appealing to British law: 'The actions and the treatments which are going on in Detention Camps mostly in Manyani are completely out of orders and laws of Queen Elizabeth the II'.[85]

VII

Many non-European peoples in the British empire grew up with the knowledge that they were British subjects and that one of their identities was being 'British'. Being British carried expectations of acceptance by whites and legal equality with them and thus entitlement to office. These were vain hopes, rapidly eroded from the late nineteenth century in the west African and the Caribbean colonies, and never much in evidence in the white settler colonies of South Africa. Black British subjects who came to Britain often had their pride in a British identity punctured when they encountered the deeply ingrained racial antipathy that permeated official and private institutions and many white individuals. The early black British political organisations argued for 'equality of opportunity for every British subject without reference to the colour of his skin, the creed he professes or the race or class to which he happens to belong'.[86] Harold Moody's League of Coloured Peoples (LCP) challenged the widely accepted view that 'true' Britons were white while promoting the idea of a British imperial identity within a progressive and colour blind empire.[87] 'We are all British subjects', wrote David Tucker, the editor of *The Keys*, the journal of the LCP, in 1934,[88] while his colleague George Brown, arguing the cause of black British seamen in Cardiff who were denied rights, argued: 'Without people of colour there would be neither Cardiff nor an Empire. For numerically and territorially this is overwhelmingly a coloured Empire, not a white one.'[89] Empire immigrants often arrived in Britain with 'a sense of cultural identification with the Motherland', a Britishness shaped by language, education, religious persuasion, the names of the places where they had grown up which 'were named after British places and personalities'. For many, it was a journey to an illusion.[90]

This essay has touched on an aspect of British imperial identity that has been little addressed. It is an area of enquiry that could be extended to take in the whole British empire and which might also look comparatively at questions of identity in other European empires. British colonial subjects could not expect to become 'citizens', which was a republican concept, as could *evolués* in the French empire, but they were subjects of the British Crown. In their disparate campaigns and pleas for equality and entitlement, black Britons often sought to become fully accepted members of the British empire, but race always excluded them from that right. An empire founded on race seemed destined to fail.

Notes

[1] Alexander Grantham, Chief Secretary of Nigeria, in honouring Canon Lackland A. Lennon, a Jamaican Anglican clergyman, recent recipient of an MBE, who for many years had worked in west Africa. *Nigerian Daily Times*, 30 March 1943.
[2] I am indebted to the ideas and arguments advanced by Colley, 'Britishness and otherness'; Wilson, *Island Race* and her edited *A New Imperial History*; Daunton and Halpern, *Empire and Others*; Hall and Rose, *At Home with the Empire*; Bridge and Fedorowich, *The British World*; Kumar, *The Making of English National Identity*; Colls, *Identity in England*; Lake and Reynolds, *Drawing the Global Colour Line*.
[3] Morgan and Hawkins, 'Blacks and the British Empire', 1–34. Also Rush, 'The Bonds of Empire'.
[4] Brubaker and Cooper, 'Beyond "Identity"'.
[5] Morgan and Hawkins, 'Blacks and the British Empire', 1.
[6] Burroughs, 'Imperial Institutions', 181.
[7] For example, *Colonial Intelligencer and Aborigines Friend*, May and June 1848, Annual Report, 15. Lowe and McLaughlin, 'Sir John Pope Hennessy', 237–39.
[8] Holt, *The Problem of Freedom*, chs 6–8.
[9] Northrup, 'Becoming African'.
[10] Fox-Bourne, *The Native Question*, 10.
[11] Goulbourne, *Ethnicity and Nationalism*, 91–96.
[12] Palmerston in United Kingdom *Hansard*, 1850.
[13] Smith, *Aggrey of Africa*, 147.
[14] Lord Ripon, the Secretary of State, to the Governor of Natal, 1894, TNA, CO179/189.
[15] Dadabhai Naoroji, as a parliamentary candidate, was presented by his white sponsor to the Liberal Association of Holborn in the late 1880s as a long-term resident who could justly be called 'an Englishman as well as an English subject'. Quoted by Holmes, *John Bull's Island*, 83–84.
[16] Westlake, 'Aliens', *Encyclopaedia Britannica*, I, 662.
[17] Ekpenyon, *Experiences of an African Air-raid Warden*, 10.
[18] Sharp, *An Appendix*, 20–28, 152–59.
[19] CO139/22 (87), quoted by Chater, 'Untold Histories', 316–18, concerning a private Act of the Jamaican Assembly in 1766 relating to the 'son of Elizabeth Fickle a free mulatto by Malcolm Laing'.
[20] Morgann, *Plan for the Abolition of Slavery*, 25–27, 33.
[21] For example, *Virginia Gazette*, 30 September 1773, 30 October 1774, quoted in Schama, *Rough Crossings*, 25.
[22] Edwards and Walvin, *Black Personalities*, 160–62.
[23] Quoted Schama, *Rough Crossings*, 14.
[24] Rippon, *Baptist Register*, II, 95.
[25] Equiano, *Interesting Narrative*, 77.
[26] Sancho, *Letters*, 177.
[27] Jea, *The Life*.
[28] Fingard, 'Race and Respectability', 169.
[29] Coleman, *Romantic Colonization*, 109.
[30] Pybus, '"A Less Favourable Specimen"', 100.
[31] Hall, 'William Knibb', 317–22.
[32] James Pinson Labulo Davies, a Lagos merchant, to Henry Venn, 9 November 1861, in Kopytoff, *Preface to Modern Nigeria*, 286. See also Skinner, *Thomas George Lawson*, 49.
[33] Schama, *Rough Crossings*, 326, 336–38, 342, 358, 366–67, 277.

[34] Kaplan and Kaplan, *Black Presence*, 85.
[35] Hammon, *Narrative*, 6.
[36] Hepple, *Race, Jobs and the Law*, 63–64.
[37] Nasson, 'War Opinion in South Africa', 257.
[38] Quoted in Adhikari, '"The Product of Civilization"', 297–98.
[39] Smith, *Jamaican Volunteers*, 163; Howe, *Race, War and Nationalism*, 193.
[40] Ranger, *African Voice in Southern Rhodesia*, 43–4.
[41] Tabili, 'We ask for British Justice'.
[42] Jackson, 'Motivation and Mobilization', 403.
[43] Ranger, 'Making Northern Rhodesia Imperial'.
[44] Bickford-Smith, 'Revisiting Anglicisation', 85.
[45] Adhikari, '"The Product of Civilization"', 289.
[46] Sapire, 'Ornamentalism in Southern Africa'.
[47] Rive, 'Buckingham Palace', 1.
[48] Peregrino, *The Political Parties*. Parsons, 'F. Z. S. Peregrino'. Saunders, 'F. Z. S. Peregrino'.
[49] Burns, 'Letters of Louisa Mvemve', 11, 103.
[50] Parsons, *Race, Resistance and the Boy Scout Movement*, 132.
[51] Bickford-Smith, 'Black Englishness'. Chalmers, *Tiyo Soga*, 488, for the multiple identities of 'A Model Kafir'.
[52] Lumsden, 'Robert Love', 136.
[53] *African Times and Orient Review* I, 1 (1912), i.
[54] *Sierra Leone Weekly News*, 24 February 1923, 9.
[55] Williams, *British Negro*, 11, 21.
[56] Schneer, *London 1900*, 215, 223.
[57] Saunders, 'African Attitudes', 143.
[58] Nasson, *Abraham Esau's War*, ch. 7.
[59] Bickford-Smith, 'Black Ethnicities', 447. Bickford-Smith reports a white visitor in 1897 asking an African dock worker whether he was a 'native' of Cape Colony. The African replied he was English, and pointing to 'coal-carrying Kaffirs', he said they were natives. Ibid., 451.
[60] *APO* (Cape Town), 3 December 1910.
[61] Karis and Carter, *Protest to Challenge*, 45–46, 49.
[62] Moody, 'Communications', 98.
[63] Sherwood, 'Caribbean Participation in the Second World War'; Busby, 'Connie Mark', 43.
[64] Schama, *Rough Crossings*, 367.
[65] Erlmann, *Music, Modernity and the Global Imagination*, 138.
[66] *Review of Reviews*, 4, 2 (September 1891), 256.
[67] Khumalo, 'Ekukhanyeni Letter-Writers', 129–31.
[68] Gandhi, *Autobiography*, 142–43.
[69] Boehmer, *Empire*, 162. Brown, *Gandhi*, 30–94; Brown and Prozesky, *Gandhi and South Africa*.
[70] Bodleian Library, Oxford, Rhodes House, Anti-Slavery Society papers, Brit. Emp. S22, G198.
[71] Omoniyi, *Defence of the Ethiopian Movement*, 23.
[72] Plaatje, *Native Life in South Africa*, 3; Boehmer, *Empire*, 128–29, 134–35, 138–40, 160–64.
[73] Molema, *The Bantu*; Starfield, '"A Dance with the Empire"', 479–503.
[74] Willan, *Sol Plaatje: Selected Writings*, 273.
[75] Gordon, *Jamaica Jubilee*. *Jamaica Advocate*, 27 July 1901, quoted by Patrick Bryan, *Jamaican People*, 261.
[76] This continued until 1939 and was then suspended but only for the duration.

[77] Scholes, *British Empire and Alliances*, 273.
[78] *The Times*, 19 June 1919, 8B.
[79] Lalouvière, *Restless Identities*, 107.
[80] Edgar and Sapire, *African Apocalypse*, 67–68.
[81] Jabavu, 'Native Disabilities', 6-7, 16-17.
[82] Sapire, 'Ornamentalism'.
[83] *The Times*, 27 May 1938, 4C; Asante, *Pan-African Protest*, 161–63.
[84] Cooper, *Decolonization*, 266.
[85] Peterson, 'Review article', 492–93.
[86] 'What We Stand For', and 'Why the *African Telegraph* Is Published', *African Telegraph*, May–June 1919, 212.
[87] Rush, 'Imperial Identity', 356–83.
[88] *The Keys*, I, 3 (Jan. 1934), 42.
[89] *The Keys*, III, 2 (Oct.–Dec. 1935), 21; Tabili, 'We Ask for British Justice'.
[90] Dabydeen and Wilson-Tagoe, *A Reader's Guide*, 80–81.

References

Adhikari, Mohamed. '"The Product of Civilization in its Most Repellent Manifestation": Ambiguities in the Racial Perceptions of the *APO (African Political Organization)*, 1909–23'. *Journal of African History* 38, no. 2 (1997): 283–300.
Asante, K. B. *Pan-African Protest: West Africa and the Italo-Ethiopian Crisis 1934–1941*. London: Longman, 1977.
Bickford-Smith, Vivian. 'Black Ethnicities, Communities and Political Expression in late Victorian Cape Town'. *Journal of African History* 36, no. 3 (1995): 443–65.
———. 'Revisiting Anglicisation in the Nineteenth-Century Cape Colony'. *Journal of Imperial and Commonwealth History* 31, no. 2 (2003): 82–95.
———. 'Black Englishness: The Case of Tiyo Soga'. Unpublished paper.
Boehmer, Elleke. *Empire, the National, and the Postcolonial, 1890–1920*. Oxford: Oxford University Press, 2002.
Bridge, Carl and Kent Fedorowich, eds. *The British World: Diaspora, Culture and Identity*. London: Frank Cass, 2003.
Brown, Judith M. and Martin Prozesky, eds. *Gandhi and South Africa: Principles and Politics*. Pietermaritzburg: University of Natal Press, 1996.
Brubaker, Roger and Frederick Cooper. 'Beyond "Identity"'. *Theory and Society* 29, no. 1 (2000): 1–47.
Bryan, Patrick.*The Jamaican People 1880–1902*. Basingstoke: Macmillan, 1991.
Burns, Catherine.'The Letters of Louisa Mvemve'. In *Africa's Hidden Histories*, edited by Barber. Karin. Bloomington, IN: Indiana University Press, 2006.
Burroughs, Peter. 'Imperial Institutions and the Government of Empire'. In The Oxford History of the British Empire Vol.3, *The Nineteenth Century*, edited by Andrew Porter. Oxford: Oxford University Press, 1999.
Busby, Margaret. 'Connie Mark, Community Activist and Caribbean Champion'. *The Guardian* (London), 43, 16 June 2007.
Chalmers, John A. *Tiyo Soga: A Page of South African Mission Work*. Edinburgh: Andrew Elliot, 1877.
Chater, Kathy. 'Untold Histories: Black People in England and Wales 1660–1812'. PhD diss., University of London, 2007.
Coleman, Deidre. *Romantic Colonization and British Anti-Slavery*. Cambridge: Cambridge University Press, 2005.
Colley, Linda. 'Britishness and Otherness: An Argument'. *Journal of British Studies* 31, no. 4 (1992): 302–29.
Colls, Robert. *Identity in England*. Oxford: Oxford University Press, 2002.

Cooper, Frederick. *Decolonization and African Society: The Labor Question in French and British Africa*. Cambridge: Cambridge University Press, 1996.

Dabydeen, David and Nanna Wilson-Tagoe. *A Reader's Guide to Westindian and Black British Literature*. Revd edn. London: Hansib Publications, 1997. Originally published 1988.

Daunton, Martin and Rick Halpern, eds. *Empire and Others: British Encounters with Indigenous Peoples 1600–1850*. London: Routledge, 1999.

Edgar Robert, R. and Hilary Sapire. *African Apocalypse: The Story of Nontetha Nkwenkwe a Twentieth Century South African Prophet*. Athens, OH: Ohio University Press, 1999.

Edwards, Paul and James Walvin. *Black Personalities in the Era of the Slave Trade*. London: Macmillan, 1981.

Ekpenyon, E. I. *Some Experiences of an African Air-raid Warden*. London: Sheldon Press, 1943.

Equiano, Olaudah.*The Interesting Narrative of the Life of Olaudah Equiano*. Edited by Vincent Carretta. London: Penguin, 1995, Originally published 1789.

Erlmann, Viet. *Music, Modernity and the Global Imagination: South Africa and the West*. New York: Oxford University Press, 1999.

Fingard, Judith. 'Race and Respectability in Victorian Halifax'. *Journal of Imperial and Commonwealth History* 20, no. 2 (1992): 169–95.

Fox-Bourne, Henry. *The Native Question in South Africa*. London 1900.

Gandhi, M. K. *The Story of My Experiments with the Truth: An Autobiography*. London: Phoenix Press, 1949. Originally published 1926.

Goulbourne, Harry. *Ethnicity and Nationalism in Post-Imperial Britain*. Cambridge: Cambridge University Press, 1991.

Hall Catherine. 'William Knibb and the Constitution of the New Black Subject'. In *Empire and Others: British Encounters with Indigenous Peoples 1600–1850*. Edited by Martin Daunton and Rick Halpern. London: Routledge, 1999.

Hall, Catherine and Sonya O. Rose, eds. *At Home with the Empire: Metropolitan Culture and the Imperial World*. Cambridge: Cambridge University Press, 2006.

Hammon, Briton. *Narrative of the Uncommon Sufferings and Surprizing Deliverance of Briton Hammon, a Negro Man*. Boston, MA, 1760.

Hepple, Bob. *Race, Jobs and the Law in Britain*. Harmondsworth: Penguin, 1970.

Holmes, Colin. *John Bull's Island: Immigration & British Society 1871–1971*. Basingstoke: Macmillan, 1988.

Holt, Thomas C. *The Problem of Freedom: Race, Labour, and Politics in Jamaica and Britain, 1832–1938*. Kingston, Jamaica: Ian Randle, 1992.

Howe, Glenford. *Race, War and Nationalism: A Social History of West Indians in the First World War*. Kingston, Jamaica: Ian Randle, 2002.

Jabavu, D. D. T. *'Native Disabilities' in South Africa*. Lovedale, 1932.

Jackson, Ashley. 'Motivation and Mobilization for War Recruitment for the British Army in the Bechuanaland Protectorate, 1941–42'. *African Affairs* 96 (1997): 399–417.

James, C. L. R. *Beyond a Boundary*. London: Stanley Paul, 1963.

Jea, John. *The Life, History and Unparalleled Sufferings of John Jea: The African Preacher. Compiled and Written by Himself*. Portsea, c. 1815

Kaplan, Sidney and Emma Nogrady Kaplan. *The Black Presence in the Era of the American Revolution*. Amherst MA: University of Massachusetts Press, 1989.

Karis, Thomas and Gwendolen Carter, eds. *From Protest to Challenge: A Documentary History of African Politics in South Africa 1882–1964*. vol 1. *Protest and Hope 1882–1934*. Stanford CA: Stanford University Press, 1972.

Keys, The Journal of the League of Coloured Peoples, 1933–39.

Khumalo, Vukile. 'Ekukhanyeni Letter-Writers'. In *Africa's Hidden Histories*, edited by Karin Barber. Bloomington, IN: Indiana University Press, 2006.

Kopytoff, Jean Herskovits. *A Preface to Modern Nigeria: The 'Sierra Leonians' in Yoruba, 1830–1890.* Madison, WI: Wisconsin University Press, 1965.

Kumar, Krishnan. *The Making of English National Identity.* Cambridge: Cambridge University Press, 2003.

Lake, Marilyn and Henry Reynolds. *Drawing the Global Colour Line: White Men's Countries and the International Challenge of Racial Equality.* Cambridge: Cambridge University Press, 2008.

Lalouvière, Paul la Hausse de la. *Restless Identities. Signatures of Nationalism, Zulu Identity and History in the Lives of Petros Lamula (c. 1881–1948) and Lymon Maling (1889–c.1936).* Pietermaritzburg: University of Natal Press, 2000.

Lowe, Kate and Eugene McLaughlin. 'Sir John Pope Hennessy and the "Native Race Craze": Colonial Government in Hong Kong, 1877–1822'. *Journal of Imperial and Commonwealth History* 20, no. 2 (1992): 223–47.

Lumsden, Joyce. 'Robert Love and Jamaican Politics'. PhD diss., University of the West Indies, Mona, 1987

Molema, Modiri. *The Bantu Past and Present.* Edinburgh: W. Green, 1920.

Moody, Harold A. 'Communications'. *The Journal of Negro History* 18 (1933): 92–99.

Morgan, Philip D. and Sean Hawkins. 'Blacks and the British Empire'. In *Black Experience and the Empire*, edited by Philip D. Morgan and Sean Hawkins. Oxford: Oxford University Press, 2004.

Morgann, Maurice. *Plan for the Abolition of Slavery in the West Indies.* London, 1772

Nasson, Bill. *Abraham Esau's War: A Black South African War in the Cape, 1899–1902.* Cambridge: Cambridge University Press, 1991.

———. 'War Opinion in South Africa, 1914'. *Journal of Imperial and Commonwealth History* 23, no. 2 (1995): 248–76.

Northrup, David. 'Becoming African: Identity Formation among Liberated Slaves in Nineteenth-Century Sierra Leone'. *Slavery & Abolition* 27, no. 1 (2006): 1–21.

Ominiye, Bandele. *A Defence of the Ethiopian Movement.* Edinburgh: J. & J. Gray, 1908.

Parsons, Q. N. 'F. Z. S. Peregrino (1851–1919): An Early Pan-Africanist'. Paper given to the Commonwealth and American History Seminar, Edinburgh University, 12 January 1970.

Parsons, Timothy H. *Race, Resistance and the Boy Scout Movement in British Colonial Africa.* Athens, OH: Ohio University Press, 2005.

Peregrino, Francis Z. S. *The Political Parties and the Coloured Vote.* Claremont, Cape Town, 1915.

Peterson, Derek R. 'Review Article: Culture and Chronology in African History'. *Historical Journal* 50, no. 2 (2007): 492–93.

Plaatje, Solomon T. *Native Life in South Africa.* London: P. S. King, 1916.

Pybus, Cassandra. '"A Less Favourable Specimen": The Abolitionist Response to Self-emancipated Slaves in Sierra Leone, 1793–1808'. In *The British Slave Trade: Abolition, Parliament and People*, edited by Stephen Farrell, Melanie Unwin and James Walvin. Edinburgh: Edinburgh University Press, 2007.

Ranger, T. O. *The African Voice in Southern Rhodesia.* London: Heinemann, 1970.

Ranger, Terry. 'Making Northern Rhodesia Imperial: Variations on a Royal Theme, 1924–1938'. *African Affairs* 79 (1980): 349–73.

Rippon, John, ed. *The Baptist Register II.* London, 1793.

Rive, Richard. *Buckingham Palace', District Six.* Cape Town: David Philip, 1986.

Rush, Anne Spry. 'Imperial Identity in Colonial Minds: Harold Moody and the League of Coloured Peoples, 1931–50'. *Twentieth Century British History* 12, no. 4 (2002): 356–83

———. 'The Bonds of Empire: West Indians and Britishness 1900–1970'. Phd diss. Washington DC: American University, 2004.

Sancho, Ignatius. *Letters of the Late Ignatius Sancho, An African.* London: Penguin, 1998, Originally published 1781.

Sapire, Hilary. 'Ornamentalism in Southern Africa: Royal Tours in the Twentieth Century'. Paper given to Imperial History seminar, Institute of Historical Research, University of London, 27 February 2007.

Saunders, Christopher. 'F.Z.S. Peregrino and *The South African Spectator*'. *Quarterly Bulletin of the South African Library* 32 (1978): 81–90.

———. 'African Attitudes to Britain and the Empire before and after the South African War'. In *The South African War Reappraised*, edited by Donal Lowry. Manchester: Manchester University Press, 2000.

Schama, Simon. *Rough Crossings: Britain, the Slaves and the American Revolution*. London: BBC Books, 2005.

Schneer, Jonathan. *London 1900: The Imperial Metropolis*. New Haven, CT, and London: Yale University Press, 1999.

Scholes, Theophilus E.S. *The British Empire and Alliances, or Britain's Duty to Her Colonies and Subject Races*. London: E. Stock, 1899.

Sharp, Granville. *An Appendix to the Representation of the Injustice and Dangerous Tendency of Tolerating Slavery, or of Admitting the Least Claim of Private Property of the Persons of Men in England*. London, 1769.

Sherwood, Marika. 'Caribbean Participation in the Second World War'. BBC broadcast 14 June 2004. Available from www.bbc.co.uk/history/war/wwtwo/colonies

Skinner, David E. *Thomas George Lawson: African Historian and Administrator in Sierra Leone*. Stanford, CA: Stanford University Press, 1980.

Smith, E. W. *Aggrey of Africa: A Study in Black and White*. London: Student Christian Movement, 1929.

Smith, Richard. *Jamaican Volunteers in the First World War*. Manchester: Manchester University Press, 2004.

Starfield, Jane. '"A Dance with the Empire": Modiri Molema's Glasgow Years, 1914–1921'. *Journal of Southern African Studies* 27, no. 3 (2001): 479–503.

Tabili, Laura. *'We Ask for British Justice': Workers and Racial Difference in Late Imperial Britain*. Ithaca, NY: Cornell University Press, 1994.

United Kingdom. *House of Commons Parliamentary Debates [Hansard]*, 3rd series, Vol. 112, 25 June 1850.

Westlake, John. 'Aliens'. In *Encyclopaedia Britannica*, vol.1. 11th edn. New York: Encyclopaedia Britannica Company, 1910, p. 662.

Willan, Brian, ed. *Sol Plaatje: Selected Writings*. Johannesburg: Witwatersrand University Press, 1996.

Williams, Henry Sylvester. *The British Negro: A Factor in the Empire*. Brighton: W. T. Moulton, 1902.

Wilson, Kathleen., ed. *The Island Race: Englishness, Empire and Gender in the Eighteenth Century*. London: Routledge, 2003.

———, ed. *A New Imperial History: Culture, Identity and Modernity in Britain and the Empire 1660–1840*. Cambridge: Cambridge University Press, 2004.

Patterns of Anglo-Hellenism:
A 'Colonial' Connection?
Robert Holland

For several decades the Mediterranean has been the poor cousin in British imperial historiography. It is generally under-represented, for example, in the *Oxford History of the British Empire* series. Passing mention in the volume on the eighteenth century is not surprising. Apart from Gibraltar, Minorca (with its successive occupations and re-occupations) and the curious experiment of Anglo-Corsican Union after 1794, the British presence in the Mediterranean up until the Battle of the Nile was in key respects receding. For later periods the sparse treatment is perhaps more striking, given the centrality of the region to the phenomenon encapsulated in the shorthand of Pax Britannica. A comparison may be made with the older *Cambridge History of the British Empire*, where Mediterranean themes found their place within the whole. One factor in this under-representation has been the modern reading back into British overseas experience of a 'Middle Eastern' category obscuring the integrity and importance of the Mediterranean proper.

In a set of essays highlighting the theme of ambiguity and empire, it is especially worthwhile ventilating a Mediterranean theme, because that area (whether defined in Braudelian terms as south of an 'olive line', or in some narrower fashion, defined, perhaps, by the fluctuating reach of the Royal Navy's gun power) is full of ambiguities from whatever angle it is viewed. This applies crucially to the variety of relationships that Great Britain as an imperial and naval power enjoyed with local populations. The Anglo-Egyptian relationship – its analysis often limited to its significance as a 'factor' in the scramble for Africa and the subsequent strategic role of Suez – is one example where critical Mediterranean experience has been marginalised by British imperial historians, if not by historians of the Middle East itself. The preoccupation of the present article, however, takes as its subject another example of an under-studied phenomenon in a Mediterranean setting. Anglo-Hellenic interactions were intense for much of the nineteenth and twentieth centuries, and straddled those grey lines separating formal empire, so-called informal imperialism and predominating influence. The following pages will therefore isolate some aspects of the connection between the British and the Greek-speaking peoples since the struggle against Napoleon.

'A really independent Greece is an absurdity' once remarked Admiral Edmund Lyons, the pugnacious British naval veteran of the struggle against Napoleon whom Lord Palmerston despatched to that country as British minister in 1835.[1] He stayed for fourteen years without leaving the country, and while in the post he acted on the principle he had enunciated (which was why he was one of Lord Palmerston's favourite diplomats). As we shall be describing, elements of subordination entered profoundly into the shaping of modern Greek statehood. In 1910, when first taking office as prime minister in Athens, Eleutherios Venizelos stated as a basic axiom that Greece had to 'conform absolutely' to the foreign policy of Sir Edward Grey as British foreign secretary. In 1936 King George II of the Hellenes went so far as to tell a British minister that Greece 'should be taken over by your civil service and run as a British colony'.[2] During September 1944 Winston Churchill instructed that Athens should be treated 'as a conquered city',[3] and shortly went there to select its *de facto* ruler. As late as April 1955 a British official at the embassy in the Greek capital stated that 'the idea that we are king-makers here dies hard'.[4] Even in the remaining decades of the twentieth century the notion did not entirely disappear, having a vicarious life among Greek conspiracy theorists who continued to allege Anglo-American plots to subvert a truly sovereign Greece. The assassination of Brigadier Stephen Saunders, British defence attaché in the Greek capital on 8 June 2000, by the Greek revolutionary organisation 17 November, was not wholly unrelated to the residues of such beliefs. The dependency of Greece under close British oversight is therefore our principal topic.

The roots of a specifically British 'protection' of Greek-speaking lands go back to the appearance of political agents from London in the southern Balkans after 1806. The presence of the latter encouraged local Christians who, perceiving the first glimmering of an opportunity to escape Ottoman rule, called openly for British intervention on their behalf. At the time British forces were too preoccupied with the security of Malta and Sicily to give such a prospect any reality. It was only reluctantly that British forces were drawn into the occupation of the southern Ionian islands after 1810, providing as these vantage points did 'an observatory on the whole of European Turkey'.[5] Even in 1815 Castlereagh as British Foreign Secretary would have been happy to see the Ionians handed over to Austria as his preferred 'guardian of the Mediterranean'.[6] He was overborne by a combination of expansionist cabinet colleagues with more pronounced Mediterranean ambitions and Tsar Alexander's determination to block further Austrian gains in the Balkans. It was the Tsar's diplomatic adviser at the Vienna Congress, the Corfiote nobleman John Kapodistrias, who made sure, however, that, in passing under British authority, the Ionian Islands did so as a protectorate – though the term at the time had no commonly understood meaning – rather than as a plain British colony. Much misunderstanding in Anglo-Ionian dealings was to ensue, as Kapodistrias fully intended.

It was widely believed after April 1821 that the Greek rebellion against Ottoman rule on the Balkan mainland had been inspired in part by the 'independence' – theoretically protected by European agreement – the Ionians now enjoyed under British supervision.[7] That the tight, not to say despotic, regime run by Sir Thomas Maitland from Corfu, stifling any expression of sympathy for the Hellenic cause, should have been the inspiration of heady Greek freedom elsewhere is an ambiguity indeed. As for Lord Liverpool's ministry in Britain, the philhellenic historian George Finlay once wrote that it responded to the Greek outbreak 'with more aversion than any other Christian government in Europe'.[8] Nevertheless, the same government, albeit one without the arch-Tory Viscount Castlereagh in its ranks, despatched Admiral Sir Edward Codrington to the eastern Mediterranean to smash the Turco-Egyptian fleet at Navarino in October 1827. According to Anglo-Hellenic legend, it was Navarino which saved the revolution from extinction and opened the way to modern Greek statehood. Yet in fact it was Russian land power in the war against Turkey in 1828–29, at least as much as British sea power earlier, which ensured that a self-standing Greek polity finally emerged. In these rival imperatives behind the 'making of modern Greece' lies a good deal of our conundrum.

When the first King of the Hellenes, Otto of Bavaria, finally arrived in the Greek capital of Nauplion on 30 January 1833, he did so, nevertheless, aboard a British warship, HMS Madagascar. The linkage between British navalism and Greek statehood we shall come back to. But the Greece that Otto came to reign, and indeed to rule, over was a small one. Almost as soon as Navarino had occurred, the Duke of Wellington as prime minister regretted it. Afterwards he wanted the emerging new polity to include nothing north of the Isthmus of Corinth, and only grudgingly permitted modest extensions to this outline. He was adamant that Crete be excluded. It was over Crete that he quarrelled with Stratford Canning,[9] but even Canning soon changed his tune towards the Greeks, and by the time he was *en route* once again to Constantinople as British minister he railed against the 'pernicious illusion' he found in Athens that Greece was destined to have borders beyond those approved by the Powers. The British, then, played a crucial role in the establishment of a Greek state under European Protection. But at the same time they wanted to keep it as small (and therefore as compliant) as circumstances allowed. Given that the vast majority of those using the Greek tongue and worshipping according to the rites of the Greek Church lay outside these frontiers, this was always likely to have ambiguous effects.

Paradoxically, too, in assisting (however grudgingly) a 'Protected' Greece into existence, the British undermined their own different variety of protection in the adjoining Ionians. It was because Wellington came to see that the very fact of an independent Greece would ultimately make the Ionians ungovernable as a dependency that his sentiments became less favourable to the struggling new state. Already by the mid-1830s the Ionian Protectorate was indeed fast becoming unviable. General Sir Howard Douglas, as lord high commissioner of the latter, defined the essential problem to be that the Protection as constituted in 1817 was 'a sort of middle state between a colony and a properly independent country without in some respects the advantages of either'.[10] The British-led Ionian regime was the first classic case of an anomalous, half-way house, or 'quasi' colony, where relations between a subordinate population and expatriate power tended to be more embittered (as in Egypt and Iraq, to quote two later instances) than in those territories where formal empire laid down relatively clear benchmarks for all concerned.

Such analogies and links merit further reflection. William Gladstone's successor as lord high commissioner of the Ionian Islands after early 1859, and the last in the post, Sir Henry Storks, struggled under very difficult circumstances to develop a new technique of administration from above which avoided any entrapment with internal political factionalism, purged corruption where it was found and concentrated on economic development. His chief aide in these tactics was Evelyn Baring, and the traces of Storks' philosophy are clearly discernible in Baring's later approach as high commissioner for so many years in Cairo. Storks ultimately failed to sustain the Ionian Protectorate, just as Baring (as Lord Cromer) in many ways failed in Egypt. The eventual integration of the Ionians into the Greek state only intensified the existing ambivalence of the latter's independence, even if the judgement that Ionian union was 'a pandora's box of British control of Greek politics' goes rather far.[11] In the 1940s a British minister still described Greece as 'an Egypt without a Cromer', meaning that the Greek polity was characterised by some of the traits of Cromerian supervision along the Nile, without the same sort of dominating figurehead personifying the relationship. It was certainly appropriate in its way that the Greek government-in-exile during the later phases of the Second World War was based in the Egyptian capital. Again, the cross-currents and analogies here indicate the great richness of Mediterranean — including 'British' Mediterranean — experience which might profitably be recaptured in the historiography.

The management of the climax of Ionian cession to Greece on 2 June 1864 may, by the same token, be seen as a prototype of modern British decolonisation, with all its contrary impulses and reactions. Above all, Storks was adamant that 'so great an event' as the transfer of the islands 'should not be marked by such a display as will lead the people of these [Greek-speaking] countries to suppose that we have been driven away or have yielded to any pressure which the Ionians have been able to impose upon us'.[12]

In short, evacuation under pressure had to be massaged into a kind of victory, or at least not allowed to be credibly portrayed as a defeat. For this reason the British garrisons were progressively concentrated in stages in Corfu Town, rather than in piecemeal fashion from the scattered islands, so that British control of the proceedings became tighter rather than more vulnerable as the great day of the hand-over approached. The day itself had all the manicured effects of flags raised and lowered, florid speeches and carefully calibrated interchanges between British troops and those of the incoming regime characteristic of more modern 'independence days'. Count Bismarck's alleged comment when he heard the news of the British withdrawal from the islands – that it was the sign of a nation in decay – reflected exactly the danger which had to be guarded against.[13] In 1897 a distinguished historian of the British empire, Walter Frewen Lord, wrote that 'our retirement from Corfu [in 1864] was generally understood to mean more than the surrender of an agreeable winter resort for people of leisure: it was the open and definite renunciation of the mastery of the Mediterranean'.[14] In fact, the renunciation (if such it was) was itself to be decisively renounced a decade or so later by the occupation of Cyprus, with its majority Greek population, during July 1878. Meanwhile, however, victory and defeat, appearance and reality, shadow and substance, defined the final paradox of British protection in the Ionian Islands, just as they were to do in the wider context of the 'end of empire' a century later.

One of the factors which had broken the British will to sustain the burden of Ionian protection had been the looming insolvency of the local state. Indeed, it was only with Gladstone's grudging help as chancellor of the exchequer that bankruptcy was staved off till the British had gone. Finance was habitually critical to Anglo-Hellenic relations and their rapid reversals. Control over the loans organised by the London Greek Committee provided the real key to who came out on top in the violent internal struggles among the Greek insurgents after 1823. The fact that the ship Florida, which in April 1824 delivered the first tranche of 'British gold', left six days later carrying Byron's body back to an English resting place he had never wished for[15] was profoundly appropriate in its encapsulation of the mixed motives and ideals characterising British engagement with the revolution. Much of the Greek foreign debt accumulated from the 1830s onwards was managed in London. That debt constrained the margins for Greek national manoeuvre, especially with regard to recurrent Balkan crises from the 1870s onwards. It is notable that such constraints did not apply to a state like Serbia, the far more autarchic and peasant character of which underpinned an authentic independence, albeit from a lower material base. In 1885 Serbia mobilised her army and kept it that way as long as necessary; Greece also mobilised, but stood her army down when the western powers, including British, cracked the financial and naval whip.[16] Similarly Greece's attempt in 1897 to precipitate war with Turkey and drag Britain and France onto her side collapsed, not least for financial reasons. The latter episode led shortly to the establishment of an international control commission over Greek finance, which still existed in the 1920s (being mentioned, for example, in William Miller's 1928 survey of contemporary Greece). John Lavandis in his later book on the history of the Greek foreign debt wrote:

> The financial control established in Greece is thorough and all-embracing. With the possible exception of the Egyptian Caisse de la Dette it is the only institution of its kind that is supervised and managed by foreign diplomatic Representatives. Unlike other countries, it possesses an International character and complexion, for it came into existence through the provision of Article II of the Greek-Turkish Preliminaries of Peace [in 1897–98].[17]

There is a contrast to be drawn here with the Public Debt Commission in Constantinople before 1914. This had a stake in Turkish fiscal arrangements and had an Englishman at its head. Crucially, however, that commission and its personnel remained under the full authority of the Sultan. In the case of the financial control mechanisms in Cairo, and later in Athens, the strict responsibility was international and, to a significant extent, British. This did not mean Greek national interests were necessarily prejudiced. The first British member of the International Control Commission was the senior city figure, dedicated philhellene and spouse of a Greek shipping heiress, Sir Edward Law. In fact, during the 1897 war Law held the view that Greece should fight to the end, even if it meant abandoning Athens to the Turks – though it might be said, as with a good deal of philhellenism, that with friends like that enemies are redundant.[18] Nevertheless, it was the reforms subsequently overseen by the commission, with Law as a prominent advocate, which came to be seen as having provided the fiscal base for Prime Minister Venizelos' military modernisation programme after 1910, thereby underpinning Greek triumphs in the Balkan wars of 1912/13. Even so, in financial terms Greece was not a 'perfectly independent country' well into the twentieth century and (although this is not our subject) arguably did not become so until relatively recently. This, too, has deeply influenced the texture and substance of Anglo-Hellenic ties.

There are two institutions (one British and the other, as we shall see, ambiguously Greek) needing special comment in this analysis. The first, the Royal Navy, has already entered our discussion. The captain of HMS Cambrian, a vessel which played a prominent role in various dramatic events during the revolution, for example, was a committed philhellene. Most of his fellow officers, however, were stringently pro-Turkish. This mixed picture aptly foreshadowed contrasting aspects of the navy's relationship to Greece and its aspirations over the following decades. During the early years of the kingdom British warships and marines helped to protect its stability. They were often more effective guarantors of law and order in coastal areas than the Greek police themselves. In the confused interregnum following the revolution of 1862, British naval intervention prevented Athens falling into complete chaos (though another motive was to protect the gold hoard in the Bank of Greece). The British Mediterranean Fleet was habitually present in force whenever the Greek kingdom was enlarged with London's blessing, or at least its acquiescence. After 2 June 1864 a powerful squadron of the British Mediterranean Fleet accompanied the young King of Greece on a tour of his newly acquired Ionian province. In 1912, in far less ordered circumstances, British warships helped to calm the acute tension in Salonica after the triumphant entry of Greek troops. Its task completed, HMS Hampshire (more famous for foundering with Lord Kitchener aboard in 1916) escorted the body of King George I back to Athens after his assassination. In 1948 – in the company now of allied American, not European, ships – the Royal Navy provided a protective shield around the formalities inducting the Dodecanese into the Greek state after a period of British military administration. On that occasion almost the entire Greek royal family, including King Paul, his consort and children (among them, Princess Sophia, today the Queen of Spain), was present.

It was inherent in the subtle ambiguity of the 'protection' of Greece, however, that if the Royal Navy celebrated and stabilised Hellenic statehood, it also at times intimidated and chastised it. The most famous occasion was provided by the so-called Don Pacifico affair, climaxing when a British squadron under Admiral Parker bombarded Piraeus in January 1850. The pretexts were various, but the essence was to impose Lord Palmerston's principle that the independence of Greece was subject to a higher law set by the inviolability of the interests of British subjects abroad. It is suggestive for our subject that the classic parliamentary evocation of mid-Victorian British supremacy in the world at large (Palmerston's *Civis Romanus Sum* conveniently turning an expected parliamentary humiliation over Don Pacifico into a resounding triumph) was made on a Greek issue. In the case of Greece, too, the conventionally assumed linkage between British navalism and humanitarianism was sometimes inverted. Royal Navy captains in Cretan waters during the Christian insurrection against Ottoman rule after 1866 were under instructions – to the disgust of some – not to take off starving women and children from the coast, even though their French and Russian counterparts were busy doing just that, the argument being that nothing should be done to prolong unnecessarily an unwanted and doomed rebellion.[19] To give some later instances, British warships blockaded Greek ports in 1886 and 1916, and came close to sinking the Hellenic Navy in Alexandria in 1944 during a Greek military mutiny. In sum, the Royal Navy was present at the creation of the modern Greek state, kept it in one piece at a succession of junctures, encouraged it to be 'a model state in the East',[20] but also hectored, bludgeoned and trained its guns on Greece and Greeks when the model provided was not the one enshrined in British expectations.

The second institution requiring further comment is the modern Hellenic monarchy. King Otho had his troubles with the British, and Palmerston once remarked that putting the Bavarian on the Greek throne was one of the worst things he ever did.[21] Even so, Otho not only arrived in Greece on a British warship, as we saw, but eventually escaped on one too, seeking the safety of British-ruled Corfu in October 1862. The ensuing Glücksberg dynasty was even more specifically British made than the Bavarian line had been. The young Danish Prince William (George I as he was shortly named) was handpicked by Palmerston when he attended the wedding of his sister, Alexandra, to the Prince of Wales in London that summer. Thereafter Queen Victoria always took a close interest in the Danish-Greek house, her abiding principle being that it should never suffer the fate of Otho and his formidable queen, who in fleeing in 1862 had brought a tarnish to their senior line. Whenever anti-dynastic feeling surfaced in Athens (as it did in 1885, 1897 and 1909) the Royal Navy speedily appeared to calm things down, and in extremis to take Greek royals off to safety if required. Such British protection ensured that, save for George I himself, members of a Greek dynasty never suffered the sometimes bloody fates of their Balkan counterparts.

The profound ambiguity surrounding the Glücksbergs in Greece itself flowed not least from this British connection. George I promised at the outset of his reign to be 'complètement Grecque',[22] but for somebody who was neither Orthodox nor Greek-speaking this was not easy. The most obvious way to signal an authentic Greekness in the circumstances was to offset a British with a Russian orientation. George I soon married a Romanoff duchess, and supported Cretan rebels in a manner which belied British hopes that he would give up entirely hopes of a greater Greece. The most unambiguously Greek action of the Glücksberg line was arguably Constantine I's neutrality in the war after August 1914, designed to protect the Hellenic gains of 1912/13 from possible reversal. All this did, however, apart from sparking civil conflict in Greece, was to bring down on him the full force of British 'ingratitude' – that visceral sense of betrayal often intruding into relationships of semi-veiled dependency. Subsequently George II worked his way back into British favour, but without the support of Winston Churchill – whose fierce loyalty to the Greek house was a coda to the cavalier royalism he displayed during the abdication crisis in Britain – the Glückbergs would almost certainly never have got back their Athenian patrimony after 1945. Indeed, the dynastic tie of Anglo-Hellenism was reinforced in 1947 by the marriage of the Princess Elizabeth to Philip Mountbatten (born in Corfu, with its British legacy), who gave up his Greek and Danish titles in order to undertake this marriage.[23] Paradoxically, in the end what helped to trigger a slow implosion of the Glücksbergs' legitimacy was an intransigent British policy over the colony of Cyprus, leaving the dynasty exposed on a key Hellenic issue. Queen Frederika's impassioned pleas on this matter to senior British figures during the 1950s were consistently brushed aside. Nevertheless, it was perfectly appropriate that – after much intervening drama – Constantine II's exile since December 1967 has been spent in London.

But why did monarchy in Greece become so central to British attempts to manage their relations with a supposedly dependent kingdom generally pictured in the metropolitan press as nonetheless unruly and unpredictable? From the 1830s onwards the British tried to work around Athenian politics, but they could never satisfactorily get inside it or work out quite what was going on. British ministers had their favourites, like Alexander Mavrocordatos in the 1840s and 1850s, or Charilaos Trikoupes (known as 'The Englishman' in Greek politics, representing London Greeks at one time in the Greek legislature) from the 1870s, and Eleutherios Venizelos most famously later on. Yet these personalities were not uniformly pliable and as instruments sometimes broke apart at crucial moments. At junctures such as neutrality in 1915–16 or the mutinies in the Royal Hellenic Forces in Egypt during 1943–4, the British felt completely confused and bewildered by Greek events. The opaqueness of Greek politics in British eyes was suggestively evoked when Churchill used the term 'notables' in speaking of Athenian political divisions in 1944, as if he was dealing with something remote and inaccessible. Even a decade later British policy-makers, and British opinion more widely, continued to oscillate in categorising Greece and its affairs as 'western' or 'eastern' by nature, with all that such categorisation implied. Over time, then, the survival of a broadly Anglophile monarchy provided the British with a relatively dependable and knowable point of reference, when so much else appeared obscure and potentially hostile.

In political terms, then, the Anglo-Hellenic tie was often 'lost in translation', and means of interpretation and clarification were not always ready to hand. In this vein it was often the more seemingly trivial incidents, especially those touching on matters of language and understanding, which indicated fundamental forces at work. One such episode is what became known in Athens as the 'Nicholson Incident', after Arthur Nicholson, who arrived as British Minister to Greece in 1884. In mid-January 1885 Nicholson went one evening for a walk on Mount Lycabettus. The mount – offering a wonderful view of the Parthenon for those who make it to the top, possible today by lift – had just been replanted with young pines, and the gendarme on duty had instructions to repel all intruders. Nicholson, barred on his ascent, asserted in his bluntest manner that he was Her Britannic Majesty's Representative. According to the subsequent account in the *Messagère d'Athènes*, the gendarme simply had not understood what was said and, when Nicholson insisted on proceeding, a brief rough-and-tumble ensued, with the diplomat emerging rather more bruised than the gendarme.[24] Afterwards Nicholson refused to accept an official apology, and pressed the issue with the Greek authorities. He reported to the British foreign secretary, Lord Granville:

> it was eventually agreed that the corps of gendarmes, about a hundred in number, should be drawn up in the public square; that a fresh order of the day should be read out, setting forth the true grounds for the dismissal of the offender and the exact nature of the offence; that, in the presence of the British representative, the men should present arms and the band play the [English] National Anthem.[25]

Granville approved of this climax, despite the fact that the parliamentary opposition forced an indignant debate in the Greek chamber lasting three days. Oddly enough, Arthur Nicholson – who ended up as permanent under-secretary of the British Foreign Service, and was the father of Harold Nicholson, one of Venizelos' most devoted foreign admirers at the Paris Peace Conference in 1919 – proved generally favourable to Hellenic interests, not least in the highly contested matter of Macedonia. Still, the incident on Lycabettus – a lone gendarme conscientiously doing his duty in an 'independent country' and a patrician British official determined to maintain 'face' at any perceived slight – conjures up the traps by which the Anglo-Hellenic link was always surrounded.

Ambiguity in the asymmetric relationship between the British and Greek-speaking populations in the eastern Mediterranean developed especially intense forms in Cyprus. Here we can only touch on some characteristic aspects. Not least among these were the fragile credibility and consistency of the strategic arguments deployed by British governments to rationalise occupation of the island. In what became a defining flourish of his premiership, Disraeli famously described Cyprus as the 'key to western Asia'.[26] There were not a few informed commentators, including in British military circles, who considered this bunkum. After all, Cyprus had no harbour and was malaria-ridden to boot. Cyprus was certainly useful, as it proved during the 1882 campaign in Egypt,[27] but whether it was anywhere near essential was another matter entirely, especially once access to Alexandria was guaranteed. Indeed, wholly contrary interpretations of the value of possessing Cyprus never went away. In two world wars after 1914 Cyprus was one Mediterranean island which was the scene of no actual fighting at all, but this did not subsequently stop it being enshrined in British military doctrine as non-negotiable.[28] Field-Marshal Sir John Harding as governor of Cyprus after October 1955 habitually shrugged off pointed questions at press conferences as to Cyprus' strategic utility by declaring 'Look at the map!', but then, as in 1878, some – including many Greek-Cypriots – did not take large-scale maps as quite so compelling.

But to what extent was the colony ever really British anyway? The island attracted such tags, after 1878, as 'Cinderella', 'orphaned' and 'peculiar' (one might as well have said 'ambiguous').[29] The British had occupied Cyprus, but left Ottoman sovereignty in place, and that sovereignty still had meaning in the early years of the twentieth century, when Joseph Chamberlain as colonial secretary remained adamant that the necessary corollary of any British departure, should it ever occur, would be a renewal of Ottoman responsibility.[30] Only annexation by Britain in November 1914 liquidated Ottoman legal rights. At the time British flags flew over a handful of public buildings, but were otherwise completely absent. The Union Jack did not become much more conspicuous after Cyprus became a crown colony proper in 1925. On that occasion the British tried to make something of the event in Nicosia, without much success. Contemporary maps of the eastern Mediterranean in Greek-Cypriot schools coloured the island blue to signify attachment to Greece, not red for inclusion within the British empire. Indeed, these schools themselves came under the inspection of the Ministry of Education in Athens. Basically this bifurcation between constitutional status, identity and popular consciousness never went away. When a British Foreign Office official travelled through Cyprus in the 'bad times' of 1958, he was struck by the impression that it had nothing 'British' about it (or, so he thought, Turkish) at all.[31] A British colony bereft of any effective tie to Britain beyond the purely titular was not the least of the paradoxes surrounding what was largely, but by no means exclusively, a Greek society.

Freezing, if not wholly abdicating, a claim to Cyprus, nonetheless, became for a long period part of the price that Greece was prepared to pay for British patronage. The Greek government spurned London's offer of Cyprus in October 1915 rather then be lured into a dangerous offensive to save Serbia. At the Paris Peace Conference Venizelos as Greek premier made only an oblique claim to the island. After serious disturbances by Greek-Cypriots in October 1931, Venizelos abandoned the island to British repression, stating baldly that the issue had to be considered 'within the traditional framework of Anglo-Hellenic friendship'. But the Greek premier added one caveat to this principle: it should operate as long, and only as long, as British maritime supremacy in the eastern Mediterranean itself survived. That supremacy finally began to expire in the first few years after 1945: the entry in strength into the Mediterranean of the American Sixth Fleet in mid-1946 began the process in earnest. The unravelling of the Anglo-Hellenic connection logically followed, though the intensity of the tie meant that it did not happen overnight. Cyprus marked the spot where this disintegration eventually did most damage on both sides.

Why, then, had the British and the Greeks cleaved together, however erratically, over such a long period of time? George Canning, as Castlereagh's successor at the Foreign Office, had engaged critically with the 'Greek question' in the mid-1820s because it offered an opportunity to 'take up an independent position in Europe',[32] meaning at that time independent of the autocratic Holy Alliance. No British statesman became a more fervent advocate of a greater Greece than Lloyd George, who, on the rebound from searing failures on the Western Front in 1916–17, came to see the Greeks (along with the Zionists) as proxies to help Britain sustain a new empire in the adjoining region. During the Second World War Churchill, despite much opposition, clung tenaciously to a Mediterranean strategy, the Mediterranean itself being, in classic Churchillian discourse, 'the soft underbelly of Europe'. Hence arose what has been termed Churchill's 'obsession' with Greek affairs[33] – an obsession which only intensified as the end of the war arrived. Greece and Greek-speaking populations, therefore, came to have a special relevance to that fundamental ambiguity of Great Britain as a great power: that it in was in Europe, and acted on Europe, but at the same time was not of it like Continental nations.

Conversely, why did Greece and the Greeks continue to need Britain for so long? The answer, simply, is that there were no alternatives, or rather those that existed either disappeared or proved unsatisfactory in practice. The modern Greek kingdom's ideal alignment, for religious and cultural reasons, was with Holy Orthodox Russia, but Russia increasingly went off in pan-Slav, not pro-Hellenic, directions. Greeks often looked to France, with a Philhellenic tradition quite as rich as that of Britain, but at crucial moments French governments had a tendency to go missing as far as support for Greek aspirations was concerned, as at the Berlin Congress in 1878. From the 1890s the possibility began to be glimpsed in Athens of dispensing with both the British and the French, and teaming up instead with other Balkan states to gorge on Ottoman territory. But such a line-up was very difficult to bring about, and, although it worked a treat in 1912, it came deeply unstuck in 1913 with Greco-Bulgarian in-fighting, and never effectively came back into the frame again. All in all, the British often let the Greeks down, but force of circumstances seemed to force the two together sooner or later, and never more so than in 1940 when Greece's 'national intoxification' in repelling Italian invasion interacted with Britain's spirit of the blitz over the skies of southern England.[34] Not even the disasters of 1941, or the bitter matter of Cyprus in the 1950s, fully eradicated these Anglo-Hellenic residues and the affinity attached to them.

What made the Anglo-Hellenic relationship so complex and erratic, however, was that superimposed on such strategic and political imperatives were countervailing rhythms of misunderstanding and deception (a word which in its Victorian sense of disappointment consistently recurs in the discourse). As always in modern Greek experience, the roots of this went back to the original revolutionary context. George Finlay in his great history already quoted, wrote with regard to the Anglo-Irish General, Sir Richard Church, who nominally at least commanded the battered revolutionary army in 1827–8:

> Both Church and the Greeks misunderstood one another. The Greeks expected Church to prove a Wellington with a military Chest well supplied from the British Treasury. Church expected the Greeks to execute his strategy like regiments of guards. Experience might have taught him another lesson.[35]

Experience certainly taught the Greeks another lesson too, since English parsimony was a frequent source of disillusionment thereafter for Hellenic populations. Ionians resented being squeezed for a military contribution to sustain a foreign garrison in their midst, while one of the emotions shared by local Christians and Muslims in Cyprus after 1878 was bitterness at the continuing extraction of tribute then conveniently recycled through the Treasury in London to compensate bondholders of the 1854 Ottoman loan. Indeed, until the early years of the twentieth century it was this British manipulation of the tribute, not any Greek-Cypriot desire for union with Greece, which was the principal motor of Cypriot politics.

In dissecting the roots of mutual deception in the Anglo-Hellenic relationship, however, imponderables of perspective and proportion also come into play. Such variables were subtle, insidious and usually revealed themselves only obliquely. They governed the astonishment of some of Gladstone's Peelite colleagues when ministers in the Derby government prevailed on him to undertake an extraordinary mission to the Ionian Islands in late 1858. 'To quell a storm in teacup is not an occupation worthy of you', James Graham wrote to him.[36] But Gladstone did think it was worthwhile to immerse himself, however briefly, in Ionian problems. He wrote later from Corfu:

> It may seem strange but so it is that my time and thoughts are as closely occupied and absorbed in the affairs of these little islands as they have been at almost any period in Parliamentary business....The complexity of the case is inverse (so to speak) as the extent of the sphere.[37]

Certainly it was not strange at all to Greeks that their modern problems should fascinate even so prestigious a figure as Gladstone. Being condescended to by those did not share Gladstone's innate interest in Hellenic affairs, as increasingly became the norm as the nineteenth century proceeded, always grated badly (and in fact the grating still goes on, as a reading of the British press on any matter concerning the public affairs of Greece generally shows). The British presence in Cyprus – also a location where complexity was seemingly inverse to physical size – got caught in the same psychological traps. The 'crisis of trust' at the heart of the breakdown in that island after 1954 was fully in line with this logic. It is these psychological and mental conundrums, as much as and perhaps even more than the more conventional questions of politics and strategy, which make Anglo-Hellenic experience, and the colonial and quasi-colonial experience of the Mediterranean more generally, with all their ambiguities, so absorbing a theme. Their echoes, indeed, are even still faintly audible within the European Union, where many of the leading participants are, in theory at least, now fully co-equal members, and in which context Turkish entry into the Union – with all the Hellenic resonances encompassing that matter – has emerged as one of the defining decisions ahead.

Notes

[1] For a treatment of Lyons' diplomatic mission to Greece see Eardley-Wilmot, *Lord Lyons*, 71–117.
[2] Koliopoulos, *Greece and the British Connection*, 8.
[3] Colville, *The Fringes of Power*, 386, 506.
[4] Hatzivassiliou, 'The British Embassy in Athens, 1951–61', 578. For these reasons the British residency in Cairo and the British embassy in the Greek capital share a similar status in the history of modern political emotion in the two countries.
[5] Quoted in Mackesy, *The War in the Mediterranean*, 12.
[6] Webster, *The Foreign Policy of Castlereagh*, 494.
[7] Pearn, 'The Ionian Islands', 156–60.
[8] Quoted in Holland and Markides, *The British and the Hellenes*, 1.
[9] Lane-Pool, *Stratford Canning*, I, 17.
[10] Holland and Markides, *The British and the Hellenes*, 15.
[11] Calligas, 'The *Rizapastoi*', 299.
[12] Holland and Markides, *The British and the Hellenes*, 75.
[13] Zetland, *Lord Cromer*, 36. Bismarck allegedly stated: 'Un pays qui a cessé de prendre et commence à rendre est dans sa decadence.'
[14] Lord, *Sir Thomas Maitland*, 289.
[15] St. Clair, *That Greece Might Yet be Free*, 179–81.
[16] On this occasion, following an ultimatum, a British naval squadron steamed into the Gulf of Corinth and anchored threateningly off Phaleron Bay.
[17] Levandis, *The Greek Foreign Debt*, 112.
[18] Morison and Hutchinson, *Sir Edward Fitzgerald Law*, 179–81.
[19] See Saab, 'The Doctor's Dilemma'.
[20] Holland and Markides, *The British and the Hellenes*, 79.
[21] Webster, *The Foreign Policy of Palmerston*, 509.
[22] Driault and Lhéritier, *Histoire Diplomatique de la Grèce*, III, 72.
[23] Perhaps residues of the themes covered in this section are not irrelevant when considering the deep interest taken by the current Prince of Wales in Greek Orthodoxy in general, and in particular the welfare of Holy Mount Athos and its monasteries. See 'Has Prince Charles found his true spiritual home on a Greek rock?', *The Guardian*, 12 May 2004.
[24] See *Messagère d'Athènes*, 12 Jan. 1885. For Nicholson's version of events, see his letter to Granville, 17 Jan. 1885, FO32/563, The National Archives (TNA).
[25] Nicholson to Granville, 19 Jan. 1885, FO32/563, TNA.
[26] The best discussion of strategic issues and the occupation of Cyprus remains Lee, *Great Britain and the Cyprus Convention*.
[27] For a useful summary, see Panayiotou, 'Strategic Origins of the British Occupation', 37–90.
[28] The growing military significance of the island from the late 1940s lay almost wholly in the fact that it was a location over which the British had a watertight *sovereign* title and where troops being evacuated from Palestine and Egypt could be re-housed in the region. The Suez campaign of 1956 re-asserted the island's strategic inadequacies for British interests.
[29] Holland and Markides, *The British and the Hellenes*, 162.
[30] Ibid., 171.
[31] Holland, *Britain and the Revolt in Cyprus*, 239–40.

[32] For George Canning and the Greek question, see Hinde, *George Canning*, 322–407.
[33] Clogg, 'Greece' in Dear, *Oxford Companion to the Second World War*, 505.
[34] Iatrides, *Ambassador MacVeagh Reports*, 540.
[35] Quoted in Holland and Markides, *The British and the Hellenes*, 9.
[36] Graham to Gladstone 24 October 1858, Add. 44164, Gladstone Papers, British Library.
[37] Holland and Markides, *The British and the Hellenes*, 13.

References

Calligas, Eleni. '*The Rizapastoi*: Politics and Nationalism in the British Protectorate of the Ionian Islands, 1815–1864'. PhD diss., University of London, 1994.

Colville, John. *The Fringes of Power: Downing Street Diaries, 1939–45*. London: Weidenfeld & Nicolson, 2004.

Dear, Ian, ed. *The Oxford Companion to the Second World War*. Oxford: Oxford University Press, 1995.

Driault Edouard, Michel Lhéritier. *Histoire Diplomatique de la Grèce à nos jours*. Paris, 1925.

Eardley-Wilmot, S. *Life of Vice-Admiral Edmund, Lord Lyons*. London: Sampson Low, 1898.

Hatzivassiliou, Evanthis. 'Heirs of the King-Makers: The British Embassy in Athens, 1951–61'. *Diplomacy and Statecraft*, 18 (2007): 573–91.

Hinde, Wendy. *George Canning*. London: Collins, 1973.

Holland, Robert. *Britain and the Revolt in Cyprus, 1954–59*. Oxford: Oxford University Press, 1998.

Holland, Robert and Diana Markides. *The British and the Hellenes: Struggles for Mastery in the Eastern Mediterranean, 1850–1960*. Oxford: Oxford University Press, 2006.

Iatrides, John O., ed. *Ambassador MacVeagh Reports: Greece, 1933–47*. Princeton, NJ: Princeton University Press, 1980.

Koliopoulos, John S. *Greece and the British Connection, 1935–41*. Oxford: Oxford University Press, 1977.

Lane-Pool, Stanley. *The Life of Stratford Canning*. London: Longmans, Green, 1888.

Lee, Dwight E. *Great Britain and the Cyprus Convention Policy of 1878*. Cambridge, MA: Harvard University Press, 1934.

Levandis, John A. *The Greek Foreign Debt and the Great Powers, 1821–1898*. New York: Columbia University Press, 1944.

Lord, Walter Frewen. *Sir Thomas Maitland: The Mastery of the Mediterranean*. London: Fisher Unwin, 1898.

Mackesy, Piers. *The War in the Mediterranean, 1803–1810*. London: Longmans, Green, 1957.

Morison, Theodore and George Hutchinson. *Life of Sir Edward Fitzgerald Law*. Edinburgh: William Blackwood, 1911.

Panayiotou, Maria. 'The Strategic Origins of the British Occupation of Cyprus and Its Role during the Arabi Revolt and the Resulting Egyptian Campaign, 1876–1882'. MPhil diss., University of Birmingham, 2006.

Pearn B. R. 'The Ionian Islands under the Administration of Sir Thomas Maitland, 1816–24', MA thesis, University of London, 1924.

Saab, Ann Pottinger. 'The Doctor's Dilemma: Britain and the Cretan Crisis, 1866–69'. *The Journal of Modern History* 49, no. 4 (1977).

St. Clair, William. *That Greece Might Yet Be Free: The Philhellenes in the War of Independence*. Oxford: Oxford University Press, 1971.

Webster, Sir Charles. *The Foreign Policy of Castlereagh, 1812–15: The Reconstruction of Europe*. London: G. Bell, 1931.

———. *The Foreign Policy of Palmerston, 1830–41: Britain, the Liberal Movement and the Eastern Question*. London: G. Bell, 1951.

Zetland, Marquis of. *Lord Cromer*. London: Hodder & Stoughton, 1932.

Missionary Manhood: Professionalism, Belief and Masculinity in the Nineteenth-Century British Imperial Field

Rhonda A. Semple

I

The modern British empire was a manly affair. Whether settler or tropical, its expatriate make-up was disproportionately male. Its formal military and civil administration and the informal infrastructure of its commercial houses, businesses and educational institutions were masculine in outlook and intent and were peopled by men. Modern British masculinities were yoked to notions of social responsibility[1] and characterised by energy, virility and strength, refined by moral notions of decisiveness, courage and endurance.

By extension, this construction of manliness can be applied to empire itself and to the new imperialism of the latter half of the nineteenth century in particular.[2] The historiography of empire has been long dominated by the lives and work of the men central to the formal action of this imperial moment. This is evidenced in the self-writing and biographies of its senior administrators, in the more recent argument that empire was possible only through the stalwart 'everyman' of the various arms of the imperial civil service and, ironically, by the dissection of imperial power relations in the 'new' imperial histories.[3] If manliness is primarily about the policing of a core set of values by the male self and for the benefit of other men, then empire and its institutions offer valuable material for the historian interested in the performance of masculinities. A reappraisal of that material will offer a valuable counterpoint to the significant volume of literature which examines women's lives and expectations of femininity in empire.

II

It is now clear that the identities of the 'manly' men who dominated imperial histories are not unproblematic. While there is a growing body of literature addressing questions of modern British masculinities, there remains much to be done.[4] Class placement and the ability to achieve a degree of respectability clearly shaped the experience and expectations of manliness. At one end of a spectrum elite cultural expression emphasised internal qualities of mind over body. At the other end of the spectrum a working man's value lay, in good part, in a variable valuation of his skill and physical strength.[5] In between sat the modern middle classes, for whom basic manly worth lay in a man's ability to train for a profession, to be employed respectably according to his own merits and to be remunerated to a level that would allow him to support a household of dependents at a socially appropriate level.[6] While across the nineteenth century the myth of middle-class independence and respectability became the measure of manhood even beyond the middle classes, that myth unravelled for families whose financial means or socio-economic positioning kept those markers out of reach. Yet, if the ability to achieve independence sits as a key manly virtue, then the farm labourers, factory workers and clerks, many of whom emigrated either independently or as part of assisted schemes precisely to gain the financial and social independence that was impossible at home, offer examples of how the imperial opportunity offered to 'men' was defined by class.[7] In addition, it was their ethnic identity, alongside social opportunity and a willingness to invest physical labour in the absence of financial or educational reserves that allowed these males to become 'men'. It cannot be ignored that their gain came at the cost of cultures and resources in new parts of the empire. Even if many British imperial institutions were homosocial, and not all were, the empire itself was not simply so and the expression of manliness was mediated by this reality.

There is a further, under-explored, ethnic dimension to the study of modern British manliness.[8] A growing body of literature on Gaelic gendered identities and on Scots in the empire emphasises just how strongly Scots in particular came to be identified with the middling expression of manliness as defined here. My own examination of Scots in missions underlines this. Callum Brown posits the importance of a particularly Scots masculine identity – the clerical hero – that is rooted in the structured nature of Presbyterianism and the intellectualism of Calvinism, but argues that it found a welcome audience both in Scotland and in England and was little linked to belief.[9] While it is possible to find ample numbers of each 'sort' of manly Englishman, 'the Irish' tended to have been defined as 'masculine' in a limiting aggressively physical manner. They were neither politically independent nor were they as individuals shaped by the ethic of non-conformity; worse, their experience of poverty was seemingly interspaced only by either mob violence or the underhanded violence – read 'unmanly' – of political assassination. They were not to be trusted, and manly men were all about trust.[10]

Modern British manliness was qualified abroad as it was at home. Away from home, the manliness of the British empire was again no monolith and the peculiarities of the different British ethnicities must be further interrogated. While degrees of social difference were, if anything, magnified abroad, instances also abound where the seemingly unbreakable social chains of home could be refashioned once away. This is true with respect to all social markers. Further, empire has long been described as offering the space for alternative forms of manliness and sexualities in particular, although that space constricted as the nineteenth century matured. While administrators in eighteenth-century Bengal cemented commercial and political relations by marrying into local elite culture, on the other side of the world fur-trade workers formed more and less stable relationships with women from first nations.[11] Across the nineteenth century such 'regularised' inter-racial relations became increasingly unacceptable, forcing such women and their families to negotiate an uncomfortable 'in between'. This in between could look remarkably dissimilar. The Indian administrator Philip Meadows Taylor hushed his wife's mixed ancestry in order to protect the respectability of his daughters; the 'railway colonies' of south Asia were peopled by the 'respectable' families of the Anglo-Indians who dominated rail jobs in twentieth-century South Asia; while the rejection in Canada of the mixed-race culture of Canadian Métis families literally forced them to the margins alongside railway rights of way in rural western Canada.[12] The above examples indicate that, while it was entirely possible for imperial manliness to be expressed in a variety of ways away from the metropole, the results of that expression were not experienced uniformly as opportunity. This is perhaps particularly true during the period that defines the era of 'new imperialism'. It is during this period that empire is described for European men at least as offering an opportunity for alterity – either as freedom from rigorously enforced forms of homo-social interaction or as flight from domesticity and the 'new woman'.[13] This literature fails sufficiently to emphasise inequities inherent in the varieties of masculine expression that empire offered. Historians have examined contemporary prescriptive literature and have found it to be particularly telling regarding this question: work by Douglas Peers on the military, by Kevin Grant and Dane Kennedy on homo-eroticism and the institutional space for administrative careers and by Philippa Levine on the regulation of prostitution argues ways in which the often problematic regulation of sexuality was central to ruling empire.[14]

However, there is a sustained unwillingness by historians, and social historians in particular, to take the theoretical and cultural particularities of religious identification seriously as they consider masculine identities. While the formal institution of the church was dominated by men in the modern period, (most) religious history does not explicitly apply a gendered analysis to the men in the pulpit. Rather, it is the women who could not preach and who filled the pews and peopled the social support systems of modern British churches whose gendered differences have been scrutinised. In reality, those very gendered expectations informed the identity not only of the women religious, but of the manly Christian as well. Additionally, while the rich body of literature which examines the role of women in the work of church extension overseas has been informed by gender analysis, with few exceptions there has been little attempt to examine critically the juxtaposition of professional and private that similarly existed for the male missionary.[15] Produced by mission societies and their supporters or by historians of missions offering analyses from a myriad of perspectives, the biographical, autobiographical and historical construction of missionary lives and work has been the subject of analysis from the eighteenth century. Yet, if feminist historians have profitably demanded an integrated consideration of the contribution of female missionaries, men remain the focus of mission history while an analysis of their manliness and masculinity has not. The reasons for this speak in part to the inherent philosophical assumption that men 'are' and it is women's difference that requires explanation, but there is more going on as well. If manliness is about a professional production that limits a man's participation in the very home that denotes his status as professional, and if manliness requires that men not talk about their private domestic lives, then historians face a paucity of information that could answer the very questions that we might like to ask of men in the past. The evangelical emphasis on the other-worldly only heightens the problems of examining questions of manliness and masculinity in self-writing. However, although the writing generated in mission societies and by mission personnel tends to underline the types of gendered separations for men that are being increasingly qualified in analyses of women's lives, in fact a careful reading of the documents is telling. Although I have resisted the intrusion of men into my analysis of peri-professional missionary women, asking similar questions of men as I have of women is useful. How did men make 'live' their faith? How did the relationship between cultural structure and personal belief play out in the privacy of home life? How many men could allow themselves to communicate in meaningful ways with their wives and with their children, boys and girls? What did the father look like in a Christian family being modelled on the frontiers of empire?

Finding answers to those questions demands the marriage of what have been divergent strands of analysis. While feminist scholars are producing some of the most exciting literature that comprises the 'new' imperial historiography, including that which focuses on the latter part of the nineteenth century, much of this analysis of modern empire has tended not to address religious issues in a meaningful manner.[16] Why this is so is a difficult question to answer, but the presumed disconnect between a secular analysis of gender and historicising belief (not religious institutions) is difficult to ignore. The study of missions is similarly not fully integrated into the study of imperial history. Norman Etherington's *Missions and Empire* companion volume to the *Oxford History of the British Empire* addresses the paucity of specific contributions dealing with mission themes in the *OHBE* as well as its failure to integrate analyses of religious material with the history of the empire as a whole. Further, despite the significant body of work that addresses women's work in missions, those arguments and approaches have not been mainstreamed in the historical study of missions, and they have not inspired the kind of evaluation of masculinities which exists in other imperial fields. In part this speaks to problems of sources. Professional male missionaries wrote to their sending societies about buildings and meetings, equipment orders and numbers of converts. While some did wrestle with faith issues on paper, their faith was expressed through institutional work and they much less rarely expressed ways in which belief informed their day-to-day interactions. The evangelical emphasis on the other-worldly challenges the secular performance of manliness and masculinity. And, although Tosh's analysis includes a consideration of domestic evangelical influences, his focus is more on evangelicalism as culture, and he does not attempt explicitly to analyse the interplay between theological belief, masculine expectation and action. That analysis is necessary to understand fully the self-writing of male missionaries in particular. There is much, then, to be explored.

Over the past thirty years Andrew Porter has produced a significant body of work that both examines the particulars and offers significant synthesis of the modern British Protestant mission movement. Some of his early writing, in particular, examined the relationship between personal belief and student evangelical activism in shaping individual professionals and colonial policy. Much of his subsequent work similarly rests on expectations about the importance of that interplay between private belief and practice and a public life, but the focus of much of his writing has been on the formal public life. I hope to re-open some of the questions posed by Porter, focusing a gendered lens on the private actions of male mission professionals in mainstream British Protestant missions in order better to understand the ways in which their personal lives were regulated by their professed faith, and how that activity shaped their professional identity and work. An examination of the lives of missionaries in the nineteenth-century British empire is essential for several reasons. Previous work on empire in general and that which addresses questions of sexuality in particular has focused on the masculine imperial environment of the soldier, administrator and commercial worlds. However, the modern British mission community played a central role in empire, on the interface between communities and cultures. This evangelical culture has been characterised as muscular Christianity, yet archival evidence suggests this definition requires revision in order to include the myriad of ways in which masculinity was performed in the modern British empire.

III

British Christianity expanded along with British activities overseas, slowly from the beginning of the eighteenth century and then exponentially in the nineteenth century. Belief travelled with settlers and expatriates, was exported through the creation of established churches – Presbyterian, Anglican, Roman Catholic – abroad and through the agency of voluntary missionary societies representing a variety of denominational perspectives. British mission organisations were never formally aligned with the institutional apparatus of empire for a number of reasons. Both home and colonial governments supported religious activity where it could buttress their authority, but, in settler and tropical colonies alike, that government-religious dynamic proved less than stable. This is true for a number of reasons: denominational conflict abroad militated against an official position of government support for any single denomination, a position that was reinforced by the nineteenth-century moves to separate church and state in Britain. Not surprisingly, missionaries who saw their work both hindered and supported by government officials at different times courted official support with caution. On their part, imperial authorities could be less than delighted with denominationally different 'excitable' evangelicals – because of their marginal status in Britain, because of the potentially destabilising effects of evangelising on other than Christian populations and because of specific instances where anti-colonial agitation had its genesis in mission communities.

Despite these official reservations, overseas mission work expanded along with the other institutions of empire – at times firmly within its framework and times stretching without. A burst of organisational activity in the 1790s resulted in the creation of several British societies established to further the work of the outreach arms of the Church of England and to build on the work of the Moravian brotherhood.[17] The end of the century saw the formation of the Baptist Missionary Society (BMS, 1792), the London Missionary Society (LMS, 1795), the Anglican Church Missionary Society (CMS, 1799) and Glasgow and Edinburgh Missionary Societies (1796). By the middle of the nineteenth century these societies had ceased to rely on the institutional support and personnel of continental religious institutions, and had created for themselves training institutions able to shape their middling-class applicants. Moderate evangelicals managed to connect the imperative to convert to both official and unofficial imperial activity. In India even some East India Company officials, formerly hostile to the efforts of western Christians, grew to recognise the value of missionary efforts. By the 1830s the governor-general of India himself had written in support of the work of British evangelicals.[18] More convincingly, missionary efforts in establishing and supporting an institutional presence in the newly created Sierra Leone and their role critiquing the slave trade and excesses of settlers in the Cape Colony and British Caribbean linked missionary efforts to the broader humanitarian movements so central to the nature of political and social reform in nineteenth-century Britain. Missionaries also found themselves linked to the 'informal' empire of commerce. Andrew Walls has written about this for Sierra Leone, Jane Samson for the Pacific and Andrew Porter for the Cape Colony. It is estimated that by 1900, 10,000 British missionaries, male and female, had plied their evangelical trade in foreign missions work.[19]

And what did this 'work' look like? Missionaries were variously writers, printers and translators – of both religious and other material. They built houses and buildings and ploughed fields (or supervised such work). After the instigation of Scots like Alexander

Duff (1806–78; India 1829), the first missionary sent overseas by the Church of Scotland and the architect of an education policy that shaped both mission in India and government education policy, they opened schools teaching in both vernaculars and English. Teaching took place in, at times, one unfurnished room or outside, but, from the 1830s to the education debates of the 1880s, missions built secondary institutions that have become universities all around the world – in India, southern Africa, New Zealand, the eastern US and Canada. At times missionaries fed the victims of famine, opened orphanages and refuges for society's outcasts – a practice that won them critiques from all sides, from evangelicals worried that their work was too secular in nature and from those who termed the resulting mission adherents believers of opportunity. Missionaries also engaged in the expressedly religious work of preaching and evangelisation, although the value such men placed on direct exhortation varied between mission societies. The evangelical revivals of the 1870s resulted in not only the creation and growth of new non- and inter-denominational faith missions; they inspired a wave of new recruits, and encouraged mission committees and supporters to re-think expensive commitments to expensive institutional work, the output of which – if quantified in converts – was less than impressive. LMS missions in north-central India were already facing criticism in the 1860s, accused of spending too much of their time working with the British expatriate settler community, but there were always those who lived ruggedly devoted lives, travelling, living and teaching in villages throughout the Himalayan foothills; however that devotion is understood by secular critics, this was men making 'live' their faith.

Beyond these formal markers of mission work, it is more difficult to understand the role allowed by notions of manliness in terms of making the real 'connections' in mission work. It is clear, however, that, for men as well as for women, separating the 'professional' from the 'private' is in no way straightforward. Whether married to the mission or as independent single workers, women have been described as the 'communicators' in mission. It is not surprising that the gendered expectations of women that limited their access to the professions and formal religious activity and instead heralded their abilities to connect emotionally led to these roles. The male missionaries described by mission biographers are quite different, whether they were, in fact, connecting with their home or mission constituents. One writer's emphasis on an adherence to reformed traditions and making a positive contribution to empire was dryly professional but hardly inspiring.[20] Various members of the mission community struggled with the need to 'sell' their work. Alexander Duff is recorded by Porter as 'struggling to balance "his moral aversion...to the ceaseless monotony of an ordinary journal" with the fact that he "scorn[ed] the idea of *dressing up common facts* into *interesting* stories, for the sake of producing an *effect*"'.[21] Women were presented in a different light. Even Mary Slessor (1848–1915; Nigeria 1876), whose work challenged men on two continents and who officially expanded territorial space and control for Britain, is characterised with the emphasis on caring and maternal, despite her remaining unmarried. She was seldom depicted with her hair cut off and wearing the 'foreign' clothes she favoured until after her death.[22] The most evocative of tract literature was written by women and it was their writing that elicited financial support. Board decisions or land purchases just did not have the same effect on mission supporters in Britain. On top of this, the importance of women's role as model of Christian wife and mother has been well described; Dana Roberts argues that such descriptions, in fact, describe a female theology of modern western Christianity. In this case, however, it is the man who, while necessary to the western nuclear family model, by the last quarter of the nineteenth century, is a presumed presence and not an actor. This reality is evidenced by LMS north Indian missionaries who candidly wrote about the mission's frustrations to its foreign secretary in London. While the LMS schools attracted students, their efforts to convert anyone were not at all successful, and on top of that the mission had ongoing staffing problems in one of their out-stations, had been plagued by staff turn-over and was chronically short of funds. However, in letters home one missionary reflected on his home life, describing in particular his role in family devotions. The description is that of a father – less a patriarch – and more, though brief, as warm and loving and worshipping alongside his wife, children and servants/mission adherents. The reflection appears to express a genuine assurance received (from God) that his evangelical call was authentic, immediate and ongoing, and it offers an assurance to the foreign secretary that his life and work were on track, despite the ongoing frustrations. This was a missionary who served in north India from the early 1840s until shortly before his death in 1890; these letters in particular span the 1860s. It is also an intriguing glimpse into the role of men in the Christian family model and certainly problematises the assertion that all men were marginal to the family home in modern British culture, and evangelical homes in particular; however, such glimpses prove rare.

In examining the professional lives of men in Protestant non-conformist missions it becomes immediately clear that separating the professional from what might be termed private is in no way straightforward, but examining the relations between the two both underscores and adds to arguments proposed by other scholars of British manliness. British men became professional by being educated both at home and in a variety of public institutions. Abrams and others have described a 'break' that occurred between the feminine-centred education of the young man and his turn to a more specifically masculine adult male role as mediated in part by the father. This is true for secular society, but mission applications can be particularly helpful in examining this process in the 'making' of a mission man. While male education was easier to quantify in relation to female education – studies by Clyde Binfield and Peter Williams offer analyses based on this fact – an assessment of men's upbringing that includes their becoming male (as opposed to assuming male as normal and not requiring analysis) is complicated. In describing their spiritual formation, men becoming missionaries across the nineteenth century most often begin their faith story with a description of their early exposure to religion by a mother or other female relative. Interestingly, this seems to hold true even in families with several generations of [male] missionaries. Laura Lauer has pointed out that a generation of scholars examining the lives of women in nineteenth-century British families have positioned women as central in those homes; it is the men who are outside looking in – either working-class men from pubs and clubs or later in the century middling-class men providing for their families in respectable employment.[23] However, John Tosh has found evidence of evangelical families in England in which fathers took an active part in not only providing, but also in early upbringing.[24] Similar evidence is thus far elusive in mission circles; in families as far-ranging as the LMS Morrisons in late eighteenth/early nineteenth East Asia, the Moffats of South Africa and various LMS families serving in South Asia in the latter half of the nineteenth century, evidence of early male religious involvement at home is scarce. The influence of 'father' is, rather, that of gatekeeper, ensuring entry to respectable professional society.

This is not at odds with other evidence about fatherly roles and can be further explained by the distances of empire: across the nineteenth century many of the children of empire were sent to boarding schools, most often in England and Scotland. Mortality figures from the LMS alone provide a rationale for getting children out of unhealthy environs simply to keep them alive; however, it is well documented that children both longed for their families and felt estranged from them as a result of this distance. Some schools or boarding situations carefully screened what could be communicated by their charges; letters to young children were most often written by mothers, unless the mothers had actually left India to be with their children. In either case the father is missing from the evidence available. Mission children recall feeling abandoned for the mission – left to fit neither at home (which was not their home) nor abroad – out of their parents' devotion to a call. That is a question beyond the parameters of this discussion, but certainly one worth further examination. For both mission children and other boarding students, education at 'home' ensured children's access to a good 'British' education and the professions, in terms of both where they were (at home and with other British children) and where they were not (in India, in Indian institutions, with mixed-race children and other expatriated children). There existed a heightened concern in empire over assuring the right placement within the categories of whiteness that existed in empire[25] that underscored the need for a boy's break from family. For girls the reality was different.[26]

But there is something unique in what future missionaries describe as part of their training. Evidence from the records of many mission bodies – the Scottish churches, the LMS, the Wesleyan Methodist Missionary Society (WMMS, 1786) and the China Inland Mission (CIM, 1865) – indicates that many men describe having become a mission candidate both as a result of formal education and as the result of a particular 'refining' incident that shaped their call to mission. Across the nineteenth century, it is in this call that there is a clear break from the non-religious pattern. However, this is both because of the particular shaping of the religious vocation, but also because this call often was preceded by a return home, or specifically acknowledges the fact that, while a boy left the influence of his mother in becoming a young man, in fact her religious influence never waned.[27] This then seems to be central in shaping a unique form of evangelical manliness that is both like and unlike that of other portions of society.

However, there exist additional important non-professional aspects of the training of male missionaries that are perhaps more similar to the training of female missionaries than they are different. It seemed possible to quantify the training of male applicants as they attended training institutions. These institutes were variable in nature: societies variously set up their own training institutions, utilised the services of institutions in ecclesiastical agreement or, in the case of the Scottish societies, also hired men who already had undergone university training. In most cases such candidates received much the same course of training as home ministers. Too often their supporting letters, which comment on their academic training, leave the historian hard-pressed to see what made them fit for mission service. What is different about women's applications is that, while their education is even more variable, what is constant is their making reference to volunteer activities as part of their application. Men did not do this. While evidence from elsewhere indicates that men did volunteer they did not consider that information important to their application to the public, professional world.

Logic suggests that these men's lives were filled with more than church and studies, but, except in the case of irregularities, neither the candidates nor the society deem it necessary either to provide information or to inquire about the type of information expected of female candidates. By the 1880s, men were actively engaged in many of the same voluntary religious activities as women but did not consider them relevant to the application procedure or, presumably, to their careers as missionaries. In the last quarter of the nineteenth century, a significant number of British men were acting as the leaders of midweek youth groups and teaching in Sunday schools, yet these activities were not considered fit 'work' to be referenced in applications. This underlines the assumption that these activities, organised under lay leadership and associated with women, were not considered part of the professional work of a church. A tension existed between the influence of the emotional, non-traditional spiritualism of revival, on the one hand, and older church traditions and secular professional influences, on the other.

Yet, while men may not have been writing about their church and volunteer activities between the 1870s and the 1920s, they were indeed engaged in such conduct. The records of several nonconformist chapels in the Reading area provide plenty of material about the degree and nature of men's involvement in voluntary chapel work, including the gendered nature of their involvement. Free Church evidence suggests similar trends.[28] Sunday school reports throughout the period indicate how closely the connections were maintained between these chapels and the LMS. The Independent Church in Abingdon used students from Highbury (Islington, est. 1826) and Hackney (Homerton, est. 1786) colleges as supply preachers and hired graduates from Cheshunt (Hertfordshire, est. 1792) as well; all three colleges were educating future missionaries at this time.[29] While there were greater numbers of female than male Sunday school teachers throughout this period, women never significantly outnumbered the men. There were repeated requests from Sunday school organisers for more teachers throughout this period, particularly for male teachers who were expected to control older boys, who, records suggest, were less than inclined to listen to their female teachers. In any case, records indicate the boys' and girls' groups followed different curricula, used different materials and behaved differently. Additional research suggests it was not only the women teachers who struggled to convince their charges how important it was to be restrained and self-sufficient. Successful or not, the attempt to lead those groups was certainly being made, and by both young men and women.[30] Despite these indications that Sunday school pupils might have welcomed fun more than being taught about their individual spiritual failings, evidence suggests that by the 1870s Cambridge student evangelicals too were teaching Sunday school, training choristers, evangelising to their fellow students and volunteering on student trips to evangelise to the children of the upper classes as well.[31] What this seems to suggest is that men's failure to reference their volunteer associations masks realities about men's position relative to their families and wider British society. This failure occurred because they had been schooled to separate home and work life and, except in explicit moments, on application or ordination, to separate emotion from business.[32] It is not until after the First World War that such attitudes changed significantly and that more than only the exceptional man became both willing and able to discuss this volunteer work in more emotive terms, and to do so in a business setting.

Similarly, while evidence exists to suggest that some men attended to and felt very connected to their children, for the most part this level of connectedness is not expressed in the correspondence of the mission archives, and was not made public. Across the nineteenth century, while men do talk about their children, it is in terms of business. The foreign secretaries of various societies were informed when children were born and died, when children were travelling home to school and, when the occasion arose, about a child needing support because of a disability. This is not because of their interest, although there is plenty of evidence that missionaries developed more than professional relations with these officials. It was because a missionary received money according to his marital status, number of children, their stage of education and, once girls were adult, whether they were working in the mission and required support. These letters, which alongside formal reports provide most of what we can know about mission life and work, are thick with the public work of the mission: monies spent and plans made for buildings, travels and personnel, meeting minutes, school curricula, lists of converts; family matters are added as a short polite aside at the end. Given the well-supported argument that the mission family served a central role as Christian witness and the evangelical argument that personal piety could not be separated from public works, this dichotomy fairly reeks of the conventions of secular professional manliness. In this regard as in others, it would seem that the insecurities of evangelical manliness are in evidence.

Male missionaries communicated their insecurities in other areas of their public/private lives as well. These concerns can be grouped together as concerns having to do with honour, and an analysis of them might border on the ridiculous if their resolution did not speak so clearly of proper manly evangelical behaviour. In nineteenth-century middling society concepts of manliness rested not only on the attainment of professional position, but on the fact that the position needed to be earned rather than inherited or granted. For missionaries that reality was not so clear. Evangelical culture was steeped in connections. Across the eighteenth and early nineteenth century, these connections had allowed non-conformist manufacturers and commercial venture to succeed in what was a hostile religious and cultural environment. For missionaries, it was the community created by faith identity in general that got them hired – their expressed religiosity had to fit – and the extensive family networks both within and between various missions are also well documented. Once hired, mission workers continued to wrestle with another fit, this one between their proffering of mission patronage and their desire to construct Christian men 'with a sense of the value of individual industry and enterprise'.[33] Gerald Studdert-Kennedy's recent study of CMS industrial work in late nineteenth-century Bengal examines such manliness, bifurcated as it was on several different fault lines. The manly identity of the Rev. Charles Bradburn is perhaps more like than unlike his mission colleagues in that he may best be described by what he was not rather than what he was. Coming from solid if not spectacular Manchester industrial money, Bradburn was not independent when he applied to the mission in the early 1880s, he had not attended university and he secured interest in and support for his work in London through the family associations of his second wife. Despite what were cultural evangelical connections, he was uncomfortable in expressing his faith directly and instead argued that his institutional efforts were what served to communicate and convince people of his Christian message that 'the boys who fill the elementary schools today will gradually become the men upon whom the position, power and prospects of Great Britain will largely depend'.[34] All the mainstream Protestant societies had hired such 'practical' men for industrial work throughout the nineteenth century, but it is this relatively late period, in the last two decades of the century, that such physical training could be celebrated as making an important and manly contribution to both mission and empire. Still, we must be reminded of the Bradburns of mission while we remember the flashier Cambridge Seven. Bradburn himself seems aware of that marginality; he argued that it was industrial training, actual training of physical movement, that would achieve his purpose. His language both celebrates the possibilities, for individuals and whole communities, 'of enterprise as faith' and speaks of constant struggles – with local Bengali Christians and his contemporary colleagues, with London for support and attention and with himself over burn-out and sexual desire.

For Bradburn, the unusual acknowledgement that sexual 'discomfort' was part of life as a missionary came in letters supporting a colleague's request to marry, arguing that 'in these matters a wife is a curtain to her husband', and men were weak enough to require that curtain.[35] In other missions this insecure manliness manifest itself in an almost puritan desire to root out 'unmanly' behaviour – unacceptable behaviour was certainly not left to the individual and God. The types of transgressions dealt with in the mission record are not limited to sexual impropriety although such instances tend to stand out. However, when transgressions of a sexual nature are grouped together with behaviours having to do with honour more broadly, they serve as evidence to support the argument that right manliness was about regulating manly behaviour. In fact the instances of sexual irregularity in the 1870s and 1880s in this mission community tended to have been dealt with surprising leniency. In one case, it was only when the offender was plagiarising sermons *as well* that it was deemed necessary to discipline him. In another case, a missionary's new wife turned out to be pregnant before their marriage; however, it was his refusal to admit and atone for his actions that was given as cause for his dismissal. Mild in comparison to the horrors of sexual crime against women in imperial armies, the treatment of these misdemeanours are alike in the assumption that, while acting out heterosexual desire was something to be controlled, it was also at the heart of Victorian masculine identity.[36] On the other hand, fiscal transgressions were taken seriously. A missionary with the LMS caught mis-spending funds to cover personal family expenditures was immediately and severely chastised; a Scots missionary was firmly reprimanded when her bank account in Edinburgh went into overdraft; and a Canadian member of the CIM went on medical leave when he was taken advantage of financially and ran into difficulties on his station. It seems almost absurd that one north Indian Presbyterian station was almost destroyed because of an altercation generated over the breaking of crockery – a happenstance that came to be seen as being about honour and could not be ignored.[37]

Finally, the issue of sexuality within marriage is one that, if not directly related to honour, is important to this argument. John Tosh has unearthed slim but telling evidence of the loving and lusty relations between English evangelical couples, as well as unhappier relations. One can only imagine the painful early negotiation of sexualities between the mission couples who met and married within weeks and/or even days of their meetings. Having said this, the inability of evangelical luminaries such as Charles Wesley to reconcile their faith with a healthy sexual identity should not be allowed to overshadow the sexual sensibilities of all missionaries, whether evangelical or not. Patricia Grimshaw's work examines the moving and even erotic letters exchanged between missionaries of the American Board of Commissioners for Foreign Missions (ABCFM, 1812) in the South Pacific. I have found nothing similar in the formal archives of the mainstream British mission societies but their absence likely speaks to the record rather than offering proof of repressed evangelical lives. Certainly missionary men had physical desire and mission societies acknowledged that as a reality requiring their attention.[38] They did so variously by hiring married men rather than single man, by arranging opportunities for men to meet potential wives or by arranging marriages for their mission men. In societies such as the Norwegian Missionary Society (NMS, 1842) and the ABCFM perceived realities of male sexual needs and the dangers of foreign constructions of sexual behaviour were quite openly discussed.

Missionaries were on a precarious footing when it came to their status in empire. From the inception of its work in South Asia the English East India Company (EIC) was hostile to Christian missionaries, believing that its commercial interests could best be met by making connections in the sub-continent producing goods and doing business as was. Despite popular perceptions, missionary ministrations were less than welcome in most barracks and particularly in *sepoy* regiments and the only groups in which any significant degree of conversion was achieved were the Gurkhas. That had arguably more to do with the displaced status of their families due to tea-plantation migration than it had to do with religious work in the ranks. In any case missionaries were interested in more than converting soldiers. Over roughly a ten-year period several of the LMS missionaries in Benares vied to become British army chaplains, and the missionary who began work in military hill stations did so because of the cantonment and despite the fact that he was warned that it was too close to a sister station. There was status to being associated with the army. This must have been attractive for any non-conforming minister, and perhaps particularly for the Scottish LMS minister in Benares who would have been well aware that his Scots Presbyterian colleagues were easily being paid twice his salary. In Benares, despite complaints from both home and local mission committees, it was not until the army appointed their own non-conformist chaplains in the late 1870s that the angling for chaplaincies among some LMS missionaries stopped. It was about pay, but also status in a situation where missionaries were really the bottom of the imperial barrel, and an appointment in the 'establishment' could have positive affect for the missionary, his family and, some argued, for the entire station.

Missionaries could observe the privilege of imperial society closely, yet their position on its fringes militated against male missionaries finding a home in the homo-social 'clubs' of empire. If such clubs existed, they consisted of the education institutions created by missionaries for mission adherents and the children of families who perceived value in a western education (and could ignore the Christian overtones). It is really not until after the Student Volunteer Movement began to influence students in British institutes of higher learning in the 1880s that missionaries like John Graham of Kalimpong began to create all-male young men's groups in the field that emphasised comradery and personal Christian commitment. In any case, those institutions consisted of one (or, at most, very few) British missionaries and 'local' mission constituents and thus do not represent a strict peer grouping. It would appear that for the most part missionaries would mostly not have participated in the type of homo-social environment so important to a manly identity in empire, a fact which could only contribute to a position of marginal masculinity.

In theory missionaries belonged to a better club than the ones from which they were excluded. While there is abundant evidence that mission men were shaped in British society, they were very particular British men, and historical evidence that explains where individuals fit as evangelicals on what is a continuum of belief and acts is perhaps the most difficult to decode. The evangelical emphasis on personal revelation and religious experience underlined at the Keswick Convention (est. 1875) for believers promised 'Christian perfection' or the possibility of a higher life to be experienced in this world. This, then, was the ultimate masculine identity – because of Christ's atonement, human perfection was possible; its expression was through personal commitment and service.[39] This prism of perfectibility was aimed with devastating effect at foreign cultures and societies, mission adherents, British expatriate imperial and sending society and self-critically. This theological 'circling-of-the-wagons' must be understood in the context of 'the age' of doubt, of questions over revelation vs. scientific evidence and in the face of textual criticism, but, for the purposes of my argument, this particular brand of British manliness is both set apart and sets itself apart from other manly identities.

IV

'Conversations with natives...are almost always mere conversations.'[40] In this gruff refusal to 'sell' his everyday interactions for the grist of mission magazines, Alexander Duff exudes a masculinity of a particular sort, and a sort that came into increasing tension with evangelical mission committees across the nineteenth century. Andrew Porter may not even remember the conversation, but as his student I recall being subjected to a similar gruff response in his office in King's – regarding my emphasis on the gendering of some mission experience or another he was, I am sure very fairly, 'not convinced'. However, his own body of work in fact offers a significant examination of evangelical manliness, in its various manifestations across the modern period; in so doing, it has much to offer the historian of British gender beyond those interested in religious society and mission in particular. Porter provides evidence that evangelical culture was no monolith in the first half of the century. Men attracted to mission work and attractive to mission societies were in the 1820s were artisans and represented the breadth of the middle classes; some men were employed because of their physical skill and others because of their theological preparation. By the 1860s the picture is no clearer; from then evangelical revivalism looks variously like the Anglican Handley Moule's attempts at Cambridge to better equip the evangelical leadership and the anti-intellectual emphasis on individual training, community building and the building of institutions and industrial work in particular. While, theoretically, evangelical masculinity shaped the new middle-class manliness that dominated Victorian society by the end of the century, in reality Porter's careful examinations of missions in society complicate this depiction of what is a religiously, ethnically and socially diverse modernising Great Britain.

In my own work on female missionaries it has become increasingly evident that the apparent dichotomy between the training of men and women that at first appeared straightforward does not in fact stand up to scrutiny. Just as Martin Francis has argued about the historical analysis of men throughout modern British society, the gendered differences in missions need be carefully investigated and the masculine expectations of male missionaries teased apart from their lived experience. Revisiting evidence existing regarding the role of masculinity in the private, in the professional and in the male role in the home domain, it is clear that across the nineteenth century men were both challenging, and being shaped by, contemporary expectations of manliness. Alexander Duff sits in a very different place in the same masculine empire from another missionary to north India, forty years later, who wrote in very moving terms to his foreign secretary about sharing the days and nights with his wife as their baby slipped away. Each man fits, in his not fitting in any kind of straightforward manner. In all, their particularities add an interesting wing to the historiography of mission and empire, and contribute in important ways to our understanding of historic British manliness more broadly.

Notes

[1] OED definition as used by Tosh, *Manliness and Masculinities*, 85.
[2] Hyam, *Empire and Sexuality*; Nagel, 'Masculinity and nationalism', 242–69.
[3] Mackenzie, 'Imperial pioneer'; Hobsbawm, *Nations*'; Koven, 'Rough lads'.
[4] Francis, 'Domestication of the Male?', 637–52.
[5] Willis, *Learning to Labour*, 52, 148; Peers, 'Privates', 823–54.
[6] Davidoff and Hall, *Family Fortunes*, 229–34.
[7] Hammerton, 'Gender and Migration', 156–79.
[8] Francis, 'Domestication of the Male?', 650.
[9] Brown 'Religion', 93, 101–3.
[10] McDevitt, 'Muscular Catholicism', 262–84.
[11] Ghosh, *Sex and the Family*; Kelm, 'A Scandalous Procession' 51–88; Van Kirk, 'Marrying-In' 1–11.
[12] Bear, 'Miscegenations', 531–48; van Kirk, *Many Tender Ties*.
[13] Foley, 'Gender and Colonialism'; Midgley, 'Gender and Imperialism'; Ware, *Beyond*; Majeed, 'Meadows Taylor's *Confessions*; 86–110; Francis, 'Domestications?', 641.
[14] Grant, 'Bones of Contention', 580–1; Peers, 'Soldiers, Surgeons', 137–60; Kennedy, *Highly Civilized Man*.
[15] Barnhart, 'Evangelicalism, Masculinity', 712–32.
[16] Nagel, 'Masculinity and nationalism'; Francis, 'Domestication of the Male?', 650–51.
[17] The LMS mission at Bethelsdorp in South Africa is indicative of the significant influence of Brethren mission methods on British mainstream protestant missions. See for example: Ross, 'Respectability and Civil Rights'. This overview relies on Porter, *Religion vs Empire?*
[18] William Bentinck as quoted in Porter 'An Overview', 49.
[19] Porter, 'An Overview', 40–63.
[20] Brown, 'Religion', 31.
[21] NLS MS7530. f.164. Alexander Duff to Inglis, 30 July 1833, quoted in Porter, 'Scottish Missions'.
[22] Pemberton, 'Imperial Mother'; Haggis, 'Meaning well', 387–99.
[23] Lauer, 'Soul Saving Partnerships'.
[24] Tosh, 'Authority', 48–64.
[25] Buettner, *Empire Families*.
[26] Semple, *Missionary Women*.
[27] For an example see the George King pamphlet collection: Aberdeen City Archives, King 269/8. 'Ordination Service of Rev. William Buyers' (Aberdeen, 1840).
[28] Aberdeen City Archives. Acc 66/II/I *Free Church Monthly and Missionary Record* 'Young men's association restarted at the church' February 1870; Yeo, *Religion*'.
[29] BRO.D/N 1/1/1/1 Abingdon Independent Chapel Minutes 1823–1873.
[30] Springhall, 'Building character'. These arguments seem to mitigate against an uncritical acceptance that middle class evangelical values 'provided a bridge between competing notions of manliness in the late eighteenth and early nineteenth centuries'. Clearly the repackaging of

missionaries as pious and hardworking had its attractions, but not for all. Hall, *White, Male*, 219 and Davidoff and Hall, *Family Fortunes*, 81–3 and 109–11.
[31] Bullock, *'History of Ridley Hall Cambridge*, quoted in Porter, 'Cambridge'.
[32] Piggin, *Making Missionaries*, 59–60. In his ordination service William Buyers asks that he have 'his actions and character be regulated by the principles of the gospel ... that he cooperate with other missionaries, and show kindness to all men' Aberdeen City Archives. King 269/8 'Ordination service of Rev. Wm. Buyers' (Aberdeen, 1840).
[33] Studdart-Kennedy, 'Evangelical Mission', 325–48.
[34] *Manual Training Teacher* September 1901, quoted in Studdert-Kennedy, 'Evangelical Mission', 338.
[35] Bradburn quoted in Studdert-Kennedy, 'Evangelical Mission', 342.
[36] Peers, 'Privates off Parade'; and Brown, 'Religion'.
[37] Semple, *Missionary Women*.
[38] Nyhagen Predelli, 'Marriage', 4–48.
[39] Porter, 'Attitudes to Africa,' 15.
[40] NLS MS7530. f.164. Alexander Duff to John Inglis, 30 July 1833, as quoted in Porter, 'Scottish Missions'.

References

Barnhart, William. 'Evangelicalism, Masculinity, and the Making of Imperial Missionaries in late Imperial Georgian Britain, 1765–1820'. *The Historian* 67, no. 4 (2005): 712–32.
Bear, Laura Gbah. 'Miscegenations of Modernity: Constructing European Respectability and Race in the Indian Railway Colony, 1857–1931'. *Women's History Review* 3, no. 4 (1994): 531–48.
Brown, Callum. 'Religion'. In *Gender in Scottish History since 1700*, edited by Lynn Abrams, Eleanor Gordon, Deborah Simonton and Eilech Janes Yeo. Edinburgh: Edinburgh University Press, 2006.
Buettner, Elizabeth. *Empire Families: Britons and Late Imperial India*. Oxford: Oxford University Press, 2004.
Bullock, F. W. B. *The History of Ridley Hall Cambridge*. 2 vols. Cambridge: Cambridge University Press, 1941, 1953.
Davidoff, Leonore and Catharine Hall. *Family Fortunes: Men and Women of the English Middle Class, 1780–1850*. New York: Routledge, 1987.
Etherington, Norman, ed. *Missions and Empire*. Oxford History of the British Empire Companion Series. Oxford: Oxford University Press, 2005.
Francis, Martin. '"The Domestication of the Male?" Recent Research on Nineteenth- and Twentieth-Century British Masculinity'. *The Historical Journal* 45, no. 3 (2002): 637–52.
Ghosh, Durba. *Sex and the Family in Colonial India: The Making of Empire*. Cambridge: Cambridge University Press, 2006.
Grant, Kevin. 'Bones of Contention: The Repatriation of the Remains of Roger Casement'. *The Journal of British Studies* 41, no. 3 (2002): 329–53.
Haggis, Jane. 'Meaning Well and Global Good Manners: Reflections on White Western Feminist Cross-Cultural Praxis'. *Australian Feminist Studies* 15, no. 33 (2000): 387–99.
Hall, Catharine. *White, Male and Middle-Class: Explorations in Feminism and History*. London: Polity Press, 1992.
Hammerton, A. James 'Gender and Migration'. In *Gender and Empire*, edited by Philippa Levine. Oxford: Oxford University Press, 2004.
Hobsbawm, Eric. *Nations and Nationalism since 1780*. Cambridge: Cambridge University Press, 1990.
Hyam, Ronald. *Empire and Sexuality: the British Experience*. New York: St Martin's Press, 1991.
Kelm, Mary Ellen. '"A Scandalous Procession": Residential Schooling and the Shaping of Aboriginal Bodies'. *Native Studies Review* 11, no. 2 (1996): 51–88.

Kennedy, Dane. *The Highly Civilized Man: Richard Burton and the Victorian World*. Boston, MA: Harvard University Press, 2006.
Koven, Seth. 'From Rough Lads to Hooligans: Boy Life, National Culture and Social Reform'. In *Nationalisms and Sexualities*, edited by A. Parker, M. Russo, D. Sommer and P. Yaeger. New York: Routledge, 1991.
Lauer, Laura. 'Soul-Saving Partnerships and Pacific Soldiers: The Ideal of Masculinity in the Salvation Army'. In *Masculinity and Spirituality in Victorian Culture*, edited by Andrew Bradstock, Sean Gill, Ann Hogan and Sue Morgan. London: Macmillan, 2000.
Levine, Philippa. 'Venereal Disease, Prostitution and the Politics of Empire: The Case of British India'. *Journal of the History of Sexuality* 4 (1994): 580–81.
Mackenzie, John M. 'The Imperial Pioneer and Hunter and the British Masculine Stereotype in Late Victorian and Edwardian Times'. In *Manliness and Morality: Middle-class Masculinity in Britain and America, 1800–1940*, edited by J.A. Mangan and J. Walvin. Manchester: Manchester University Press, 1987.
Majeed, Javed. 'Meadows Taylor's Confessions of a Thug: The Anglo-Indian Novel as a Genre in the Making'. In *The Literature of British India*, edited by B. Moore-Gilbert. Manchester: Manchester University Press, 1996.
McDevitt, Patrick F. 'Muscular Catholicism: Nationalism, Masculinity and Gaelic Team Sports, 1884–1916'. *Gender and History* 9 (1997): 262–84.
Midgley, Clare, ed. *Gender and Imperialism*. Manchester: Manchester University Press, 1998.
Nagel, Jane. 'Masculinity and Nationalism: Gender and Sexuality in the Making of Nations'. *Ethnic and Racial Studies* 21, no. 2 (1998): 242–69.
Nyhagen Predelli, Line. 'Marriage in Norwegian Missionary Practice and Discourse in Norway and Madagascar, 1880–1910'. *Journal of Religion in Africa* 31, no. 1 (2001): 4–48.
Peers, Douglas M. '"Privates off Parade": Regimenting Sexuality in the Nineteenth-Century Indian Empire'. *The International Review* 20, no. 4 (1998): 823–54.
———. 'Soldiers, Surgeons and the Campaigns to Combat Sexually Transmitted Disease in Colonial India, 1805–1860'. *Medical History* 42 (1998): 137–60.
Pemberton, Carrie. 'Imperial Mother or Liberating Sister? Mary Slessor in Post-colonial Perspective'. *NAMP/CWC Position Papers* 95 (1996).
Piggin, Stuart. *Making Evangelical Missionaries: The Social Background, Motives and Training of British Protestant Missionaries to India*. Sutton: Courtney Press, 1984.
Porter, Andrew N. 'Cambridge, Keswick and Late Nineteenth-Century Attitudes to Africa'. *Journal of Imperial and Commonwealth History* 5, no. 1 (1976): 5–34.
———. 'Evangelical Enthusiasm, Missionary Motivation, and West Africa in the Late Nineteenth Century: The Career of G.W. Brooke'. *Journal of Imperial and Commonwealth History* 6, no. 1 (1977): 23–46.
———. 'Scottish Missions and Education in Nineteenth-Century India: The Changing Face of "Trusteeship"'. *Journal of Imperial and Commonwealth History* 16, no. 3 (1988): 35–57.
———. '"Cultural Imperialism" and Protestant Missionary Enterprise, 1780–1914'. *Journal of Imperial and Commonwealth History* 25, no. 3 (1997): 367–91.
———. 'Language, "Native Agency", and Missionary Control: Rufus Anderson's Journey to India, 1854–5'. In *Missions and Missionaries. Studies in Church History: Subsidia 13*, edited by Pieter N. Holtrop and Hugh McLeod. Oxford: Oxford University Press, 2000.
———. 'The Universities Mission to Central Africa: Anglo-Catholicism and the Twentieth Century Colonial Encounter'. In *Missions, Nationalism, and the End of Empire*, edited by Brian Stanley. London and Grand Rapids, MI: Eerdman 2003.
———. *Religion versus Empire? British Protestant Missionaries and Overseas Expansion 1700–1914*. Manchester: Manchester University Press, 2004.
———. 'An Overview, 1700–1914'. In *Missions and Empire*, edited by Norman Etherington. *Oxford History of the British Empire Companion Series*. Oxford: Oxford University Press, 2005.

———. 'Missions and Empire, c.1873–1914'. In *The Cambridge History of Christianity*, Vol. 8, *World Christianities c.1815–c.1914*, edited by Sheridan Gilley and Brian Stanley. Cambridge: Cambridge University Press, 2006.

Roberts, Dana. *American Women and Missions*. Macon, GA: Mercer University Press, 1998.

Ross, Robert. 'Missions, Respectability and Civil Rights: The Cape Colony, 1828–1854'. *Journal of Southern African Studies* 25, no. 3 (1999): 333–45.

Semple, Rhonda. *Missionary Women: Gender, Professionalism and the Victorian Idea of Christian Mission*. Woodbridge: Boydell & Brewer, 2003.

Springhall, John. 'Building Character in the British Boy: The Attempt to Extend Christian Manliness to Working-Class Adolescents, 1880–1914'. In *Manliness and Morality*, edited by J.A. Mangan and J. Walvin. Manchester: Manchester University Press, 1987

Studdert-Kennedy, Gerald. 'Evangelical Mission and the Railway Workshop Apprentices: Institutionalizing Christian Presence in Imperial Bengal, 1885–1914'. *Journal of Imperial and Commonwealth History* 33, no. 3 (2005): 325–48.

Tosh, John. 'Authority and Nurture in Middle-Class Fatherhood: The Case of Early and Mid-Victorian England'. *Gender and History* 8, no. 1 (1996): 48–46.

———. *Manliness and Masculinities in Nineteenth-century Britain*. London: Pearson Education, 2004.

van Kirk, Sylvia. *Many Tender Ties: Women in Fur-Trade Society, 1670–1870*. Winnipeg: Watson & Dwyer, 1980.

———. '"From Marrying-In" to "Marrying-Out": Changing Patterns of Aboriginal/Non-Aboriginal Marriage in Colonial Canada'. *Frontiers: A Journal of Women Studies* 23, no. 3 (2002): 1–11.

Willis, Paul. *Learning to Labour: How Working Class Kids Get Working Class Jobs*. Farnborough: Saxton House, 1977.

Yeo, Steven. *Religion and Voluntary Organizations in Crisis*. London: Croom Helm, 1976.

The Ambiguous Amir: Britain, Afghanistan and the 1897 North-West Frontier Uprising

Keith Surridge

In July 1897 India's border region with Afghanistan, the famous north-west frontier, was set ablaze by tribal revolts against the British that eventually took nearly a year to suppress. The ferocity of the uprising forced the British to deploy over 60,000 troops, more than the combined totals of the armies used in the two earlier wars against Afghanistan in 1838-42 and 1878–81. The outbreak of tribal hostility had taken the British by surprise, as had the scale of the revolt and the cooperation shown by the tribes. During those first shocking weeks the British sought to understand why such an event had occurred and one answer that emerged was the alleged complicity of the Afghan ruler, the Amir Abdur Rahman Khan. While this charge was never proven, the suspicion revealed the ambiguous position the amir held in British perceptions. On the one hand, he was a duplicitous enemy of Britain, who, in the opinion of one viceroy, was 'a cantankerous and suspicious old savage'. On the other hand, however, in the words of another viceroy, the amir, 'in spite of his uncertain temper and insolent language, [was] a consistent friend of the British alliance'.[1] Indeed, keeping the amir friendly was seen by some as vital to Britain's wider interests. As one of the few surviving independent Muslim rulers left in the world, whose territory was close to India's Muslim millions, the amir's attitude towards the British was regarded as crucial. When the tribal revolt began, Britain was engaged, often violently, in consolidating its rule over the Islamic regions of Aden, Sudan, Somaliland and northern Nigeria. The ripple of Muslim outrage from one frontier reaching out to the others, perhaps encouraged by an important figurehead, and provoking a pan-Islamic uprising was to be feared. Thus events on India's periphery revealed British sensitivity to Muslim opinion.

The north-west frontier has been the subject of numerous works during the time of empire and after. These have perhaps been of three types: those that have dealt with frontier policy; those that have discussed the 'great game' with Russia, and those that have examined the military aspects of the frontier.[2] There has, to my knowledge, been only one modern biography of the amir and this does not give much attention to the 1897 frontier uprising.[3] This article, therefore, intends to shed light on how Britain handled the amir at a critical time, when relations were already strained, and on the problems the British faced along their most turbulent frontier. It will also emphasise the nagging concern felt by the British that events on the north-west frontier were somehow part of a wider conspiracy.

I

Abdur Rahman Khan had gained the amirship of Kabul in 1880 after years of exile in Russia. He owed his position to the British who were then in occupation of much of eastern Afghanistan, during what became known as the Second Afghan war (1878–81). As in the first war (1838–42), the British had indulged in a process of regime change with dire consequences. Although Abdur Rahman had not been their first choice, by the time of his accession he was their only viable candidate. Nevertheless, certain conditions were imposed on the new amir: first, a British agent would now be resident permanently in Kabul, a British concession being the Memorandum of Obligation of July 1880 stipulating that he would be a Muslim. This was to avoid the same fate as that of the last British agent sent to Kabul, Major Sir Louis Cavagnari who, along with his escort, was slaughtered in 1879. Second, the amir was not permitted to make treaties of alliance with foreign powers and all foreign relations were to be overseen by the British, thus limiting his chance to do any business with the Russians. While these terms were not particularly onerous, the British were, in fact, making the amir accept the Treaty of Gandamak, which had been signed on 26 May 1879 by Yakub Khan, Abdur Rahman's predecessor, cousin and bitter enemy. Moreover, as part of the deal, the new amir had to accept the loss of some territory to the British, notably the strategic Kurram valley.[4] Thus Abdur Rahman did not actually inherit the kingdom of his grandfather, Dost Mohammed Khan, who had been the subject of the earlier regime change and whose forces had wiped out the British garrison. At that point Abdur Rahman was not in a position to resist British demands because once he was installed the British left Afghanistan. The new amir of Kabul now saw his first task as uniting his grandfather's kingdom and from 1881 he embarked on a series of campaigns against the rulers of Kandahar and Herat to cement his authority throughout the country. This he achieved, but not without a great deal of bloodshed and repression. By 1890 Abdur Rahman was firmly in control and now had time to consider his relations with the British.

It was in Britain's interests to see the amir with a firm grip on the country that might easily fracture along dynastic or ethnic lines. In many ways Afghanistan was a geographical expression and any troubles within might easily have after-shocks that could affect its frontiers and beyond. Stability in Afghanistan suited Britain's best interests because there would be little to generate agitation among the tribes, while a powerful amir, who might seek to impose his rule, was something the tribes themselves feared. However, by the time the amir had consolidated his hold on Afghanistan, relations with the British were at an all-time low. In 1892, Sir H. Mortimer Durand, then foreign secretary to the government of India, wrote despairingly:

> The Amir is behaving worse than ever, and I cannot see where it is to end. He has taken Asmar, in spite of our prohibition against meddling with Bajaur. He tells us he is King of the Afridis, and almost admits that he stirred them up against us. He does admit that he has let his tribes go at Kurram, where he is in fact waging an unofficial war against our friends the Turis. He is threatening Dir, and the Diris have applied to us for protection ... He treats our envoy like a prisoner. On the north, instead of following our advice, he is pushing forward on the Pamirs, courting another Penjdeh. And he won't come and meet the Viceroy 'Like an Indian Chief'.[5]

The reasons for the amir's intransigent attitude were fourfold: first, the process of consolidating his kingdom had led him to deal with his enemies ruthlessly and this had elicited the scorn of Lord Lansdowne, the viceroy, who in 1893 sent a letter of complaint to the amir about his methods. The amir regarded this as blatant meddling and, in the words of Sir Percy Sykes, 'He bitterly resented it and never forgave it'.[6] Second, the surveyor Sir T. Hungerford Holdich observed that, having pacified Afghanistan, 'it was inevitable that the military instincts of the Kabul Court should be directed towards the outlying tribes who never yet have been subdued from either side'. The Afghan government began to interfere with the frontier tribes and actively campaigned against the Bajauris and the pagan Kafirs of Kafiristan. If the amir took over any tribal territory this would bring his frontier directly in contact with British India, without the tribal cushion in between. To the British this was unacceptable.[7] A third source of strain was caused when the British began to build a railway in Baluchistan to the south in disputed territory and towards the Afghan city of Kandahar. The amir evidently reacted furiously and described the project as 'just like pushing a knife into my vitals'.[8] A fourth reason was the rejection of an Afghan embassy in London by Lord Salisbury's government. The amir apparently wanted to bypass dealing with what he considered to be an unfriendly government of India, but Salisbury would consider an Afghan ambassador only when a British, that is Christian, counterpart was installed in Kabul. The amir's disappointment was said to be profound.[9]

The solution to this crisis in relations, after some tortuous negotiations, was the mission sent to Kabul under Durand in October 1893. Durand and his team, which included Holdich, managed to establish officially the boundary between Afghanistan and British India and the resulting frontier became known as the 'Durand' line or boundary, or even the 'scientific frontier'. While this agreement was applauded as a valuable improvement in Anglo-Afghan relations, Holdich was not convinced and later wrote: 'It requires no great strain of the imagination, and not much reading between the lines of official correspondence, to conceive that the Amir disliked the boundary exceedingly'.[10] A fixed boundary now meant that the amir could not meddle in tribal affairs with impunity and was obliged to withdraw troops from Baluchistan. In spite of a sweetener of six extra lakhs of rupees, bringing his subsidy up to eighteen lakhs per annum, 'He did not like it, but he signed the agreement all the same...silently reserving to himself the right of disputing the boundary in detail when it should come to the process of actual demarcation'.[11] Indeed, for the next four years the demarcation process dragged on and the frontier itself became increasingly unsettled.

II

The area of the north-west frontier that today is Pakistan's border with Afghanistan runs for some 400 miles south west of the Hindu Kush mountains in the north to the Sulaiman range in the south. Further south still are the deserts of Baluchistan. The north-west frontier area, which would be turned into a province in 1901, is mountainous and split by several passes and river valleys, the most famous being the Khyber pass and the Kurram river valley. The peoples of this region are Pushtuns, or more familiarly Pathans, who are of the same group, and speak the same language, as many in eastern Afghanistan. Most tribes are Sunni Muslim, although a few are Shia, like the Turis. In 1893, the tribes were neither governed directly by Afghanistan nor Britain, and those on the British side of the frontier were paid to keep the peace and their men recruited into local defence forces. More often than not the tribes fought each other, with occasional forays against the settled, wealthier lowlands that were directly under British control. This would lead to British retaliation in the form of 'butcher and bolt' operations, which meant the destruction of tribal villages and crops and then a hasty withdrawal. Fighting in the mountains was hazardous for the British and constantly exercised the skills of their military men.[12] When the Durand line became the official demarcation between Afghanistan and Britain, those tribes on the British side now came under Britain's jurisdiction and could no longer appeal to the amir if they so desired. While this appeared to change nothing for the British, in that they continued to pay subsidies and refused to interfere in tribal domestic squabbles, the affected tribes resented their new status. Indeed, from 1895, as one later authority put it, the frontier was 'abnormally disturbed', first, because of the Durand agreement and, second, because of the 'intrigues of the Amir'.[13]

The first major problem facing the British in 1895 was in the kingdom of Chitral to the north, where the British residency was besieged owing to a dynastic dispute. Once the problem was dealt with the British established, for the first time, a garrison in Chitral and a base at the Malakand pass in the territory of Swat and Bajaur. For Sir George Robertson, who had conducted the defence of the residency, the pretender to the Chitrali throne had been the candidate of the amir:

> Putting aside all sophistry, it was certain that Sher Afzal would not have attempted his adventure without the tacit consent of the Amir, and was, in short, the Afghan nominee. Abdur Rahman obviously sought to obtain directly through this prince what the Indian Government had disallowed – the suzerainty of Kabul over Chitral.[14]

Nevertheless, nothing was ever proven.

But from 1896 the amir's attitude did seem to bother London and the secretary of state for India, Lord George Hamilton, referred the matter to the new viceroy, Lord Elgin. Elgin, however, thought the Amir not 'especially unfriendly' and, although there were 'questions as regards Chitral' among others, he was 'not sure that his [the amir's] attitude is very different from that which he has always maintained'.[15] Thus, while, as yet, the conduct of the Amir was not a cause for concern, he continued to prove difficult, particularly over the boundary of the Mohmand tribe, one of the largest on the frontier. Unfortunately for the Mohmands the new boundary cut through their territory, leaving half the tribe on the Afghan side and the other half on the British. This was intolerable to both the Mohmands and the amir who wanted the tribe to be on the Afghan side. Indeed, in May 1896 the amir told Elgin that the Durand convention had left the Mohmand country in his hands and had never mentioned the area. Also, the line drawn on the convention map did not conclusively define the boundary. Naturally, the British rejected this interpretation and so throughout 1896 the dispute rumbled on, especially as the amir was apparently urging his local commander-in-chief, or sipah salar, Ghulam Haidar Khan, to encourage the Mohmands to protest. Furthermore, the British became aware that a local mullah, the Hadda, or Adda, Mullah, was doing his best to incite the Mohmands by urging them not to trade with the British on pain of death. The amir was also in correspondence with the Afridis of the Khyber Pass, another of the large tribes and was urging them to accept his protection. A stiff note from Elgin asserted British claims and brought a more passive attitude from the amir. In 1897, after the British offered an unobtrusive demarcation process and a few villages, the amir backed down altogether. Nevertheless, the amir's nit-picking had not endeared him to the British authorities. 'In negotiating small questions', wrote Hamilton, 'he is as sharp as any Jew attorney, and it is difficult to deal with such a nature, unless you put the subject in dispute as a whole, and exercise pressure either by threat of force or withdrawal of subsidy'.[16]

III

The outbreak on the frontier began on 26 July 1897 with an attack on the British garrison at the Malakand Pass by the Swatis, who were soon joined by the Bunerwals and Mamunds (different from the Mohmands). On 7 August 1897, the Mohmands launched an attack on the fort at Shabkadr, while on the 23rd the Afridis attacked British garrisons in the Khyber Pass and three days later were joined by their neighbours the Orakzais. Thus within a few weeks the northern half of the frontier area had risen in revolt against British overlordship. In each of these cases a mullah or holy man was heavily involved. In Swat, a fakir called Sadulla, known to the British as the 'mad fakir' or to his followers as the 'sartor' (bare-headed) fakir, had called for jihad. The Mohmands were led by the Hadda Mullah, Najm-ud-din, while the Afridis were influenced by Mullah Sayed Akbar. As the British were caught totally unawares and so many tribes were involved at once, the suggestion was that the whole affair had been planned and was being coordinated. With the amir on unfriendly terms with the British he was immediately suspected of being the culprit, especially as there were reasons which suggested his involvement other than those above. But first the uprising needs to be put into its wider context to show why its scale caused so much alarm, and why the attitude of the amir was considered so important.

A frontier uprising anywhere in the empire might be considered to be nothing more than a local affair that could easily be dealt with. The revolt on the north-west frontier in 1897, however, went beyond such complacency as its magnitude became apparent. For the British, as Winston Churchill put it, this was evidence 'of secret workings.... Civilisation is face to face with militant Mohammedanism'.[17]

This feeling that the British empire confronted the menace of Islam, both along and inside its borders, was prevalent at the time. One reason was that by the 1890s the British ruled more Muslims than any other empire and were sensitive to any signs of dissent. As India held the most it was here that the British remained acutely alert for any sign of trouble. Modern scholars are now aware how important intelligence gathering was to the British. The recent works of Christopher Bayly and Richard Popplewell have shown how information, and the ability to access and interpret it, was crucial both to the rule of the East India Company and the British government. This was needed to counter threats posed by nationalists and, crucially, the British remained heavily dependent on indigenous sources.[18] Indeed, a lack of reliable knowledge had contributed greatly to the outbreak of the Indian Mutiny in 1857. Ever since then the British authorities remained wary of Muslims, whom they blamed for causing the trouble. These fears were compounded in 1872, when the viceroy, Lord Mayo, was assassinated by a Muslim. So for the British it was imperative that India's Muslims be given no cause to revolt by either domestic or external policies. According to Peter Hardy it was Lord Lytton, the architect of the Second Afghan War in 1878, 'who first introduced the Indian Muslims into the consideration of Middle Eastern policy, where indeed they remained until the days of Churchill, sometimes as a ghoul, sometimes as a phantom, sometimes as Frankenstein's monster, but always as a bogy'. And, as Lytton himself explained to Lord Salisbury, then foreign secretary in Disraeli's government:

> There is no getting away over the fact that the British Empire is a Mahomedan power, and that it entirely depends upon the policy of Her Majesty's Government, whether the sentiment of our Mahomedan subjects is to be an immense security or an immense danger, to us.

Thus, as Hardy asserts, 'The "Indian Mahomedan" bugaboo in British foreign policy had been born'.[19]

The advent of pan-Islamic feeling brought about by the threat posed by the European powers to Muslim polities was of much concern to opinion in Britain and India. Certainly, by 1882 it was acknowledged in Britain that the Ottoman empire was at the heart of the pan-Islamic movement, from where propaganda and agents could spread the message.[20] For some in Britain, Islam seemed resurgent after decades of decline, and to the missionary movement, as Andrew Porter has found, it now posed a serious challenge in both Asia and Africa.[21] In Europe, the Turkish victory over the Greeks in early 1897 seemed to justify these fears and led to a major crisis involving many of the great powers, including Britain. In the end, however, the Turks were prevented from making any gains at Greece's expense and actually lost full control of Crete. This caused outrage within the Sultan's empire and, as one contemporary Muslim writer, Rafiüddin Ahmad, commented, this was evidence that 'Christendom had not shaken off its ancient animosities against Islam'. Nevertheless, according to Ahmad, this engendered an Islamic revival that owed its origins to 'a perception of reasonable and probable dangers to Islam and the Islamites engendered by the Greco-Turkish war and the attitude of Christendom towards Islam during recent years'. Even Lord Salisbury, the prime minister, acknowledged the effects of the Turkish victory might have on the Muslim world: 'A slight ... an exaggerated victory, has recalled to them their past of a thousand years ago, when they were victorious in every part of the world ... they cannot but believe that that glorious period of their history is to be repeated.'[22]

Thus one of the first concerns for the British at the start of the north-west frontier uprising was the possible role of pan-Islamic feeling among the tribes, among Indians, and the possible involvement of the Turks. Indeed, five days before the outbreak Hamilton asked Elgin whether the sultan had sent emissaries to India, such as 'two Turks, and other Mussalmans from Java, selected by Ottoman Consul-General there. ... Are you taking steps to watch such matters in India?' Elgin's reply was that pan-Islamic propaganda was watched, but there was a shortage of Muslim agents.[23] Once the uprising was under way anxiety grew: Hamilton warned Elgin to 'keep watch for Temaledin Effendi, dervish of Constantinople, tall and thin, reddish beard, acquiline [sic] nose, eloquent, supposed to have gone recently to India via Karachi'. Later he expressed his concerns about Turkish newspapers getting into India as 'the tone is virulent'. Consequently, the Turkish newspapers *Sabah* and *Malumat* were prohibited by the viceroy.[24] None of this was lost on the commander-in-chief in India, Sir George White, who wrote, 'I fear the rapprochement between Constantinople and Kabul and the hostile tone of the Turkish press may cause us trouble with the Mussulmans of India'.[25] There was, therefore, a great deal of apprehension among the highest British authorities in London and Calcutta that there was more to the uprising than a local disturbance. Consequently, attention focused on whether the amir was part of a pan-Islamic conspiracy or not. The long-serving political agent to the Afridis, Sir Robert Warburton, wrote later that in May 1897, just before the uprising:

> reports were circulated in Peshawar [in British territory] that an agent from Constantinople had reached Caubul [sic], had interviewed the [amir], who had

sent for all the noted Mullahs in his country, had introduced them to this agent, and after telling them to go to their homes and preach a religious war ... to their people and secure one out of every eight males as reservists for his army, had permitted them to leave.[26]

Moreover, Rafiüddin Ahmad certainly equated some of the amir's actions with helping the pan-Islamic revival. Following the demarcation of the Durand line, much of the area known as Kafiristan was given over to the amir, who promptly and ruthlessly set about converting the pagan population: 'So long and so frequently have [Muslim] princes been losing territories that this annexation, little as it is, was hailed with unbounded joy by the people of Afghanistan and their friends and well-wishers.'[27]

A more potent concern for the British about the amir was with regard to two titles he had assumed, and two books he had written years earlier. In 1889, he called himself 'King of Islam' and in 1896 'Light of the religion and of the faith'. His two books were entitled *Rectification of the Faith* and more importantly, given events on the frontier, *Inducement for a Holy War*. It was reported that about sixty copies of the latter were sent to the Hadda Mullah by the Afghan Hakim of Kunar for distribution among the Mohmands prior to the outbreak.[28] Later, India Office officials reviewed a third book, *Advice to Afghans*, published sometime after 1893. The tone of the book was disheartening for one official who noted: 'It would be easy to compile a citizen of Afghanistan from this excellent treatise, but without a chapter on duty to my neighbours for that duty is summed up – "If he is a Christian you must kill him".'[29]

IV

Circumstantial evidence existed, therefore, to show that the amir had an interest in encouraging the uprising. And, as the disturbances escalated, some on the British side were too ready to see the amir's involvement. One was Major H. A. Deane, the political agent in charge of the Malakand agency, which encompassed the areas of Dir, Swat and Chitral. In his official diary Deane wrote that he had heard that the amir had paid 40,000 rupees 'to an influential Mulla in India to work up this business ... My own opinion is that both Kabul and India are concerned in the matter'. Moreover, Deane, to back up his case in a subsequent letter, attached a report from a local agent, Abdul Hamid Khan, who argued:

> Since the commencement of the Greco-Turkish war the Amir of Afghanistan has sent Maulvis and Talibs to excite frontier Muhammadan [sic] tribes by distributing among them books on jehad [sic]. The Amir has opened shops to sell rifles and cartridges cheap to the different tribesmen. If there were no movement from his [the amir's] side, Muhammadan [sic] tribes would never dare to disturb the British Raj.[30]

Deane's contention was supported by others. The commissioner of Peshawar, Sir Richard Udny, was, however, more forthright in his condemnation because he reported that Afghan sepoys, dressed in plain clothes, were joining the tribesmen, and Afghan officials were doing nothing to stop them. 'It is quite certain' he wrote, 'that the people would never have moved in such a general way, if it had not been universally understood that they had the permission of the Amir.'[31]

When asked for his opinion Lord Roberts, the former commander-in-chief of the Indian Army, had no doubts that the Amir was involved:

> The Amir is a clever, cunning, treacherous, unscrupulous Mahomedan, and, like many of his race and creed, is becoming more and more [deranged] by the fanatical tenets of his religion as he gets on in years. He firmly believes that we are afraid of him, and ... he thinks the more he troubles us, the more pliable he will find us.

Roberts called for a firm hand to be shown to the amir, just as the British had recently dealt with the Boers in South Africa. It was time to tell the amir 'that we stand no more nonsense' because '[a]n Oriental yields ungrudging admiration to firmness and determination not to be trifled with'. Roberts hoped that if proof were found of the amir's intrigues then it would be better to have an 'open enemy ... in the long run than a disloyal friend'.[32]

The amir's position was not helped by the mullahs leading the revolts for they told their followers that they had his backing and could expect Afghan assistance. The fakir was certainly proclaiming Afghan support, while the Hadda Mullah was particularly assiduous in using the amir's name to stir up trouble. In letters to the Mian Guls, the grandsons of the famous Akhund of Swat and nominal leaders of the Swatis, and to several Afridi mullahs and maliks, he liberally promised help from Afghanistan, and said that the amir urged patience while he consulted his officials. The amir apparently promised the Afridis that he, or his son, would join them once they had decided on their course of action.[33]

Moreover the supposed role in the disturbances of the sipah salar, Ghulam Haidar Khan, added to the resentment of the amir. He was well known to the British having earlier been involved in the boundary demarcation, during which he had proved to be very obstructive. To Colonel Holdich, who knew him quite well, he was good natured and hospitable, but 'at heart an intensely bigoted Mahomedan' and was 'too openly hostile to British interests'. Holdich felt the sipah salar to be too much his own man which accounted for the rumours about his conduct during the uprising.[34]

Others though felt that the sipah salar was too much the amir's man. Even before the outbreak, in April 1897, a memorandum stated that the amir, through the sipar salah, was intriguing with the Afridis. Once the fighting began the sipah salar's name became prominent as various charges were laid at his door. He supposedly told the fakir to launch his attack and he would receive help; a British agent, Ahmad Mian, evidently saw a man passing between the sipah salar and the fakir; later the sipah salar apparently sent 25,000 rupees to the Hadda Mullah and another sum to help towards the funeral of a mullah killed in action against the British. The role of the sipah salar in the uprising was to rumble on in British correspondence for the next few months and be the subject of discussion between the amir and the British authorities.[35]

V

As the rising on the frontier escalated, questions about the complicity of the amir and the sipah salar were in need of answer. The British realised that to accuse the amir of openly supporting the enemy was 'a very serious matter' and that certain proof was needed. From early enquiries it was clear that Afghan subjects had helped attack Shabkadr and the viceroy, through the deputy commissioner of Peshawar, demanded the amir 'recall his subjects and render it impossible for them to repeat an offence so exceedingly grave as this deliberate violation of British territory'. Moreover, the amir was also warned that he should deal with the Sipah Salar, remove him, or 'His Highness must be held responsible for the Sipah Salar's actions'.[36] The amir denied any complicity and rejected the charge that Afghan regulars were with the Hadda Mullah: he did acknowledge that Afghan tribesmen, if they had joined, had done so secretly. In a somewhat exasperated tone the amir indicated his own troubles by 'violently denouncing mullas [sic]', who had caused him trouble for fourteen years and had gone over to the British side of control. While accepting the amir's denials, the viceroy wanted the amir to denounce publicly any tribesmen joining the uprising and to order his officials to stop any movements towards the frontier. This the amir had already done: in a public durbar on 17 August 1897 he had voiced his anger at the sipah salar and swore that he had always stayed loyal to his British commitments. The assembly to whom the amir had addressed his remarks subsequently approved his conciliatory reply to the British.[37]

Elgin gave a copy of the amir's reply to the press who were already discussing the uprising in some detail. The amir's denial of any involvement was warmly received, as the correspondent of *The Standard* remarked, 'The Ameer [sic] is far too astute to start on a losing game'. The *Daily Graphic* was even more forthright: 'Abdur Rahman is too astute a statesman not to know that the fantastic designs attributed to him by feather-pated Islamophiles are rank madness even if he had not arrived at an age when large ambitions of every kind must cease to tempt'.[38]

Elgin's release of the amir's announcement, or *firman*, came at a difficult time for him and it was done, it seems, in the hope of gaining much-needed support for his own position. For, as Elgin confided to Hamilton, he felt himself 'to be standing in a very isolated position as regards our attitude towards the Amir'. The military, the civilians, that is Udny and Deane, and even the India Office, especially Lee Warner, the secretary of the Political and Secret Correspondence Department, were all ready to see the amir in a bad light. Elgin pointed out that he had on more than one occasion had to speak sharply to the amir over some incident or other, but he was concerned that London, under Durand's advice, was calling for an alteration in the current relationship with the amir. While acknowledging that relations were unsatisfactory he believed they should be kept unchanged until the amir's death, and 'when all is said and done, has not the Amir played the part assigned to him when he was named ruler of Afghanistan?' And, if Britain was thinking of altering the current arrangements, '[a]re we going to reduce him from the position of a subsidised ally to that of a feudatory like one of the Native States in India?' The outcome would be war and a large increase in the army. Even so, Elgin was prepared to investigate the allegations made against the amir 'with all honesty'.[39]

The uprising of the Afridis and Orakzais between 23 and 26 August 1897 inflamed the frontier revolt and re-heated suspicions about the amir just as things seemed to be cooling down. By early September, the British were beginning to understand the uprising as 'fanatical' in nature, that is the tribes revolted owing to their own religious fundamentalism, stirred up by credible mullahs. Nevertheless, the names of the amir and the sipah salar were still being mentioned in British appraisals of the situation. For example, Deane reported that the sipah salar had told the amir that the British would invade Afghanistan once they had dealt with the tribes.[40] All this served to do was to keep the amir and the sipah salar under the spotlight and now that the Afridis had joined the revolt the intensity increased. On 7 September 1897, the deputy commissioner at Kohat told Udny and Sir William Cuningham, the foreign secretary to the government of India, that two spies saw two Afghan regiments in mufti bringing ammunition, sent by the amir, to the Afridis.[41]

An immediate test of the amir's friendship now arrived as the British concentrated first on dealing with the Hadda Mullah and the Mohmands. The amir had already ordered the mullah to disperse his force, or lashkar, but now the British informed him that if the mullah fled to Jarobi, where he had 'established his abode', as this was now on the Afghan side since an agreement signed in November 1896, the British would still 'follow him up and destroy him and his habitation'. If, however, the mullah fled across the mountains into the Kunar valley, which was in Afghanistan proper, then the viceroy expected the Afghans to deal with him.[42]

Thankfully for the British the amir appeared keen to conciliate and accede to their demands. He despaired of 'the statements of foolish persons' who believed the military build-up at Peshawar was aimed at Afghanistan and he approved of the hot pursuit policy although he hoped the troops would not advance too far.[43] All in all it was a rather satisfactory response and at every level it seemed the amir was cooperating fully and maintaining his friendship with Britain. This brought forth a resigned, yet understanding response from Hamilton. The amir, he ventured:

> Has a double game to play. He evidently has no more love of these firebrand Mullahs than we have, but with fanaticism so deeply rooted and so volcanic he must be careful in not taking action which would bring him in conflict with such religious enthusiasm. It may be that this was one of the reasons which made him so tiresome over the delimitation through the Mohmand country. For the future I shall take a more lenient view of his double-facedness, for it is due more to the situation he is in than to the man himself.[44]

The irony of the last sentence was lost on Hamilton, who only now it seemed appreciated that the amir was caught in a cleft stick, having to appease his mullahs and the British at the same time. The amir was not helped by British attitudes that had always been double-edged, as the subtle difference between Hamilton and Elgin testifies. Whereas Hamilton seemed to promote the views of those who would treat the amir more as a lackey than an ally and seek to impose British demands on Kabul,

Elgin represented a more restrained side of British policy. He realised that it was better to humour the amir, to keep him friendly towards Britain and to treat him as an independent sovereign. The problems of the Durand line agreement made Elgin's job more difficult because to the amir, and for many on the frontier, this represented a move forward by the British, perhaps the first stage of a more sustained advance. Thus the ambiguity of the amir reflected the ambiguous nature of British frontier policy.

Yet the rumours refused to go away. The deputy commissioner at Kohat once more passed on intelligence that the amir was somehow in league with the Afridis and Orakzais, having agreed to protect them if they became his subjects and paid him revenue.[45] These stories continued to plague the relations between the British authorities and the amir, who came under increasing pressure to show his loyalty to the British. On 13 October 1897, the amir informed Elgin that orders had been given to arrest the Hadda Mullah, who was now on Afghan soil. However, he said he could not prevent tribesmen coming into Afghanistan from the British side, especially as many had relatives across the frontier, and that he would face their hostility if he tried to prevent this 'natural intercourse'. The amir promised that any Afridis and Orakzais who fled to his domain would be prevented from using it as a base from which to launch attacks against the British. In more practical terms, the amir was to be tested when the following day a deputation of 200 Afridis and Orakzais arrived in Kabul seeking his help.[46] Again, the amir acted as the British hoped and expected he would. He rejected the tribal petitions, which listed their grievances against the British, but offered his services as a mediator. It was somewhat of a relief for the British to discover that the main reason behind the Afridi and Orakzai uprising was not religious fanaticism, but more parochial concerns relating to trade and affronts to tribal dignity. Subsequently, the viceroy related to the amir that General Sir William Lockhart, commander of the British forces, had called on the Afridis and Orakzais to surrender and would discuss matters with them once he had arrived in the Afridi heartland of Tirah.[47]

Once the amir had rejected the pleas of the Afridis and Orakzais they lost their last hope. As November came, and the weather grew colder, the two tribes began to lose heart and sought an agreement with Lockhart. The amir had in the end proved loyal and cooperative and his attitude had certainly contributed to the termination of hostilities between the British and the Afridis and Orakzais. The Khyber Pass had been closed during the fighting and once the tribes acknowledged their defeat the amir was keen to re-open it, although he hoped that while he waited the Tartara route would be opened as an alternative. The viceroy was eager to accommodate the amir and explained to Hamilton that:

> We have received no direct evidence of the Amir's complicity in the disturbances. On the contrary, all the evidence which is forthcoming is in his favour, and I propose to reply that we shall forthwith reopen the Khyber line, and permit the passage of His Highness's stores as formerly.[48]

While relations with the amir managed to remain fairly satisfactory as far as the British were concerned, this could not be said of relations with, or perceptions of, the sipah salar, Ghulam Haidar Khan. Throughout the months following the start of the uprising his alleged continual double dealing meant that he never had the benefit of any doubt from the British. His plotting also meant that Britain's relations with the amir would never be perfect. As mentioned earlier, the sipah salar had annoyed the British over the boundary demarcation and was suspected of aiding the Hadda Mullah. Despite the amir's protestations of innocence, no such undertakings appeared from Ghulam Haidar Khan. Sir George White, the British commander-in-chief in India, perhaps reflected opinion among the higher authorities when he told Elgin that Deane was too quick to blame the amir, but 'I believe the Sipah Salar to be steeped in intrigue against us'.[49] Even when the Hadda Mullah and his allies had suffered crushing defeats, rumours about the sipah salar had continued; the Khan of Nawagai, a British ally, openly accused him of sending rifles to the Hadda Mullah. Deane wanted to write to Ghulam Haidar Khan to make him stop Afghan subjects from joining the tribesmen, but was warned by Cuningham that he could do this only as long as 'there is no doubt as to the gathering coming from Afghan limits'. Furthermore, the amir would be notified of any such correspondence.[50] At the time Major-General Sir Bindon Blood, commander of the Malakand Field Force, was trying to come to terms with the Mamunds, but it seems the whole process was being interfered with by the sipah salar, who wanted to direct the tribe during the negotiations. But the Mamunds had been totally defeated and even with the sipah salar in close proximity they were determined to surrender to the British. On being reassured that their country would not be annexed they accepted British terms.[51]

While the sipah salar was certainly unfriendly towards the British, his attempts to stir up trouble, perpetuate what had already started or hamper peace negotiations did not work. During the tribal rising the sipah salar was a bogeyman whose influence was exaggerated. The only decisive support he might have provided was to have invaded the British side with his army, but even he was not independent enough of the amir to risk such a venture. The actions he took, such as promoting the Hadda Mullah, sending some material help and providing volunteers to help the tribes, were just enough not to risk the wrath of the amir. Once the fighting ended, however, the sipah salar was summoned to the amir's presence, but before he could answer his sovereign he became ill and died. A last word on the sipah salar came from Elgin. On 21 July 1898, he reminded Hamilton that he had wanted 'full particulars' on the sipah salar's activities regarding the Mamunds. 'In view of the death of Ghulam Haidar, it appears unnecessary to pursue this question, the more so as the evidence obtainable is scanty and inconclusive.'[52]

VI

The presence of an independent Muslim state, Afghanistan, on the border of India was always a concern for the British considering the volatility of the tribal area. When the 1897 tribal uprising began it was too easy for the British to believe that the amir and his local sipah salar were behind the whole business. While there were many on the frontier who felt this, those in higher positions, notably the viceroy himself, refused to consider the notion and argued that the amir had done nothing to warrant British hostility. In this regard he was supported by Winston Churchill, who suggested afterwards that 'the advantages which the Amir would derive from a quarrel with the British are not apparent'.[53] Nevertheless, the amir had apparently increased the temperature on the frontier through his writings and assumption of titles that seemed to incite Muslims to jihad. For those who pointed out these failings, there were perfectly reasonable explanations that had more to do with the nature of Afghanistan itself, than the frontier or British fears. The amir himself had problems with mullahs, even the Hadda Mullah, who had described him 'as one of the most oppressive rulers who was hated by the people of Afghanistan'. The amir's recent biographer, Hasan Kawim Kakar, suggests that the amir, through the sipah salar, might have encouraged the Hadda Mullah with false promises, only to let him suffer the ignominy of defeat at the hands of the British. Moreover, he further maintains that the amir used the concept of jihad as a rallying point for his people at a time when Afghanistan seemed beset on all sides by infidels, and when relations with the British were poor. The amir's version of jihad was not to launch holy war against the infidels, but to cement his own position in the country.[54]

The focus on Abdur Rahman Khan as complicit in the uprising revealed British sensitivity over a temperamental and vital frontier. The belief that the uprising might have wider antecedents clearly affected British perceptions at the start, especially as there was some truth in the assertion that Muslims abroad were linked to Muslims within the Indian empire and on its borders. Yet, once the initial shock had worn off, a calmer appreciation took hold. Forty years later Churchill remarked that the tribes' hostility was 'easily explainable on quite ordinary grounds'.[55] These grounds, once the dust had cleared, seemed to be Britain's frontier policy as a whole. The tribal revolt had immediately re-awakened a debate that was then carried out in the letter pages of the press and in articles in leading periodicals. This argument had been around since the first Afghan conflict and centred on whether Britain should pursue a 'forward' policy by establishing the frontier within Afghanistan itself. Britain would thus be ready to meet a Russian invasion before it got to India. The other side of the dispute ventured that Britain should pursue a policy of 'masterly inactivity' by leaving the frontier zone in the hands of the tribes and Afghanistan in the hands of its own rulers. They would then disrupt any Russian advance. Many of the correspondents and writers attacked the 'forward policy'. To an old Indian soldier like General John Adye, writing in The Times, this was the cause of the recent trouble: 'that is of forcing ourselves and our authority upon the independent border tribes'. He was supported in this by General Neville Chamberlain in the pages of The Saturday Review, whose editorial criticised the pronouncements of Lord Roberts – a well-known advocate of the forward approach. Sir Lepel Griffin, who had helped put the amir on the throne, wrote in The Nineteenth Century that the tribal revolt had been caused by the 'breakdown of the "forward" frontier policy'.[56]

To Lord George Hamilton, however, these 'controversialists' ignored 'the fact that the inherent difficulty of the situation consists of the extraordinary fanatical and unreliable mass of humanity with whom we have to deal'. And it was in the area where non-interference had been the main policy that British authority had completely collapsed. In the short term, Hamilton could see one positive aspect: 'We have now the opportunity of raising our prestige, and I fear that in governing Orientals an assertion of strength and fighting power is periodically necessary.'[57]

In the end the uprising did not sever links between the amir and the British and to all intents and purposes relations carried on as before. For Britain, though, a new policy was needed on the frontier if it was not to be caught napping again and be charged with interfering in tribal life. Whatever happened in India and the wider world among Muslims, the British were determined that the tribes should have no reason to launch jihad. When Elgin was replaced by Lord Curzon in 1899, the new viceroy set about restructuring the frontier. In the teeth of opposition from officials in the Punjab, who would no longer oversee the tribal area, Curzon created the North West Frontier Province, in his view the best way to administer the tribes with as light a touch as possible. While no policy could eradicate friction with the tribes totally this was fairly successful until the outbreak of war in 1914, when all the old demons of pan-Islam and fanaticism on the frontier, in India and in other Muslim areas of the empire, surfaced once more.

Notes

[1] Newton, *Lord Lansdowne*, 106; Curzon, *Tales of Travel*, 54.
[2] See, for example, Davies, *Problem of the North-West Frontier*, still the best overall view of Anglo-Afghan relations during that period; Johnson, *Spying for Empire*; Moreman, *The Army in India*; and especially Barthorp, *Frontier Ablaze*.
[3] Kakar, *Government and Society in Afghanistan*.
[4] Robson, *Road to Kabul*, 210, 214; Sykes, *History of Afghanistan*, II, 137.
[5] Quoted in Sykes, *Sir Mortimer Durand*, 202.
[6] Newton, *Lord Lansdowne*, 106; Sykes, *Afghanistan*, II, 169.
[7] Holdich, *Indian Borderland*, 227–28.
[8] Ibid., 228; Khan, *Life of Abdur Rahman*, II, 159–60.
[9] Sykes, *Afghanistan*, II, 193–94.
[10] Holdich, *Indian Borderland*, 230.
[11] Ibid., 231.
[12] For more, see Moreman, *The Army in India*.
[13] Davies, *Problem of the North-West Frontier*, 71.
[14] Robertson, *Chitral*, 33.
[15] Hamilton to Elgin; Elgin to Hamilton, 17 Jan. 1896 and 5 Feb. 1896, Elgin Papers, MSS EUR/F84/14, British Library, India Office Records, Africa and Asia Collections (BL, IOR, AAC).
[16] Hamilton to Elgin, 12 March 1897, Elgin Papers, ibid. For more on the disputes of 1896, see Memorandum of Information Regarding Affairs Beyond the North-West Frontier of India, (1896), L/PS/20/MM3, BL, IOR, AAC.
[17] *Daily Telegraph*, 6 Nov. 1897, in Woods, *Young Winston's Wars*, 67.

[18] Bayly, *Empire & Information*; Popplewell, *Intelligence and Imperial Defence*. For a useful discussion of the work of Bayly and others, see Ballantyne, 'Colonial Knowledge', esp. 187–95.
[19] Hardy, *Muslims of British India*, 119.
[20] Landau, *Politics of Pan-Islam*, 40–44, 60, 69.
[21] See Porter, *Religion versus Empire?*, 211–24.
[22] Ahmad, 'A Moslem's View', 17–20; Salisbury quoted in Steele, 'Lord Salisbury', 11; Grenville, *Lord Salisbury and Foreign Policy*, 89–96; Roberts, *Salisbury*, 648–51.
[23] Hamilton to Elgin; Elgin to Hamilton, tels, 21 and 25 July 1897, L/PS/7/93/Nos 739 & 671, BL, IOR AAC. See also note by unknown India Office official.
[24] Hamilton to Elgin, tels, 12, 16 & 18 Aug. 1897; Elgin to Hamilton, tels, 17 & 20 Aug. 1897, L/PS/7/94/873/12, 16, 17, 20–21, BL, IOR, AAC.
[25] White to the Duke of Cambridge, 11 Aug. 1897, Sir George White Papers, MSS EUR/F108/20/No.102, BL IOR AAC.
[26] Warburton, *Eighteen Years in the Khyber*, 290–91.
[27] Ahmad, 'A Moslem's View', 520.
[28] Walters, *Operations of the Tirah Expeditionary Force*, 15–16; Commissioner of Peshawar to Foreign Secretary, Simla, 3 Aug. 1897, L/MIL/7/15860/f.58, BL, IOR, AAC.
[29] Cuningham to Lee Warner, 24 Feb. 1898, L/PS/7/101/1898/351. See also Government of India: Home Department Memorandum, 9 Dec. 1897, L/PS/7/98/1225, BL, IOR, AAC.
[30] Deane, Diary, 29 July 1897, L/PS/7/98/1293/No.81; Deane to Foreign Secretary, 31 Aug. 1897, L/PS/7/96/1043/Encl. 166/Appendix IV, BL, IOR, AAC.
[31] Commissioner of Peshawar to Foreign Secretary, Simla, tel., 10 Aug. 1897, L/PS/7/98/1293/No.220, BL, IOR, AAC.
[32] Roberts to Lee Warner, 14 Aug. 1897, L/PS/7/94/762, BL, IOR, AAC.
[33] Deane to Foreign Secretary, Simla, 7 Aug. 1897, L/PS/7/98/1293/No.171; Deane, Diary, 12 Aug. 1897, L/PS/7/95/939/No.119; Deane to Foreign Secretary, 24 Sept. 1897, enclosing letter from Mulla Adda [sic] to the Mian Guls, 2 Sept. 1897, L/PS/7/97/112/299; General Lockhart to Foreign Secretary, 20 Nov. 1897, enclosing letter from Mulla of Adda [sic] to mullahs and maliks and 'other people of Tirah', 5 Sept. 1897, L/PS/7/99/205/No.131, BL, IOR, AAC.
[34] Holdich, *Indian Borderland*, 281–82.
[35] Memorandum, *Khyber*, 4 April 1897, L/PS/7/91/491; Deane to Foreign Secretary, Simla, 4 Aug. 1897, L/PS/7/98/1293/No.144; Deane, Diary, 12 & 31 Aug. 1897, L/PS/7/95/939/Nos 119 & 223, BL, IOR, AAC.
[36] Cuningham to Udny, tel., 11 Aug. 1897; Elgin to Hamilton, tel., 13 Aug. 1897, L/PS/7/98/1293/nos 229 & 252, BL, IOR, AAC.
[37] Elgin to Hamilton, 23 & 25 Aug. 1897, L/PS/7/94/873, 25, 27, BL, IOR, AAC.
[38] *The Standard*, 16 Aug. 1897; *Daily Graphic*, 16 Aug. 1897, cuttings in Elgin Papers, MSS EUR F84/79A, 55 & 59, BL, IOR, AAC.
[39] Elgin to Hamilton, 24 Aug. 1897, Elgin Papers, MSS EUR F84/15/XXVII, 83–86; see also Elgin to Hamilton, 10 Aug. 1897, ibid., XXV, 75–78, BL, IOR, AAC.
[40] Deane to Cuningham, 4 Sept. 1897, L/PS/7/95/939/no. 175, BL, IOR, AAC.
[41] Dep. Comm. Kohat to Udny and Cuningham, 7 Sept. 1897, L/PS/7/95/939/No.228, BL, IOR, AAC.
[42] Elgin to Hamilton, tel., 6 Sept. 1897, L/PS/7/94/874. Also Elgin to Hamilton, 7 Sept. 1897, Elgin Papers, MSS EUR F84/15/XXIX, 91–93, BL, IOR, AAC.
[43] Elgin to Hamilton, 21 Sept. 1897, L/PS/7/95/925, BL, IOR, AAC.
[44] Hamilton to Elgin, 30 Sept. 1897, Elgin Papers, MSS EUR F84/15/XXXI, 63–64, BL, IOR, AAC.
[45] Dep. Comm. Kohat to Udny, 28 Sept. 1897, Enclo. No.14. See also Officer on Special Duty, Kurram, to Udny, 29 Sept. 1897, Enclo. No.19, L/PS/7/97/1142, BL, IOR, AAC.

[46] Amir to Viceroy, 13 Sept. 1897, Enclo.126; British Agent, Kabul to Cuningham, 19 Oct. 1897, Enclo. 118, L/PS/7/97/1142, BL, IOR, AAC.
[47] British Agent, Kabul, to Cuningham, 16 & 18 Oct. 1897, Enclos., nos 133, 163; Elgin to Amir, 28 Oct. 1897, Enclo. 183, L/PS/7/97/1142, BL, IOR, AAC.
[48] Elgin to Hamilton, tel., 21 Dec. 1897, Elgin Papers, MSS, EUR F84/20/No.943, 310, BL, IOR, AAC.
[49] White to Elgin, 28 Sept. 1897, White Papers, MSS EUR F108/20/115, BL, IOR, AAC.
[50] Diary, HQ Malakand Field Force, 16 & 17 Sept. 1897, L/PS/7/97/112; Deane to Cuningham, tel., 6 Oct. 1897; Cuningham to Deane, tel., 7 Oct. 1897, L/PS/7/97/1118/Enclos., Nos. 29, 30, BL, IOR, AAC.
[51] Deane to Cuningham, 8 & 9 Oct. 1897, L/PS/7/97/1118/Enclos., Nos. 38, 39, BL, IOR, AAC; Walters, *Operations of the Malakand Field Force*, 71.
[52] Elgin to Hamilton, 21 July 1898, L/PS/7/105/754, BL, IOR, AAC. Holdich, *Indian Borderland*, 281, 339.
[53] Churchill, *Story of the Malakand Field Force*, 149.
[54] Kakar, *Government and Society*, 156–57, 176–78.
[55] Churchill, *My Early Life*, 139.
[56] For cuttings see Elgin Papers, MSS EUR F84/79A & 79B/pp. 54 & 78B, BL, IOR, AAC. Griffin, 'The Breakdown of the "Forward" Frontier Policy', 501–16.
[57] Hamilton to Elgin, 9 Sept. 1897, Elgin Papers, MSS EUR F84/15/XXVIII, 54–55, BL, IOR, AAC.

References

Ahmad, Rafiüddin. 'A Moslem's View of the Pan-Islamic Revival'. *The Nineteenth Century* 42 (1897): 517–26.
Ballantyne, Tony. 'Colonial Knowledge'. In *The British Empire: Themes and Perspectives*, edited by Sarah Stockwell. Oxford: Blackwell, 2008.
Barthorp, Michael. *The Frontier Ablaze: The North-West Frontier Rising 1897–98*. London: Windrow & Greene, 1996.
Bayly, C. A. *Empire & Information: Intelligence Gathering and Social Communication in India, 1780–1870*. Cambridge: Cambridge University Press, 1996.
Churchill, Winston S. *The Story of the Malakand Field Force: An Episode of Frontier War*. London: Mandarin Paperbacks, 1990.
———. *My Early Life: A Roving Commission*. London: The Reprint Society, 1944.
Curzon of Kedleston, Marquess. *Tales of Travel*. London: Century Hutchinson, 1988.
Davies, C. Collin *The Problem of the North-West Frontier 1890–1908*. Cambridge: Cambridge University Press, 1932.
Grenville, J. A. S. *Lord Salisbury and Foreign Policy: The Close of the Nineteenth Century*. London: The Athlone Press, 1964.
Griffin, Lepel. 'The Breakdown of the "Forward" Frontier Policy'. *The Nineteenth Century* 42 (1897): 501–16.
Hardy, Peter. *The Muslims of British India*. Cambridge: Cambridge University Press, 1972.
Holdich, Sir T. Hungerford *The Indian Borderland 1880–1900*. London: Methuen, 1901.
Johnson, Robert. *Spying for Empire: The Great Game in Central and South Asia, 1757–1947*. London: Greenhill Books, 2006.
Kakar, Hassan Kawim. *Government and Society in Afghanistan: The Reign of Amir 'Abd al-Rahman Khan*. London: University of Texas Press, 1979.
Khan, Mir Munshi Sultan Mahomed, ed. *The Life of Abdur Rahman: Amir of Afghanistan*. Vols 2. London: John Murray, 1900.
Landau, Jacob. *The Politics of Pan-Islam: Ideology and Organisation*. Oxford: Clarendon Press, 1990.

Moreman, T. R. *The Army in India and the Development of Frontier Warfare, 1849–1947.* Basingstoke: Macmillan, 1998.
Newton, Lord. *Lord Lansdowne: A Biography.* London: Macmillan, 1929.
Popplewell, Richard J. *Intelligence and Imperial Defence: British Intelligence and the Defence of the Indian Empire, 1904–1924.* London: Frank Cass, 1995.
Porter, Andrew. *Religion versus Empire? British Protestant Missionaries and Overseas Expansion, 1700–1914.* Manchester: Manchester University Press, 2004.
Roberts, Andrew. *Salisbury, Victorian Titan.* London: Weidenfeld & Nicolson, 1999.
Robertson, Sir George. *Chitral: The Story of a Minor Siege.* 5th edn. London: R. J. Leach, 1991.
Robson, Brian. *The Road to Kabul: The Second Afghan War 1878–1881.* Staplehurst: Spellmount, 2003.
Steele, David. 'Lord Salisbury, the "False Religion" of Islam, and the Reconquest of the Sudan'. In *Sudan: The Reconquest Reappraised*, edited by Edward Spiers. London: Frank Cass, 1998.
Sykes, Sir Percy. *Sir Mortimer Durand.* London: Cassell, 1924.
———. *A History of Afghanistan.* Vols 2. London: Macmillan, 1940.
Walters, Captain G.H. *Operations of the Tirah Expeditionary Force 1897–98.* Simla: Intelligence Department, 1900.
———. *The Operations of the Malakand Field Force and the Buner Field Force, 1897–98.* Simla: Intelligence Branch, 1900.
Warburton, Colonel Sir Robert. *Eighteen Years in the Khyber, 1879–1898.* London: John Murray, 1900.
Woods, Frederick, ed. *Young Winston's Wars: The Original Despatches of Winston S. Churchill.* London: Sphere, 1972.

The Church of the Three Selves: A Perspective from the World Missionary Conference, Edinburgh, 1910

Brian Stanley

The most obdurate challenge confronting Christian missions in the nineteenth century was how to bring to fulfilment the goal described by Henry Venn of the Church Missionary Society (CMS) in 1865, namely 'to establish in each district and especially where there are separate languages, a self-supporting, self-governing, self-extending native Church'.[1] Though most famously expounded by Venn and (independently) by his American Congregationalist contemporary Rufus Anderson, the 'three-self' ideal was in substance, if not in precise wording, shared by the Protestant missionary movement as a whole. The Liverpool missionary conference of 1860, for example, affirmed that the supreme object of the missionary enterprise was the establishment of churches which should depend, 'not upon distant and foreign Churches, but upon their own exertions and their own spiritual graces'.[2] Parallel statements can be found in the writings of Catholic missionary spokesmen such as François Libermann or Daniel Comboni.

Historians of the missionary movement have devoted considerable attention to the three-self theory and to the multiple ambiguities which Venn and Anderson encountered when they sought to implement it through the policies of their respective missionary agencies, the CMS and the American Board of Commissioners for Foreign Missions.[3] What scholars have yet to attempt is a more comprehensive survey of how far, and with what regional or denominational variations, the three-self principle was translated into practice over a longer period of time. The continuing significance of the 'three selves' has been emphasised mainly by historians of Christianity in China, whose long history of anti-foreignism dictated that Christian missions had a greater vested interest in the implementation of the principle than anywhere else. Thus the 'Christian Manifesto' drawn up in 1950 by Wu Yaozong (Y. T. Wu) and eighteen other Protestant leaders as a basis for negotiation with Zhou Enlai and the new Communist regime conceded that '[t]he movement for autonomy, self-support, and self-propagation hitherto promoted in the Chinese church has already attained a measure of success', though it also urged that this task should be completed 'within the shortest possible period' – an objective realised through the Three-Self Patriotic Movement, which was formally constituted in 1954 and became the voice of the 'official' state-regulated Protestant church in Communist China.[4] In this way a slogan devised in the west by nineteenth-century missionary society administrators paradoxically became central to the self-understanding of an indigenous expression of Christianity which took rapid and controversial strides to sever almost all ties with the churches of Europe and North America.

I

One partial, flawed, but nevertheless instructive answer to the question of how far three-self principles moved from rhetoric to reality is provided by the evidence submitted to Commission II of the influential World Missionary Conference held in Edinburgh in 1910 and the particular interpretation which the commission placed on that evidence. The conference was the third in a series of ecumenical conferences organised by the Protestant missionary movement, the first two being held in London in 1888 and New York in 1900. It is remembered today in a way that its two predecessors are not, because it established a continuation committee which gave birth to some of the most important Protestant internationalist structures of the twentieth century, culminating in the formation of the World Council of Churches in 1948. Of the 1,215 official delegates at Edinburgh, 509 were British, 491 were North American and only nineteen were from the non-western world, eighteen of them from Asia.[5] The business of the conference was prepared by eight study commissions. Commission II, given the task of reporting to the conference on 'The Church in the Mission Field', sent a questionnaire to 217 serving missionaries, mission executives and national church leaders seeking their views on the current state of health of the churches planted by Protestant missions.

The commission's report began by asserting that the most important general conclusion to be drawn from the replies submitted to its questionnaire was that an individualistic view of the missionary task as a story of the heroic struggle of missionaries rescuing 'little groups of unimportant people' from the forces of heathendom must now be 'entirely abandoned'. The church on the mission field could no longer be regarded as 'an inspiring but distant ideal, nor even as a tender plant or a young child'. On the contrary, 'the child has, in many places, reached, and in others is fast reaching, maturity; and is now both fitted and willing, perhaps in a few cases too eager, to take upon itself its full burden of responsibility and service'.[6]

The assertion that in many lands the objective of a genuinely independent 'three-self' church was now within reach and in places already achieved was perhaps the central claim of the report. The chairman of Commission II, and also the person responsible for drafting its report,[7] was the Revd Dr J. Campbell Gibson (1849–1919), an eminent missionary of the Presbyterian Church of England from Lingtung, in southern China. The stamp of Gibson's progressive ideas and sanguine personality on the report are evident, although the absence of any surviving records of the commission's deliberations makes it impossible to identify the particular contributions that other members of the commission, some of them people of more conservative inclination than Gibson, may have made to its text. It is, for example, worthy of note that one member was the Revd Frederick Baylis, Africa secretary (and later Far East secretary) of the CMS, and that Appendix K of the report reproduced the 'Memorandum on Development of Church Organisation in the Mission Field', adopted by the CMS in 1909, which Baylis wrote.[8] Baylis has been characterised as a cautious and pragmatic thinker who steered the CMS away from its earlier commitment to make rapid progress towards the appointment of native bishops; his memorandum was sadly remarkable for its advocacy of distinct mission structures in India rather than immediate progress towards synodical government, and for its total silence on the subject of an indigenous episcopate.[9] Nevertheless, it is clear that the commission was particularly anxious for the respondents to its questionnaire to supply evidence of the extent of their progress towards a three-self church: number 4 of the very long list of questions on the questionnaire requested respondents to describe the working of their church organisation in regard to self-government, self-support and self-propagation.[10] Edinburgh 1910 thus gives no reinforcement to the supposition that the commitment of leading missionary strategists to the *principle* of the three-self formula had weakened by the Edwardian period. It may, however, strengthen the case that commitment in principle was one thing and the will to achieve practical implementation quite another.

Gibson was chosen as chairman of the commission on the basis of his role as one of two vice-chairmen of the China Centenary Missionary Conference held in Shanghai in 1907; he had also chaired that conference's committee on the Chinese church.[11] The sentiments and in places even the phraseology of the 1910 Commission II report correspond closely to the precedent set three years earlier at Shanghai. Thus the claim of the report that a mature church with its own independent life and institutions 'presented itself no longer as an inspiring but distant ideal' echoed Gibson's report on the Chinese church to the Shanghai conference which had concluded that self-support was 'no longer an ideal for a distant future, but a practical object to be immediately worked for and speedily realized ... we have already in China a Church which in a substantial degree is already [sic], and which is perfectly able soon to be entirely, self-governing, self-supporting, and self-propagating'.[12] The Edinburgh report also included repeated quotations on a number of topics from the records of the Shanghai conference, and printed all of its resolutions in an appendix.[13] The commission followed the Shanghai conference in exuding Gibson's optimism that a three-self church could be achieved within the foreseeable future. However, this confidence was significantly tempered by three concerns which are given more or less emphasis in the report. The first of these will be summarised briefly, and more sustained consideration given to the second and third.

II

The first anxiety expressed by the report was the fact that the patterns of constitutional development of the indigenous church described in the questionnaire replies appeared to conform so closely to the models familiar from western denominational tradition. The report observed with evident disappointment the complete absence of what it termed 'an Indian system, a Chinese method, or an African type of church organisation'. Instead, the denominational affiliation of the sending mission defined the ideal and method of the emerging local church organisation with depressing predictability. What would today be regarded as a failure in cultural sensitivity was interpreted in 1910 as an inability to treat the innate characteristics of different races as a fruitful resource for the development of authentic church life. The report expressed disappointment that 'the native mind in the countries concerned has not made a deeper mark on Church organisation'.[14] As if to underline the regrettable dominance of western ecclesiological traditions, the bulk of the first chapter of the report, on the 'constitution and organisation of the Church', was devoted to a laborious discussion of how each of nine different models of western Protestant church polity was handling the issue of church-mission relationships.[15] In fact the commission overlooked the substantial evidence afforded by the questionnaire replies that considerable modification of western denominational polities was taking place. There was also a measure of romanticism in its wistful longing for distinctively 'native' church forms that would somehow be essentially 'Indian', 'Chinese' or 'African' and a reluctance to acknowledge that ecclesiastical models that drew any features from the West could be fully authentic.

III

A second and very specific concern of the commission was that the level of remuneration being offered to church workers in Asia and Africa was alarmingly and consistently low.[16] The Commission II questionnaire asked questions about the salaries currently being paid to ordained clergy, preachers and catechists, male and female schoolteachers and Bible women, and how these compared to wage levels outside the church paid to those of similar or lower levels of education. The majority of respondents had reported that all these categories of church workers were receiving considerably less than they could have earned in secular employment. A few examples will have to suffice:

William Campbell of the English Presbyterian mission in Formosa reported that 'the salaries paid to Church employees are small, very small compared with the earnings of men following other occupations, and with the average standard of living in society'. Pastors received a basic wage of 16 dollars a month, plus a children's allowance of a dollar a child and an additional dollar for living in a market town. Preachers were paid 8 dollars a month if single, and 10 if married, plus the same additional allowances as applied to pastors. Those who were ranked as second-grade, being deemed 'less efficient', received even less. If these church workers had joined the postal, telegraph, railway or customs services in Formosa, Campbell observed, they could easily have obtained 15 to 40 dollars a month.[17] From Rajpur in the United Provinces in India, Canon S. Nihal Singh of the CMS mission replied that salaries of catechists and teachers were less than half of what those of similar competence earned in secular employment, and in some cases as little as one quarter. Rates for catechists and male teachers began at only 10 rupees a month and rose to a maximum of 30 for senior catechists and 20 for higher grade teachers; Bible women and women teachers started on just 8 rupees, rising to a maximum of 12 for Bible women and 10 for teachers. Church pay compared 'very unfavourably' with average wage levels.[18] The situation was no better, sometimes worse, in most African churches. At Ngombe Lutete (Wathen), the principal Baptist Missionary Society (BMS) station in the lower Congo, there were as yet no African pastors, but evangelists were paid the equivalent of 6 shillings a month if single, or 9 shillings and 3 pence if married. The resident missionary, J. R. M. Stephens, estimated that these rates were no more than one-fifth of what the men could have earned as railway or traders' clerks.[19] In the Free Church of Scotland's Livingstonia Mission in Nyasaland, evangelists' wages were between a quarter and three-quarters of equivalent secular rates.[20] In the Church of Scotland's Blantyre Mission, African clergy earned only about half of what they could have earned in secular callings, and teachers less by an unspecified amount; evangelists, however, were, according to Alexander Hetherwick, paid 'about the same as they would get in secular employment'.[21]

The general picture painted by these figures will not surprise anyone familiar with mission history. What is of interest in this evidence supplied to the Edinburgh conference is not so much the fact of the low levels of church workers' remuneration as the source of the remuneration and the interpretation placed on the evidence by the commission. The great majority of the church workers reported on in the questionnaire replies were still supported in large part, if not in their entirety, from mission funds. In China, Korea and Japan, and in some places in India and Africa, ordained national pastors – who even in Asia were still very few in number in 1910 – were now generally regarded as the financial responsibility of the church, even if evangelists and teachers were supported by the missionary society. Indeed, the commission's report explicitly commended the principle advocated by some respondents that ordination to the pastoral ministry should be made dependent on the existence of financial guarantees of support from the congregation or group of congregations that would benefit from the prospective pastor's ministry.[22] Evangelists and schoolteachers, on the other hand, were in most cases still a charge on mission funds. Both the Livingstonia Mission and the BMS lower Congo mission were noteworthy partial exceptions, with all evangelists' salaries being entirely supported by the indigenous church. Even in such cases, however, the level of their salaries still tended to be fixed, either directly or indirectly, by the mission. From Livingstonia W. A. Elmslie replied that '[t]he Livingstonia Mission Council, as having at first paid all workers fixed the salaries. Since congregations support their evangelists and preachers they have accepted the rates fixed.'[23] Stephens reported that at Ngombe Lutete 'the Church *with the advice of the missionary* fixes the amount of pay'.[24]

The report drew the conclusion from the evidence submitted to it that the prevailing rates of payment to all classes of national workers were usually too low. It then proceeded to suggest that 'the time has clearly come for considering whether grave injustice is not being done to native workers in many mission fields, – an injustice which must unavoidably have a most injurious effect upon the character of the work that is done by their means'.[25] The suggestion that an injustice was being committed was clearly premised on the fact that in most cases it was the mission, not the church, that was the paymaster. The report warned that 'we must beware of the tendency, which has undoubtedly sometimes existed, to make the control of the purse the basis of authority exercised by missions over the local Church and its workers'.[26]

Thus far the logic of the commission's argument might appear to lead to the conclusion that missions ought to take steps to reduce the yawning gap that invariably existed between the stipends of European missionaries and those paid to national workers.[27] In fact, however, the report then pursued its argument in precisely the opposite direction by warning missions against taking any action to remedy the problem of underpayment from their own resources:

> while it may be recognised that, generally speaking, the salaries of native workers in the mission field are lower than they ought to be, it does not follow that the deficiency ought to be made good from foreign funds. It should everywhere be impressed upon the members of the Church in the mission field that the remedy lies with themselves. They should be taught to regard the contributions of the foreign Church as a temporary aid, cheerfully given during infancy, but not as the main or permanent basis of support. If the subject is patiently and persistently treated in a Christian spirit, it will be found that the cases are very rare in which a growing Christian community is not able to give adequate support to the ministrations by which it is spiritually nourished.[28]

If in 1910, as many of the questionnaire replies suggested, the second leg in the stool of the self-governing, self-supporting and self-propagating church was still looking decidedly wobbly (which usually meant that the first leg was wobbly also), the principal fault and hence also the remedy was said to lie, not with the foreign mission boards, but with the national Christians on the mission field. Almost in the same breath the report had said that missions were doing the indigenous church a repeated injustice and then that the solution to that injustice lay with the injured party rather than the perpetrator of the injustice. The inconsistency is blatant to the modern ear, but appears not to have been noticed by the conference delegates. The point was not specifically taken up in the discussion of the report at the conference session on 16 June. The speakers who came closest to the issue were, not surprisingly, the Asian representatives of the national churches, who, in different ways, all emphasised the inescapable connections between self-support and self-government. Bishop Honda Yoitsu of the Methodist Church of Japan, speaking through a translator, warned that missionary work 'which does not recognise the national spirit and the spirit of independence will make weak-kneed and dependent Christians, and it will give rise to persecution'.[29] From China, Cheng Jingyi, the youthful and sole Chinese delegate of the London Missionary Society (LMS), acknowledged that the Chinese church was weak and poor, but insisted that 'experience shows that out of deep poverty Christian liberality may abound'. Self-support and self-government, urged Cheng, were to be regarded as a privilege and a joy, not a burden.[30] Yun Ch'iho, former vice-minister of foreign affairs in the Korean government, questioned the widespread assumption that all work carried on by foreign money must be under foreign control and urged that national leaders be consulted in the distribution of mission funds.[31] One of the Indian delegates, J. R. Chitambar, from the American Methodist Episcopal Church in Lucknow, addressed the issue of support of national workers, but was more concerned to rebut as unwise and divisive the suggestion that the best educated among them should be given the title of 'missionaries' and employed by the mission boards, leaving the inferior grade of national workers to be supported by their churches.[32]

Just how concerned the commission really was about the chronic under-payment of the main body of national Christians in mission or church employment is debatable. The issue received no more than a passing mention in the summative chapter VIII of the report, and then only as one of the reasons for the dearth of candidates for higher-level theological training. The report regarded the lack of clergy trained to a high level as a grave deficiency in 'the great civilised countries, such as India, China, and Japan', for here the Christian message was being challenged by alternative philosophies, especially those fashioned in the west.[33] The chapter accordingly gave particular emphasis to the need for wealthy friends of missions to endow teaching posts and scholarships in non-western theological institutions, since it was unrealistic to expect young and poor churches 'struggling with the initial problems of self-support' to make such provision a priority.[34] The likelihood of such institutions aggravating those problems was not contemplated. The logic of the questionnaire replies received by the commission in fact suggested that, even if such higher-grade institutions were more widely established on the basis of foreign funding, their graduates would in many cases prove beyond the limited financial capacity of the indigenous church to support. The commission had in effect concluded that national workers were ill paid because they were insufficiently educated to merit being well-paid.

IV

The third and more general concern to surface in the commission's report was the evident inability or unwillingness of some churches to match the vigour and enthusiasm for self-support which Gibson had observed in south China. The report of the committee on the Chinese church submitted to the Shanghai conference in 1907 had made extensive reference to Gibson's own mission in Shantou (Swatow), where by 1905 80 per cent of the costs of supporting the entire staff of Chinese clergy, preachers and teachers were being met by Chinese contributions.[35] In point of fact the majority of churches even in China were less far advanced towards self-support than was the Shantou church, and Gibson's wording of a resolution on the Chinese ministry was amended by the Shanghai conference on the grounds that it was too optimistic: the words 'This Conference rejoices that the Chinese Church already supports its own ministry entirely in many cases, and partially in nearly all' were amended to read 'and partially in others'.[36] The conference also recommended that 'every effort be made by Missions and Chinese Churches, to place the salaries of Chinese brethren engaged in church work on a scale adequate to the requirements of their position'.[37]

Hence at Shanghai in 1907 Gibson's statements on self-support had had to be toned down as being too optimistic to describe the reality of the Chinese church as a whole. Nevertheless, at Edinburgh sufficient evidence was submitted from various respondents in China, Formosa, Japan and Korea to the Commission II questionnaire to give substantiation to Gibson's confidence that the day of the self-supporting church was indeed at hand. Albert Lutley, reporting on the China Inland Mission churches in Shanxi province, recorded that the churches were governed by an annual provincial conference, in which Chinese outnumbered missionaries by two to one, and with two elected chairmen, one being Chinese. Each country or village church was, according to Lutley, 'practically self-supporting', and the church also supported some village schoolteachers and a few evangelists. Lutley attributed the prominent role of Chinese in the government of the Shanxi churches to the example and influence of the remarkable late Pastor Hsi (Hsi Shengmo), though he also observed that there were as yet no signs among church leaders of a desire for a rapid transfer of full authority.[38] William Campbell supplied evidence from Formosa that, despite the admittedly low level of salaries, the Presbyterian Church still received nearly twice as much for general church work from national contributions as it did from foreign mission funds.[39] From Japan, Dr Ibuka Kajinosuke reported that the *Nihon Kirisuto Itchi Kyokai*, the (Presbyterian) United Church of Christ in Japan, now had some ninety congregations formally constituted as financially independent churches, supporting their own pastors; any church which failed to maintain its financial independence would automatically lose its voting rights in the presbytery.[40] Self-support was well advanced in the Japanese Protestant churches, the majority of whose leaders, as well as many of the members, were from the traditionally dominant *samurai* class. Most Japanese Christians were urban and middle class. The resulting spirit of self-reliance was particularly strong in the United Church of Christ in

Japan.⁴¹ Similarly, the young Presbyterian Church in Korea, constituted on a national basis as recently as 1907, had been reared on the principles of self-support: the church already had more Korean ministers than missionaries in the presbytery, all of whom were fully supported by church contributions, despite the fact that all church members were, in the words of the Revd J. E. Adams from Taiku, 'about equally poor'. Other workers, known as 'helpers', were supported in some cases by the church and in others from mission funds. It is worthy of note that Adams recorded that the salary rates for the former were 'rather higher' than for the latter.⁴²

Prominent churches in East Asia, particularly those of Gibson's own Presbyterian polity, thus supplied corroboration for what he already believed to be the case on the basis of his own experience in Shantou: namely, that the attainment of full self-support was within the grasp of the indigenous church. From parts of the African church similarly encouraging reports were forthcoming. One of the pioneers of African independency, Pastor Mojola Agbebi, founder of the Native Baptist Church of Lagos and President of the Native Baptist Union of West Africa, was able to describe his churches as being self-governing, self-supporting and self-propagating, for he had agreed to link his network of independent churches with the Southern Baptist Convention's Foreign Mission Board only on condition that African leadership was maintained.⁴³ A correspondent from the Basel Mission church on the Gold Coast reported that the church's two synods had recently more than doubled the set rate of communicants' contributions to church funds, and was confident that within a few years the church would be 'entirely self-supporting'.⁴⁴ From Uganda, Bishop Alfred Tucker reported that self-support (as well as self-government and self-propagation) in the Anglican Church was already 'fully secured': the thirty indigenous clergy, plus all 2,000 lay readers and teachers, were entirely supported from native sources. Although stipends were low, all clergy, lay readers and teachers were also given a house, a garden for cultivation and grazing, and had their hut tax paid by the church.⁴⁵ In the American Board mission in Natal, all foreign funding for the support of native pastors had been discontinued in about 1894; all churches with ordained pastors, and some with lay pastors, were now self-supporting.⁴⁶

These examples were, however, probably unrepresentative of Africa as a whole. More typical was Livingstonia, where only the oldest church at Bandawe was fully self-supporting, and there were as yet no African pastors,⁴⁷ or the Baptist churches of the Ngombe Lutete district, which remained firmly under missionary control, even though the churches now supported between fifty-five and sixty-seven of the 155 Bakongo teachers (the remainder being voluntary).⁴⁸ At Rustenberg in the Transvaal W. Behrens of the Hermannsburg Mission claimed that members of the native congregations were 'being educated up to Self-Support' through a per capita levy of five shillings per annum, and insisted that self-government and self-support must be 'the eventual goal'. Yet Behrens warned that 'we foreign Missionaries', in contrast to some 'unruly but educationally advanced natives' who had imbibed 'Ethiopianism', 'fear that this is a long way off still with the South Africa natives, who had no culture worth speaking of, until the white man came to this country'.⁴⁹ Nonetheless, there was enough evidence of a contrary kind in the Africa replies to persuade the members of

Commission II that what worked in East Asia could work in Africa also, given the right determination of mind on the part of both missionaries and national Christians.

In East Asia, and even in parts of Africa, the gap between Gibson's own experience in Shantou and that of many mission churches seemed to be bridgeable. The commission's deepest underlying concern was that in much of India this was not the case. The BMS Indian secretary, Herbert Anderson, recorded that his society employed some 500–600 Indians as evangelists, teachers, 'assistant missionaries' and 'missionaries' serving a total of 200 churches, all of whose salaries were fixed and paid by the London committee, and cited only one church, in Cuttack in Orissa, as being wholly self-governing, self-supporting and self-propagating. Anderson's claim that, in accordance with Baptist ecclesiological principle, the society possessed 'no authority' over local churches and that therefore no transfer of power was necessary, disguised the extraordinary influence which the power of the purse still exercised.[50] In the CMS Punjab mission 80 per cent of the central fund from which church salaries were paid still came from London, and no congregation as yet supported its own pastor.[51] Also in the Punjab, in the American Presbyterian church at Hoshiarpur, though the ideal of self-support had been taught from the inception of the mission in 1875, monthly subscriptions from communicants (many of them from the depressed classes) were still inadequate to support the pastor without foreign aid.[52] In the Society for the Propagation of the Gospel's (SPG) church in Delhi, according to Sushil K. Rudra, the notable Bengali principal of St Stephen's College, 'self support – in the real sense of the word does not exist, and for a long time cannot exist'. Nine-tenths of the congregation came from the depressed classes, being menial servants or from the humblest class of wage earners.[53] The Methodist Episcopal mission, located mainly in western and central India, had encouraged tithing and other means of systematic proportionate giving, but had to report that among a poor and illiterate membership repeated famines and epidemics 'have interfered sadly with the development of self-support'.[54]

The situation was a little better in the stronger Christian Tamil communities in the south. There were a few instances where mature congregations had become self-supporting. In the CMS Tirunelveli mission, two of the fourteen 'Circles' of village pastorates were fully self-supporting, and one was nearly so.[55] In the LMS mission in south Travancore, founded by W. Ringeltaube as early as 1809, there were now seventeen self-supporting and self-governing pastorates, comprising some sixty-nine congregations.[56] The Wesleyan Methodist Tamil church at Royapettah in Madras had for the past ten years been independent of all financial help from the mission.[57] Bishop Alfred Whitehead of Madras pointed out in his response that self-support was further advanced among the long-established urban Tamil congregations, which contained numbers of educated and well-to-do members, than among the recently planted rural Telegu congregations, where the Christians were very poor and from the depressed classes. In the SPG mission 12,000 baptised Tamil Christians contributed 15,000 rupees a year towards their pastoral work, while 13,000 baptised Telegu Christians contributed only 5,200 rupees a year. The CMS was rather more successful than the SPG in developing self-support among the Telegu Christians, with 25,000 baptised

Christians contributing 12,000 rupees annually. Whitehead attributed the noticeable but not large difference in per capita giving partly to the greater poverty and susceptibility to famine of the SPG districts, but also to the greater progress made by the CMS in giving Indians a share in church government through a system of district church councils.[58] In the Lutheran church in Madras, where more than two-thirds of the 1,009 members were 'cooly earning poor people' (*sic*), one-third of the salary of the pastor, N. Devasahayam, was still paid by the Leipzig Mission. Only a few of the mission's churches had risen to the duty of supporting their pastors, 'and that not fully as yet'. 'The duty of selfsupport', reflected Devasahayam ruefully, 'was not impressed upon the converts from the beginning.'[59] Similarly, in the American Baptist Telegu mission, self-support was making 'very slow progress in most places', although the churches had organised a Home Missionary Society, which had several missionaries at work among the hill tribes, and one operating overseas, namely, John Rangiah, working among the Telegu sugar workers in Natal, who was present at the Edinburgh conference.[60]

V

It was the preponderance of Indian examples of the continuing dependence of churches on foreign funds that led Commission II to warn against the dangers of increasing foreign support as a solution to the underpayment of national church workers, even though the members of the commission, as representatives of the western missionary agencies that employed the bulk of those workers, felt morally responsible for the problem. Having witnessed the development of a successful system of self-support among a rural Christian population in south China, and learnt of similar achievements in Japan and Korea, Gibson evidently found the far slower progress of the Indian churches in this respect perplexing. His sixty-three-page response to his own questionnaire included a lengthy extract from his report to the Shanghai Centenary Conference, concluding with the claim that '[t]here is more money among our people than we sometimes suppose... we have now reached a stage where there should be no long delay in the complete attainment of self-support'.[61] Gibson's questionnaire response went on to attribute the energy of the Shantou church in propagating itself to '[t]he conditions of social life, the entire absence of caste divisions, and perhaps the national temperament of the people'.[62] It thus comes as no surprise to find that the only attempt at a systematic explanation of the Indian Christian failure in the Commission II report is in a passage headed 'Racial Characteristics': the difficulties in India of raising up 'strong, independent, self-supporting Churches' were blamed on 'the gentle and submissive nature of the Hindu temperament'. In China on the other hand, both 'racial characteristics' and 'the fabric of social observances' were deemed to be more favourable to mission work. In the absence of the caste system, there was greater scope for individual will and action, and hence it had proved easier to 'lead the Chinese Church to take upon its own shoulders its own burdens without leaning upon foreign help than it has been in India'.[63] The section of the report devoted to 'support of workers' accordingly began by arguing that the view taken of these matters by the national church depended, not simply on the teaching of the early missionaries, but also on 'the characteristics of the race of people among whom the Church is being formed'.[64] The same report which castigated national churches for failing to reflect their own racial characteristics in their patterns of organisation thus resorted, in the case of the largest single Protestant mission field, India, to blaming racial characteristics for the financially dependent condition of the Indian church.

Modern commentators would no doubt accuse the report of falling back on a crude form of racial essentialism in an attempt to excuse a lamentable failure of missionary policy. However, if, as Devasahayam's response suggested, missions in India (to a much greater extent than missions in China) had omitted from the beginning to insist on the priority of self-support, that omission is to be understood as a failure of collective nerve in a context shaped, first by the uniquely inhibiting constraints of caste solidarity and later by the irruption into the church of large numbers of the depressed classes (Dalits), whose poverty in relative if not absolute terms was unusual, even for Asia. Dependency has thus been a feature of modern Indian Christianity to an extent not matched elsewhere in Asia or in Africa.

VI

The Edinburgh Commission thus tended to explain what was a complex problem of economic dependency and missionary paternalism by appeal to supposed differentials in innate racial characteristics. These racial distinctions might ultimately be bridgeable (indeed, if they were not, the foundational premise of Christian missions stood in question).[65] Nevertheless, it seemed to follow that the only remedy lay in protracted and rigorous strategies of Christian nurture and church discipline. Hence chapter II of the Commission II report was devoted to the topic of 'Conditions of Membership' and chapter III to 'Church Discipline'. Because of their focus on the criteria determining admission to, and exclusion from, the Christian community, these are the sections of the Edinburgh documents which come closest to an analysis of the intensifying cultural and ethical problems confronting the missionary movement as processes of conversion to Christianity began to acquire an independent and accelerating momentum that had been absent for most of the nineteenth century. However, the degree of emphasis and amount of space given to church discipline – a theme which Gibson reiterated strongly in introducing the report to the conference – tended in practice to overshadow the commitment of the commission to the goal of building a three-self church.[66]

Ultimately the failure of so many South Asian and African churches to adopt three-self principles was treated as indicative of a deeper failure of spiritual and mental initiative. The report's disappointment that 'the native mind ... has not made a deeper mark on Church organisation' in the mission fields was symptomatic of a broader and more fundamental regret that there was as yet so little sign of the 'younger' churches developing their own forms and patterns of theological thinking. The report discussed this theme twice, first in relation to theological training in chapter V on 'Training and Employment of Workers' and then more fully in chapter VII on 'Christian Literature and Theology'. The commission concluded that the church in the mission field showed, with only a few exceptions, 'very little sign of literary power, and still less of any original and formative thought on the great questions of the Divine revelation and of spiritual life'.[67] The commission cited various respondents, mainly from India, in support of this judgement. One leading India missionary commented: 'I have hardly known one Indian Christian thinker whose theology has revealed definite constructive thought, who has been able to shake himself away from the trammels of the West.'[68] From Delhi, Sushil K. Rudra identified the problem as being the paucity of Christians among 'the better classes' who could act as thinkers and leaders of the community, and hinted that the low rates of pay attached to mission employment were partly to blame: 'in the present state of western dominance and supremacy they cannot do so. They have enough to do to seek an honourable livelihood in the world and maintain their position in Indian society generally'.[69] The report also cited an unnamed foreign missionary who was more explicit than Rudra in asserting that intellectual dependence was inevitably linked to financial dependence: 'The hand of the foreign padris who hold the purse strings is too heavy for anything like original and formative thought, or any other sort of real originality in India....Till Indians get loose from the bondage to foreign money, it is useless to expect much or any really inspired general literature.'[70]

The report was not afraid to print and endorse these accusations that the dominance of the missionary lay at the root of the matter, but this theme was expounded in a fashion that used racial stereotyping to throw at least some of the collective blame back onto Asian shoulders. The report implied that the underlying reason that missionaries were so dominant was that they came from the 'vigorous' and 'progressive' European races, full of 'bustling activity'.[71] Conversely, oriental (and especially Indian) Christians possessed a more contemplative and mystical spirituality which was apt to be dismissed by Westerners as 'inert and idle'.[72] The impression had thus been given that 'the masterful leadership of the European nature is an effectual barrier to any free expression of opinions which may not be in complete harmony with the missionary teaching'.[73] The commission was in no doubt that the stultifying tradition of foreign missionary dominance must be eroded and that a more sympathetic appreciation of the distinctive features of eastern spirituality was required, but the resort to inherent racial characteristics in analysis of the problem implied a protracted time scale. Though self-support might be just round the corner, it would inevitably be 'a long time' before Asian Christians – let alone African ones, who scarcely receive a mention in these sections of the report – would be emancipated from European statements of Christian doctrine and forms of Christian organisation. This was not necessarily a matter of regret, for the report reflected that such long-term tutelage might be 'one of the means God in His providence has ordained for preserving the substantial unity of the faith in its transmission from generation to generation and from race to race'.[74] European 'masterfulness' was blamed for the slow rate of progress towards the achievement of a three-self church, but it had its value as a preservative of orthodoxy.

The Edinburgh report thus employed the notion of race loosely and inconsistently, in a manner which Andrew Porter has identified as typical of the missionary movement at the time.[75] The report had drawn a clear distinction between the racial qualities of Chinese and Indians, yet ultimately made appeal to ethnically undifferentiated caricatures of oriental mysticism and indolence to explain why European dominance was paradoxically both the root of the problem and yet also indispensable to the solution. Race tended to be invoked in the general absence of any serious attempt to reflect on the variations in social and economic structure or dynamics of colonial rule between different societies. Recourse was made to the category of race for multiple and contradictory purposes. Indeed, as I shall argue in my forthcoming study of the World Missionary Conference, the notion of race was in fact integral to the arguments of the most 'progressive' voices at Edinburgh who desired to see the emergence of distinctively Asian (not yet African) forms of Christian theology and worship.[76] While Jeffrey Cox is strictly correct in his recent judgement that 'of anything that could be labelled "scientific racism" there is no hint whatsoever' at Edinburgh,[77] the language of race was undoubtedly much more prominent than it had once been in missionary discourse; whether the consequences of this were as deleterious as is generally assumed is not a simple question.

To an extent that may seem surprising given the high imperial climate of 1910, the commission had unambiguously endorsed the goal of a three-self church. Its membership covered a broad range, both of denominational affiliation from Anglo-Catholic to Baptist and of nation – it included Scottish, English, Welsh, American, Swedish and German mission leaders. Yet the evidence suggests that, at the level of the policy-makers who manned the mission boards, and probably also among the more progressive missionaries who were privileged by their selection as questionnaire respondents, there was near-universal consensus in favour of the *principle*, made famous by Henry Venn half a century earlier, that missionary societies should aim for their own euthanasia in any particular field (how far missionary societies in the early twentieth century implemented their own principles is another matter). Furthermore, the commission had even expressed a firm commitment to the achievement of what current Christian missiological theory sometimes terms the 'fourth self' of 'self-theologising', meaning the capacity and inclination to shape Christian theology according to the contours of eastern philosophies. Nevertheless, the report had to concede that, for all the signs of progress towards self-support in China and some other parts of East Asia, the goal of a three-self church was some way from realisation, above all in India. Similarly, the commission was compelled to acknowledge that the more ambitious objective of churches that had the confidence to engage in their own independent theological reflection still looked frustratingly distant; it was indeed considerably more distant than the goal of autonomy in finance and governance, about whose achievement the report, as has been seen, was so generally, if unrealistically, sanguine. It is hard to escape the conclusion that, in this respect also, the report was faithfully reflecting Gibson's own experience in Shantou. It is also clear that, if the report seriously underestimated the obstacles that still lay in the path of the achievement of self-support for most younger churches, it equally overestimated the permanence of the obstacles which in 1910 appeared to prevent those churches from speaking with their own distinctive voice, in tones that would soon prove to be political as well as theological.

Notes

[1] Venn, *Retrospect and Prospect*, 4–5, cited in Porter, *Religion versus Empire?*, 167.
[2] *Conference on Missions*, 310.
[3] See Williams, *Ideal of the Self-Governing Church*, and Harris, *Nothing but Christ*.
[4] Hayward, *Christians and China*, 50; see Wickeri, *Seeking the Common Ground*, 129–33.
[5] The one black African delegate was Dr Mark Christian Hayford from the Gold Coast.
[6] World Missionary Conference, 1910, *Report of Commission II* (henceforth *Report of Commission II*), 2–3, also 38.
[7] Maclagan, *J. Campbell Gibson*, 28.
[8] *Report of Commission II*, 317–20.
[9] On Baylis, see Williams, *Ideal of the Self-Governing Church*, 202–03, 213, 230–51; Farrimond, 'Policy of the Church Missionary Society', 79, 100–11.
[10] *Report of Commission II*, 277.
[11] Maclagan, *J. Campbell Gibson*, 28; Hood, *Mission Accomplished?*, 153.
[12] *Records: China Centenary Missionary Conference* (henceforth *Records*), 12, 18.
[13] *Report of Commission II*, 328–36, and see index entries at 375, 379.
[14] Ibid., 12.
[15] Ibid., 14–30.
[16] Ibid., 202.
[17] World Missionary Conference papers, series 1 (henceforth WMC), box 12, folder 5, item 72, 24–25, Missionary Research Library Collection 12, Union Theological Seminary, New York.
[18] WMC, box 12, folder 1, item 312, 20–21.
[19] WMC, box 11, folder 4, item 558, 25.
[20] WMC, box 11, folder 2, item 412, 16–17. Response of W. A. Elmslie.
[21] WMC, box 11, folder 2, item 424, 17–18.
[22] *Report of Commission II*, 201. See, for example, James D. Taylor from the American Board mission in Natal in WMC, box 11, folder 3, item 462, 3.
[23] WMC, box 11, folder 2, item 412, 16.
[24] WMC, box 11, folder 4, item 558, 25. Italics added.
[25] *Report of Commission II*, 202–03.
[26] Ibid., 203.
[27] For example, in the Norwegian Zulu mission, where missionary stipends were up to five times those of ordained African ministers; WMC, box 11, folder 1, item 395, 16 (Bishop Nils Astrup).
[28] *Report of Commission* II, 204–05.
[29] Ibid., 349.
[30] Ibid., 352.
[31] *Report of Commission II*, 358–59.
[32] Ibid., 362–63.
[33] *Report of Commission II*, 197. The report here was influenced by the Shanghai conference; see *Records*, 450–51.
[34] *Report of Commission II*, 271–72.
[35] *Records*, 12, 32–33.
[36] Ibid., 469–70. See Hood, *Mission Accomplished?*, 146, 149.
[37] *Records*, 441.
[38] WMC, box 13, folder 2, item 139, 1–2, 4–5, 21–2.
[39] WMC, box 12, folder 5, item 72, 4.
[40] WMC, box 12, folder 5, item 17, 1–2.
[41] Drummond, *History of Christianity in Japan*, 169, 180; Brown, *Mastery of the Far East*, 647.
[42] WMC, box 12, folder 5, item 1, 1–3, 13–14, 16; see Brown, *The Mastery of the Far East*, 521–22.
[43] WMC, box 11, folder 2, item 434, 1. See King, 'Co-operation in Contextualization', 2–21; Ayandele, *Visionary of the African Church*.

[44] WMC, box 11, folder 1, item 422, 1–2 (Rev. B. Groh).
[45] WMC, box 11, folder 3, item 464, 2, 4, 6, 22–23.
[46] WMC, box 11, folder 3, item 462, 3 (Rev. James Dexter Taylor).
[47] WMC, box 11, folder 1, item 412, 1 (Rev. W. A. Elmslie). The first pastors were ordained in 1914; see McCracken, *Politics and Christianity in Malawi*, 244.
[48] WMC, box 11, folder 4, item 468, 2, item 558, 2–3, 5. The two respondents from Ngombe Lutete gave differing figures: John Weeks (468) reported that fifty-five out of 153 teachers were supported; J. R. M. Stephens (558) said sixty-seven out of 155.
[49] WMC, box 11, folder 1, item 399, 1, 3.
[50] WMC, box 11, folder 6, item 214, 1, 4, 5, 7, 22–23. By 1913 forty-seven Indian pastors and thirty evangelists were supported by the churches associated with the BMS; see Stanley, *History of the Baptist Missionary Society*, 155.
[51] WMC, box 12, folder 1, item 362, 6 (E. F. E. Wigram); see also box 11, folder 6, item 213, 1, 15 (Rev. J. Ali Baksh).
[52] WMC, box 11, folder 7, item 233, 1, 4 (Rev. K. C. Chatterjee).
[53] WMC, box 12, folder 2, item 329, 2. On Rudra, see O'Connor, *A Clear Star*.
[54] WMC, box 12, folder 1, item 325, 'Constitution and Organisation', 1 (Bishop J. E. Robinson).
[55] WMC, box 11, folder 6, item 228, 3–4 (Rev. E. S. Carr).
[56] WMC, box 11, folder 8, item 270, 6–7 (Rev. I. H. Hacker).
[57] WMC, box 12, folder 1, item 322, 1 (Mr Krishna Ram).
[58] WMC, box 12, folder 3, item 375, 5–9.
[59] WMC, box 11, folder 7, item 250, 1–2, 12.
[60] WMC, box 11, folder 6, item 261, 2 (Rev. W. L. Fergusson).
[61] WMC, box 13, folder 1, item 98a, 15, citing *Records*, 15–16.
[62] WMC, box 13, folder 1, item 98a, 16.
[63] *Report of Commission II*, 91–92.
[64] *Report of Commission II*, 199.
[65] Porter, *Religion versus Empire?*, 285.
[66] *Report of Commission II*, 343–44.
[67] Ibid., 258.
[68] *Report of Commission II*, 259.
[69] WMC, box 12, folder 2, item 329, 18, cited in part in *Report of Commission II*, 260.
[70] *Report of Commission II*, 260–61.
[71] Ibid., 262.
[72] Ibid., 210. The report here is dependent on Herbert Anderson's reply in WMC, box 11, folder 6, item 214, 24.
[73] *Report of Commission II*, 260.
[74] Ibid., 262.
[75] Porter, *Religion versus Empire?*, 285.
[76] See Stanley, *World Missionary Conference*. This article is based in part on chapter 6 of the book.
[77] Cox, *British Missionary Enterprise*, 229.

References

Ayandele, E. A. *A Visionary of the African Church: Mojola Agbebi, 1860–1917*. Nairobi: East African Publishing House, 1971.
Brown, Arthur John. *The Mastery of the Far East: The Story of Korea's Transformation and Japan's Rise to Supremacy in the Orient*. London: G. Bell, 1919.
Conference on Missions Held in 1860 at Liverpool. London: James Nisbet, 1860.
Cox, Jeffrey. *The British Missionary Enterprise since 1700*. New York and London: Routledge, 2008.
Drummond, R. H. *A History of Christianity in Japan*. Grand Rapids, MI: Eerdmans, 1971.

Farrimond, K. J. T. 'The Policy of the Church Missionary Society concerning the Development of Self-Governing Indigenous Churches 1900–1942, 2004. PhD thesis, University of Leeds.

Harris, Paul W. *Nothing but Christ: Rufus Anderson and the Ideology of Protestant Foreign Missions*. Oxford and New York: Oxford University Press, 1999.

Hayward, V. E. W. *Christians and China*. Belfast: Christian Journals, 1974.

Hood, George. *Mission Accomplished? The English Presbyterian Mission in Lingtung, South China: A Study of the Interplay between Mission Methods and their Historical Context*. Frankfurt: Peter Lang, 1986.

King, Hazel. 'Co-operation in Contextualization: Two Visionaries of the African Church – Mojola Agbebi and William Hughes of the African Institute, Colwyn Bay'. *Journal of Religion in Africa* 16 (1986): 2–21.

McCracken, John. *Politics and Christianity in Malawi 1875–1940: The Impact of the Livingstonia Mission in the Northern Province*. Cambridge: Cambridge University Press, 1977.

Maclagan, P. J. *J. Campbell Gibson, D.D. Missionary of the Presbyterian Church of England: A Biographical Sketch*. London: Religious Tract Society, n.d. 1922.

O'Connor, Daniel. *A Clear Star: C. F. Andrews and India 1904–1914*. New Delhi: Chronicle Books, 2005.

Porter, Andrew. *Religion versus Empire? British Protestant Missionaries and Overseas Expansion, 1700–1914*. Manchester and New York: Manchester University Press, 2004.

Records: China Centenary Missionary Conference Held at Shanghai, April 25 to May 8 1907. Shanghai: Centenary Conference Committee, 1907.

Stanley, Brian. *The History of the Baptist Missionary Society 1792–1992*. Edinburgh: T. & T. Clark, 1992.

———. *The World Missionary Conference: Edinburgh 1910*. Grand Rapids, MI, and Cambridge: Eerdmans, 2008.

Venn, Henry. *Retrospect and Prospect of the Operations of the Church Missionary Society 1865*. London: Church Missionary House, 1865.

Wickeri, Philip. *Seeking the Common Ground: Protestant Christianity, the Three-Self Movement and China's United Front*. Maryknoll, NY: Orbis Books, 1987.

Williams, C. Peter. *The Ideal of the Self-Governing Church: A Study in Victorian Missionary Strategy*. Leiden: E. J. Brill, 1990.

World Missionary Conference, 1910. *Report of Commission II: The Church in the Mission Field*. Edinburgh, London, New York, Chicago and Toronto: Oliphant, Anderson & Ferrier and Fleming H. Revell, n.d. [1910].

Distance and Proximity in Service to the Empire: Ulster and New Zealand between the Wars

Keith Jeffery

At Mesen, or Messines, in Belgium there are two First World War memorials in perhaps unexpected juxtaposition. One is an Irish 'Peace Tower', dedicated on 11 November 1998 to commemorate the Irish from all over the island who served and died in the war. During the Battle of Messines in June 1917 (though not, as it happens, at this specific location) the 36th (Ulster) Division, a strongly unionist formation, fought alongside the 16th (Irish) Division, a nationalist one. Next door is a New Zealand Memorial Park, commemorating the part taken (and at this precise location) by the New Zealand Division in the same battle. In the park is an obelisk designed by the New Zealand architect S. Hurst Seager, identical to other national battlefield memorials at 's-Graventafel (near Passendale) in Belgium and Longueval (on the Somme) in France. Each of these three obelisks carries the poignant inscription: 'From the uttermost ends of the earth.' In geographical terms, nevertheless, the distance New Zealanders had travelled was not so much an impediment to be regretted as an endeavour to be celebrated, since the very distance travelled amplified and confirmed the unstinting loyalty of their imperial service. Reflecting on the adjacent memorials at Mesen, the observation has been made that 'the New Zealanders came further, geographically, than anyone else', but 'the nationalist Irish also came a long way, at least in political terms, and found it even further going home'.[1] The proximity of these two monuments, and the distance travelled by at least some of those commemorated, raises questions about the factors of distance and proximity, and the extent to which perceptions of national or communal identity might be affected by them. Does a Kiwi identity become less distinct the further one goes from New Zealand, and, at a distance from Ulster itself, is 'Ulster-ness' subsumed within 'Irishness' or 'Britishness', and, if so, to what extent? There is some historiographical literature on the question of what one historian has called 'western historiography's ongoing preoccupation with issues of distance and proximity'. In this context 'historical distance' is generally understood in a temporal or chronological sense, but it can also include distances of form and ideology.[2] These considerations are not irrelevant to the subject of this essay, but it will focus on the more geographical or locational connotations of 'distance' and 'proximity'.

Issues of national or communal identity crop up frequently in the characterisation of New Zealand, Ulster and Irish participation in the First World War. Writing from London in January 1917 W. F. Massey, the New Zealand Prime Minister, complained that, while New Zealand soldiers had been given a good deal of publicity, 'unfortunately the public in many instances mixes them up with Australians, and think they are one and the same. New Zealand itself is hardly ever mentioned, and the country suffers accordingly'.[3] This quotation was used in an interesting article by James Bennett which in part explores the respective identities of Australian and New Zealand Anzacs. But, when Bennett looks for comparators among other empire troops, the Tommies are invariably English or British. There is no sense in Bennett's study that the *British* army might be disaggregated in the way he insists the Anzac Corps ought to be. Discussing the attitudes of evidently non-New Zealand commanding officers, Bennett links the British corps commander at Gallipoli, Sir Alexander Godley, with the Kiwi hero, Lieutenant-Colonel William Malone, without any apparent awareness that the former was, by his own estimation, an 'Irish soldier', and the latter (albeit English-born) the product of an Irish Catholic family.[4] Sometimes New Zealanders disappear altogether. In *Realities* [sic] *of War*, Sir Philip Gibbs managed to discuss the contribution made by the dominions without mentioning them at all.[5] These days historians are alive to the understandable sensitivities of New Zealanders about being lumped willy-nilly into some essentially Australian Anzac formation, as illustrated in a remark in a recent study of Gallipoli historiography where the author compared 'the British heroic-romantic myth' with 'the more familiar Australian (and New Zealand) Anzac legend'.[6] But however well-intentioned the writer may have been, here New Zealand is consigned to the tyranny of brackets, in a kind of limbo of what we might call 'parenthetical history'.

National identity was equally elusive for Irish and Ulstermen. Following the terribly costly 'V' Beach landings at Gallipoli on 25 April 1915, the divisional commander, Major-General Aylmer Hunter Weston (who had Scottish lineage), congratulated the survivors of the Royal Dublin Fusiliers on the terrific achievement of their success. 'It was', he affirmed, 'done by men of real and true British fighting blood.'[7] Ulster's most specific contribution to the British imperial war effort was most readily identified with the 36th (Ulster) Division, which first saw serious action on the first day of the Somme, 1 July 1916, when it suffered some 5,000 casualties. The Ulster Division was exceptionally close-knit – it was a sort of 'pals' formation – and after the war its sacrifice came to be associated particularly with the freedom of Ulster unionists to run their own territory in what emerged as Northern Ireland (comprising six of the nine counties of the old province of Ulster). But sometimes it took a little teasing out. On 1 November 1922 Sir James Craig, the first Prime Minister of Northern Ireland, unveiled a war memorial at Coleraine, County Londonderry. The monument depicts a soldier at ease, placed on a high plinth. Below him is (according to the sculptor) 'a hooded figure of Erin' holding a wreath. 'Erin' or not, what Craig said at the memorial's dedication was that those who had died had 'left a great message to all of them to stand firm, and to give away none of *Ulster*'s soil'.[8]

But these are, as it were, separate and parallel expressions of autonomous identity. And, indeed, for both New Zealand and Ulster (or Northern Ireland), there was often a reluctance to over-emphasise any sort of separate (or separatist) identity. For both territories the predominant political stance in the interwar years was one which rejoiced in 'Britishness', celebrating a willing subordination within the 'greatest empire the world had ever seen'. For the Northern Irish, or Ulster people, or whatever the unionists chose to call themselves, there was a fluctuating need to distinguish themselves from the 'Irish', or at least those Irish nationalists (North and South) who espoused a separatist desire for the whole island of Ireland to be an independent state. This essay will investigate some of these perceptions and aspirations concerning New Zealand and Northern Ireland in the context of a number of what might be called reciprocal visits between the two places: that of the Northern Ireland premier, Viscount Craigavon (as he became in 1927), to New Zealand in 1929–30 and the visits of three New Zealand premiers to Northern Ireland between 1923 and 1930, exploring along the way how 'distance' and 'proximity' might in differing ways affect and modulate opinions and mutual perceptions expressed by both visitor and visited.

According to Craigavon's official biographer, among the reasons for his trip to Australia and New Zealand in 1929–30 was that, when he had 'entertained two Prime Ministers of New Zealand, W. F. Massey and Joseph Gordon Coates' in Northern Ireland, their 'accounts of their country had made him very eager to see it'.[9] The New Zealand visit, moreover, had something of the air of a royal progress or state visit. It could be put in the context of royal visits to the dominion, such as those of the Duke and Duchess of Cornwall and York in 1901; the Prince of Wales in 1920; the Duke and Duchess of York in 1927; and the Duke of Gloucester in 1935.[10]

A closer analogy might be Leopold Amery's tour as colonial secretary in November–December 1927, the first visit ever to New Zealand of a serving British cabinet minister.[11]

The Craigavons arrived at Auckland (from Australia) on 18 November 1929. Lord Craigavon, reported *The Times*, 'will make a careful examination of New Zealand farming and the dairy produce trade in the anticipation that he will gain much useful information on problems of interest to Northern Ireland'.[12] The pattern of the tour was set at the start: civic reception, speeches of mutual self-admiration and celebration of the British empire, visits to local places of interest, and meetings with groups of Irish and/or Ulster people. We are fortunate, too, that Lady Craigavon kept a diary, which provides a particularly vivid (and comparatively unrestrained) account of the tour. Early on, at New Plymouth, Craig assured the assembled civic dignitaries that 'we look upon New Zealand as a right-hand brother in a community which goes to form the great British Empire'.[13] Next day there was a reception in New Plymouth by Ulster people of the district. Here Craigavon spoke of:

> that close touch between the two [places] and the fact that Ulster and New Zealand were one as loyal as the other, that had made their visit so very enjoyable. Sometimes [he said] at Home there might be just a little fear that the Dominions were not quite so alive to the grandeur of the British Empire as of old, but thank God he had been cheered to know that there had been no diminution of New Zealand's loyalty.

The same day Craigavon wrote home to his cabinet secretary, remarking 'It is wonderful the number of men & women of Ulster blood out here, it is the backbone of the Dominion; they are a splendid lot.' Culturally, there was a distinctly *Irish* dimension to the occasion. Lady Craigavon was presented with a bouquet 'in the shape of a harp' (*not* a Red Hand), and during the evening 'two little girls, Misses Joan Austin and Mary Walsh, danced an *Irish* jig'.[14] It is perhaps worth pausing for a moment to reflect on what was culturally believed to be appropriate to celebrate the visit of the prime minister, and arguably the creator, of Northern Ireland, a fierce and professional (as it were) Ulsterman.

The next day, a Sunday, they moved on to Wanganui, where they toured the city. Lady Craigavon wrote in her diary:

> On our return to the hotel [we] found about thirty or forty Ulster people had turned up hearing that we were there. Our hearts sank as we were dropping with fatigue, but, of course, had to receive them all in the lounge. Luckily their spokesman was a clergyman who was due to take a service at half past six, so this helped to shorten the proceedings![15]

The Craigavons' exhausting schedule was relieved by a three-week stay over Christmas and New Year at the Grand Hotel, Rotorua. Here they relaxed as tourists, and Craig put in a lot of trout-fishing.[16] They arrived in Wellington on 3 January, and at once went to call on the prime minister, Sir Joseph Ward, 'at his house at Heretaunga, a charming little home with a nice garden looking over the golf links'.[17] Later that day Craigavon visited S. Hurst Seager's memorial to the Ulster-born W. F. Massey – the mausoleum of 'his friend and fellow-countryman', as *The Times* put it[18] – at Point Halswell on

Wellington Harbour. 'The Memorial', noted Lady Craigavon, 'was not quite finished, but will be magnificent. High up on the most prominent point of land, jutting out into the Bay, they have erected an oval monument of marble and granite in the centre of which is the tomb.' It was approached 'by a flight of steps and a narrow alleyway, the idea being to represent the chancel of a church and thus make people realise the sanctity of the spot'.[19] Lady Craigavon did not remark that there is, in fact, no mention whatsoever of Ulster (or Ireland) on the memorial. After laying a wreath (on which was inscribed 'A tribute of affection and esteem to a great Imperialist and a firm friend from the people of Ulster'),[20] Craigavon naturally marked the occasion with another speech. He observed that it had given him 'great pleasure to visit New Zealand, which reminded him more of Northern Ireland than any other part of the world he had seen'. He also dwelt on Northern Ireland's own memorial to Massey:

> As a tribute to the memory of the late Mr. Massey, the drive leading up to the Ulster Houses of Parliament had been named Massey avenue. 'I had to decide upon a name,' said Viscount Craigavon,[21] 'and it occurred to me that Mr. Massey was the greatest living Ulsterman of his day. I am glad to say I was able to advise him of the fact that his name had been given to the drive, and to hear from him before he died.[22]

What might be observed here, is that in the same speech, Craigavon, apparently indiscriminately, referred to 'Northern Ireland' and 'Ulster', for unionists, perhaps, synonyms, but scarcely so for Irish (or Ulster) nationalists.

The rest of the tour was spent largely on the South Island. The Craigavons were given a warm welcome at Greymouth on the west coast, where the deputy mayor, J. B. Kent, declared that it was the 'first occasion on which a member of Parliament from any part of Great Britain [sic] had honoured Greymouth with a visitor [sic]'.[23] There was a particular concentration in this locality of Catholic Irish inhabitants, of which Craigavon had clearly been advised, and he implicitly addressed it in his speech. He 'could not tell how delighted he was, since being on the West Coast, to have met such a large number of Irishmen by birth and Irishmen by lineage'. He was glad to say that 'they all appeared to be playing their part and were a credit to the country'. Once again he mentioned Massey Avenue in Belfast, along which 'for all time, so long as the Parliament buildings stood, every person who trod the path to them would walk'. There was a striking degree of confidence in the future here – 'for all time, so long as the Parliament buildings stood' – though, despite the highest hopes of Ulster Unionists, the two things were by no means the same.

In his peroration, Craigavon not only addressed the relations between Northern Ireland and New Zealand within the British imperial system, but also those between Northern Ireland and the Irish Free State. 'We belong', he said, 'to the same country, for while the one flag flutters over us we are one'. Ulster was 'not jealous of New Zealand's progress. On our part, we have passed through horrible times, but they have now passed away, and we have peace and prosperity. Premier Cosgrave and myself are on the best of terms, and both working for the good of the country.'

There could not, he concluded, 'be peace, prosperity and progress unless memories of the past were thrown behind'.[24] This speech at Greymouth took up a theme he had introduced at one of his main Australian speeches in Sydney two months previously. Reflecting then on the

> prevailing conditions in Ireland, Lord Craigavon said that the relationship between all classes and creeds to-day was better than he could ever remember. Irishmen had gone through an extraordinary time of trouble – trouble that had been heartbreaking at a certain period. They had got over it, and nobody was the less friendly for it. Probably the crisis had brought Irishmen closer together, for they had all been struggling for a principle – a principle for which Australians would have fought for equal ardour. There was now a great cheerfulness about the people, and they had emerged from eight years of domestic and commercial strife better men and women.[25]

This amiable and optimistic vision of conditions in Ireland was literally fantastic, describing years during which one historian has written that 'North-South relations were characterised by a pervasive cold war'.[26] In Craigavon's Greymouth speech, moreover, along with a separate reference to 'Ulster', he used the word 'country' in two distinct senses: the first apparently covering the whole empire; the second connoting Ireland, North and South.

A couple of days later the focus on Northern Ireland, and the politics (on the New Zealand side at least) were unequivocally unionist. At Christchurch (where there was a particular concentration of Ulster settlers) the mayor, R. S. Black, 'said it was visits such as this which made them feel they belonged to one glorious Empire and one flag. The fight', he added. 'which their guest had put up in the past 30 years was viewed with admiration and envy.'[27] Moving on to Dunedin, the Craigavons were taken to see 'the old settlers Museum containing', remarked Lady Craigavon condescendingly, 'some interesting relics, and a good deal of rubbish as well; but in a new country it is, of course, hard to collect together much of real interest, though in future years these Victorian souvenirs will no doubt be much appreciated'.[28]

At Timaru (a centre of Catholic Irish settlement with a history of sectarianism),[29] the visitors were greeted by the mayor, Mr W. Angland, who told them he was especially glad to welcome them as Ireland was the land of his birth. This prompted Craigavon to an effusion of Irishness. 'We all revere the land of our birth,' he declared, 'and I am pleased to see that Irish stalwarts who have come to New Zealand have assisted to build up this country to its present unbounded prosperity', potentially a problematic comment to make in a country by all accounts slipping badly into economic recession. Indeed, throughout the Craigavons' tour there was no sense of the economic problems which dominated much contemporary New Zealand political debate. 'Like New Zealand,' continued Craigavon, 'I think Ireland has a wonderful future. We have passed through troublous and exciting times, but I am sure that now that all lies behind us, and both North and South will rally round and join in taking the road to prosperity.' They were, he concluded, 'a small community in Ulster – small but desperately Imperialistic'.[30]

At Masterton the emphasis shifted to Northern Ireland's recent history, and Craigavon took a more ostentatiously party political line:

> They were in every way a loyal people in Ulster. People here in New Zealand would have done the same as Ulster did in the same circumstances. There was no law that could compel a British citizen to give up his citizenship unless he desired to give it up. (Applause) Suppose someone passed a law that Masterton should no longer belong to the Empire. It would be ultra vires. The people of Masterton would say: 'You can go, but we remain British citizens and no law can drive us out.' That was all the people of Ulster did. (Applause).[31]

Craigavon's final speech was at a reception hosted by the Ulster Association of New Zealand in the Wellington Town Hall concert chamber. Elsewhere in the building a boxing tournament was being held which inspired Craigavon to use a sporting simile to describe intra-Irish relations. On this occasion the Ulsterman began on a wider, more inclusively 'Irish' tack, but ended with the old certainties of loyalist rhetoric, reverting to Ulster unionist type. He asked his audience

> to believe him when he said that there was not an Ulster man or woman who was not just as delighted to know that the South was prospering under the new regime as those who came from the South themselves. (Loud applause) Both sides had come through very anxious and very troublesome times, but just like those who were taking part in a boxing contest next door, blows had been given and received, and at the end of it all there was the usual shaking of hands.[32]

He finished, however, with words directed specifically at those Ulster folk living in what he hoped he might call 'the New Ulster', and he wanted to take the opportunity of saying

> 'Good-bye to Ulster in New Zealand.' So long as they were loyal to the old flag – as he was sure they ever would be – they could always be depended on to a man. (Applause.) He assured them that the walls of Derry were still standing, that 'Roaring Meg' was still there, and the Walker monument still towering up above the city. (loud applause.)[33]

This summoning-up of the 1689 Siege of Derry, among the most potent of the unionist 'foundation myths', came from a man who, scarcely a month before, had assured the Irish people of Greymouth that 'peace, prosperity and progress' could be possible only if 'memories of the past were thrown behind'. But was it the distance from home, and remoteness from the sterile tropes of exclusivist 'Ulsterness', which enabled Craig's intermittently more ecumenical attitude?

Not much was reported at home about the Craigavons' Antipodean tour. The *Irish News*, however, Belfast's nationalist daily, representing the political views of approximately a third of the Northern Ireland population, protested against what it called Craigavon's 'hypocritical utterances'. 'Addressing audiences largely composed of people of Irish blood,' it complained, 'a great proportion of them Catholics, he has consistently represented the Six Counties as a prosperous, happy land, its inhabitants at peace and fully contented with his Administration.' There was, it declared, danger that his speeches might 'delude a people ill-informed of the real state of affairs' in Northern Ireland.[34]

At the beginning of January 1930 the *Irish News* printed 'The Triumph of Tyranny' by P. J. O'Regan, an 'Irish-New Zealander', which had originally been published in the *New Zealand Tablet*. O'Regan, described as 'perhaps the leading lay Irish Catholic in the country', was the son of Cork immigrants who had been elected an independent MP in the 1890s for the west coast mining district of Inangahua, near Greymouth. After losing his seat in 1899, he had become a successful lawyer representing working men and a prominent supporter of Irish republican causes.[35] O'Regan dismissed Craigavon's claim that Northern Ireland was 'harmonious and prosperous' as a 'daring travesty of the facts'. He summarised how the rights of the Catholic minority in Northern Ireland 'had been trampled under foot' by the abolition of proportional representation for parliamentary elections, in sharp contrast, he observed, to its existence in independent Ireland where it worked to the benefit of the 'antinational and Protestant minority' there.[36]

At the end of the month the *Irish News* returned to the topic of Craigavon's New Zealand tour, accusing him of taking a 'five-months holiday abroad' where he was able to 'bandy about rhodomontade about Northern Ireland', celebrating its 'Loyalty and Prosperity'.[37] It also published an article by a prominent New Zealand journalist, B. Magee, who asserted that if Craigavon had come to New Zealand six years earlier when 'a dour North of Ireland man', Massey, had been prime minister, he 'would have been lionised, for then the cloven foot of bigotry was painfully apparent'. Now, however, matters in New Zealand had greatly improved. The current governor, Sir Charles Fergusson, albeit a prominent Presbyterian, had done much 'to emphasise the desirability of eliminating bigotry from the country'. Lord Craigavon, argued Magee, could not have come to New Zealand 'at a more opportune time to have his mind opened and his vision widened to the inflow of new thoughts and ideas'. In New Zealand, where Catholics constituted only a small percentage of the population, he had been welcomed by Sir Joseph Ward, a Catholic prime minister (with a Southern Irish background), and, asserted Magee, he would have found that, unlike Northern Ireland, 'in all the departments of State and private employment ... religion was not a bar to preferment, much less subject to penalisation on that account'. Craigavon had 'assured all and sundry' that he hoped 'that the trip will be of benefit to the North'. For Magee, in New Zealand Craigavon had had a grand 'opportunity to learn' the possibilities and benefits of religious tolerance.[38]

Between 1923 and 1930 three New Zealand prime ministers, Massey, Forbes and Coates, came to Northern Ireland, on each occasion following attendance at imperial conferences. Massey's visit in December 1923 was his second to Ulster as prime minister (he also came in November 1916), but it was his only visit to *Northern* Ireland as a separate political entity. Massey came as an official guest, the Belfast government having agreed to meet all the expenses of his five-day visit.[39]

There were four main themes of the visit. First, there was a general celebration of the British empire and the sense of imperial partnership which Northern Ireland and New Zealand shared. Speaking at a Chamber of Commerce lunch in Belfast, Massey declared that he looked upon 'New Zealand and Northern Ireland as two countries in some respects very much alike – similar in their characteristics and actuated by the same patriotic spirit of loyalty to the Crown and love and appreciation for the Empire which our ancestors built up'.[40] Second was an emphasis on the importance to both places of trade. At the same Belfast luncheon, the local minister of commerce, H. M. Pollock described Massey as 'the greatest commercial traveller in the British Empire, one who believed in pushing Empire Goods for Empire Consumption'.[41] One of the strongly expressed hopes, indeed, of this visit was that increased inter-imperial trade, and Imperial Preference, would work to the great advantage of the economies of Northern Ireland and New Zealand, and there were specific hopes that New Zealand, which already 'grew flax for linseed purposes', might also be able to grow flax 'to supply fibre for the Belfast linen industry'.[42]

Third, obviously, was the returning emigrant, 'roots' dimension of the visit. Massey duly went to Limavady, where he inspected the War Memorial Institute, 'revisited a number of scenes of his boyhood', met up with some 'old schoolmates and friends of bygone days' and went to morning service in the Second Limavady Presbyterian Church, where he and his parents had 'worshipped in far-back days'.[43] After the service he inspected a church parade of the Royal Ulster Constabulary 'B' Specials (the exclusively Protestant paramilitary reserve police force) and 'congratulated them on the notable part they played in restoring peace to Ulster'.[44] Speaking in Limavady, Massey said that New Zealand 'had plenty of room for settlers, he said, "Give me a quarter million Ulstermen and women and I will take the blessed lot." (Applause.) They wanted to keep the race pure.'[45] At an official luncheon in Derry, Massey was unambiguously unionist. He was introduced as 'a strong man and an Orangeman'; and he told his audience he was 'glad that Ulster had remained part of the United Kingdom', adding, however, that this should not be taken as any reflection on the government of Southern Ireland. 'He would like to think', he said, 'that there would be peace and friendship between the different countries of the British Empire, including Southern Ireland'.[46]

Massey came in for some criticism for his evident pro-unionist sympathies. The *Irish News* ticked him off for plunging into British and Irish controversies:

> He 'boosted' Baldwinite Protection ... he accepted praise as 'a strong Man and an Orangeman'; he babbled nonsense about 'Ulster and the United Kingdom'; in short, there was nothing left undone or unsaid ... that a self-respecting citizen of a remote free country would not have scrupulously avoided while dwelling amongst people living under another Government.

Massey's 'exhibitions of *Ulsteria*' (a word evidently to rhyme with 'hysteria') were 'ill-mannered, uncouth and reprehensible'.[47]

The fourth theme was one of how New Zealand was perceived in Ulster, as most extravagantly expressed at Queen's University, Belfast, on Friday 30 November 1923. Lord Craigavon recalled that:

> Queen's University, amid scenes of unprecedented enthusiasm, proclaimed him as one of her own. I was privileged to be present when the students, attired in Maori dress elected him their paramount Chief and escorted him through the Town, cheered by an admiring multitude voicing a welcome from the heart of all Ulster.[48]

The most extensive account of this remarkable event appeared in a souvenir brochure produced after Massey's visit by one of the big Belfast department stores. It described how Massey was greeted formally by the acting vice chancellor (Professor Symmers) 'in the way of the old Celtic greeting' with 'a hundred thousand welcomes' (*cead mile fáilte*).

> A more dramatic welcome still awaited 'the great white chief' of the New Zealand Dominion. The whole front area of the University was in possession of the Maori tribe, and their chieftains, seated on a dias [sic], called the premier to the place of honour at their table. The Maori warriors were painted after the manner of the native race, and were apparelled after the fashion of the tribe.
>
> The presentation of gifts followed, these including an *Irish Shillelagh with green ribbon*.
>
> It transpired that the cook had no feast in readiness, and envoys were despatched to bring in a few missionaries to form food for the repast. These were tested in turn, and eventually one of the number was consigned into a big pot, under which a huge fire was lighted.
>
> **WAR DANCE AND HOWLING CHORUS**
>
> The war dance came next. There were three advances and three retreats, the former being characterised by a howling chorus, which reverberated over the landscape, and the latter by a silence that was almost uncanny....
>
> Mr. Massey was obviously delighted with the Maori reception, and, when acknowledging the presents, he referred to the fact that the race had great warlike traditions, that they never surrendered, and that they played a great part in the World War. They were now civilised citizens of a great country.[49]

There was an Ulster resonance in Massey's final remark about the Maori people. Bearing in mind the broad 'Irish military tradition', the Siege of Derry shout of 'No Surrender!' and the recent heroics of the 36th (Ulster) Division at the battle of the Somme, he could as well have said of Ulster loyalists that they 'had great war-like traditions, that they never surrendered, and that they played a great part in the World War'. Whether, of course, he might have asserted that 'they were now civilised citizens of a great country', is, perhaps, a rather different matter.

This student demonstration was clearly based on the haka, as performed, for example, on 'All Blacks' rugby tours, and which would have been seen in Belfast in November 1924 when the New Zealand touring team defeated Ulster.[50] The All Blacks' haka was (and is) taken very seriously, but pantomime performances of the Belfast sort, in which identikit 'savages' (who looked more Zulu than Maori in this instance) leap about in a grotesque (if supposedly affectionate and admiring) parody of a 'native dance', raise serious issues of cultural engagement and contemporary western attitudes to the exotic 'other'. At the time few people thought the matter very remarkable. The New Zealand press reported the occasion as 'an amusing and excellently organised "rag"', in which five hundred students 'dressed in all sorts of weird variants of Maori costumes' gathered outside the university and 'installed Mr. Massey as "Big Chief"'(see Figures 1 and 2).[51] Maori singing and poi dancing had become popular at 'smoke concerts' and celebrations in New Zealand from the turn

After Mr. Massey had the Degree of LL.D. conferred on him, and was passing out of the University Buildings, he was received by 500 Students dressed as Maoris. Photograph shows the Chief asking Mr. Massey to ascend the throne.

Figure 1 From Bank Buildings (Belfast) Ltd. Souvenir Brochure 'Premier Massey's Ulster Visit'.

of the century,[52] and Pakeha New Zealand students frequently indulged in mock war dances. In the late 1920s members of the Hongi Cub at Auckland University favoured mock hakas as a way of disrupting Student Christian Movement sing-alongs.[53] But Maori tolerance for the racism inherent in white parodies of the haka declined, demonstrated most dramatically when in May 1979 members of the radical Maori 'Waitangi Action Committee' violently broke up the mock haka which engineering

Mr. Massey entered into the spirit of the Students' "rag" and is seen on throne between the "King" and "Queen" of Maoris.

Figure 2 As Figure 1.

students at Auckland University had performed for over twenty years as part of their annual 'capping day' festivities.[54] In the 1920s and 1930s, however, the public discourse remained dominated by essentially British assumptions of Caucasian cultural superiority.

While Massey was the only dominion prime minister to combine a visit to Northern Ireland with the 1923 conference, two premiers came after the 1926 meeting, Walter Stanley Monroe of Newfoundland and J. G. (Gordon) Coates of New Zealand. Unlike Massey in 1923, both men visited Dublin before travelling on to Belfast, thus to an extent validating the position of the Irish Free State as a fellow dominion. Both men also received honorary degrees at Trinity College in Dublin (where Monroe (a Protestant) had been born).[55] When he came to Belfast, Monroe affirmed how very loyal Newfoundland was. In sharp contrast to the separatist tendencies being displayed by some dominions (though not New Zealand), Monroe had told the imperial conference that 'Newfoundland had no desire to be consulted regarding Britain's foreign policy. They gave the British Government a blank cheque, whether they were Conservative, Liberal or Labour, and in the event of war Newfoundland would join in feeling sure they were doing so in a just cause.'[56]

Coates arrived in Belfast on Saturday 11 December, the day after he had been awarded his honorary degree (when the Trinity College Public Orator introduced him as 'the worthy successor of those great men Robert [*sic*] Seddon and Joseph Ward',[57] Massey's greatness evidently not having registered in Dublin). The *Weekly Northern Whig* remarked that Coates, like Massey, 'comes of Ulster stock'.[58] In fact Coates's main family base in the 'Mother Country' was in England, but he had an uncle, William Coates, working in the Belfast linen business, whom he met while in the province.[59] Coates, however, had a more intriguing Ulster link (and one not picked up at all during his 1926 visit) through his maternal grandmother, Agnes Casement-Aickin, one of the prominent Casement family from County Antrim, and a relative of Sir Roger Casement, the Irish republican leader executed in 1916, though more recently also celebrated as an Irish gay icon.[60]

Coates was taken to Derry, where he toured the city walls and visited the Apprentice Boys' Memorial Hall, where he was 'shown a 16-foot effigy of the traitor Lundy in course of preparation for the 18th December anniversary'.[61] In Belfast at a public meeting sponsored by the Overseas League he, like Massey, celebrated the imperial link, reaffirmed New Zealand's fidelity to the empire, and spoke of the economic advantages to be had from imperial preference and increased inter-imperial trade. He touched briefly on Irish matters, remarking that while in Dublin staying with the governor-general (the veteran Irish nationalist Tim Healy) he 'had had the opportunity of hearing quite a lot about Ireland – quite a lot which one did not know at first-hand previously' about 'the aspirations, the objects, the intentions, and the desire of the people of being able to develop this country even more than it had been developed. He [Coates] sincerely believed that with goodwill and tolerance this country would progress more than it had ever done in the past.' In this reference to 'goodwill and tolerance', is there a hint that the New Zealander appreciated the strength of sectarian animosities in contemporary Ireland? Coates went on to speak of his own country, and assured his audience that 'though some 13,000 or 14,000 miles' separated them from the Mother Country,

> New Zealanders still had close affection, sympathy, and loyalty for the people in this part of the world. (Applause.) He said that as a Britisher, but they had other Britishers in New Zealand who were of a darker colour – the Maories [sic], and even they claimed close relationship with the Mother Country, but they claimed it from another point of view altogether. They said that relationship had been brought about through the process of absorption, and quite recently one of his Ministers, in describing how that happened, explained to his audience that his great grandfather had eaten a Presbyterian minister. (Laughter.)[62]

Thus Coates expounded in Northern Ireland the prevailing New Zealand public ideology of Maori and Pakeha as one people living in harmony, an attitude which reflected James Craig's assertions of all-Ireland harmony in some of his 1929–30 speeches in New Zealand.

In a leading article, 'A Message from the Britain of the Pacific', the *Weekly Northern Whig*, while accepting some conventional contemporary stereotypes of Pakeha-Maori relations, commended Coates for his cheerful optimism, and congratulated New Zealand for its marvellous recent history of development and the highly creditable way it had coped with what it delicately called 'the problem of the original owners of the soil'. What in the early nineteenth century had been 'two practically unknown islands, inhabited by a scanty population of warlike cannibals', had become 'a highly organised Dominion of the Empire, in which upwards of a million people live under exceptionally happy conditions'. Extremes of wealth and poverty were unknown, and there was 'little room for either the leisured sybarite or the "work shy" loafer'. The Maoris, it was noted, although cannibals, 'were, nevertheless, a race with many noble qualities', who in the years following the arrival of British colonists 'never seem to have aroused the feelings of intense dislike and repulsion which long embittered the relations between the red men of North America and the "pale faces"'. Throughout New Zealand, maintained the *Whig* (perhaps with more certainty than was absolutely warranted), 'there is no such thing as the "colour prejudice" which has been responsible for so much wrong and misery both in North America and South Africa'.[63]

Not everyone was quite so pleased with Coates and his visit. The nationalist *Irish News* complained about 'the old and dishonourable practice of utilising eminent strangers as cogs in the elaborate machinery devised for bolstering up and maintaining in power the indefensible Ascendancy Clique who dominate the Six Counties'. Surely, it commented, the prime minister of New Zealand, 'if he is not more innocent of worldly guile than any contemporary ruler of a State', would by now have realised that he had not been invited to Northern Ireland for his own sake, but merely 'to act as an advertising agent for a discredited Government'. Neither Coates nor the Newfoundlander Monroe had been 'allowed to learn a solitary essential fact about the state of affairs in the Six Counties'. If, alleged the *Irish News*, Coates returned home 'convinced that the Six Counties are inhabited by a million and a quarter of happy, prosperous and contented people', in part it would have been because he had toured the province 'without discovering that the Chamber of Commerce, or Chamber of Trade, or whatever sub-committee of [the] U.U.C. [Ulster Unionist Council] may have entertained him, has carefully excluded every citizen of all the thousands opposed to the U.U.C.'s policy from the public functions in which he has participated'.[64]

There was some truth in this. During his visit to Derry, for example, Coates was accompanied by Sir James Craig, and at the city the party was met exclusively by Unionist civic leaders (representing through gerrymandered electoral divisions a city with a Catholic and Nationalist majority). Coates's tour, moreover, included purely Protestant historic sites. On the other hand, there is some doubt whether representatives of the minority community would, in any case, have accepted invitations to participate in meeting the New Zealander. For obvious and understandable reasons, Northern Nationalists tended to boycott official Northern Ireland government occasions, and it was only after the tripartite Boundary Agreement of December 1925, which secured partition and the existence of Northern Ireland for the foreseeable future, that Nationalist MPs began to take an active part in the Northern Ireland parliament.

The 1930 imperial conference brought four dominion prime ministers to Ireland, though only three came north. The South African, Hertzog, visited Dublin but not Belfast. The first to come north was Richard Bennett of Canada who came for a busy day of engagements before departing for Scotland. That the political climate in Northern Ireland had somewhat changed was demonstrated by Craigavon at lunch reading a letter from Joseph Devlin, the veteran Nationalist MP, apologising for being unable to attend.[65] The next premier to come was James (J. H.) Scullin, the first Catholic to have become prime minister of Australia. In Dublin he not only met the Irish premier, William Cosgrave, but also the republican leader, Eamon de Valera.[66] He received an honorary degree, not from Trinity College with its Ascendancy connotations, but from the National University of Ireland.[67] Being a strong Irish nationalist with Ulster forebears, moreover, he provides a sharp contrast with William Massey. Scullin's parents were both from the North, his father coming from Bellaghy, County Londonderry.[68]

Like Bennett, Scullin was given a civic reception in the city hall, followed by a government luncheon. At the former, Scullin spoke in general terms about the unity of Ireland. He said that he and his wife (whose family were from County Cork) in their marriage united North and South. While he did not want to trespass in the 'politics of any part of this country' (which was a rather different line from the one he adopted at home in Australia), he hoped 'that in spirit and in friendship Ireland will be united, because within this Commonwealth of Nations we want unity'. At the lunch, Scullin was welcomed not only by Craigavon, but also by Joe Devlin, a first for any Northern Ireland Nationalist MP. Devlin thanked Craigavon 'for his kindness in asking him to come there with his colleagues representing a different section of opinion to his'. The leader writer of the *Irish News* added that 'without lessening our appreciation' of Craigavon's 'act of courtesy', 'we, and those for whom we speak, would be happier still if the hand of fellowship could be stretched forth on more important occasions'.[69] In all, Scullin's visit permitted an unusual (for the still new state of

Northern Ireland) combination of public ceremonial and Catholic celebration (Scullin's visit included a meeting with the Catholic primate, Cardinal MacRory), in welcoming a visitor whom the Unionist government was ostensibly pleased to have in the province.

The New Zealander George W. Forbes was the last dominion premier to visit Northern Ireland in 1930, and after the minority excitements of the Scullin visit, it was something of a return to the *status quo ante*. The reception committee comprised Craigavon, four cabinet ministers and the lord mayor of Belfast, all Unionists. At the city hall, the lord mayor said that 'to refer to politics is outside the scope of this formal but very sincere welcome', and promptly made an explicitly political remark. 'I am only stating the truth', he said, 'when I mention that the attitude which New Zealand has always displayed in Imperial matters has found a warm echo in the heart of the loyal people of this city.' Forbes responded in terms which can only have pleased the Unionists: 'He felt that in coming to Belfast he was coming to a city that had a sentiment which was very strong in New Zealand – the sentiment of affection for the Old Country and loyalty to the Crown. (Hear, hear.)...The British Empire', he continued (and in contrast to Scullin's usage), 'is a term that we like very much better than the Commonwealth of Nations.'[70] During his visit, the commercial possibilities of trade between Northern Ireland and New Zealand, given point by the prevailing economic recession, were addressed in a couple of engagements. Forbes toured the Belfast Ropeworks – the largest in the world – for which New Zealand might be able to supply raw material, and he also went to the Linen Research Centre (where the economic possibilities of flax were investigated).

Like Massey, Forbes was given an honorary degree by Queen's University, and, like his predecessor, he was treated to a 'Maori' demonstration. 'The students', wrote Lady Craigavon in her diary, 'staged a Maori Rag which was quite amusing, but not as good as the one they originally did for Mr Massey'.[71] It was on a smaller scale than in 1923, the *Belfast Telegraph* reporting that 'upwards of a hundred students in weird costumes, with awesome headgear and grim warpaint, made the welkin ring with their whoops, howls, and yells'. Under the headline 'A Maori Welcome. "Wild Tribesmen" Greet Mr. Forbes at Queen's', the *Weekly Northern Whig* provided a more detailed description of the events. This time there was no missionary, but Forbes was presented with 'a magnificent bouquet of cauliflower' and also a wife: 'The bride, a strapping wench of some six feet odd, was brought forward and handed over with all the mysterious rites associated with such an occasion. With the coy damsel it was a case of love at first sight, for she threw her arms around her new husband in empassioned [sic] embrace.' In order to facilitate 'feasting and merriment', Forbes was then presented with a plate of herrings and potatoes, along with a bottle of Guinness (the *Irish News* said it was Bass – an English beer).

> It was evident [continued the *Whig*] that Mr. Forbes had enjoyed the 'rag' immensely, and when he was given an opportunity of replying he assured the tribesmen that the Belfast Tribe was the best in the world. How they had reached such a high degree of perfection was a mystery, but he ventured to suggest that some of the cries would have made a normal Maori turn pale.[72]

Forbes, like Massey, was also presented with a 'shillelagh', so the cultural cocktail was complete, the exotic and the familiar combined in an event which celebrated exuberant high spirits and martial enthusiasm, apparently characteristic of both Ulster and New Zealand.

The emergence between the wars of a regular series of imperial conferences, though intended to exploit the centripetal common bonds of empire, in fact served to stimulate centrifugal forces as well. Although the meetings provided ample photographic and rhetorical opportunities for public manifestations of imperial unity, they also gave 'status-seeking'[73] dominion leaders a chance to promote their individual territories' interests, as well as establishing the limits of imperial power and codifying dominion autonomy. Naturally this varied from dominion to dominion, with South Africa and Canada, for example, being more independent-minded than Newfoundland or New Zealand.[74] But inevitably, paradoxically even, proximity to fellow dominion leaders could serve to emphasise mutual 'distance' in social, economic and political terms, as much as any closeness there may have been within the imperial or commonwealth 'family', a situation illustrated in the sometimes acerbic debates during the 1930 imperial conference.[75]

As demonstrated by the Northern Ireland example, the tours (with their associated rituals) which dominion premiers took of Britain and Ireland on the occasion of inter-war imperial conferences are themselves also very revealing of inter-war imperial relationships (and mutual perceptions), between the 'Mother Country' (or countries) and what might be called the sibling states which comprised the emerging 'British commonwealth of nations'. Lip service was consistently paid to the strength of imperial loyalty (and there is no reason to suppose that this did not genuinely reflect the sentiments of most Ulster unionists or Kiwi imperialists), but the visits of successive New Zealand premiers to Northern Ireland also sought to promote the alleged practical benefits which both communities hoped would accrue from the imperial link. Possible trading opportunities – especially based round the potentialities of empire flax-growing to supply raw material for the linen industry – were a constant theme in public speeches, and the itineraries arranged for visiting politicians.[76] Nevertheless, reflecting changing economic circumstances, G. W. Forbes in 1930 did not repeat W. F. Massey's expansive, and perhaps visionary, 1923 call for 250,000 migrants, even in the high cause (as Massey had asserted) of keeping the race 'pure'.[77]

There were also clear promotional aspects to these tours. A common factor in Craigavon's visit to New Zealand and J. G. Coates's 1926 visit to Northern Ireland was the presentation of an idealised vision of their home countries, which certainly in Craigavon's case was intensified by his distance from home and his proximity to non-Protestant Irish migrants in New Zealand. For Craigavon the liberation of 'distance' gave him the freedom to celebrate Irishness to an extent almost inconceivable back in Northern Ireland. Massey and Forbes, in turn, could cheerfully (or apparently so) submit to the folderol of mock Maori greetings more readily than was perhaps becoming possible at home.

The centrifugal tendencies displayed in inter-imperial relations during these years have to be understood in the context of the extraordinary and, for some, apparently whole-hearted imperial war effort of 1914–18.[78] Indeed, in some ways the quest for autonomy was enabled by the experience of the Great War. Among the rituals associated with the 1923, 1926 and 1930 imperial conferences in London was the marking of that great collective sacrifice by the formal participation of dominion premiers in Armistice Day ceremonies in Westminster Abbey and the laying of wreaths at the cenotaph in Whitehall.[79] And the shadow of the Great War fell across the visits of New Zealand premiers to Northern Ireland. It is not clear precisely where the 'Maori' demonstration for Forbes took place at Queen's University. By the time of his visit in December 1930 a large and imposing war memorial (with an angel tending a dying soldier) had been erected directly in front of the main university buildings, exactly where the students had danced for Massey and the 'missionary' had been 'cooked'. The proximity of that memorial might well have constrained the precocious posturings of the undergraduates in 1930. And yet their 'war dance' and the gift of the shillelagh (a weapon) provided a facetious echo of the martial virtues celebrated and commemorated in that monument. Three New Zealand premiers attending imperial conferences in London took the opportunity to visit Northern Ireland between the wars. Forbes and Coates also visited war graves along the Western Front, which brings us back to where we began. There the national differences, such as they were, and the distances travelled – geographical, political, psychological (or whatever) – became irrelevant in the common experience of the war and what might be called the 'perpetual proximity' of those Ulstermen and New Zealanders commemorated in the imperial – and commonwealth – cemeteries and monuments to the missing.

Notes

[1] Jeffery, *Ireland and the Great War*, 138–41; McGibbon, *New Zealand Battlefields*, 6–7, 26–32.
[2] Taylor, 'Introduction', 120; see also Phillips, 'Histories'.
[3] W. F. Massey to James Allen (defence minister and acting prime minister), 2 Jan. 1917, quoted in Bennett, '"Massey's Sunday School Picnic Party"', 23.
[4] Ibid., 35, 42. Godley entitled his autobiography, *Life of an Irish Soldier*.
[5] Gibbs, *Realities of War*, 470.

[6] Macleod, 'British Heroic-Romantic Myth', 83.
[7] Wylly, *Neill's 'Blue Caps'*, 42.
[8] *Belfast Telegraph*, 11 Nov. 1922, emphasis added.
[9] Ervine, *Craigavon*, 519.
[10] For the 1901 tour, see Bassett, 'A Thousand Miles of Loyalty'.
[11] Amery, *My Political Life*, II, 402–73.
[12] *The Times*, 19 Nov. 1929.
[13] *Taranaki Herald*, 7 Dec. 1929, clipping in diary of Lady Craigavon (henceforward Craigavon diary), Public Record Office of Northern Ireland, (PRONI) D.1415/C/3.
[14] Ibid., 9 Dec. 1929, emphasis added; Craigavon to Charles H. Blackmore, 7 Dec. 1929, PRONI, PM 9/24.
[15] Lady Craigavon diary, 8 Dec. 1929, PRONI, D.1415/C/4.
[16] 'I have just come in from a long day's trout fishing—Bag 23 between the two of us, *averaging* 2 1/2 lbs., other days 3, 11 & 12 & *one* of mine was a 6 1/4 lbs.' Craigavon to Blackmore, 17 Dec. 1929, PRONI, PM 9/24.
[17] Craigavon diary, 3 Jan. 1930, PRONI, D.1415/C/4.
[18] *The Times*, 4 Jan. 1930.
[19] Craigavon diary, 3 Jan. 1930, PRONI, D.1415/C/4.
[20] *Londonderry Sentinel*, 4 Jan. 1930 (I am grateful to Brian Mitchell for this reference).
[21] This was not strictly true. The road leading up to the south entrance to the Stormont estate (where the parliament buildings were erected) was called 'Killeen Road', before being renamed 'Massey Avenue' in 1925.
[22] *Wellington Evening Post*, 4 Jan. 1930, clipping in Craigavon diary, PRONI, D.1415/C/4.
[23] *Grey River Argus*, 9 Jan. 1930, clipping in Craigavon diary, PRONI, D.1415/C/4.
[24] Ibid.
[25] *Sydney Morning Herald*, 11 Nov. 1929.
[26] Barton, 'Northern Ireland, 1925–39', 199.
[27] *Otago Daily Times*, 13 Jan. 1920, clipping in Craigavon diary, PRONI, D.1415/C/4.
[28] Craigavon diary, 11 Jan. 1930, PRONI, D. 1415/C/5.
[29] See Brosnahan, '"Battle of the Borough"'.
[30] *Timaru Herald*, 29 Jan. 1930, clipping in Craigavon diary, PRONI, D.1415/C/6.
[31] *Wairarapa Age*, 21 Jan. 1930, clipping in Craigavon diary, PRONI, D.1415/C/6.
[32] *Dominion*, 5 Feb. 1930, clipping in Craigavon diary, PRONI, D.1415/C/6.
[33] *Evening Post*, 5 Feb. 1930, clipping in Craigavon diary, PRONI, D.1415/C/6.
[34] *Irish News*, 3 Jan. 1930.
[35] Brosnahan, 'Parties or Politics', 74–75.
[36] *Irish News*, 3 Jan.1930.
[37] Ibid., 4 Feb. 1930.
[38] Ibid., 3 Feb. 1930.
[39] C. A. Blackmore to Cecil Litchfield (a senior official in the Ministry of Commerce), 14 Nov. 1923, PRONI, PM10/3.
[40] *Irish Times*, 30 Nov. 1923. The Irish politician Kevin O'Higgins had a different view of the similarities of the two territories. 'New Zealand', he wrote to his wife from the 1926 Imperial Conference, 'must be rather like Northern Ireland – it produces the same type of Jingo reactionary.' White, *Kevin O'Higgins*, 222.
[41] Quoted in 'Premier Massey's Ulster Visit' brochure, produced by the Bank Buildings, Ltd, PRONI, PM 6/13.
[42] *Irish Times*, 30 Nov. 1923.
[43] *Londonderry Sentinel*, 4 Dec. 1923.
[44] *Irish Times*, 3 Dec. 1923.
[45] *Weekly Northern Whig*, 8 Dec. 1923.

[46] *Irish Times*, 3 Dec. 1923.
[47] *Irish News*, 4 Dec. 1923, emphasis in original.
[48] 'Introduction by Viscount Craigavon' (for a planned biography of Massey by E. A. James), 10 Mar. 1930, PRONI, PM 6/13.
[49] 'Premier Massey's Ulster Visit', PRONI, PM 6/13, emphasis in original. The estimated 500 students involved constituted about half of the entire student body of 1,077 in 1923–24. A British Pathé newsreel of the occasion ('Great Maori Demonstration') can be found at http://www.britishpathe.com (Film ID: 324.16) (accessed 30 March 2008).
[50] The score was 28–6. *The Times*, 6 Nov. 1926. On 2 Dec. 1935 Ulster held the All Blacks to a draw (one try apiece), *The Times*, 2 Dec. 1935.
[51] Similar reports, all evidently drawn from the same Press Association communiqué, appeared in the *New Zealand Herald*, *Dominion* and *Press*, 4 Dec. 1923.
[52] Phillips, 'Musings in Maoriland', 531.
[53] O'Sullivan, *Long Journey*, 45.
[54] Walker, *Ka Whawhai Tonu Matou*, 220–24.
[55] *Weekly Northern Whig*, 11 Dec. 1926.
[56] *Belfast Telegraph*, 4 Dec. 1926.
[57] Ibid., 11 Dec. 1926.
[58] *Weekly Northern Whig*, 18 Dec. 1926.
[59] See 'Schedule for visit of Mr. J. G. Coates', PRONI, PM 6/7.
[60] For Coates' family background, see Bassett, *Coates*, 10–14; for Casement, see Dudgeon, *Roger Casement*.
[61] *Belfast Telegraph*, 13 Dec. 1926.
[62] *Weekly Northern Whig*, 18 Dec. 1926. Another route to integration is suggested by the rumours that Coates had fathered children by Maori women (Basset, *Coates*, 26).
[63] *Weekly Northern Whig*, 18 Dec. 1926.
[64] *Irish News*, 13 Dec. 1926
[65] Ibid., 19 Nov. 1930.
[66] Robertson, *J. H. Scullin*, 286–87.
[67] *The Times*, 24 Nov. 1930.
[68] *Irish News*, 13, 29 Nov. 1930.
[69] Ibid., 28 Nov. 1930.
[70] *Weekly Northern Whig*, 6 Dec. 1930.
[71] Typescript extract from Lady Craigavon's diary, 2 Dec. 1930, PRONI, D.1415/B/38, fol. 683.
[72] *Belfast Telegraph* and *Irish News*, 3 Dec. 1930; *Weekly Northern Whig*, 6 Dec. 1930.
[73] Nicholas Mansergh's phrase; see his discussion of interwar dominion relations in Mansergh, *Commonwealth Experience*, ch. 8.
[74] For the role of the Irish Free State in the progressive definition of dominion autonomy, see Harkness, *Restless Dominion*, and the sharp critique of his thesis in Martin, 'The Irish Free State'.
[75] This was especially so on economic issues. See Holland, *Britain and the Commonwealth Alliance*, ch. 7.
[76] For the Northern Ireland side of these expectations, see Ollerenshaw, 'Businessmen in Northern Ireland'.
[77] At the 1917 Imperial War Cabinet Massey had been instrumental in securing a United Kingdom commitment to empire settlement schemes; see Drummond, *Imperial Economic Policy*, 25–26, and, for the subsequent history of empire settlement, chs 2–3.
[78] Sir Charles Lucas asserted that it was 'not Great Britain alone, but the whole – the heartwhole – British Empire' which declared war against Germany in 1914; see Lucas, *The Empire at War*, I, 293. For a more nuanced assessment, see Holland, 'The British Empire and the Great War'.
[79] *The Times*, 12 Nov. 1923, 12 Nov. 1926, 12 Nov. 1930.

References

Amery, L. S. *My Political Life*. 2 vols. London: Hutchinson, 1953.
Barton, Brian. 'Northern Ireland, 1925–39'. In *A New History of Ireland*, vii, *Ireland, 1921–84*, edited by J. R. Hill. Oxford: Oxford University Press, 2003, 199–234.
Bassett, Judith. 'A Thousand Miles of Loyalty: The Royal Tour of 1901'. *New Zealand Journal of History* 21 (1987): 125–38.
Bassett, Mike. *Coates of Kaipara*. Auckland: Auckland University Press, 1995.
Bennett, James. '"Massey's Sunday School Picnic Party": "The Other Anzacs" or Honorary Australians?'. *War & Society* 26 (2003): 23–54.
Brosnahan, Seán. '"The Battle of the Borough" and the "Saige O Timaru": Sectarian Riot in Colonial Canterbury'. *New Zealand Journal of History* 28 (1994): 41–59.
———. 'Parties or Politics: Wellington's IRA 1922–1928'. In *The Irish in New Zealand: Historical Contexts and Perspectives*, edited by Brad Patterson. Wellington: Stout Research Centre for New Zealand Studies, 2002, 67–87.
Drummond, Ian M. *Imperial Economic Policy 1917–1939: Studies in Expansion and Protection*. London: Allen & Unwin, 1974.
Dudgeon, Jeffrey. *Roger Casement: The Black Diaries*. Belfast: Belfast Press, 2002.
Ervine, St John. *Craigavon: Ulsterman*. London: Allen & Unwin, 1949.
Gibbs, Sir Philip. *Realities of War*. Revd edn. London: Hutchinson, 1929.
Godley, Sir Alexander. *Life of an Irish Soldier*. London: John Murray, 1939.
Holland, R. F. *Britain and the Commonwealth Alliance 1918–1939*. London: Macmillan, 1981.
———. 'The British Empire and the Great War, 1914–1918'. In *The Oxford History of the British Empire*. vol. 4. *The Twentieth Century*, edited by Judith M. Brown and Wm. Roger Louis. Oxford: Oxford University Press, 1999.
Harkness, D. W. *The Restless Dominion: The Irish Free State and the British Commonwealth of Nations, 1921–31*. London: Macmillan, 1969.
Jeffery, Keith. *Ireland and the Great War*. Cambridge: Cambridge University Press, 2000.
Lucas, Sir Charles, ed. *The Empire at War*. 5 vols. London: Oxford University Press, 1921–26.
Macleod, Jenny. 'The British Heroic-Romantic Myth of Gallipoli'. In *Gallipoli: Making History*. London: Frank Cass, 2004, 73–97.
Mansergh, Nicholas. *The Commonwealth Experience*. London: Weidenfeld & Nicolson, 1969.
Martin, Ged. 'The Irish Free State and the Evolution of the Commonwealth, 1921–49'. In *Reappraisals in British Imperial History*, edited by Ronald Hyam and Ged Martin. London: Macmillan, 1975, 201–23.
McGibbon, Ian. *New Zealand Battlefields and Memorials of the Western Front*. Auckland: Oxford University Press, 2001.
Ollerenshaw, Philip. 'Businessmen in Northern Ireland and the Imperial Connection, 1886–1939'. In *'An Irish Empire'? Aspects of Ireland and the British Empire*, edited by Keith Jeffery. Manchester: Manchester University Press, 1996, 169–90.
O'Sullivan, Vincent. *Long Journey to the Border: A Life of John Mulgan*. Auckland: Penguin, 2003.
Phillips, J. O. C. 'Musings in Maoriland – or was there a *Bulletin* School in New Zealand?' *Historical Studies* 20 (1983): 520–35.
Phillips, Mark Salber. 'Histories, Micro- and Literary: Problems of Genre and Distance'. *New Literary History* 34 (2003): 211–29.
Robertson, John. *J. H. Scullin: A Political Biography*. Nedlands, WA: University of Western Australia Press, 1974.
Taylor, Barbara. 'Introduction: How Far, How Near: Distance and Proximity in the Historical Imagination'. *History Workshop Journal* 57 (2004): 117–49.
Walker, Ranginui. *Ka Whawhai Tonu Matou: Struggle without End*. Auckland: Penguin, 1990.
White, Terence de Vere. *Kevin O'Higgins*. Tralee: Anvil Books, 1966.
Wylly, H. C. *Neill's 'Blue Caps'*, vol. 3, *1914–1922*. Aldershot: Gale & Polden, n.d [1923].

Law, Politics and Analogy in Akan Historiography

Richard Rathbone

In the 1960s some of the dominating figures in imperial history and the pioneers of the new field of African history eyed one another with wary hostility.[1] Many of the latter had of course been nurtured by the former; to some extent what was afoot was little more than one of the cyclical Oedipal turf wars that characterise most fields of scholarship. The hostility was, however, not without justification on either side. Some Africanists railed against what they regarded as the marginalisation by imperial historians of the histories of the human subjects of empire and most especially Africans. At the same time some historians of empire regarded the search for an African-centred history as a Quixotic enterprise given that the written and hence more easily verified sources for such reconstructions were thin on the ground. But it is fair to say, as with all too few turf wars, that accommodation followed by a degree of mutual admiration succeeded the sharp hostility of the 1960s. It is, however, also fair to say that some historians of Africa, a misguided, fundamentalist minority, continue to eschew whenever possible archival sources when their authors were involved in what is regarded negatively as 'the colonial project'.

Most modern scholars would today regard the colonial period as an enormously significant if ambiguous period in the broader sweep of African history[2] and would understand the record of African thoughts and deeds as being profoundly imbricated not only within the history of empires but also within the histories of metropolitan powers. Earlier suspicions have thankfully given way to infinitely more productive debates. This chapter is, however, much more concerned with some of the fall-out of those earlier wrangles. It is concerned with the ways in which African processes have frequently been described and understood, ways which consciously and unconsciously borrow from the taxonomies of European history. It is about the rather easy-going use of analogy by which some Africanists have attempted to explain the quiddities of the African past to those supposedly more versed in the categories deployed by historians of Europe; the assumptions such authors and their publishers implicitly made about the potential readership is immediately instructive for the target readership was manifestly western rather than African. Such analogies were certainly trotted out, often entirely reasonably but sometimes outrageously, to serve such explanatory purposes. But they also did some service to historians of Africa seeking to place the agency of their chosen subjects of study – Africans – in historical studies on at least an equal footing with that of the colonial powers. Among the ambiguities of empire there are few which are quite so ironic as the choice of such analogy being largely derived from the pasts of the imperial powers. An aspect of that irony is that such comparisons had loomed large in the frequently disparaging imperial commentaries on the supposedly backward nature of African civilisations. If analogy really was perceived as necessary, were there other analogies available to modern scholars? The answer must be that there were: African historical studies grew in the second half of the twentieth century within a scholarly environment which was less and less ignorant about the non-European pasts of the Middle and Far East, South and Southeast Asia and even central America.

The argument begins with an anecdote the details of which are less important than the mind sets it reveals. Fifteen years ago Augustus Casely-Hayford and I were drafting an article on the important but neglected history of Freemasonry in west Africa.[3] In the course of this we needed to contextualise institutions an earlier scholar had called 'fraternities'[4] within a broader spectrum of what west Africanists then called 'voluntary associations'.[5] All of the scholarship we read asserted that voluntary associations had played a vital role in the generation of popular nationalism in the aftermath of the Second World War; however, none of the scholars who were so confident about this link seemed to have bothered to do any serious research on any such association. There was little published evidence of their search for, let alone consultation of, society records, of interviews with society officers, of serious examination of the contemporary press for references to society membership and activities. Nonetheless scholars were happy to claim that, for example, 'each of these little societies was an active nucleus of an anti-chief, anti-colonial movement, quick to acquire new life as a radical commoners' party'[6] or that the work of such societies resembled 'the way that Nonconformist and working-class associations trained the new Labour leadership in nineteenth-century Britain'.[7] The explicit analogy in that second quotation was derived from a set of implicit assumptions which, like most assumptions, were not value free.

Pioneering scholars interested in Africa in the mid-twentieth century were mostly liberal Christian and/or radical-liberal in intellectual orientation. It was not a randomly recruited army of scholars; most shared hostility to colonialism as well as sympathy for Africans. Some, like Thomas Hodgkin, were considerably more radical than liberal.[8] They were convinced that the political developments in west Africa which they were so privileged and excited to witness were a further set of episodes of a romantic and inspiring universal story which had seen the toppling of *anciens régimes*, monarchies and colonial despotisms from Buenos Aires to Beijing, from Caracas to Calcutta. This is not the place to challenge the acuteness of that assumption. But it is the place to raise the historiographical point that the inference was derived from analogy and in turn that analogy was derived from particular, even parochial references. To begin with the analysis is unmistakably British – radical French scholars would almost certainly not have made the same points;[9] the analogy is restricted to the experience of nineteenth-century Britain. It is, for example, clear that, despite his political and personal cosmopolitanism, Hodgkin's conclusions were essentially derived from the work of J. L. and B. Hammond and a cursory content analysis shows that he was especially dependent upon their *Age of the Chartists*. He and other scholars were undoubtedly reading into African phenomena inferences and assumptions about political development which were derived from British urban experience in the early industrial era despite the manifest dissimilarity in cultures and the critical fact that west Africa had not enjoyed – and, as we now know, was not about to enjoy – an industrial revolution of any sort.[10]

The significant point is that this aspect of west African history was not being understood in its own terms but, rather, as similar if not quite identical to processes which had occurred in Bradford or Manchester a full century earlier. This was both understandable and sympathetic; like historians of other eras and other places they had found it hard to explain an important aspect of the political movements they were watching. Without recourse to examples drawn from better-documented processes they could not 'altogether explain how people knew what to do, how the libretto for such an opera was so thoroughly internalized'.[11] Few of us would fail to recognise that there were palpable historical linkages between these processes; few scholars would deny the role of Africa and Africans in the making of modern Bristol or Liverpool, for example. But such links might, rather than constructing identity, have actually emphasised diversity. Accra was not and never would be Manchester, Lagos was not to be Birmingham but the particular use of analogy came close to suggesting that there was more evolutionary similarity than dissimilarity.

The treatment of west African voluntary associations is only one example of the overbearing and, more arguably, distorting force of analogy. The late Geoffrey Elton was surprised[12] when he learnt about the adoption of his celebrated thesis of a

'Tudor revolution in government' in the first extensive elaboration of the development of the administration of the west African forest kingdom of Asante by Ivor Wilks.[13] Wilks was to be taken to task by some reviewers for his uncritical use of the descriptive word 'bureaucratization' for the gradual reform of a pre-literate court in a pre-literate kingdom, a kingdom moreover in which there was to be a profound suspicion of literacy when it actually became a possibility in the early twentieth century.[14] Wilks defended his position in the new edition of his book. 'I do not take seriously comments that in speaking of ... "bureaucratization" in Asante, I am inappropriately importing concepts from a European context .... To speak of "bureaucratization" in Asante is not to imply that the process was identical with that in, say, Prussia, but it to say that comparisons are possible between the two.'[15] Wilks was not alone among historians of Africa in deploying comparative examples in a commendable attempt to help readers to comprehend the African past. Nor is he to blame for the ways in which some of us consciously or unconsciously have transformed comparators into actual descriptions of process. Seeing African history through the prism of other times and other places is a generalised process. Its roots are diffuse and very deep but understanding them is potentially enlightening.

In part those roots obviously grew from the understandably aggressive response to the manifest inferiority complex shared by many pioneer historians of Africa. For many professional historians before the last quarter of the twentieth century, academic history was essentially a matter of the recovery and then the analysis of texts. In some respects the formal assumptions about what was and was not possible for professional historical research had meant that the study of the histories of African peoples was to be narrated in print for decades by historians of empires. Aspiring to be taken seriously in such company, historians who worked upon the pasts of peoples who mostly did not read or write and left few or no literary remains felt forced to be assertive as there were many professional historians who were condescending at best and dismissive at worst about their ambitions. These struggles were not always a matter of somewhat abstracted philosophy but were in some cases matters of concrete competition for scholarly recognition on university validating committees. The Africanist assertion[16] insisted upon the respectability of their project which was, *inter alia*, to be seen as a contribution to world history. Part of the proof of that respectability was the categoric similarity of their case studies to those of what was widely regarded as 'mainstream history'. Thus the reforms of government introduced by Asantehene Osei Kwadwo were to be seen and understood to be *like* those instituted by Henry VII and his successors. The attraction of simile was no passing fashion. In a relatively recent article Ivor Wilks writes that the royal court in Kumase 'became a *manhyiamu*, a parliament in European terms. Thus Asante in the eighteenth century replicated aspects of the mediaeval European experience'.[17] The implicit smoothing over of 'cultural specificity' was a consequence of this strategy. But it was also informed by real sensitivity, by a perception that emphasising what could easily be misunderstood to be 'exotic' or egregiously 'other' ran the risk of distancing African history from other, better-established histories; in addition 'exotic' practice could all too easily be ignorantly read as 'savage' or 'primitive'[18] practice in rather the same way as today 'world music' tends to suggest, however debatably, the 'innateness' of percussion rather than the cerebral order of string quintets and counterpoint.

These positions were not arrived at solely within the confines of universities. It was also an historiographical context which came to early maturity in the midst of widespread anti-colonial agitation in which histories were being energetically recruited to serve to legitimate claims for self-determination; it was understandably not thought to be demeaning to fashion readings of the past which showed that this or that people had been as capable of self-rule as those who had long enjoyed self-rule by commanding institutions very like those of 'older' states. Nationalists and those fascinating expatriate scholars who laudably supported their project felt obliged to portray African institutions as well as African achievements as, at the very least, equal to and hence similar to those of better-known and more obviously esteemed societies and polities. It seemed hard to express admiration for the institutions of these remote others in terms of their local meanings not least because we knew all too little about those meanings and, when we learnt a bit more, those meanings were not merely numerous but often contradictory.[19] And lastly these allusive and evasive narratives fitted in neatly with one of the demands of structural-functional anthropology which played a major part in shaping how historians came to see the pre-colonial past in this part of the world. That demand was firmly specified by the Gold Coast/Ghana's most significant enthnographer, Robert S. Rattray, when he wrote that the essence of his life's work had been 'to trace out how things hang together consistently in a given social system'. [20]

The foregoing is intended to provide one element, a very general element, of a context for the central concern of this paper. The reasons for using extra-African and especially European historical taxonomies are, as we have seen, contingent and complex. The practice appears to have been widespread among the early historians of Africa. But not all such borrowings are the same. I want now to look at the specificity of the ways in which particular elements of the descriptive language of European history have been deployed in the foundational literature on one specific African culture, that of the Akan of Ghana. The use and abuse of the idea of 'bureaucracy' has already been touched upon and it provides me with a useful shoe-horn. As I understand Weber's idea of bureaucracy, the first prerequisite for the generation of any bureaucracy, was the presence of embedded and understood laws and legal rules. This part of this article is dedicated to one troubling question: what explains the salience of the law and legalism which have been such centripetal elements in scholarly attempts to understand the Akan of pre-colonial Ghana? In the process of looking at these two entwined questions, I hope to be able to show that the historiography of southern Ghana/the Gold Coast is *sui generis*, the product of its own particular scholarship and not simply the outcome of more general tendencies. The Akan polities are described in quite particular ways, ways which are strikingly dissimilar from the ways in which other African kingdoms such as those of the Zulu or Baganda were described. Is this particularity simply the product of singularity or is it part a function of the interests and mind-sets of those who pioneered the study of those polities?

Although the presence of anything other than a rather contrived reading of 'bureaucracy' in pre-colonial Asante and other Akan speaking polities is improbable, there is much less point in contesting the existence of legislation, laws and jural custom in the pre-colonial polities in what became southern Ghana. From the point of view of the development of Akan historiography, there is no doubt whatever about the centrality of law and legal institutions to those who from within and without 'native society' observed the area in the nineteenth and early twentieth centuries. Reflections upon African legal systems, on African jurisdiction are notable in British documents dealing with the Gold Coast from the last years of the Company of Merchants in the first quarter of the nineteenth century; and by mid-century such reflections were central to James Stephen's ideas about British policy in west Africa.[21] In this broader context it is very important to stress that this official and informal literature has a time depth which is unusual for tropical Africa. It is no less important to stress that the descriptive and analytical literature, as opposed to the European-dominated travel literature, was initiated by west Africans in the second half of the nineteenth century. What is beyond doubt is their constructive impact upon a century's worth of subsequent scholarly enterprise. It mattered greatly that the professional Africanist scholarship of the second half of the twentieth century was built upon a considerable corpus of knowledge and, even more importantly, ways of understanding that knowledge laid down by two generations of African intellectuals.

Much the most significant of the nineteenth-century ethnographers were John Mensah Sarbah and J. E. Casely-Hayford. Both men were western-educated and extremely well-read coastal west Africans, the scions of Gold Coast merchant families.[22] Both had eventually studied in London and both had been called to the Bar, a matter which was undoubtedly of considerable significance.[23] Both produced sophisticated, scholarly studies of African society; and both regarded law and legal procedure as the organising principles of Akan society and used law as a way of explaining its nature. Nationalists *avant le lettre*, both Mensah Sarbah and Casely-Hayford were naturally eager to underline the un-recognised or at least under-recognised claims of Africans to racial equality; and a significant aspect of that cluster of claims was the clear evidence they produced that the Africans about whom they wrote were not 'lesser breeds' because they were most assuredly not 'without the law'. Law, they argued, was central to the nature of these societies and their members; it set out what they, institutions as well as individuals, could and could not do, provided guarantees of liberty alongside the constraint of anti-social selfishness and applied to all.

Appropriately these bodies of law were not portrayed as being intrinsic and static but, rather, the outcome of evolution. That process began with 'usage', wrote Sarbah, 'which developing into custom, becomes apparently crystallized and merged into native law'.[24] Custom, it seems, became law and law is implicitly seen as being somehow a higher form of custom. And, continuing with the theme of analogy, Sarbah defined custom as being something 'to which the memory of man runneth not to the contrary'.[25] Understandably, part of Sarbah's intention was to demonstrate the gravity, the dignity of 'native law' and to help 'the newly arrived European' see the error of his ways if he were to say 'that there were no customary laws'.[26]

Sarbah is less of an evolutionist and is less convincing in his insistence upon the unchanging nature of native law. Taking the recorded observations of W. A. Bosman[27] as his datum, Sarbah wrote that '[c]ustomary law and other usages ... have not altered to any extent up to the present day'. Now this is a pretty startling claim about immutability over a time-scale of nearly 300 years. While one can readily understand his motivations in making such a case, we can see (as he could not) that such arguments fitted in all too neatly with the multi-purpose western tool-kit which built the myths of 'historyless people'.

Casely-Hayford's *Gold Coast Native Institutions*[28] was also much taken up with the central significance of law; and he was no less excited by analogy. 'The King', he wrote, 'is the Chief Magistrate of the community and ... there are minor courts .... You have first the Courts of Headmen, the Chiefs' courts and finally the King's court which is both a court of first instance and a court of appeal.'[29] The stress upon system, on routine, and its fundamental similarity to the British system which he knew so well is notable. Casely-Hayford even sought by the invocation of western science to rationalise what to us might seem to be both unscientific and irrational.

> Where there is a strong conflict of evidence and the Court is unable to arrive at a decision, the ordeal is resorted to, which consists of drinking a large quantity of a herbal preparation ... if [he] returns the stuff he is declared free ... If he retains the Edum[30] he is found guilty .... I have heard this explained on physiological grounds as being highly scientific.[31]

The author fails to point out that Odom is a poison and, if the accused failed to vomit, his eventual death was frequently forestalled by public decapitation.

This is a literature which insists that membership of 'the tribe' implied undeviating acceptance of a necessarily singular and normative 'native law'. In some respects their position was not far removed from that of the appalling E. Sidney Hartland who insisted that 'the primitive African' (and in such pejorative texts it is always '*the* African' rather than 'Africans') 'accepts it [the corpus of law] as a whole, a unity, the thought of analysing which has never entered his head'.[32] Disregarding the absence of class and gender as well as individualism in such essentialist accounts, what is of much greater importance is the marginalisation of the role of power and, more prosaically, the mechanics of learning about, transcription of and practical use of 'native law'. At the same time an empathetic reading allows us readily to understand why sensitive African scholars, justly enraged by the arrogance as well as the ignorance of racialism, should wish to emphasise that, well before the advent of Europeans, Africans were in full possession of what was so frequently presented as the absolute proof of civilisation, and the organising principle of empire, the rule of law. Just as *Pax Brittanica* was so frequently presented as the heir to *Pax Romana*, African scholar-lawyers in the nineteenth century were also to draw upon Justinian and Clarendon in making specific and manifestly political cases.

Matters, however, were not to stop there. While Sarbah and Casely-Hayford may have been dissimilar in many respects, they, and others, provided a rough template, a frame within which Akan society was to be set by many subsequent scholars and administrators.

Evolving colonial authority began to mirror African ideology. To put it briefly and crudely, the initial expansive ambitions of colonial officials had been stymied by a dearth of revenue. For largely economic reasons, administration and the tasks of maintaining law and order, labour supplies and what might loosely be called 'development' would henceforth be carried out by 'traditional authorities', the successors of the old kingdoms and chieftaincies of the pre-colonial era. For this to be presented as legitimate rather than paradoxical required a rapid makeover; these organs had, after all, long been stigmatised as barbaric, portrayed as being in large measure responsible for the continuation of slavery, judicial kidnapping and human sacrifice. Expunging these phenomena, held to be repugnant and alien to natural justice, had been a loudly proclaimed rationale for colonial annexation in west Africa. Now these institutions which had been regarded in the past as closely related to the forces of darkness were to become the new allies. That legitimation involved the recognition of customary law and customary tribunals as full players in everyday life. One of Casely-Hayford's demands in his Gold Coast native institutions reads: '[You must] give full sway to the working of the Native State System by candidly recognising the authority of the Kings and Chiefs, strengthening their influence and working through them.'[33] In many respects this was exactly what was now to happen. That development required from its beginnings that the colonial authorities took native law seriously.

The drift is apparent not merely in legislation but also in mood. And it began quite early; for example, Sir James Marshall, the first puisne judge of the Gold Coast's Supreme Court said[34] that customary law was based upon 'ideas, equally ancient and equally deep rooted which permeate the native mind ... a system of laws and customs'. Such ideas were very different from those to be found in, for example, the *Report of the Select Committee on West Africa of 1842*.[35] In a short time published authorities like Sarbah and Casely-Hayford were to loom large in the ongoing task of discovering what was – and as importantly what was not – 'native law' and the earnest transcription of the results.[36] And, as the process progressed, a handful of western-educated chiefs, most notably Nana Sir Ofori Atta,[37] were to be looked upon by the colonial authorities as the authentic authorities on, and arbiters of, native law. Colonial authority's tendency to rely upon towering, articulate chiefly figures was not just a vice of those who governed the Gold Coast; in Fiji and Uganda, for example, one can see Sir Lala Sukuna[38] and Sir Apollo Kaggwa[39] playing similar roles. This reliance upon the legal authority of traditional rulers was to lead, ironically, to the political alienation of precisely the class of which Sarbah and Casely-Hayford were such interesting exemplars. They, like most nationalists, were committed modernisers and democrats. For the most part 'chiefs and kings' were almost inevitably traditionalists but even more importantly they were to exploit every chance to extend their jurisdiction, power and wealth, 'to command service, obedience and respect' as R. S. Rattray was to put it,[40] under the protection of the colonial state. Their views on what was and what was not 'customary law' were intimately related to their own well-honed sense of personal advantage. But in some senses their 'take' on customary law conformed rather well to harsh reality.

The historical record neither confirms nor denies any suggestion that there had indeed been a good deal of localised, tacit social agreement about the kinds of issues of everyday life covered, for example, in *Leviticus* in the deeper past. But before the colonial period issues like succession, inheritance, taxation, land-tenure – the brutal matters of politics – seem more frequently to have been governed by the sequential making and unmaking of laws by the owners of the means of coercion, most notably chiefs. This unsurprising dictatorial tendency was naturally facilitated by the lack of written legal records. As in most parts of the lost world of *anciens régimes*, those monarchs who were strong enough to do so went on to legitimate their actions by an insistence upon their legality; and they were strong enough, frightening enough to encourage other people to assent. Among the Akan, the entourages of chiefs had always included executioners and the exercise of chiefly power ultimately rested upon the threat and reality of frequent life-taking; at specific moments in the histories of southern Ghanaian pre-colonial states, these executioners were very busy men.[41] For weaker rulers, challenges to such claims emerged and when counter-claimants were powerful enough, alternative versions of legality could prevail. In such circumstances it is unsurprising that many laws came in multiple and sometimes contrary versions over time, a matter that is abundantly evident in the wonderful court records of colonial and post-colonial Ghana. But laws were now to be codified and through the colonial period it was the versions sanctified by trusted monarchs that came to be transcribed and then embodied in what was now to be written customary law. Those versions were now deodorised, shorn of the aspects of customary law that colonial law officers had deemed to be repugnant, most especially those involving torture and life-taking, although, rather surprisingly, trial by ordeal survived this purge. The process of taming customary law and its codification produced a rickety structure which in part survives today. But it cannot, and more importantly should not be read back into the pre-colonial period.

The close relationship between law, administration and ethnography was nicely to be brought out by another lawyer-scholar. A Scot rather than an African, R. S. Rattray was the Gold Coast government's first official government anthropologist. Originally a linguist and folklorist, Rattray had eventually trained in anthropology in Oxford.[42] Like many other scholars who became enchanted by Asante, he became both an enthusiast for traditional government and a romantic who was deeply suspicious of innovation. Significantly for my argument about the role of law in the scholarly construction of the Akan, he was also a qualified but non-practising barrister. The fusion of these roles and ideas is immediately apparent in the preface to his fascinating *Ashanti Law and Constitution*.[43] There he insisted that 'a knowledge of Akan-Ashanti law is of paramount importance to the local Administration, engaged as it is in framing "Native Jurisdiction Ordinances", in schemes for the working of "Native Tribunals", and in plans for "Indirect Rule"'.[44]

Rattray was a complex man whose intellectual, administrative and personal lives were tempestuous and fascinating.[45] His premature death in a gliding accident caught something of his life-long propensity for drama. His enduring significance lies in his early detailed work on the Akan.[46] Along with Sarbah and Casely-Hayford his works have gradually evolved to become primary sources and they are very frequently cited in modern law courts in the course of the internecine legal wrangles which still ensnare

Ghanaians, as well as in the work of modern historians and anthropologists. Like his African predecessors, Rattray was an habitual analogist. For example in his influential studies of land tenure and land alienation he claims that the Asante system was 'parallel to feudalism'.[47] His authority on feudalism was Sir Henry Maine's *Ancient Law*. Like Maine, Rattray seems to regard feudalism as a period, a developmental stage. Although I make no claim to expertise in mediaeval history, I can discern virtually nothing in the recovered history of the Akan which suggests anything even remotely like any variant of feudalism about which I have read; but his *aperçus* were eagerly seized upon by the handful of Soviet historians of pre-colonial Africa. Although Ivor Wilks, following the earlier arguments of J. B. Danquah, was to drive a persuasive coach and horses through Rattray's claim,[48] there are innumerable other examples of analogy; but let us hang on to one of his most important assertions, that which is embedded in his book's title. That insisted that the Asante state had a constitution.[49] Rattray, following his legally trained predecessors, portrayed Akan states largely in terms of their legal structures, processes and procedures. Although his notion of constitution is largely confined to a static description of institutions and their functions, he certainly implies that Asante was ideally governed by an agreed body of laws maintained by regular procedures. Of course these laws and routines could be defied but there was, he argued, something palpably there to be defied, something recognisable by the reasonable man to be a constitution. This was not an invention of Rattray's; a couple of decades earlier J. E. Casely-Hayford had suggested that his book *Gold Coast Native Institutions* would be: 'useful to the aborigines anxious to know the constitutional history of their country'.[50] And this tradition was carried into the modern era by the greatest intellectual of twentieth-century Ghana, Dr J. B. Danquah. At the risk of being repetitious, Danquah like Mensah Sarbah, Casely-Hayford and Rattray, was a barrister.[51] Unlike them, he was a member of a royal family, half-brother to the most authoritative of chiefs in the colonial period, Nana Sir Ofori Atta. Danquah's celebrated study, *Akan Laws and Customs*, bears the immediately suggestive sub-title 'and the Akim Abuakwa Constitution'.[52] His very interesting if less well-known *Akim Abuakwa Handbook*[53] also devotes an entire section to that state's 'constitution'. There is nothing archaic about this descriptive language; it is still very much alive. Nana Arhin Brempong (Professor Kwame Arhin), in a relatively recent and largely historical piece on 'the nature of Akan government', takes only three pages before coming up with a sub-heading which reads 'Constitution'.[54]

The burden of the argument is that this sequence of scholars, each of them with their own discernible and understandable agenda, collectively if unconsciously constructed, for lack of a better phrase, an enduring intellectual climate. It was a very particular intellectual climate which led to a snowballing and particular perception of the Akan. That perception appears to be *sui generis*. It differs considerably from historical understandings of, for example, the Yoruba, the Zulu or the Manding. It is a vision of a set of histories of states in which those polities are essentially seen in terms of their supposed 'laws and constitutions' neither of which is, or probably could be, historicised. The idea of constitution which was being articulated by west African intellectuals from the late nineteenth century was not historically an Akan idea. It was, after all, a relatively modern British construction elaborated in the century after 1689.

Among other things the idea of constitution was usefully suggestive of the systematic and a deal of subsequent historical scholarship has sought evidential support for the systemic because its authors implicitly believed that system and civilisation were synonymous. The treatment of, for example, the frequent 'destoolments' in most Akan polities, the graceless term for the relatively frequent removal of kings, has often tried to routinise usurpations and *coups d'état* (some of which were notably violent) as evidence of something like traditional democracy. The notion of sensitive, accountable *anciens régimes*, the invocation of a pre-colonial golden age, was an appealing one for those opposed to the decidedly un-democratic, unaccountable and externally imposed colonial regimes, but it does not chime in with what we know of that past. It is true that one can hunt for apparently supportive evidence in what Wilks calls 'the unwritten history' of the Akan. The problem with that concept, however, is that the 'unwritten' has undoubtedly been shaped by the written accounts, which, as we have seen, have been available and, more importantly, have been extensively used in legal and political skirmishing for well over a century.[55] More significantly, closer study of conflict within these kingdoms provokes two conclusions. First, even if one succumbs to the notion of a discernible legal system, the evidence suggests very strongly indeed that there were numerous versions of what or was not 'the system'. The fact that the colonial state and its successors endorsed the version favoured by those who were momentarily hegemonic should not confer upon that version any sense of its orthodoxy, its 'authenticity' or its 'correctness' through time; that is the only possible conclusion to be drawn from close study of court cases in the twentieth century. Even more subversively perhaps, a great deal of the closely researched contingent history of the Akan summons up a world in which the frequently arbitrary exercise of power governed the lives of ordinary people.[56] These were authoritarian states, often very authoritarian states in which defiance of chieftaincy risked painful punishment and lingering deaths.

We can explain and even historicise the evocation of European exemplars and analogies; my concern here has been to emphasise the deep African roots as well as the imperial provenance of those ways of seeing. But that helps us not at all to understand the Akan, their cultures, their states and their histories. Historians might find many of these analogies ahistorical and unreflective. Much more importantly it is not helpful to regard the Akan and their institutions as being 'like' other peoples and their institutions; to do so is to ignore their meanings. And, as damagingly, it diverts us from a recognition that, in Ernest Gellner's words, 'The difference between the agrarian religious world and the industrial scientific one has always been absolutely central to understanding the world'.[57]

Notes

[1] This is a fair description of the relationship in the 1960s between the predecessors of Andrew Porter and myself at King's College London and the School of Oriental and African Studies respectively, the formidable Professors Gerald Graham and Roland Oliver.
[2] A point John Parker and I elaborate upon in our *African History: A Very Short Introduction*.

[3] It appeared in Ade Ajayi and Peel, *People and Empires*.
[4] See Acquah's *Accra Survey*.
[5] This was long before the widespread scholarly use – and misuse – of the idea of 'civil society'.
[6] Austin, *Politics in Ghana*, 26–27.
[7] Hodgkin. *Nationalism in Colonial Africa*, 84–85.
[8] See his biography, *Thomas Hodgkin* by Michael Wolfers.
[9] The limited amount of contemporary radical literature in French seems to suggest that they placed much more emphasis upon labour solidarity and ideology rather than upon the role of churches for example.
[10] Ivor Wilks might, however, disagree. He writes of southern Ghana: 'So, too one may refer to an "industrial revolution" if by that...is meant...the rapid expansion of gold production.' *Forests of Gold*, 95.
[11] Patrick Collinson, *The Reformation*, 140
[12] And considerably dismayed.
[13] Wilks, *Asante*. Wilks somewhat complicates matters by extending the cross-reference when he writes on p. 468 that the '"revolution in government" [is] a bureaucratic one' and footnotes both Weber and Gerth and Mills to support the point.
[14] See, for example, Lucy Mair's review in *Times Literary Supplement*, 4 July 1978.
[15] Wilks, *Asante*.
[16] And it goes without saying that we are all deeply indebted to those who made this case so powerfully.
[17] Wilks, '"Unity and Progress"', 45.
[18] An ambiguous word widely used to disparage as well as to connote *pre-modernity* by respectable scholars. In 1956 the BBC 3rd Programme commissioned a series of broadcast talks under the title of *The Institutions of Primitive Society* and the speakers included E .E. Evans-Pritchard, Raymond Firth, Edmund Leach, Max Gluckman and Meyer Fortes.
[19] Ignorance of African languages remains a serious barrier to comprehension of African pasts.
[20] The emphasis is mine. For more on Rattray, see Rathbone, 'Rattray, Robert Sutherland', and Allman and Parker's recent *Tongnaab*.
[21] Decades of much discussed conflict between the legal systems practised within the environments of the coastal forts and those of the African states which surrounded them were part and parcel of the mess that was the context of eventual British annexation in 1874.
[22] Roger Gocking provides a very helpful background to their communities in his *Facing Both Ways*. See also Edsman, *Lawyers in Gold Coast Politics*.
[23] Sarbah read for the Bar at Lincoln's Inn and was called to the Bar in 1887 aged only 23 which made him the youngest west African to qualify at that time. Casely-Hayford was an Inner Temple man and was called in 1896.
[24] Sarbah, *Fanti Customary Law*, 25.
[25] The derivation of this particular idea becomes clearer when he writes that 'time immemorial' dates from the return of Richard I from the Crusade.
[26] Ibid., vi.
[27] Bosman, *A New and Accurate Description of the Coast of Guinea*.
[28] The title continues 'with thoughts upon a healthy imperial policy for the Gold Coast and Ashanti'.
[29] *Gold Coast Native Institutions*, 93.
[30] Current orthography would call this *Odom*.
[31] Ibid., 94.
[32] Hartland, *Primitive Law*, 9.
[33] *Gold Coast Native Institutions*, 114.
[34] During an address to the Colonial Exhibition in London in 1886.
[35] Which talked, for example, about 'the arbitrary decision of native chiefs' and '"the wild justice" of private revenge'.

[36] And thus fatally ensuring that a conservative inflexibility was henceforth to constrain what was presumably once a more dynamic process.
[37] For more on him, see Rathbone, *Murder and Politics in Colonial Ghana*.
[38] For more on him, see Nayacakalou, *Leadership in Fiji*. On the general point, see Newbury's admirable *Patrons, Clients and Empire*.
[39] See Low and Pratt, *Buganda and British Overrule*.
[40] Rattray, *Ashanti Law and Constitution*, xii.
[41] See, for example, McCaskie, 'Death and the Asantehene'.
[42] Where he studied with R .R. Marett (1866–1943).
[43] Oxford, 1929. The Negro Universities Press edition of 1969 unaccountably dates the first edition to 1911.
[44] *Ashanti Law and Constitution*, v.
[45] The late R. S. Machin's unpublished biography of Rattray is available electronically at http://lucy.ukc.ac.uk/MACHIN/machin_toc.html.
[46] A good account of some of this is to be found in McCaskie, 'R. S. Rattray'.
[47] In his major work *Ashanti* and in *Ashanti Law and Constitution*.
[48] See his *Forests of Gold*, 92–95. Wilks, however, begins the book in which this demolition is undertaken by writing about '[o]ld systems [in Africa] not unlike the feudalisms of mediaeval Europe'.
[49] Ibid., 1.
[50] xiii.
[51] He studied in the Inner Temple and was called in 1922.
[52] Akim Abuakwa was a large Akan state lying to the south of the better known Asante. In the text this structure includes, written in upper case, an Executive Council, a Court of Appeal and an Assembly. Danquah, *Akan Law and Customs*, 10–11.
[53] Which was also published in London: Foster, Groom, 1928.
[54] Arhin, 'Nature of Akan Government', 72.
[55] Well-thumbed copies of all the works mentioned here and others are commonly found on the shelves of the palaces of Akan chiefs to this day.
[56] This is brought out powerfully in Boni's excellent *Le strutture della disuguaglianza*.
[57] Davis, 1.

References

Acquah, Ione. *Accra Survey*. London: University of London Press, 1958.
Ajayi, J. F. Ade, and J. D. Y. Peel , eds. *People and Empires in African History: Essays in Memory of Michael Crowder*. Harlow: Longman.
Allman, Jean and John Parker. *Tongnaab: The History of a West African God*. Bloomington, IN: Indiana University Press, 2005.
Arhin, Kwame. 'The Nature of Akan Government'. In *Mondes Akan: Identité et pouvoir en Afrique occidentale*. edited by P. Valsecchi and F. Viti. Paris: L'Harmattan, 1999.
Austin, Dennis. *Politics in Ghana, 1946–1960*. Oxford: Oxford University Press, 1964.
Boni, Stefano. *Le strutture della disuguaglianza: Capi, appartenenze e gerarchie nel mondo Akan dell'Africa occidentale*. Milan: FrancoAngeli, 2003.
Bosman, W. A. *A New and Accurate Description of the Coast of Guinea*. London, 1705.
Casely-Hayford, J. E. *Gold Coast Native Institutions with Thoughts upon a Healthy Imperial Policy for the Gold Coast and Ashanti*. London: Sweet & Maxwell, 1903.
Collinson, Patrick. *The Reformation*. New York: Random House, 2003.
Danquah, J. B. *Akan Laws and Customs and the Akim Abuakwa Constitution*. London: Routledge, 1928.
———. *Akim Abuakwa Handbook*. London: Foster Groom, 1928.

Davis, John. Interview with Ernest Gellner *Current Anthropology* 32, no.1 (1991).
Edsman, Björn. *Lawyers in Gold Coast Politics, c.1900–1945; From Mensah Sarbah to J. B. Danquah.* Uppsala: Acta Universitatis Upsaliensis, 1979.
Gocking, Roger. *Facing Both Ways: Ghana's Coastal Communities under Colonial Rule.* Lanham, MD: University Press of America, 1999.
Hartland, E. Sidney *Primitive Law.* London: Kennikat Press, 1924.
Hodgkin, Thomas. *Nationalism in Colonial Africa.* London: Muller, 1956.
Low, Donald and C. R. Pratt. *Buganda and British Overrule, 1900–1955: Two Studies.* Oxford: Oxford University Press, 1960.
Machin, R. S. unpublished biography of Rattray. Available at http://lucy.ukc.ac.uk/MACHIN/machin_toc.html.
McCaskie, T. C. 'R. S. Rattray and the Construction of Asante History: An Appraisal'. *History in Africa* 10 (1983): 187–206.
———. 'Death and the Asantehene: A Historical Meditation'. *The Journal of African History* 30 (1989): 417–44.
Nayacakalou, R. R. *Leadership in Fiji.* Melbourne: Oxford University Press, 1975.
Newbury, Colin. *Patrons, Clients and Empire: Chieftaincy and Over-Rule in Asia, Africa and the Pacific.* Oxford: Oxford University Press, 2003.
Parker, John and Richard Rathbone. *African History: A Very Short Introduction.* Oxford: Oxford University Press, 2007.
Rathbone, Richard. *Murder and Politics in Colonial Ghana.* New Haven, CT: Yale University Press, 1993.
———. 'Rattray, Robert Sutherland (1881–1938)'. *Oxford Dictionary of National Biography.* Oxford: Oxford University Press, 2004, online edn, May 2006. Available at http://www.oxforddnb.com/view/article/40722.
Rathbone, Richard and Augustus Casely-Hayford. 'People, Families and Free-Masonry in Colonial Gold Coast'. In *People and Empires in African History: Essays in Honour of the Late Michael Crowder.* edited by J. F. A. Ade Ajayi and John Peel. Harlow: Longman, 1992.
Rattray, R. S. *Ashanti Law and Constitution.* London: Constable, 1911.
———. *Ashanti.* London: Oxford University Press, 1923.
Sarbah, J. M. *Fanti Customary Law: A Brief Introduction to the Principles of the Native Laws and Customs of the Fanti and Akan Sections of the Gold Coast with a Selection of Cases thereon Decided in the Law Courts.* London: W. Clowes, 1897.
Wilks, Ivor. *Asante in the Nineteenth Century.* Cambridge: Cambridge University Press, 1975.
———. *Forests of Gold: Essays on the Akan and the Kingdom of Asante.* Athens, OH: Ohio University Press, 1993.
———. '"Unity and Progress": Asante Politics Revisited'. In *Mondes Akan: Identité et pouvoir en Afrique occidentale*, edited by P. Valsecchi and F. Viti. Paris: L'Harmattan, 1999.
Wolfers, Michael. *Thomas Hodgkin: Wandering Scholar.* Monmouth: Merlin Press, 2007.

Leaders, Dissidents and the Disappointed: Colonial Students in Britain as Empire Ended

A. J. Stockwell

Andrew Porter has called the British Empire 'the world's greatest-ever educational enterprise'.[1] This is not to suggest that educational provision was monolithic in design, or a government priority, or even that it naturally contributed to imperial solidarity. On the contrary, the British government harboured misgivings about the misfits which the promotion of education might produce and, until the Second World War, its approach was generally pragmatic, cheese-paring and cautious. As often as not, it left education to settlers, missionaries and philanthropists. Like so much else in the empire, educational development was rarely systematic; it was rather the product of interaction between official and non-official bodies, between metropolitan organisations and local interests, between western ideas and indigenous cultures. It reflected as much the diversity of empire as any sentiment of common purpose and, as colonial peoples selected those features of British learning best suited to their needs, they challenged the imperial order and exposed its fragility.[2]

Institutions of higher education in colonies of settlement shadowed developments at home. Harvard, William and Mary, Princeton, Yale, Brown, Rutgers and Dartmouth were all founded before 1776. McGill University in Montreal (1821) and Cape Town's South African College (1829) were near contemporaries of London's University College (1826) and King's College (1829). Sydney (1850), Melbourne (1852) and Otago (1869) coincided with the launch of the Victorian civic universities such as Manchester (1851) and Newcastle (1852). Overseas institutions reflected different British types but the influence of London University predominated in India where universities were set up in Calcutta, Bombay and Madras in 1857. By contrast, only four universities had been founded in the other non-European territories of the empire before the Second World War: Malta, Jerusalem, Ceylon and Hong Kong. Although it was expected that institutions of lesser status would evolve into universities, this was constrained by prevailing attitudes to non-European peoples, lack of resources, the dearth of English-medium secondary schools and experience in India where, it was held, universities had produced numerous overqualified, unemployable, politically ambitious and intractable young men.[3] When Lord Hailey was asked in July 1939 what he would do 'if he were educational dictator of the Empire', he replied that he would continue on 'present lines', promoting popular, vernacular education. It would not be possible, he argued, to frame a coherent policy for higher education until the government had decided 'what it was going to do with the educated product'.[4]

I

In the absence of a university in his own country, a colonial student might pursue higher education elsewhere, principally in Britain, if he had private means or a government scholarship. From 1901 colonial scholars in Britain were charges of the director of scholars, one of the crown agents who disbursed funds allocated by colonial governments, monitored students' academic progress and supervised their pastoral care. These tasks involved liaison with colonial administrations, university authorities, voluntary organisations and student associations. A leading voluntary body was the Victoria League which promoted closer union between British subjects throughout the world and took an interest in the welfare of students in the United Kingdom, particularly those from Malaya.[5] The most influential student organisation was the West Africa Students' Union (WASU) which was founded in 1925 by Herbert Bankole-Bright (Sierra Leone) and Ladpido Solanke (Nigeria). WASU became the centre for the social, cultural and political activities of west African students. In 1930 Hanns Vischer (joint secretary of the secretary of state's Advisory Committee on Education) mounted a campaign to establish a London club for African students. In spite of the economic depression and WASU's decision to set up its own hostel in Camden, the project went ahead and Aggrey House opened in Doughty Street in 1934.[6] Retired colonial administrators acted as student guardians. Home stays with caring families – country parsonages provided reliable billets – eased the transition into British society. When the future prime minister of independent Malaya, Tunku Abdul

Rahman, came to England in 1920 he was placed with half-a-dozen other students in the care of the Reverend Edgar A. Vigers of Little Stukeley, where he was groomed for entry to St Catharine's College, Cambridge.[7]

Piloting princes occasionally hit the rocks of love and marriage. In the spring of 1940 Tengku Indra Petra (the son of the Raja of Kelantan and nephew of the sultan) contracted a secret marriage on the eve of his return to Malaya. The Tengku's guardian, J. R. Innes, identified the bride as 'a Bournemouth girl belonging to the small shopkeeper class', 'an impudent adventurous' and 'an unscrupulous and headstrong young woman'. It was, he wrote, 'an act of amazing folly' because Kelantan law required princes to marry Muslims.[8] Colonial Office officials found a way round this particular impasse but drew a general moral from such 'recurring incidents': Malay princes 'had best be educated in Malaya' while Malay girls should also be educated 'so that there may be an adequate supply of eligible wives for the better educated young men'.[9] Such disappointments are the stuff of colonial literature: the fate of Hari Kumar (anglicised to Harry Coomer) in Paul Scott's *The Raj Quartet* or of Raja Muhammad Saleh (anglicised to Sally) in a two-part fable by the Malayan administrator Hugh Clifford. The warm welcome which Saleh received from his hosts froze as his love for an English girl went unrequited. 'Unfitted by training to be a Raja, unfitted by nature to be an Englishman', he returned to his father's court, drifted into rebellion and was killed running amok. The political officer responsible for this educational experiment concluded sorrowfully: 'May God forgive us for our sorry deeds and for our glorious intentions.'[10]

Even those who thrived in the inclusive liberalism of British universities, as did Eric Williams at Oxford, or Tunku Abdul Rahman at Cambridge, or Jomo Kenyatta at the London School of Economics, ran into racialism. Williams was convinced that it 'disposed of' him in the competition for an All Souls Fellowship.[11] Slights and injustice fomented resentment. As the governor of Nigeria observed in 1937, 'The harm that can be done, on his return to his own country, by one African student who has managed to accumulate a store of real or fancied grievances during his stay in England far outweighs the good done by a dozen students who come back successful and satisfied.'[12] Whether or not the experience of higher education in Britain was pleasant, however, it was limited to a small number before the Second World War. In the 1930s there were in any year between 5,000 and 6,000 overseas students of whom 400 to 500 came from the colonial empire compared with a rough average of 1,400 from India.[13]

The Second World War marooned many students in Britain. When their studies ended some found employment, as did Mohamed Suffian bin Hashim (later Lord President of the Malaysian judiciary) who became head of the Malay section of both the BBC and All India Radio.[14] Falling on hard times, WASU received assistance from the welfare committee of the Anti-Slavery Society and the Dean of Westminster's Appeal Fund before the decision was taken in 1944 to stabilise its finances by making it a limited company with Lord Listowel as chairman of trustees.[15] The war revealed flaws in the mechanisms for handling student needs and those of Britain's wider colonial community, which expanded as munitions workers, foresters and servicemen arrived in Britain from Africa, the West Indies and other parts of the empire. The Colonial Office now assumed responsibility for colonial residents in the United Kingdom. In May 1941 the director of scholars was transferred from the Crown Agents to the Colonial Office where he led the new welfare branch of the social services department. As welfare officer, he was to look after the interests of colonial students, colonial seamen and race questions generally. Such was the growth of its business, particularly following the arrival in Britain of Caribbean RAF volunteers, that the welfare branch was upgraded to a Colonial Office department in 1943.[16] The new director of scholars and welfare officer was John L. Keith who had served in Northern Rhodesia from 1919 to 1937 when he had been seconded to Chatham House to assist Lord Hailey in the research for *An African Survey* (1938). Keith's deputy was Ivor Cummings. The son of a doctor from Sierra Leone and an English nurse, Cummings had been born and brought up in England, worked for a time for the United Africa Company in Freetown and later as warden of Aggrey House.[17] Another wartime initiative was the Advisory Committee on the Welfare of Colonial Peoples in the United Kingdom. Appointed by Lord Cranborne in September 1942, it was intended to ensure that the new concept of partnership was 'a fact and not a phrase' and that colonial visitors would in due course return to their own lands 'with an abiding impression of the tolerance, seemliness, and good will of the English way of life'.[18] To this end the Colonial Office courted WASU, which joined a number of MPs, including progressives such as Arthur Creech Jones, Haden Guest and Reginald Sorensen, in forming the West Africa Parliamentary Committee. The parliamentary under-secretary, Harold Macmillan, visited WASU twice in 1942 to discuss west African problems and on another occasion Clement Attlee addressed its members on the implications of the Atlantic Charter.

At the same time dramatic measures were being planned for the post-war expansion of higher education in the colonies. When in July 1943 Oliver Stanley vowed 'to guide Colonial people along the road to self-government within the framework of the British Empire', he committed government 'to build up their social and economic institutions', not least universities which would be essential 'if our goal of Colonial self-government is to be achieved'.[19] He launched a comprehensive review of higher education comprising a commission chaired by Sir Cyril Asquith and subsidiary enquiries on west Africa and the West Indies. Another on Malaya followed a few years later.[20] Together they recommended the early establishment of universities or university colleges in 'special relationship' with London University. Resources for this ambitious project were found from Colonial Development and Welfare funds and within a few years university colleges were set up in the West Indies, the Gold Coast, Ibadan and Makerere, while an autonomous university opened in Singapore.

II

It was expected that the flow of students coming to Britain would be stemmed once colonial universities launched their teaching programmes.[21] This did not happen. Although the statistics are not exact, they do indicate a remarkable and sustained influx. Precise figures were kept for those on government scholarships but information on private students – those who funded themselves and came under their own steam – was far less accurate. By 1954 'privates' were said to outnumber official scholars three to one. Some counts included those in further and technical education and also trainee nurses and teachers. In approximate terms the total, which had remained pretty constant during the 1930s, rose from 500 in 1939 to 1,000 by May 1946, to 3,000 by July 1947, to 5,000 by 1951. In 1949 colonial students in the United Kingdom overtook those from the Indian sub-continent (3,500 compared with 3,450). By the start of 1955 the figure had advanced to 10,000 which marked a twenty-fold increase since 1939 and represented perhaps 10 per cent of the entire coloured colonial population of Britain. By 1959–60 the total had reached 29,000.[22]

There are many reasons for the expanding numbers: a back-log of candidates had accumulated since 1939; the horizons of a new generation had been enlarged by world war; post-war development plans required a trained workforce; funding was now forthcoming from Colonial Development and Welfare and other sources; the capacity of infant colonial universities could not keep pace with the demand for higher education; friends and relatives had gone before; British subjects and British-protected persons had the right to come to the United Kingdom. In the immediate post-war years the largest contingents were from the West Indies and west Africa. The West Indian student body grew from 166 in 1939 to 1,114 by 1950. Special scholarships were awarded to ex-servicemen, like Roy Augier from St Lucia, who became a pioneering historian of the Caribbean and pro vice-chancellor of the University of the West Indies. Another holder of an ex-serviceman's scholarship was Michael Manley, son of Norman, who was taught by Harold Laski and Arthur Lewis at the London School of Economics and became prime minister of Jamaica in the 1970s. The west African total increased from seventy in 1939 to over 700 in 1947 to more than 2,000 in 1950, or 43 per cent of colonial students in the United Kingdom. Whereas in 1947 the sixty Malayan students felt overshadowed by Africans and West Indians and neglected by the Colonial Office, their position was rapidly transformed by Malaya's booming economy and job opportunities. By 1953 the number of Malayans had risen to 1,200, compared with about 1,700 Nigerians and 750 from the Gold Coast.[23]

Colonial students registered at institutions across the United Kingdom. There were significant contingents in Manchester, Liverpool, Birmingham, Nottingham, Edinburgh, Glasgow, St Andrews and Aberdeen.[24] Approximately half the total at any time was in London on account of its allure as imperial capital as well as the range and reputation of its colleges and courses. At the end of the 1950s and before the post-Robbins expansion of higher education in the United Kingdom, colonial students on average accounted for 5.7 per cent of a university's student body. In London University as many as 2,881 or 11.5 per cent originated from the colonies or new Commonwealth. Courses in medicine, engineering and especially law were in great demand. The number of students from the colonies studying law in the United Kingdom rose from eighty-two in 1943 to over 600 in 1949, to 1,451 by the end of 1954. In 1951–52 it was reckoned that 827 colonial students had enrolled for law in

London alone.[25] Nevertheless, students who arrived without the guarantee of a place risked disappointment, especially in the late 1940s when 90 per cent of university places were reserved for ex-servicemen. Private students of few means were especially vulnerable but might remain unknown to the authorities until they got 'into trouble by running out of money or in other ways'.[26] Whether they were official scholars or indigent 'privates', however, overseas students were exposed, as the secretary of state noted, to 'new and often disturbing' social and political conditions which were 'bound to exercise an influence on them for good or ill'.[27]

It was not until the mid-1950s that systematic surveys of the experiences of colonial students were produced.[28] They revealed ignorance and prejudice across British society and charted the disillusionment of Britain's 'disappointed guests'.[29] Be it overt or sly, discrimination occurred at work and at play, and ranged from a 'colour tax' (surcharge on rentals) to outrage over mixed marriages. Years after his own student days in the Britain of the 1930s, Eric Williams (the first prime minister of independent Trinidad) contended that the University College of the West Indies had been founded 'in order to prevent West Indians going to England and associating with white women'.[30] In fact, there were numerous marriages of colonial students with British women. One of the most felicitous was that between the Ghanaian Joseph Appiah and Peggy Cripps (daughter of Stafford); while it caused a predictable flutter in the press, Appiah claimed to have experienced no racial prejudice in Britain.[31] A mixed marriage did not incur official opprobrium unless, as in the case of the prince of Kelantan in 1940, it was judged to contravene custom or jeopardise policy. Thus, although Tunku Abdul Rahman was censured by members of the Kedah royal family for what turned out to be a short-lived marriage to Violet Coulson, British officials did not interfere.[32] On the other hand, when Seretse Khama (chief of the Bangwato) married Ruth Williams in September 1948, the Commonwealth Relations Office claimed he had flouted the custom of Bechuanaland and forced the couple into exile. This shabby treatment by a government anxious to avoid trouble from white supremacists in southern Africa was denounced not least by African and West Indian students in Britain.[33]

Central to students' well-being was accommodation. The problems of providing adequate lodgings and social amenities were particularly acute in the war-damaged capital of 'austerity Britain'. In his novel, *The Lonely Londoners*, Sam Sevlon, who arrived from Trinidad in 1950, presented an 'ironic reversal of the El Dorado myth', encapsulating 'the romance and disenchantment of an imagined city that was both magnet and nightmare for its new colonial citizens, a promised land that despite its lure turned out to be an illusion'.[34] News of these conditions provoked outcry in the colonies: 'Many colonial students at British universities, colleges and technical institutions are living in slums and deriving the worst possible impression of the British way of life.'[35] Places in hostels were at a premium. London House in Mecklenburgh Square did not accept coloured students until 1949 and the Colonial Office was forced to close Nutfield House near Marble Arch on account of declining financial contributions from colonial governments. In the autumn of 1949 the Colonial Office locked horns with the Board of Trade over the use of Hans Crescent Hotel in

Knightsbridge. Harold Wilson (president of the Board of Trade) was determined to de-requisition it so that it might earn dollars from North American visitors. Arthur Creech Jones (colonial secretary) pointed out that the colonies were themselves contributing handsomely to dollar earnings and that the Colonial Office had already relinquished accommodation in Soho, because of 'undesirable influences' in the area, and also in Seven Dials which was dangerously 'near the Communist headquarters'. His argument that it was essential to provide stable conditions for 'potential leaders' in the colonies won the day.[36]

The presence of unprecedented numbers of colonial students in post-war Britain placed the Colonial Office in a novel position. It was now obliged to deal at first hand, rather than at arm's length, with the grievances and ambitions of colonial peoples. Students may not have been wholly representative of their countries, but they were representative of elites whose desire for self-rule was driving colonial politics and re-shaping British policies. The farsighted recognised that arrangements for students' welfare should take into account not only their problems in the United Kingdom but also aspirations for their homelands. With the onset of the Cold War, however, the official approach to colonial students shifted, at least for a time, from pastoral care to surveillance.

III

British security services closely monitored the membership and activities of international youth organisations that sprang up at the end of the Second World War. In November 1945 the World Students' Congress in London spawned the World Federation of Democratic Youth (WFDY) and the International Union of Students (IUS), both of which shifted their focus from anti-fascism to anti-colonialism. From December 1948 MI5 investigated the Co-ordinating Council for Colonial Students' Affairs (CCCSA) which had been set up in London on the initiative of the National Union of Students. In February 1949 the CCCSA organised demonstrations against military action by the Dutch in Indonesia and the British in Malaya. In the same month it was the prime mover behind the Convention on Colonial Affairs at Holborn Hall to discuss the difficulties of colonial students in the United Kingdom as well as the problems of education, economic development and self-government in the colonies. In May the CCCSA arranged another gathering at Holborn Hall, this time to receive reports from the World Peace Congress in Paris (April 1949). Later in the year it sponsored a number of colonial students attending the World Youth Festival in Budapest. While none of its constituent organisations was known to be communist-controlled, MI5 claimed there was 'plenty of evidence to show that the Co-ordinating Council will be exploited by the [Communist] Party'.[37] In short, any student consorting with the WFDY, IUS, or CCCSA was under suspicion as a fellow traveller. Not surprisingly, colonial students expected to be watched, and, wrongly crediting the Colonial Office with the capacity to keep a file on the political inclinations of each one of them, they grew increasingly suspicious of its welfare department.[38]

West Africans were the most politically engaged of the colonial students in post-war Britain. Having welcomed the advent of the Labour government in July 1945, they were soon frustrated by its refusal to discuss policy with them and Marxists rose to the fore in the West African Students' Union.[39] WASU supported the general strike by Nigeria's government employees in June–August 1945 and in October sent delegates to Manchester for the Fifth Pan-African Conference which called for an end to colonial rule. WASU also affiliated with the World Federation of Democratic Youth and the International Union of Students. In April 1949 MI5 reckoned that 'for some years' WASU had had 'a fairly strong minority of Communist sympathisers'.[40] A kindred organisation, the West African National Secretariat (WANS), was formed in December 1945 with Bankole Awooner-Renner as chairman and Kwame Nkrumah as general secretary. Nkrumah had arrived in Britain from the United States in May 1945 and registered in quick succession at the London School of Economics, University College and Gray's Inn. He also immersed himself in radical student politics. Having tapped his phone and intercepted his mail, the security services concluded that Nkrumah was in contact with the British Communist Party and in November 1947 passed this information to the police in west Africa whither he was then bound.[41] Joe Appiah, who would become president of WASU at the end of 1949, was well aware that the police had searched WANS and was himself questioned by special branch when he disembarked at Newhaven after attending the inauguration in France of the Congress of Peoples Against Imperialism (1948).[42]

Sir John Macpherson, governor-designate of Nigeria, was more relaxed in his assessment of the threat posed by the student leaders with whom he spoke at the WASU hostel in December 1947. While there were 'some fairly tough customers in the group', he noted that 'they were all very quick to laugh – even at themselves'.[43] Macpherson was the herald of the new policy which ministers and officials had been developing for west Africa. Principally associated with Arthur Creech Jones and Andrew Cohen, the plan was to modernise local government and employ western-educated Africans in it. The rationale for new policies was developed in the CO's African Studies Branch led by George Cartland who drew attention to the importance of training Africans 'for their high calling as leaders and eventually rulers of their people'.[44] There was Colonial Office consensus on this. For example, Harry Bourdillon of the Far Eastern Department accepted the 'principal contention that wise and sympathetic handling of the colonial student in this country, during the formative years when he is all too susceptible to mischievous propaganda, may be of incalculable importance in the whole future political development of the Colonial Empire'.[45] Sir Charles Jeffries (deputy under-secretary with responsibility for personnel) convened an informal group of officials to consider the causes of students' dissatisfaction and ways of winning their trust, such as providing them with opportunities to witness liberal institutions in action and savour the British way of life at weekends and in vacations. It met for the first time in mid-January 1948.[46]

Within a week of this meeting, Creech Jones encountered the full force of student anti-colonialism at a conference organised by the Fabian Colonial Bureau. As a witness vividly recorded, the secretary of state 'stopped a bucketful of bolshie stuff from some of the Colonials present'. Creech Jones came away 'distinctly stirred up' and 'full of "something must be done"'.[47] David Rees-Williams (parliamentary under-secretary) was appalled by the pervasive influence of communists. They were said to meet students on arrival in Britain and, he had been informed, were even 'working through prostitutes in London and other big cities in order to get their message across'. Rees-Williams called for restrictions on student entry into the United Kingdom, a vigorous campaign against communism in Britain and the colonies, and rigorous improvement in the pastoral care offered especially by the Inns of Court which, he fulminated, 'have commercialised the whole business, turned entry to the Bar into a farce & been quite stupid over the whole thing'.[48] The riots which erupted in Accra on 28 February 1948 appeared to vindicate a hard-line approach to colonial students. Both the governor and the Colonial Office were taken by surprise and feared the worst: that the Gold Coast was on the edge of a communist-led revolution. Since it was widely suspected that these disturbances had been planned in London, the security services intensified their surveillance of colonial students and attempts were made to isolate them from communist influences.[49]

Four months after the upheaval in the Gold Coast, a state of emergency was declared in Malaya. Malayan students now came under observation. Before the war, the Malay Society of Great Britain (formed in 1927) had been far less substantial than WASU; it had lacked premises, excluded Malayan students who were not Malays and confined itself to social and cultural activities. Its stance was transformed by the Japanese occupation and Britain's post-war Malayan Union scheme which Malays resisted because it drastically curtailed their political rights. The communist insurrection, which broke out soon after the Malayan Union had been replaced with a federal constitution, induced the Malay Society to work out a non-communist, non-communal agenda in co-operation with non-Malay students of the Malayan Students' Union (formed in 1946). The Malayan Forum, which acted as a bridge between the groups, offered a more radical programme for political advance. Its leading lights included Abdul Razak (future prime minister of Malaysia) and Goh Keng Swee (future minister and deputy prime minister, Singapore), while Lee Kuan Yew and Toh Chin Chye (respectively future prime minister and deputy prime minister of Singapore) attended from time to time. In 1953 the Eurasian lawyer and intellectual John Eber (who had fled to Britain after a period of detention in Singapore) became the Forum's secretary and Mohamed Sopiee (future member of the government of independent Malaya) assumed the editorship of its magazine, *Suara Merdeka* (voice of freedom).[50]

The security services took no action against the Malayan Forum but they were exercised by the Democratic Malayan Students' Organisation. This organisation was shunned by most Malayan students because it claimed to represent the views of the Malayan People's Liberation League which had been proscribed in Malaya. Its leader, H. B. Lim (Lim Hong Bee), had come to Britain in the mid-1930s and was said to be still reading for the Bar in 1949.[51] In 1947 he started the *Malayan Monitor*, a cheaply produced magazine which supported the communist struggle, and in 1949 he attended the World Youth Congress and fourth annual council of the IUS in Sofia as Malayan representative.[52] In February 1949 the liaison officer for Malayan students, O. T. Dussek, reported that a Malayan student had been unsettled by an anti-British speech delivered by Lim at the London School of Economics. Dussek, who had been the first principal of Sultan Idris Training College and assistant director of education in the Federated Malay States during the inter-war years, had 'a profound distrust of the L.S. of E. & [disliked] his Malayan students being sent there'.[53] The next month, there was uproar during a meeting at the Royal Empire Society addressed by the Conservative MP and former Malayan Civil Servant L. D. Gammans. Colonel Aubrey Wallich, businessman and member of the federation's executive and legislative councils who had been to the fore in urging the eradication of communism, denounced the *Malayan Monitor*'s 'seditious' allegation that British soldiers had slaughtered defenceless Chinese villagers at Batang Kali in December 1948.[54] Batang Kali was a murky episode in British counter-insurgency which the authorities tried to hush up but which remains unresolved.[55] The colonial governments of Malaya and Singapore banned the *Malayan Monitor* and, together with the Association of British Malaya, urged London to close the press and deport Lim from Britain.

Those most closely involved with student matters were not persuaded that colonial radicals posed a threat either at home or overseas. Colonial Office personnel felt that hard-liners in the International Relations Department of the Foreign Office were inclined 'to exaggerate the influence and success of Communist propaganda with our students'.[56] They objected to a tendency to single out colonial students in discussions of travel restrictions and insisted on vetting any student 'black list' drawn up by MI5. Subsequent investigation revealed that connections between communists, African students in Britain and the Gold Coast disturbances were less clear than had first been assumed. A month after the riots Creech Jones took the view that the west African student community was not controlled by communists but was liable to be manipulated by communists in order 'to embarrass the "Imperialist" powers and to work for Colonial independence'.[57] By the end of the year, Sir Percy Sillitoe (director of MI5) appeared to adopt the Colonial Office perspective that there were more 'potential troublemakers' among private students than scholarship holders on account of the fact that they were more likely to suffer from inadequate finance, accommodation and social amenities.[58] In 1950 the Foreign Office survey of communism in Africa confirmed that WANS, which appeared 'to have died a natural death' in 1949, 'was never under Communist control'.[59]

The Colonial Office was reluctant to jump to conclusions about student involvement in the Malayan insurrection. Officials doubted whether the *Malayan Monitor* was seditious and reckoned that its proscription posed a greater risk than inaction. They preferred to counteract the 'subversive influences to which students are at present exposed' by providing reading matter which gave reliable news of Malaya, although they baulked at the airmail costs of *Majlis* and were unimpressed by the 'stodgy fare' of the *Malayan Bulletin* produced by the Association of British Malaya.[60] ABM members were encouraged to welcome students into their homes, but, as one official remarked, the Colonial Office itself fell down on hospitality, leaving colonials very much to themselves in the office canteen.[61] As for Lim, he seemed to be a loner rather than a leader, the 'only one well-known bad man from

Malaya in this country at the moment'. Since 'he wd. not return to Malaya anyway for fear of arrest', he was 'in a different category from those who will return to their territories of origin'.[62] In any case, Lim was immune from deportation by dint of being a British subject.

While Lim was left alone, we might note one notorious instance of trafficking in students: that of Rawson M. Macharia, the main prosecution witness in the show trial of Jomo Kenyatta at Kapenguria in 1952–53. Because his 'firm stand ... against terrorism' placed him 'in grave danger', Macharia was whisked out of Kenya as soon as he had testified. An officer from special branch accompanied him onto the aircraft and his whereabouts in England were to remain secret. The Kenyan attorney-general's department paid for him to study local government at Exeter University. Although he failed the first year, he stayed on because it was 'undesirable' for him to return to Kenya. It was later revealed that Macharia had perjured himself at the trial and that the judge had been corrupt. Macharia himself publicly confessed that he had been coached by the prosecution and had been bribed by the offer of a university course and a job in local government.[63]

As H. B. Lim continued to publish the *Malayan Monitor* and tour British universities, the Colonial Office kept special branch at bay and avoided the tough action demanded by old Malaya hands and the Malayan government.[64] In 1953, when communist influence on colonial students was believed to be on the wane, the Colonial Office bridled at devious attempts by the Malayan government (working through its own special branch, MI5 and Scotland Yard) to discover whether the Malayans, who came to the United Kingdom for training in trade unionism, were being suborned by their tutors. Ever anxious 'to avoid any suggestion that the Colonial Office is spying on student activities', officials objected to 'any too obvious "tailing" of our students by heavy-footed coppers'. They were surprised by the implication in one MI5 report that students should avoid the company of Lady Hilda Selwyn-Clarke.[65] Lady Selwyn-Clarke was the wife of Sir Percy, the progressive governor of the Seychelles. A member of the Fabian Colonial Bureau and the Labour Party, she had stood as a parliamentary candidate in Clapham South. Colonial Office officials were also unmoved by the forceful demands of Sir Gerald Templer to prevent Dr Victor Purcell from 'infusing poison into successive batches of students from Malaya, and into any other students who come his way'.[66] On retirement from the Malayan civil service, Purcell had become a lecturer in far eastern history at Cambridge but had clashed publicly with Templer over the treatment of the Chinese in Malaya.

IV

Whereas the security services gauged the political significance of colonial students according to their nuisance value, others were more inclined to measure it in terms of their leadership potential. An editorial in *The Times* declared: 'they are the intellectual or hereditary elite of the colonies and the leaders of tomorrow' and 'the principle should be that, if it is worth allowing them over here at all, it is worth looking after them well'.[67] Convinced that the attractions of communism could not be countered by propaganda alone, successive colonial secretaries made it their priority to improve living conditions and eradicate racial discrimination. By 1949, however, the plight of colonial students was causing public concern. Those not fortunate enough to reside with families or in university halls of residence were assigned lonely lodgings or bleak Colonial Office hostels. Although they were temporary sojourners whose specific problems hardly coalesced with those of resident immigrants, colonial students were becoming a domestic issue and the Colonial Office was now called upon to perform a role for which it was ill equipped. Solutions to these problems were beyond the reach of both its welfare department and the well-meaning but unsystematic contributions of voluntary bodies. Changes in the administration of student welfare were recommended by the Cabinet's official committee on overseas students, which had been set up following a report from Sir Charles Jeffries' informal group.[68] It was decided that, from January 1950, the British Council would co-ordinate all student welfare schemes and manage Colonial Office hostels, such as Hans Crescent, the women's hostel at Collingham Gardens and others outside London. The British Council appeared well suited to these tasks: it had long specialised in promoting social and cultural relations with overseas visitors and it maintained a network of branches across the country. Its unofficial status was expected to dissipate the distrust which impaired relations between students and the Colonial Office. Observers were heartened by the Council's remit to bring hostels to the standard of university halls of residence, to improve the quality of recommended lodgings and to end ghettoisation by the ploy of dispersing students into the community after an initial spell of hostel life.[69]

Student grievances did not subside, however, and protests over accommodation were led by West Indians. Michael Manley had earlier challenged the welfare regime of the Colonial Office and now the West Indian Students' Union (WISU) resisted the British Council's plans. West Indian consciousness, as opposed to ingrained loyalty to individual islands, was a relatively recent response to racial prejudice in Britain as well as to Caribbean-wide developments, such as cricket, the federal movement and the inauguration of the university college.[70] Formed in December 1946, WISU was a relative newcomer among student unions. Keith was impressed by its 'good work in bringing West Indians over here together and in breaking down parochialism among them'.[71] Although the union had some contact with international communism through the IUS, it focused on student welfare. Its *cause célèbre* was the crisis at Hans Crescent Hostel. In 1951 the British Council decided to restrict the hostel to first-year students, partly because of pressure on space and partly because of its commitment to integrate students into the wider community. Residents objected to having to surrender their rooms to freshmen at the start of the new academic year and in July 1951 forty-three of them staged a 'stay-in strike'.[72] They sought justice from the secretary of state and enlisted the support of MPs and other sympathisers, such as Harold Laski's widow who was dismayed by the 'deplorable' conditions and colour prejudice suffered by colonial students.[73] John Keith only increased the tension by threatening to withdraw the malcontents' allowances but James Griffiths (secretary of state) ignored the advice of his civil servants and agreed to meet a student delegation. Griffiths was an approachable but shrewd negotiator and, assisted by his parliamentary under-secretary, Thomas Cook, who came from a background of trade unionism and workers' education, he succeeded in allaying agitation.

The Hans Crescent incident caused such public embarrassment that Griffiths decided to reduce the risk of repetition by replacing the wartime advisory committee (on the welfare of colonial peoples in the UK) with one better suited to current issues. On account of the general election and student reluctance to appear over-eager to participate, the Consultative Committee on the Welfare of Colonial Students in the United Kingdom was not convened until the end of November. It was chaired by Lord Munster (parliamentary under-secretary for the colonies in the new Conservative government) and included members of the three main parliamentary parties, London University's adviser to overseas students, officials from the Colonial Office and British Council, and student representatives. Reginald Sorensen represented the Labour Party. For years he had championed the cause of west African students and provided a link between them and officialdom. Mary Trevelyan was full-time adviser to overseas students at London University and the prime mover behind conferences for part-time advisers at other universities. Since the 1930s she had been warden of Student Movement House (in Russell Square and later Gower Street) and she campaigned for the establishment of International Students' House which opened in Great Portland Street in 1965. Sister of John (educator and film censor) and the diplomat Humphrey (later Lord Trevelyan), Mary Trevelyan was also an accomplished musician.[74]

There was considerable discussion over which students to invite and whether union leaders were genuine representatives. Exchanges on this issue had the flavour of pre-war debates about the composition of colonial legislatures and of later battles over student participation in the governance of British universities. Mary Trevelyan opposed the permanent membership of students on the grounds that it was impossible to find reliable spokesmen, that 'their presence limits plain-speaking' and that they 'easily misunderstand English - & they talk!'[75] John Keith described M. A. Oyewole (Nigerian Students' Union) and Joseph Appiah (West African Students' Union) as 'difficult', 'disaffected' and 'Communistic fellow travellers'. Appiah was 'a really poisonous person' who had made 'libellous' speeches against Churchill and was 'by no means representative of WASU'. Oyewole, who 'professed' to be reading law but was more heavily engaged in the running of a number of student boarding-houses which he owned, was 'hardly a person who would [be] acceptable to the Government of Nigeria'.[76] In the end invitations went to each students' union and all were represented at the first meeting of the consultative committee: Abdul Nazerali (East African Students' Federation), S. A. Onyinah (Gold Coast Students' Union), Maurice Baker (Malayan Students' Union), M. A. Oyewole (Nigerian Students' Union), Joseph Appiah (West African Students' Union), Dudley Thompson (West Indian Students' Union). Thereafter, student membership changed according to the cycles of union elections and study programmes. By and large, west Africans were the most engaged, whereas Malayans were frequently too engrossed in their studies to attend meetings. As the chairman struggled to win student co-operation, Mary Trevelyan sensed her fears had been justified:

> I am sure that endless 'hot air' must still be expected and will have to be endured – and that we shall all need endless patience. I suppose that almost everything must be 'taken' rather than a risk a breakdown. But I feel myself that there is a limit to lying down and being walked over, and I hope that the time will come when the Colonial representatives will trust us sufficiently to allow us to give them our own views in a form they will accept![77]

J. B. Williams of the Colonial Office, who had 'never believed that there was any real hope that student representatives on the Committee would prove easy or reasonable', was more pragmatic: 'the chance for them to blow off steam to us may do more good than is apparent at the meetings'.[78] Indeed, the committee soon blew itself out. It convened seven times in 1952 but thereafter its agenda withered and attendance declined. It met for the last time in November 1955 and was formally wound up in July 1960.[79]

Meanwhile, the British Council redoubled its efforts to provide for student welfare, especially in London. The warden of Hans Crescent, Hugh Paget, made it 'a model of what an inter-racial centre for students should be' and one which the secretary of state and the president and director of the British Council were proud to show off to the Queen and Duke of Edinburgh in December 1955.[80] The British Council still restricted hostel accommodation to short-term occupancy and first-year students but endeavoured to place others alongside British students in university halls of residence. The social and cultural role of hostels expanded. Additional recreational facilities were provided in London by colonial governments: Malaya Hall, which opened in Bryanston Square in December 1949, was followed in 1950 by East Africa House in Great Cumberland Place. The British Council arranged home stays and events in vacations; in 1953 alone it issued 9,500 invitations to overseas students in London to meet British people in their homes, clubs or societies.[81] It also drew upon the resources of some seventy voluntary organisations, including the Victoria League, Over-Seas League, League of Coloured Peoples, Rotary, East and West Friendship Council, Workers' Educational Association, YMCA, YWCA, various Christian and Muslim bodies, local authorities and learned societies.

When James Griffiths visited Hans Crescent, as opposition spokesman on colonial affairs, two years after the 'stay-in strike', he told students: 'I measure our success or failure by whether you leave this country with happy memories or otherwise.'[82] Much of the effort, however, was still under-funded and haphazard and the results were mixed. While the experiences of colonial students varied, surveys conducted in the 1950s indicated widespread bitterness over care in a community that was marked by racial prejudice and ignorance of other cultures.[83] Hospitality could appear coldly functional or cause acute embarrassment. One Trinidadian, the fictional Collis in George Lamming's *The Emigrants*, who was entertained to supper by a middle-class English couple, departed as soon as he sensed that 'there seemed to be an understanding that this evening had been an ordeal which was drawing to a close'.[84] Recalling encounters with the British Council during his student days, a real-life Trinidadian commented:

'The British Council exists to provide organized kindness at five shillings a year. As such, it satisfies felt needs. Because the organization supplies needs which an integrated society would have found fulfillment in human relationships, it remains, like the accommodating woman, curiously unloved, even in use.'[85] The worst off were the large numbers of private students who lacked sponsorship and requisite qualifications. Unready for what awaited them, they might reach Britain as stowaways and have to make shift with lodgings that were 'either brothels or indescribably dirty'.[86]

The problems of the 'privates' originated in the colonies. Time and again, colonial governments were exhorted in the press to prevent them from embarking for Britain or at least to prepare them for what lay ahead. They were also criticised for their failure to reintegrate returning students within their own communities. With the scholarship elite in mind, Creech Jones warned governors that they:

> miss the varied social contacts and the amenities to which they have become accustomed, and unless they can be made to feel that their personal dignity is respected as [he hoped] it has been in the United Kingdom they may quickly develop a sense of injustice and racial discrimination with very obvious and unhappy results.[87]

This was the experience of John Eber, a Eurasian who had been educated at Harrow, Cambridge and the Inns of Court and had been 'completely accepted in English society'. On his return to Singapore, however, he encountered 'all kinds of subtle discrimination against him' which turned him bitterly anti-British.[88] In 1947, while on an official visit to Lagos, John Keith witnessed the sort of welcome which a British-educated African might suffer even in a non-settler colony. Keith's assistant, Ivor Cummings, was barred from registering at the Bristol Hotel because he was black. This incident provoked a mass demonstration which Kayode Eso has called 'the first true test of people's power against the colonialist's hold on Nigeria'.[89]

The subsequent speed of political change, starting in west Africa and Malaya, resulted in the early devolution of student affairs from the Colonial Office to student units. These units were run in London by agents of national governments-in-waiting and in due course were subsumed within the high commissions of independent states.[90] More significantly, accelerated decolonisation meant that the British-educated, and not untried products of new colonial universities, were the principal beneficiaries of the localisation of public services. Almost all the leaders of the emerging nation-states whom Mary Trevelyan met during her tour of west Africa in 1955 had been trained in Britain.[91] When independence drew near, they appeared to discard their student radicalism; as one of them observed, they were 'proletarians in Westminster and bourgeois in Lagos'.[92]

The end of empire did not, however, halt the flow of students to Britain. Just as numbers from India more than doubled during the decade after 1947, so those from the former colonies continued to rise. By and large they came for the reasons which had motivated previous generations of visitors: the desire for qualifications and advancement; the availability of scholarships and other funds; the reputation of the British degree and its inexpensiveness compared with higher education in North America. On arrival, they encountered many of the social problems which had disturbed their predecessors. And, like their predecessors, they would discover in some quarters of Britain a concern for their well-being. For, having reclassified them as overseas students, the 'mother country' continued to value them, though increasingly in terms of the fees they paid and the potential they offered as future customers.

Notes

[1] Porter, 'Empires in the Mind', 194.
[2] Cf. Porter, *Oxford History of the British Empire*, 1, 4, 24–25.
[3] For the principles and practice of colonial educational policies before the war, see Whitehead, 'Education in British Colonial Dependencies, 1919–39'. See also Ashby, *Universities: British, Indian, African*.
[4] Minutes of the 96th meeting of the ACEC, 20 July 1939, CO 859/2/7, The National Archives, Kew (TNA).
[5] Report of the Colonial Students Committee appointed by the secretary of state, 1938, CO 885/92.
[6] Aggrey House, which was named after Dr J. E. K. Aggrey, the leading African educationalist in the Gold Coast, lost its separate identity when it was absorbed into a system of hostels run by the CO's Welfare Department. WASU's hostel, which moved to the Chelsea Embankment after the war, was run by Solanke and his wife until the mid-1950s. See CO 554/83/3, CO 554/109/4, CO 554/143/8, CO 847/5/11, CO 847/72, CO 859/21/3; Adi, 'West Africa Students in Britain'; Garigue, 'The West African Students' Union'; Olusanya, *West African Students' Union*.
[7] Miller, *Prince and Premier*, 37–38.
[8] Innes to J. E. W. Flood (director of colonial students), 4 March, 13 March, 3 April, 7 April 1940, CO 717/144/10.
[9] Ibid., J. M. Martin, minute, 1 May 1940.
[10] Clifford's *Saleh*, was originally written and published in two parts, *Sally: A Study* (1904) and *Saleh: A Sequel* (1908). They were combined in a single volume in 1926 with the title *A Prince of Malaya* and this was reprinted in 1989 with an introduction by J. M. Gullick.
[11] Williams, *Inward Hunger*, 46.
[12] Sir Bernard Bourdillon to W. G. A. Ormsby-Gore (secretary of state), 10 Dec. 1937, CO 554/109/4.
[13] Carey, *Colonial Students*, 28–29; Lee, 'Commonwealth Students', 3; Keith, 'African Students in Great Britain', 65.
[14] Barlow, 'Obituary', 1–3.
[15] Note by CO Welfare Department on WASU, 2 Apr. 1948, CO 554/143/8; minute by J. L. Keith, 15 March 1941, CO 859/43/7.
[16] Thurston, *Sources for Colonial Studies*, I, 321, 343–44.
[17] Wilmer, 'Ivor Cummings'.
[18] *The Times*, 24 Sept. 1942.
[19] Oliver Stanley, 13 July 1943, *House of Commons Debates*, 391, cols 48–52, 57–59, 62–64, 66–69.
[20] Sir Cyril Asquith, son of the former prime minister, was a high court judge. The enquiries on west Africa, West Indies and Malaya were chaired respectively by Walter Elliot (who had been a minister in the National Governments of Baldwin and Chamberlain), Sir James Irvine (vice-chancellor of St Andrew's University) and Sir Alexander Carr-Saunders (Director of the London School of Economics). See *Report of the Commission on Higher Education in the Colonies*, Cmd. 6647 (1945), *Report of the Commission on Higher Education in West Africa*, Cmd. 6655 (1945), *Report of the West Indies Committee of the Commission on Higher Education in*

the Colonies, Cmd. 6654 (1945); *Report of the Commission on University Education in Malaya*, Colonial No. 229 (London, HMSO, 1948).

[21] Keith, 'African Students in Great Britain', 65.
[22] Official statistics are scattered across Colonial Office files. The first survey of colonial students in Britain, *Colonial Students in Britain*, was published in 1955 by PEP (Political and Economic Planning), a non-governmental research organisation to which CO files, minutes and statistics had been made available. This was followed by Carey's *Colonial Students*. See also Lancaster, *Education for Commonwealth Students*.
[23] Minutes by A. Chamier, 23 July 1947, and Keith, 24 July 1947, CO 537/2578; H. T. Bourdillon, 17 Oct. 1947, CO 537/2572; Keith to Raja Sir Uda bin Raja Mahmud, 24 Sept. 1953, CO 1028/27.
[24] For a case study, see Hargreaves, 'African Students in Britain'.
[25] Keith to T. Harvatt (secretary, Council of Legal Education), 17 Oct. 1949, CO 876/117; memorandum by the director of colonial scholars on arrangements for sending colonial students to the United Kingdom for higher education, June 1953, CO 1028/1; PEP, *Colonial Students in Britain*, 215; Carey, *Colonial Students*, 104.
[26] Minute by K. Blackburne, 21 Feb. 1949, CO 537/5138.
[27] Circular despatch from the secretary of state to governors, 10 June 1948, CO 537/4276.
[28] PEP, *Colonial Students in Britain*; Carey, *Colonial Students*. Cf. Singh, *Indian Students in Britain*.
[29] See Tajfel and Dawson, *Disappointed Guests*.
[30] Minute by Dr Edith Mercer including 'the extraordinary allegation' by Dr Williams, 19 June 1957, CO 1031/2402.
[31] *Evening Standard*, 27 July 1954. See also Appiah, *Autobiography*; CO 554/1062. Having qualified as a lawyer, in 1954 Appiah returned to Ghana with his wife and son. The following year he switched support from Nkrumah's Convention People's Party to the predominantly Ashanti National Liberation Movement.
[32] Miller, *Prince and Premier*, 48, 52–55.
[33] Seretse Khama arrived in England in September 1945 and, after a brief period at Balliol College, he enrolled at the Inner Temple. He lived at Nutford House, a CO hostel in London, and was a member of WASU. The Khamas were allowed to return to Bechuanaland in the late 1950s and in 1966 he became the first president of Botswana. See Williams, *Colour Bar*. For a vindication of British handling of the issue in the interests of Africans, see Hyam and Henshaw, *The Lion and the Springbok*, 168–97.
[34] Susheila Nasta, introduction to the 2006 edition of Sevlon, *The Lonely Londoners* (first published in 1956), v.
[35] *East Africa and Rhodesia*, 12 Feb. 1948.
[36] Minutes and accompanying papers for the meeting of the Cabinet Production Committee (chaired by Stafford Cripps), 4 Nov 1949, CAB 134/640, TNA, CO 537/4272.
[37] MI5 to Sir Marston Logan (CO), redacted, 8 April 1949, CO 537/4381. See also CO 537/4313, 4382.
[38] Braithwaite, *Colonial West Indian Students*, 107.
[39] In August 1945 George Hall endorsed the view of his Conservative predecessor (Oliver Stanley) that WASU was not an organ for the discussion of general policy and declined to see a deputation on west African matters, CO 554/143/7.
[40] MI5 to Sir M. Logan (CO), redacted, 8 April 1949, CO 537/4381. Cf. 'A survey of communism in Africa', FO Research Dept. memorandum, June 1950, para. 224, in Rathbone, *Ghana*, I, 270.
[41] For example, Sir Percy Sillitoe to J. N. Ferguson, Senior Assistant Commissioner of Police, Gambia, 10 Nov. 1947, KV 2/1847, TNA. See also CO 537/3566; Rathbone, 'Nkrumah'; Sherwood, 'Kwame Nkrumah'.
[42] Appiah, *Autobiography*, 167, 175.

[43] 'Note by Sir John Macpherson on his visit to WASU Hostel on 13th December, 1947', CO 554/143/7.
[44] 'The Political Significance of African Students in Great Britain', n.d. [July 1947], CO 537/2572. Cartland served in the Gold Coast 1935–44, the Colonial Office 1944–49 and Uganda 1949–63. He then embarked on a second career in university administration as registrar of the University of Birmingham 1963–67 and vice-chancellor of the University of Tasmania 1968–77.
[45] Bourdillon, 17 Oct. 1947, CO 537/2572.
[46] Minutes of 1st meeting of the informal group investigating the political significance of colonial students in the UK, 13 Jan. 1948, CO 537/5138.
[47] H. P. Elliott to J. L. Keith, 13 Feb. 1948, enclosing a note on the Fabian Colonial Bureau Conference of 17–18 Jan. 1948, CO 537/2574.
[48] Ibid., Rees-Williams to Sir Thomas Lloyd, 20 Feb. 1948.
[49] Rathbone, *Ghana*, xliv. See CO 537/4312.
[50] See Carey, *Colonial Students*, 90–93; Yeo, 'Student Politics in University of Malaya', 366ff.; Lee, *Singapore Story*, 121–22; Shaw, *Tun Razak*, 71ff.
[51] J. D. Higham (CO) to N.R. Jarrett (secretary to Association of British Malaya), 21 Dec. 1949, CO 537/4312.
[52] O.H. Morris, 3 Nov. 1949, CO 537/4381, number 28, CO 537/4382.
[53] Sir Marston Logan, 26 Feb. 1949, CO 537/4782. In his minute Logan appears to have confused Dussek with Dusart.
[54] Ibid. The offending issue of *Malayan Monitor* was volume 2, no. 2, Feb. 1949.
[55] Bayly and Harper, *Forgotten Wars*, 449–56; Stockwell, 'Chin Peng and the Struggle for Malaya', 290–91.
[56] W. S. Morgan to Sir M. Logan and J. L. Keith, 11 June 1949, CO 537/4381.
[57] Creech Jones to Sir Gerald Creasy, 28 March 1948, Rathbone, *Ghana*, part I, 72.
[58] Sir P. Sillitoe to Sir Orme Sargent (FO), 23 Dec. 1948, CO 537/4312.
[59] 'A survey of communism in Africa', FO Research Dept. memorandum, June 1950, para. 224, in Rathbone, *Ghana*, part I, 270.
[60] See CO 537/3749, CO 537/4781.
[61] Higham to Jarrett, 21 Dec. 1949; minute by Trafford-Smith, 3 Nov.1949, CO 537/4312.
[62] O. H. Morris, 3 Nov. 1949, CO 537/4381.
[63] Correspondence in the recently released but redacted file CO 1028/29. See Anderson, *Histories of the Hanged*, 63–68; Lapping, *End of Empire*, 414ff.
[64] See CO 1022/119, CO 1022/146.
[65] Minutes by T. C. Jerrom, 24 Nov. 1953, J. D. Higham, 8 Jan. 1953, Sir J. Shaw (MI5) to Barton, 27 March 1953, CO 1022/197.
[66] Minutes by R. L. Baxter and T. C. Jerrom on discussions with Sir Gerald Templer and Sir Donald MacGillivray on 11 and 14 Nov. 1953, CO 1022/85, CO 1022/197. Stockwell, *Malaya*, III, 13–16.
[67] *The Times*, 9 May 1949.
[68] Lee, 'Commonwealth Students', 13.
[69] For the role of the British Council, see Lee, 'Commonwealth Students', 9–11; Lee, 'British Cultural Diplomacy', 114, 117.
[70] For WISU, see Braithwaite, *Colonial West Indian Students in Britain*, 127–67. It appears that Braithwaite, a CDW-funded Trinidadian student who came to Britain in 1945, wrote this account in the mid-1950s.
[71] Minute by J.L. Keith, 30 Nov. 1950, CO 876/155.
[72] See CO 876/194, 195.
[73] Hilda Laski to Griffiths, 19 Aug. 1951, CO 537/6702.
[74] Lee, 'Commonwealth Students', 11, 22.

[75] Mary Trevelyan to T. Cook, 11 Sept. 1951, CO 537/6702.
[76] Ibid., minutes by Keith, 29 Aug., 4 Sept., 2 Nov. 1951, CO 537/ 6702.
[77] Mary Trevelyan to Lord Munster, 11 Feb. 1952, CO 537/7617.
[78] Minute by J.B. Williams, 30 Jan. 1952, CO 537/7617.
[79] For the establishment, papers and disbandment of this committee, see CO 537/6702, CO 537/7617, CO 1028/28 (1952–53), CO 1028/41 (1954–56), CO 1028/100 (1960).
[80] *The Times*, 6 July 1954, 14 Dec. 1955.
[81] Sir Paul Sinker, director general, British Council, to *The Times*, 6 Dec. 1954.
[82] *The Times*, 1 July 1953.
[83] PEP, *Colonial Students in Britain*; Carey, *Colonial Students*.
[84] Lamming, *The Emigrants*, 145. See also Schwartz, *West Indian Intellectuals in Britain*, 9ff.; Chamberlain, 'George Lamming'.
[85] Ramchand, 'Colour Problem at the University', 30. Ramchand studied at Edinburgh University, 1959–63.
[86] Mary Trevelyan to Lord Munster, 11 Feb. 1952, CO 537/7617.
[87] Circular despatch from the secretary of state to governors, 10 June 1948, CO 537/4276.
[88] Minute by J. D. Higham, 9 July 1951, CO 717/202/7. Eber was detained without trial in 1951 and, on release, went into voluntary exile in Britain where he became secretary of the Malayan Forum and eventually general secretary of Fenner Brockway's Movement for Colonial Freedom.
[89] Flint, 'Scandal at the Bristol Hotel'; Eso, *Mystery Gunman*, 21–24.
[90] See CO 1028/27 and secretary of state for the colonies, circular 1001/56, 20 Sept. 1956, CO 1028/74. In 1961 the Colonial Office's residual interest in student affairs passed to the Department of Technical Co-operation.
[91] Trevelyan, 'African Student at Home', 38, 40–41. Much the same could be said of the government which Tunku Abdul Rahman formed in Malaya in the same year; six of the ten key ministers had qualified in Britain and a seventh had graduated in medicine from the University of Melbourne.
[92] Quoted in Adi, 'West African Students in Britain', 125.

References

Adi, Hakim. 'West African Students in Britain'. In *Africans in Britain*, edited by David Killingray. Special issue of *Immigrants and Minorities* 12, no. 3 (1993): 107–28.

Anderson, David. *Histories of the Hanged: The Dirty War in Kenya and the End of Empire*. London: Weidenfeld & Nicolson, 2005.

Appiah, Joseph. *Joe Appiah: The Autobiography of an African Patriot*. New York, London: Praeger, 1990.

Ashby, Eric. *Universities: British, Indian, African: A Study in the Ecology of Higher Education*. London: Weidenfeld & Nicolson, 1966.

Barlow, Henry. 'Obituary of Tun Mohamed Suffian bin Hashim 1917–2000'. *Journal of the Malaysian Branch of the Royal Asiatic Society* 73, no. 2 (2000): 1–3.

Bayly, Christopher, and Tim Harper. *Forgotten Wars: The End of Britain's Asian Empire*. London: Allen Lane, 2007.

Braithwaite, Lloyd. *Colonial West Indian Students in Britain*. Barbados, Jamaica, Trinidad & Tobago: University of West Indies Press, 2001.

Carey, A. T. *Colonial Students: A Study of the Social Adaptation of Colonial Students in London*. London: Secker & Warburg, 1956.

Chamberlain, Mary. 'George Lamming'. In *West Indian Intellectuals in Britain*, edited by Bill Schwartz. Manchester: Manchester University Press, 2003, 175–95.

Clifford, Hugh. *Saleh: A Prince of Malaya*. Introduction by J. M. Gullick. Singapore: Oxford University Press, 1989.

Eso, Kayode. *The Mystery Gunman*. Ibadan: Spectrum, 1996.
Flint, John. 'Scandal at the Bristol Hotel: Some Thoughts on Racial Discrimination in Britain and West Africa and its Relationship to the Planning of Decolonisation, 1939–47'. *Journal of Imperial and Commonwealth History* 12, no. 1 (1983): 74–93.
Garigue, Philip. 'The West African Students' Union: A Study in Culture Contact'. *Africa: Journal of the International African Institute* 23, no. 1 (1953): 55–69.
Hargreaves, John. 'African Students in Britain: The Case of Aberdeen University'. In *Africans in Britain*, edited by David Killingray. Special issue of *Immigrants and Minorities* 12, no. 3 (1993): 129–44.
Hyam, R., and P. Henshaw. *The Lion and the Springbok: Britain and South Africa since the Boer War*. Cambridge: Cambridge University Press, 2003.
Keith, J. L. 'African Students in Great Britain'. *African Affairs* 45, no. 179 (1946): 65–72.
Lamming, George. *The Emigrants*. London: Michael Joseph, 1954.
Lancaster, Patrick. *Education for Commonwealth Students in Britain*. London: Fabian Society, 1962.
Lapping, Brian. *End of Empire*. London: Granada, 1985.
Lee, J. M. 'British Cultural Diplomacy and the Cold War: 1946–61'. *Diplomacy & Statecraft* 9, no. 1 (1998): 112–34.
———. 'Commonwealth Students in the United Kingdom, 1940–1960: Student Welfare and World Status'. *Minerva* 44 (2006): 1–24.
Lee Kuan Yew. *The Singapore Story*. Singapore: Times Editions, 1998.
Miller, Harry. *Prince and Premier: A Biography of Tunku Abdul Rahman Putra Al-Haj First Prime Minister of the Federation of Malaya*. London: Harrap, 1959.
Olusanya, G. O. *The West African Students' Union and the Politics of Decolonisation, 1925–1958*. Ibadan: Daystar Press, 1982.
PEP. *Colonial Students in Britain: A Report by the PEP*. London: Political and Economic Planning, June 1955.
Porter, Andrew. 'Empires in the Mind'. In *The Cambridge Illustrated History of the British Empire*. edited by P. J. Marshall. Cambridge: Cambridge University Press, 1996: 185–223.
———. 'Introduction'. In *The Oxford History of the British Empire*, vol. 3, *The Nineteenth Century*. Oxford: Oxford University Press, 1999: 1–28.
Ramchand, Kenneth. 'The Colour Problem at the University: A West Indian's Changing Attitudes'. In *Disappointed Guests: Essays by African, Asian, and West Indian Students*, edited by Henri Tajfel and John L. Dawson. London: Oxford University Press for the Institute of Race Relations, 1965.
Rathbone, Richard, ed. *Ghana: British Documents on the End of Empire*. London: HMSO, 1992.
———. 'Nkrumah, Kwame (1909?–1972)'. *Oxford Dictionary of National Biography*. Oxford: Oxford University Press, 2004.
Schwartz, Bill, ed. *West Indian Intellectuals in Britain*. Manchester: Manchester University Press, 2003.
Sevlon, Sam. *The Lonely Londoners*. Introduction by Susheila Nasta. London: Penguin, 2006.
Shaw, William. *Tun Razak: His Life and Times*. London: Longman, 1976.
Sherwood, Marika. 'Kwame Nkrumah: The London Years, 1945–47'. In *Africans in Britain*, edited by David Killingray. Special issue of *Immigrants and Minorities* 12, no. 3 (1993): 164–94.
Singh, Amit Kumar. *Indian Students in Britain: A Survey of their Adjustments and Attitudes*. New York: Asia Publishing House, 1963.
Stockwell, A. J., ed. *Malaya: British Documents on the End of Empire*. London: HMSO, 1995.
———. 'Chin Peng and the Struggle for Malaya'. *Journal of the Royal Asiatic Society* 16, no. 3 (2006): 279–97.
Tajfel, Henri, and John L. Dawson, eds. *Disappointed Guests: Essays by African, Asian, and West Indian Students*. London: Oxford University Press for the Institute of Race Relations, 1965.
Thurston, Anne. *Sources for Colonial Studies in the Public Record Office*, vol. 1. London: HMSO, 1995.
Trevelyan, Mary. 'African Student at Home'. *African Affairs* 54, no. 214 (1955): 37–41.

Whitehead, Clive. 'Education in British Colonial Dependencies, 1919–39: A Re-Appraisal'. *Comparative Education* 17, no. 1 (1981): 71–80.
Williams, Eric. *Inward Hunger: The Education of a Prime Minister.* Introduction by Colin Palmer. Princeton, NJ: Markus Weiner, 2006.
Williams, Susan. *Colour Bar: The Triumph of Seretse Khama and His Nation.* London: Allen Lane, 2006.
Wilmer, Val. 'Ivor Cummings'. *Independent,* 4 Dec. 1992.
Yeo Kim Wah. 'Student Politics in University of Malaya, 1949–51'. *Journal of Southeast Asian Studies* 23, no. 2 (1992): 346–80.

The Central African Federation and Britain's Post-War Nuclear Programme: Reconsidering the Connections

L. J. Butler

Two of the defining developments in post-war British history were the disengagement from empire and the decision to embark on an ambitious programme of nuclear research and development, both military and civil. It has long been argued that the two may have been connected. For example, an increasing emphasis on a nuclear deterrent as the basis of British defence policy involved (possibly unanticipated) costs, but, by enabling the phasing out of National Service after 1962, it may also have limited the operational flexibility of the British armed forces, robbing them of the manpower required to engage in future colonial wars, even had these been politically acceptable.[1] The fact that Britain's determined acceleration of decolonisation after 1959 developed alongside a critical phase in British nuclear policy certainly appears to be more than coincidental. A further possible link between the nuclear and decolonising themes is that emphasis on Britain's continuing status as the world's third leading power, derived from its possession of nuclear weapons, may have compensated for the retraction from empire, soothing what might otherwise have been a politically difficult issue for the government of Harold Macmillan.[2]

The purpose of this article is to take these speculations further, by asking whether these two strands may have converged even more closely than has previously been appreciated. It takes as its focus the interest shown by successive British governments in securing an independent source of uranium, that precious and enigmatic fuel without which so many of Britain's post-war aspirations faced frustration. Specifically, it investigates the enthusiasm shown by London for developing a uranium source within what became the Central African Federation, an unusual and important example of Britain's approach to colonial policy in the 1950s, famously described as the 'most controversial large-scale imperial exercise in constructive state-building ever undertaken by the British government', bringing together Northern and Southern Rhodesia and Nyasaland.[3] Yet this was an initiative whose purpose has long been clouded by a fundamental ambiguity. This article's key proposition is that, in addition to the predominantly political explanations advanced for Britain's commitment to the federation, above all a desire to pre-empt the entrenchment of Afrikaner influence in central Africa, an important subsidiary influence on British government thinking when London opted to proceed with this experiment was growing concern about the long-term security of uranium supplies, particularly in view of likely competition from the United States.[4] The idea that strategic minerals may have loomed large in policy-makers' thinking on central Africa is not, of course, novel. In a pioneering and influential study, written before the relevant government records became available, the late Professor Partha Gupta proposed that the attractions of strategically vital chrome from Southern Rhodesia were prominent in London's decision in favour of a federation.[5] It is suggested here that it was the lure of uranium, rather than chrome, which exercised British policy-makers. Given the extreme reticence of Whitehall concerning the entire subject of Britain's post-war nuclear programme, it is perhaps unsurprising that a possible 'nuclear dimension' to contemporary discussions on central Africa has not featured prominently in the historical literature.[6]

Wartime Anglo-American co-operation in the Manhattan Project had been enshrined in highly personal, if ambiguous agreements between Churchill and Roosevelt. When the prospect of continuing co-operation was dashed by the McMahon Act in 1946, Britain was obliged to embark on its own programme of nuclear research.[7] While the wartime allies continued to work together, through the Combined Development Trust, on allocating precious supplies of uranium for their respective nuclear programmes, the exchange of nuclear technology was effectively blocked. Attempts by Britain, at the highest level, to gain information on, and even influence over, US nuclear planning, captured most vividly by Attlee's talks with Truman in December 1950, proved fruitless. Similar initiatives by senior British military figures were equally unrewarding. Washington remained sceptical that Britain could contribute significantly to NATO's nuclear capability, tending to view British nuclear aspirations as creating undesirable competition for raw materials. Such attitudes seemed only to reinforce the importance of Britain pressing on with its own independent efforts to produce an atomic weapon.[8] On his return to power in 1951, Churchill initially believed that he could suspend the British bomb project, since a revived 'special relationship' would lead to Britain being supplied with the weapons it needed by the US. Disabused of this notion during his visit to Washington early in 1952, Churchill concluded that work on Britain's project must proceed.[9]

Under the 'Modus vivendi', agreed by the Combined Policy Committee in January 1948, the Combined Development Trust became the Combined Development Agency, representing the United States, Britain and Canada. Under these arrangements, the entire world, with the exception of the United States and the British Commonwealth, constituted 'CDA territory', with the agency having a prior claim on all 'Free World' discoveries and development of uranium. It was primarily for this reason that British interest grew in identifying Commonwealth sources of the mineral. This ambition could only intensify as difficulties surfaced with the CDA regime, threatening Britain and its plans.

The interest shown by post-war British governments in the development of colonial mineral and other raw material resources is well established. Symbolising it was Foreign Secretary Ernest Bevin's brief, but intense, preoccupation with the mineral wealth of Africa.[10] As Sarah Stockwell has recently made clear, the optimism shown about the colonies' potential by Attlee's colleagues after 1945 persisted well into the 1950s, and was cultivated with enthusiasm by the same Conservative administration which acted decisively, unlike its predecessor, on the question of central African territorial integration.[11] London's interest in colonial resources was not confined to the more 'conventional' minerals such as copper and gold, but extended to uranium. A measure of Britain's desire to tap colonial, and Commonwealth, reserves of uranium was the speed with which post-war steps were taken not only to identify possible sources, but to bring them under state control, where possible.[12] Immediately after the Second World War, there began an episode of intense prospecting for viable uranium deposits. In 1947, reserves were discovered in South Australia. Two years later, Britain offered to buy, at guaranteed prices, small lots of uranium found in the Commonwealth. This offer was subsequently amended in 1951 to encourage prospectors to intensify their searches. Meanwhile, ore deposits were found in South Africa in 1950 which promised to yield the most substantial deposit of any find made since the war. Further investigations were made in Ceylon, Canada, British Guiana, the Gold Coast, British Honduras, India, Kenya, Malaya, New Zealand, Nigeria and Nyasaland, to complement the investigations being conducted in Britain itself.[13] By 1951, development work was under way at Rum Jungle, in Australia's Northern Territory, and at Radium Hill in South Australia. By the early 1950s, then, a veritable uranium 'rush' was in progress, reflecting the concern of both the British and US governments.[14]

Although Britain tried to maintain the basic principle that Commonwealth uranium sources were 'domestic', and exempt from CDA arrangements, it was eventually forced to abandon this position, simply because it lacked the financial resources to develop these sources, an underlying, and recurring, problem in Britain's entire post-war development strategy.[15] In practice, therefore, South Africa, Radium Hill and Rum Jungle came to be treated as 'CDA territory'.[16] This reinforced Britain's interest in locating colonial sources of uranium unambiguously *outside* the agency's remit. One candidate, in which British experts had long shown interest, was central Africa. The Belgian Congo was an established supplier of uranium even before 1939, followed in importance by the United States and Canada. In the summer of 1940, thirty tons of uranium ore had been shipped from the Belgian Congo to New York, for eventual use in the Manhattan Project.[17] In 1944, the CDT had concluded a contract with the African Metals Corporation to buy Congolese uranium oxide.[18] Late in the war, strong suspicions developed that uranium might be found in Southern Rhodesia on a large scale, comparable with the richest existing known deposits. This seemed a compelling argument for ensuring that the Southern Rhodesian government retained control of any deposits.[19] But equally significant was the interest which arose in the uranium-producing potential of Northern Rhodesia, prompted by the territory's proximity to the uranium-rich Belgian Congo, and the two colonies' very similar geology and mineralisation.[20] Although the London Group of the CDT discussed the exploration of Northern Rhodesia in June 1945, the initial prospects seemed discouraging, since much of the territory had already been explored thoroughly by the established copper industry.[21] Four years later, the question resurfaced, with British officials reassuring the CDA that the Northern Rhodesian mining companies grasped the importance of finding uranium, but adding that no workable deposit had yet been found.[22] Nevertheless, optimism about central Africa's potential gained renewed strength in 1950 following a visit by C. F. Davidson, senior geologist with the Ministry of Supply's Atomic Energy Division. While in Salisbury, Davidson commented that the geological structure of Rhodesia suggested that 'this part of the world may be as rich in radioactive minerals as any in the Commonwealth'.[23] Ironically, with the Belgian Congo's uranium reserves expected to dwindle by the mid-1950s, its neighbour's potential would attract growing interest.[24] Davidson's suspicions were long held. He had been saying much the same thing since 1941 and was convinced that the Copperbelt was the most promising area of the British Commonwealth for the discovery of the prized radioactive minerals.[25] Although Davidson acknowledged that much was being done to locate them, and that the copper companies' geologists were keen, he judged that the colonial government in Lusaka, which still had no geological survey department, could give a stronger lead. Since the companies' existing holdings were relatively well known, the main hope of important new finds appeared to lie in the unexplored region of Northern Rhodesia, the Western Concession.[26]

Highly significant, and potentially alarming to London, was the interest shown by the United States authorities in Britain's efforts in central Africa. Press reports of Davidson's activities immediately attracted the notice of the US Atomic Energy Commission (USAEC), which was reportedly 'very anxious to know more on this'.[27] At a meeting of the CDA in February 1951, the American side asked if more could not be done to promote Commonwealth uranium exploration. The British side responded cautiously, arguing that the area in which London could initiate uranium prospecting was limited, although work was progressing, for example, in Nigeria and Uganda. The possibility of accelerating these efforts was being considered. Nevertheless, the

Americans pressed their British counterparts for information on the likelihood of finds being made in Northern and Southern Rhodesia.[28] Among the practical steps being taken, early in 1951, were arrangements made by the Ministry of Supply, through the Colonial Office and the Northern Rhodesian government, for the Royal Air Force to conduct, as a priority, an aerial survey of the Western Concession. Further co-operation with the copper companies was also envisaged.[29] At the Atomic Energy Division, C. F. Davidson was defensive of recent initiatives. He emphasised continuing efforts to alert mining companies, prospectors and others to the region's possibilities, and the provision of equipment, training and surveys by government. He noted, pointedly: 'Perhaps we might remind the American members of C.D.A. that the Rhodesias have a surface area of 438,000 square miles – one seventh of that of the U.S.A. – and that Northern Rhodesia is larger than Texas.' He thought it unlikely that short-term initiatives, such as expeditions from London or Washington, would achieve much: rather, the discovery of a workable deposit of uranium, about which Davidson remained optimistic, would more likely arise from an 'accidental' encounter in the search for gold or copper. In effect, he concluded, London was doing all that it could.[30] Yet there were further echoes of basic problems familiar in the entire post-war colonial development initiative. One practical constraint on progress was the shortage of trained geologists employed by the Atomic Energy Division. Even by late 1951, only nine were available, still eight below the complement authorised in 1946.[31] American officials appeared content with British reassurances. The general consensus, expressed at the CDA's meeting, was that London had a carefully planned and well-rounded programme of uranium prospecting within the Commonwealth.[32]

During 1951, Davidson's activities in central Africa gained momentum. Following visits to the Rhodesias by his team of geologists, his principal aim was to maintain regional interest in uranium prospecting.[33] An atmosphere of increasing excitement was reflected in the *Rhodesia Herald*'s announcement, late in April, that uranium had been found by a lone prospector at Beitbridge in Southern Rhodesia. However, this find was subsequently judged commercially unviable. A fresh disappointment followed when ore samples from Broken Hill in Northern Rhodesia revealed no potential for uranium as a by-product from zinc mining. It remained possible, however, that this, and the Beitbridge discovery, might be attractive, if they proved to be 'enormous'.[34] By the end of 1951, interest in uranium prospecting in Northern Rhodesia was outstripping that shown in any other British colonial territory. Although uranium had been found in most of the large copper deposits, it was not present in quantities considered economically workable. Similarly, the known Southern Rhodesian deposits were geographically remote and lacked any high-value by-product, and, given current uranium costs, were therefore unattractive.[35]

Despite these setbacks, US enthusiasm seemed undiminished. At the CDA's meeting in October 1951, the Americans stressed that the USAEC was keen to assist with prospecting work in Britain's territories, possibly by providing equipment and assay facilities, and even finance. The commission, they emphasised, was 'obviously' concerned to investigate all possible sources of uranium.[36] This US interest was particularly evident in Washington's enthusiasm for the expansion of South African uranium production. Late in 1950, a secret agreement was reached between South Africa, the United States and Britain for the Union's gold-mining companies to supply uranium to the CDA. It was hoped that output would reach 3,000 tons by 1956. Washington and London were to contribute respectively two-thirds and one-third each of the necessary finance, as loans, with payment for the uranium being on the same basis. Within the Foreign Office, 'powerful reasons' were seen for Britain to endorse this scheme: it was, above all, important not to undermine Anglo-American co-operation in the CDA by failing to support Washington's attempts to boost production. Highly revealing, however, was the rider that it would be 'unfortunate' if Britain left the US to negotiate alone with a Commonwealth member. Moreover, the bulk of South Africa's uranium would probably be needed by the US, allowing Britain to reap the resulting dollar-exchange advantage.[37] Equally, and humiliatingly, since Britain remained 'entirely dependent' on the CDA for all its requirements of uranium, there were good, practical reasons not to 'annoy the Americans'.[38]

Propelling this American interest were growing US defence requirements of uranium, linked to the mammoth rearmament drive inspired by the Korean War, Washington's response to the Soviet Union's unexpected atom bomb test in 1949 and the subsequent US decision to develop thermonuclear (or 'hydrogen') weapons. That defining document of Washington's strategy in the Cold War, 'NSC-68', presented to President Eisenhower in April 1950, assumed an enormous increase in US military strength, centred on US atomic superiority over the Soviet Union, which would require a constant supply of uranium.[39] As Sir Christopher ('Kit') Steel, Britain's minister in Washington noted, the resulting US emphasis on strategic stockpiling raised the real possibility that, in a scramble for resources (which seemed likely once the *civil* applications of atomic power became feasible), Britain's needs might be eclipsed.[40] An early foretaste of the US government's determination to secure the uranium it sought had come in March 1950, when Washington negotiated a new contract with Canada for the purchase of most of the latter's uranium oxide output for the next eight years.[41] The extent of British concern, and the potential for Anglo-US tension, became increasingly clear during 1952, as preparations began to determine the two countries' uranium allocations. Plans to expand the US atomic programme threatened to trigger a shortage of uranium, which might in turn affect the quantities available to Britain.[42] By early 1952, rapid growth in US military requirements for atomic weapons led the Pentagon to argue that the entire expansion programme hinged on the supply of raw materials, procurement of which had become 'an operation of supreme importance' for 'the whole strategic policy and defence of the U.S.'. American officials, particularly Marion Boyar (General Manager of the USAEC and the senior US member of the CDA), had hinted to their British counterparts that US requirements would be vastly in excess of anything previously sought, and even *more* in excess of likely available supplies. For the Defense Department, uranium procurement had become the top priority facing the US armed forces, to be treated on a wartime basis and promoted without regard to cost or conventional commercial considerations. British officials feared that the US might use its military requirements as a pretext to abandon current CDA procurement arrangements. The Defense Department had complained periodically to the State Department that the CDA's methods were 'too dilatory and too commercially minded'. The Americans were reported to see the British in the CDA as an impediment to US drive and initiative, perennially detecting problems (especially financial ones) in any scheme to obtain more uranium.[43]

The extent of the United States' apparently insatiable requirement for uranium, and the resulting implications for Britain's own atomic programme, startled the Cabinet Office in London when it became known during 1952. Informal discussions with the Americans revealed that there was no ceiling to US requirements of atomic weapons, and therefore of uranium. Henceforth, atomic weapons were 'to be treated as ordinary ammunition'.[44] When its existing expansion programme had been completed, US annual consumption of uranium was predicted to exceed 10,000 short tons. The prospective supplies available in 1952, however, totalled only 3,650 tons, and a further expansion programme was shortly to be put before Congress. The USAEC was therefore under intense pressure from the Defense Department, Congress and the president to procure the maximum possible quantity of uranium. Inevitably, it seemed, world uranium production would fall 'considerably short' of the amounts Britain and the US needed.[45] Admittedly, the President's Materials Policy Commission (the Paley Commission) accurately predicted domestic discoveries of uranium in its June 1952 report. Moreover, arguably, with the first sizeable deliveries of South African uranium during 1952, US anxieties over uranium supplies might diminish, but this did not mean that Washington's efforts to guarantee supplies would relax. Certainly, the British government could not afford to make any such assumption.[46]

A further important consideration, adding to the complications facing Whitehall during 1952, was the impending strategic review by the Chiefs of Staff, partly inspired by the British government's growing economic difficulties, themselves largely the result of the rearmament programme begun by the previous Labour government. The review, conducted between late April and early May 1952, resulted in the 'Report on Defence Policy and Global Strategy', circulated to the Cabinet Defence Committee in June 1952 and approved by it on 9 July.[47] Emphasising the importance of deterrence in conducting a long-term period of Cold War, the paper cautioned against any British assumption that the US would devote resources to eliminating Soviet targets particularly threatening to Britain: this role would have to be undertaken by Britain itself. While assuming that in time of war, the US would supply Britain with nuclear weapons, the chiefs of staff nevertheless emphasised that the British weapons programme should be accelerated.[48] Such a prospect had already caused alarm in Whitehall, where concern had been voiced about the 'difficult' uranium supply situation which such a recommendation would create.[49]

The clear US emphasis on the *military* applications of atomic energy, and the stockpiling of uranium which this encouraged, not only raised the possibility that shortages of uranium would impinge upon Britain's own nuclear programme, but served to underline the overriding intention of the existing CDA allocation arrangements. All CDA contracts specified that the uranium supplied was to be used for defence or research purposes, leaving Britain potentially without the resources it needed to develop its civil nuclear programme, unlike the US, which enjoyed its own unrestricted domestic uranium sources.[50] Thus uranium from the Belgian Congo could be used only for defence purposes, and an 'understanding' existed that similar limitations should apply to ore from South Africa and Australia.[51] US preoccupation with the military applications of atomic energy encouraged British officials to dissemble with the Americans about the uses to which Britain's allocations of uranium would be put, in a curious inversion of the later received wisdom that the civil nuclear programme was largely a convenient cloak for Britain's military programme.[52] Yet the possible industrial applications of atomic energy, particularly electricity generation, had featured prominently in post-war British efforts from an early stage, giving Britain what would become the most ambitious civil nuclear programme in the world.[53] The attractions of such a programme, to a country facing the apparently irreversible decline of its coal industry, and increasingly concerned about the security of its oil supplies, seemed indisputable at the time.[54] The construction of two reactors, capable of producing plutonium for the weapons programme, was decided upon as early as 1947, and by 1950 these were in use, demonstrating that a useful by-product of their operations was heat. Arguably marking the start of Britain's civil nuclear energy programme was the decision in 1949 to replace these two Windscale reactors with two more, capable of generating electricity. In 1952, on Churchill's orders, work began to design what became the pioneering Calder Hall plant, where construction began in August 1953 following the announcement by Duncan Sandys, the minister of supply, that a nuclear power programme was planned.[55]

Britain's concerns during 1952 were aggravated by the apparent readiness of the Australians to negotiate directly with the US over uranium supplies.[56] Ironically, in view of Prime Minister Robert Menzies' extraordinarily accommodating attitude over British nuclear weapons testing in Australia (soon to be seen in the detonation in October of Britain's first device, off the Monte Bello Islands), his government's position on uranium development proved to be unpalatably independent for London's tastes. In August 1951, Menzies approached the US government, hoping to interest Washington in the new uranium deposit at Radium Hill.[57] In March 1952, Professor Marc Oliphant, a key figure in the Manhattan Project and chairman of the Australian government's atomic energy advisory committee, wrote to Lord Cherwell, the paymaster-general and Churchill's personal adviser on nuclear matters, concerning the agreement concluded between Canberra and Washington over US purchases of South Australian uranium. Remarkably, Oliphant's committee had not been consulted about these arrangements.[58] Understandably, perhaps, given the precedent of Canada's apparently attractive uranium contracts, pressures emerged within the Australian government to ensure that Australia derived the maximum possible financial return on the exploitation of its natural resources. Some ministers argued, parenthetically, that higher dollar earnings would benefit the Sterling Area as a whole. Equally, on political grounds, Canberra could not accept a price for Rum Jungle uranium which was lower than that already negotiated by the government of South Australia for ore from Radium Hill.[59]

Whitehall's official committee on atomic energy agreed on 28 April 1952 that Britain should participate in CDA purchases of uranium from Radium Hill and in the development of ore from Rum Jungle.[60] By May 1952, the CDA had agreed to buy the entire output of Radium Hill, until early 1961, and to buy ore from Rum Jungle for three years. The price in each case was around 97 shillings per pound of ore, compared with the 41 shillings 6 pence paid for the higher grade Belgian Congo ore, and an average 72 shillings for the chemically similar South African ore.[61] The chancellor of the exchequer noted the financial implications arising from Britain's membership of the CDA (along with the 'insatiable hunger' of the US 'for more and more production'). While he had approved a 'relatively modest' (£600,000) additional commitment to the Rum Jungle project, and acquiesced in the government's general line that Britain should continue to take its share of any further CDA developments within the Commonwealth, provided that the costs were not 'totally unreasonable', he concluded that any further schemes arising *outside* the Commonwealth ought to be treated with caution.[62] More immediately, Lord Cherwell would set out his growing concerns when he held discussions with Menzies in Australia in October 1953. Among these, unsurprisingly, was the sheer scale of Washington's appetite for uranium, despite the devastating stockpile of nuclear weapons the US already possessed (enough to destroy the Soviet Union 'two or three times over'), and the indication that American purchases of uranium from any source, and, crucially, at any price, would continue. Given that Britain contributed one-third of the CDA's funds, Cherwell added, London thought it reasonable for Britain to secure one-third of the uranium acquired by the agency.[63]

It was not only cost, nor the fact that the Americans had a taken the lead in negotiations with Canberra, which irked London. There were also suspicions that Washington was attempting to steal a march on Britain in its dealings with Australia by offering to share civil nuclear technology with the Australians as an added inducement to accept US terms on the Rum Jungle contract, to secure for the US a larger share of available Australian uranium. This apparent American willingness to modify the terms of the McMahon Act, when it suited Washington, threatened to undermine Britain's long-term plans to capitalise on what promised to become a lucrative export market.[64]

Having previously drawn most of its uranium from the Belgian Congo and Portugal, which between them yielded the cheapest sources then available, Britain in mid-1952 faced the prospect that its long-term supplies would come from relatively expensive suppliers, South Africa and, possibly, South Australia.[65] It was against this background, combined with growing British concern about the US appetite for uranium, and misgivings about the Australian government's stance on uranium development, that London showed renewed interest in possible colonial sources of the mineral. In July 1952, Lord Cherwell approached the colonial secretary, Oliver Lyttelton, to remind him of the government's concern about the uranium supply position. 'It would be particularly valuable', he wrote, 'if we could find a source in the Colonies, as we have an agreement with America by which we share anything which is bought outside metropolitan or Colonial areas.' Cherwell knew only of Nigeria as a colonial source, but here there were technical and geographical difficulties, 'but we cannot help hoping that there must be richer deposits in some part of the Colonial Empire'. Aware that the Colonial Geological Service was doing what it could, Cherwell could not resist noting that there were currently some 500 US geologists scouring the planet for uranium, and asking if Britain could not do more.[66] Involved in Britain's research programme from its inception, Cherwell exercised great influence over Churchill on nuclear policy matters.[67] His anxieties about Washington's capacity to overwhelm Britain in a scramble for uranium have already been noted. It was Cherwell who, with a rhetorical flourish reminiscent of Curzon, had warned Churchill that only atomic weapons could prevent imperial states such as Britain declining to the status of colonized subjects: 'If we are to rely entirely on the United States ... for this vital weapon, we shall sink to the rank of a second-class nation, like the native levies who were allowed small arms but no artillery.'[68]

Coincidentally with Cherwell's initiative, new possibilities appeared to be emerging in Northern Rhodesia. At the Mindola section of the Nkana copper mine, operated by the Anglo American group, a sizeable (125,000 tons) deposit of uranium ore had been unearthed. Like Anglo American, the Division of Atomic Energy concluded that this discovery justified the construction at Mindola of a uranium plant.[69] Also in 1952, a DAE report on Northern Rhodesia reinforced optimism in London about the territory's potential, described as being 'of considerable importance'.[70]

During the spring and summer of 1952, then, there coalesced a number of factors which had potentially alarming implications for the British nuclear programme. Clear evidence of a disturbingly high US appetite for uranium, far-reaching discussions on Britain's entire global strategy and disappointing experience of the scope for favourable access to Commonwealth supplies all helped to prompt renewed British enthusiasm for the potential of Northern Rhodesia as a secure source. It was precisely at this point that plans for the future of Britain's central African territories were being finalised in London. While Churchill's Cabinet had agreed in principle in November 1951 to support the idea of a federation,[71] the necessary preparations were made during the first half of 1952. These involved not only a conference in London during April and May, but also less than convincing attempts to 'consult' African opinion in the region. The White Paper embodying the federal proposals was agreed by Cabinet in June 1952, at the height of concerns about uranium supplies. While the cabinet secretary's notes of the Cabinet's discussion make no reference to uranium, it seems unlikely that this aspect escaped ministers' notice.[72]

The Americans swiftly revealed their interest in Northern Rhodesian developments, pressing London for details. If the Mindola project could be brought under CDA auspices, then US technical and personnel support was assured: CDA finance might also be available. Key US officials considered Northern Rhodesia's potential to be of 'considerable importance' to the joint Anglo-American effort.[73] Highly revealing, however, were the contrasting reactions of officials in London. As the Ministry of Supply's Atomic Energy Division confided to the Washington Embassy, 'there has been a great deal of talk here in high circles about the advantages of discovering, in Colonial territory a source of uranium which could be outside [Combined Development]

Agency arrangements in the way that Colorado uranium is outside them'. The Mindola deposit in Northern Rhodesia appeared to be 'just what people had hoped for'. It was understandably disconcerting, therefore, for British officials to discover that a DAE official had 'blown the gaff' by telling the Americans about it.[74]

To the DAE, it soon appeared that the new Northern Rhodesian find was of 'real importance', and a senior geologist was quickly despatched to the territory to conduct a six-week investigation. Late in 1952, the DAE informed the CDA that, although the precise prospects were not yet clear, the indications were that Northern Rhodesia might produce fifty to 100 tons of uranium ore a year, with operations expected to commence in 1954.[75] Galvanised by this prospect, London made every effort to ensure that the new deposit was assessed rapidly and thoroughly, and developed without delay. In December 1952, the Atomic Energy (Official) Committee requested the Ministry of Supply to conclude a uranium-producing contract with the Rhokana Corporation as quickly as possible.[76] Although it was resolved to keep the Americans fully informed about progress, and to seek US technical help if necessary, the Official Committee decided that the Mindola project should be developed by the Ministry of Supply, *outside* the remit of the CDA. The uranium produced at Mindola was to be purchased direct by the British government. Like indigenous production in the US (at Colorado, for instance), which the US government bought direct, Northern Rhodesian uranium would be taken into account in determining CDA allocations.[77] As Stockwell has noted, during the 1950s Britain was keen, as a general principle, to maintain colonial mining operations in British hands, where possible.[78] London's interest in developing an independent uranium supply could, arguably, be seen as an example of this larger tendency.

Late in 1953, with the federation now established, the desirability of establishing Northern Rhodesia as an independent source of uranium for Britain was greater than it had ever been. South Africa's output (expected to match the Belgian Congo's), while welcome, and ultimately of critical importance to Britain's plans, came with the complication that all its production would be committed to the CDA until 1964.[79] This fact, together with difficulties over Australian uranium and Washington's increasingly proprietorial position regarding 'Free World' supplies, only highlighted the importance, to Britain, of Northern Rhodesia's potential: 'This seems the only other possible source of major supply for civil purposes at present in sight.'[80] The election of Eisenhower, and the promise this brought of a modest relaxation of the constraints on US military nuclear co-operation, did nothing, therefore, to diminish London's anxieties about the ambitious civil programme's security.[81] Fresh from his meeting with Menzies in Australia in October 1953, where he had described US rivalry in the atomic field, especially the latter's bottomless purse when buying uranium, Cherwell was soon seeking reassurances from the Ministry of Supply that all possible was being done to explore Northern Rhodesia's potential.[82] From London's viewpoint, the major concern, late in 1953, was to secure the maximum possible supplies of uranium for the civil programme, a problem which the official committee on atomic energy discussed on 4 November 1953. As the 'vague' offer of Australian uranium was thought inadequate, 'uncommitted' sources of uranium were being examined. The overriding British objective was to guarantee uranium supplies for industrial purposes unrestricted by any arrangements with the US, since, as Pierson Dixon of the Foreign Office explained, 'it is distinctly unpalatable to think that our major source of power in 30 years' time might be subject to the vacillations of American policy'.[83]

Even as late as the summer of 1954, an official of the newly formed United Kingdom Atomic Energy Authority, successor to the Atomic Energy Division of the Ministry of Supply, could note: 'We still think that there is a good chance of the Rhodesias making an important contribution to our uranium needs.' The authority's geologists, like their predecessors, retained faith that, given the similarity of Northern Rhodesia to the Belgian Congo, a uranium find was still possible, even though, given local circumstances, it might prove to be a relatively expensive source. Moreover, to fail to proceed with a scheme like that at Mindola would, it was believed, undermine all Britain's recent efforts to encourage the search for colonial uranium.[84] Still, rapid returns seemed unlikely. The outlook for Britain accordingly appeared bleak by summer 1954, as the Federation of Rhodesia and Nyasaland approached its first anniversary. Ministers concluded with resignation that there was little prospect of securing uranium supplies independent of the CDA, ideally within the Commonwealth, 'for at least the next five years'.[85]

The aim of this article has been to propose not a jettisoning of existing interpretations of the Central African Federation's origins: its purpose is far more modest. It suggests that the inclusion of the 'nuclear dimension' may help to produce a more nuanced reading of British motives in creating the federation, or at least, a broader awareness of the preoccupations of the British government at this time. The particular constellation of pressures confronting London in 1952, the year in which Cabinet authorised definite action on the long-delayed federal proposal, is striking. Rivalry with the United States, faltering ties with the 'Old' Commonwealth and strategic reassessments which demanded an enhanced British nuclear capacity all threw into relief the desirability of an indisputably 'British' source of the commodity against which national power would increasingly be measured. It is conceivable that, *inter alia*, Britain's preference for federation, rather than amalgamation in central Africa, was shaped by the fact that Northern Rhodesia would remain subject to continuing, direct, British influence. Specifically, the difficulties recently encountered with the Australians over the development of the Rum Jungle uranium deposit were less likely to be experienced in the case of a Northern Rhodesia firmly under British control. More generally, in addition to the obvious hopelessness of any attempt by Britain to compete with the United States for uranium, the apparent eclipsing of British interests in Commonwealth supplies, suggested by the dominant role adopted by Washington in negotiating contracts with Australia and South Africa, and its pre-emptive securing of Canadian output, arguably served to emphasise the fragility of Commonwealth links and dwindling British influence at a time when fundamental changes in the association's very nature seemed possible, given recent developments towards self-government in the Gold Coast (liable to strain London's relations with Pretoria) and the impending possibility of an application for Commonwealth membership from the Sudan. In this context, an added incentive arose to avoid 'dominion' status for the Central African Federation in the near future (although this ultimate possibility was dangled at local settler politicians to ensure their co-operation), and to guarantee unrestricted access to Northern Rhodesia's uranium potential by keeping the territory securely under Colonial Office control. As with so much else associated with the federation, that most ambiguous of British initiatives in late-imperial management, London's hopes would, ultimately, be disappointed. Yet, rather like the confidence apparently evident in Britain's decision to create the federation, the bid for independence enshrined in Britain's quest for a secure colonial source of uranium adds to the sense that, far from meekly accepting the inevitability of post-war decline, British policy-makers in the 1950s were keen to hold the line, and still saw an important role for the colonial territories in achieving their ambition.

Notes

[1] See, e.g., Holland, 'The Imperial Factor', 179.
[2] Holland, *Pursuit of Greatness*, 281–82.
[3] Hyam, 'Geopolitical Origins of the Central African Federation', 145.
[4] On the origins of the federation, Hyam, 'The Geopolitical Origins', can now be supplemented by Murphy, *Central Africa*, and the same author's '"Government by Blackmail"'.
[5] Gupta, *Imperialism and the British Labour Movement*, 340.
[6] It is largely ignored in Margaret Gowing's still otherwise authoritative study of the post-war nuclear programme, *Independence and Deterrence*. For an innovative study of early atomic diplomacy, see Kelly, 'No Ordinary Foreign Office Official'.
[7] The standard accounts of the British project remain Gowing, *Britain and Atomic Energy* and the same author's two-volume *Independence and Deterrence*.
[8] Paul, *Nuclear Rivals*, 3; Ball, 'Military nuclear relations', 445–47.
[9] Best, *Churchill: A Study in Greatness*, 309.
[10] Hyam, 'Africa and the Labour Government', 149.
[11] Stockwell, 'African Prospects', *passim*.
[12] Stockwell, 'African Prospects', 81–82.
[13] Geological Survey and Museum Atomic Energy Division, *Annual Report for the Year 1951*, EG 1/38, The National Archives (TNA).
[14] Stockwell, 'African Prospects', 81.
[15] See, especially, Hyam, *The Labour Government and the End of Empire*, xlii–xlvii.
[16] Sir Roger Makins to Sir Pierson Dixon, 21 Nov. 1953, EG 1/71, TNA; ibid., W. K. Ward to E. J. S. Clarke, 3 Dec. 1953 enc. Summary of various agreements with uranium-supplying countries.
[17] Gowing, *Independence and Deterrence*, I, 350.
[18] 'Sources and supplies of uranium', memo. by M. W. Perrin and D. C. Gattiker, 17 Dec. 1943, AB 1/537, TNA; ibid., Major-General L. R. Groves (Chairman, CDT) to Henry L. Stimson (Sec. of War and Chairman, CPC, Washington), 24 Nov. 1944.
[19] R. S. Sayers (DSIR) to W. Gorell Barnes (Privy Council Office), 3 June 1944, AB 1/586, TNA.
[20] F. C. How (Ministry of Supply) to Lord Cherwell, 25 Nov. 1953, EG 1/119, TNA. The *World Survey of Uranium Sources*, prepared for the CPC in 1944, concluded that uranium might be found in Northern Rhodesia.
[21] Combined Development Trust, 13th meeting of London Group, 12 June 1945, AB 1/507, TNA.
[22] Minutes of meeting of CDA, 12 Jan. 1949, AB 16/306, TNA.
[23] *Rhodesia Herald*, 6 June 1950. Davidson repeated the orthodox conclusion, drawn on the geological similarity between the Northern Rhodesian Copperbelt and the neighbouring Belgian Congo, where the world's largest deposits of uranium had been found.

[24] Helmreich, *Gathering Rare Ores*, 260; see also Stockwell, 'African Prospects', 82, citing SMC 23, 'Uranium Supply and Demand', circulated 8 Feb. 1950, AB 16/1918, TNA.
[25] Davidson to Peirson, 20 June 1950, AB 16/982, TNA.
[26] C. F. Davidson to P. J. Eaton (British Embassy, Washington), 21 June 1950, AB 16/306, TNA; ibid., R. A. Thompson (Ministry of Supply, Department of Atomic Energy) to Eaton, 23 Feb. 1951.
[27] J. A. Hall (USAEC) to P. J. Eaton, 13 June 1950, and Eaton to R. A. Thompson (Ministry of Supply, Division of Atomic Energy), 14 June 1950, AB 16/306, TNA.
[28] Minutes of meeting of CDA, 15 Feb. 1951, AB 16/306, TNA.
[29] R. A. Thompson to Eaton (Washington), 23 Feb. 1951, AB 16/306, TNA.
[30] C. F. Davidson to R. A. Thompson, 2 March 1951 and 6 March 1951, AB 16/306, TNA.
[31] Geological Survey and Museum Atomic Energy Division, *Annual Report for the Year 1951*, EG 1/38, TNA. A further difficulty surrounded the use of Geiger counters during Northern Rhodesia's notorious rainy season: see *The Mining Journal* No. 5969 (1950), 30.
[32] R. E. Leahy (USAEC) to P. J. Eaton, 13 April 1951, AB 16/306, TNA.
[33] Eaton to Leahy, 17 April 1951, AB 16/306, TNA.
[34] *Rhodesia Herald*, 30 April 1951; Geological Report by A. E. Phaup, 27 April 1951; Davidson to Eaton (Washington), 26 July 1951, enc. Report by Chief Geologist, Mufulira Copper Mines Ltd., on Cimbavi Betafite Prospect, Lundazi District, Northern Rhodesia, AB 16/306, TNA; ibid., Davidson to J. C. Ferguson (Geological Survey of Southern Rhodesia, Salisbury), 18 Aug. 1951.
[35] Geological Survey and Museum, *Annual Report for the Year 1951*, EG 1/38, TNA; P. F. G. Twinn (Division of Atomic Energy) to P. J. Eaton (Washington), 8 Jan. 1954, AB 16/306, TNA.
[36] P. J. Eaton to R. A. Thompson (Ministry of Supply, DAE), 18 Oct. 1951, AB 16/306, TNA. Meanwhile, US finance was being made available to develop other colonial mineral resources. For example, in May 1951, plans were approved to use £3 million of Economic Co-operation Administration funds to develop new copper and cobalt capacity at the Chibuluma mine in Northern Rhodesia. Here, the possibility of finding uranium was also being kept in mind: see Davidson to R. A. Thompson, 2 July 1951, AB 16/306, TNA; see also Butler, *Copper Empire*, 139–42.
[37] Sir Roger Makins to Lord Cherwell (Paymaster-General), 'Top Secret', 12 Nov. 1951, EG 1/38, TNA; ibid., minute by Cherwell, 12 Nov. 1951.
[38] E. J. S. Clarke (Paymaster General's Office) to N. Pritchard (Commonwealth Relations Office), 2 Nov. 1953, EG 1/71, TNA. It could, of course, be reasoned that although, for Washington, Britain's atomic programme was a potential competitor for a limited supply of uranium, the US also looked to Britain for co-operation in securing some of that uranium. Paul, *Nuclear Rivals*, 3–5.
[39] Paul, *Nuclear Rivals*, 172–75.
[40] Sir Christopher Steel to Sir Roger Makins (Deputy Under-Sec. of State, Foreign Office), Top Secret and Personal, 30 Oct. 1952, EG 1/38, TNA.
[41] Eckes, *The United States and the Global Struggle*, 181; Helmreich, *Gathering Rare Ores*, 240.
[42] ANCAM 509 Secret, BJSM Washington to Cabinet Office, 13 Feb. 1952, EG 1/38, TNA.
[43] F. W. Marten (British Embassy, Washington) to W. Harpham (General Dept., Foreign Office), 18 March 1952, EG 1/38, TNA.
[44] BJSM to Cabinet Office, Top Secret, 3 June 1952, EG 1/38, TNA. Washington's intention to regard nuclear weapons as an unexceptional form of munitions would eventually be enshrined in Eisenhower's 'New Look' strategy, adopted late in 1953. The 'Basic National Security Policy' (NSC-162-2), approved by the president in October, was itself driven partly by the search for economies in the conventional defence budget. See Baylis, *Ambiguity and Deterrence*, 158.
[45] Sir Christopher Steel (British Embassy, Washington) to Sir Roger Makins (Foreign Office), Top Secret, 23 May 1952, EG 1/38, TNA; ibid., CANAM 399, Top Secret, Cabinet Office to BJSM Washington, 28 May 1952.
[46] Helmreich, *Gathering Rare Ores*, 225.

[47] Baylis, *Ambiguity and Deterrence*, 126–51.
[48] Ibid., 143.
[49] R. E. France to Sir Roger Makins, 9 July 1952, AB 16/359, TNA.
[50] J. C. C. Stewart to E. J. S. Clarke, 5 May 1954, EG 1/71, TNA.
[51] Atomic Energy Board, AEB (52) 3rd meeting, 29 May 1952, AB 41/557, TNA.
[52] E. J. S. Clarke (Paymaster General's Office) to N. Pritchard (Commonwealth Relations Office), 2 Nov. 1953, EG 1/71, TNA.
[53] Edgerton, *Warfare State*, 105. Gowing's *Independence and Deterrence* remains indispensable on the civil programme. The UKAEA's pamphlet, *Atomic Energy in Britain*, is a less daunting introduction. The imbalance in available studies which privileges the military aspects of the programme, at the expense of its equally important civil dimension, is discussed in Arnold, 'Letter from Oxford'.
[54] On the coal industry, Ashworth, *History of the British Coal Industry* is authoritative. On oil supplies, Bamberg, *British Petroleum and Global Oil* is particularly informative.
[55] *The Times*, 27 Jan. 1953.
[56] Gowing, *Independence and Deterrence*, I, 374–88.
[57] Paul, *Nuclear Rivals*, 182–83.
[58] E. J. S. Clarke (Paymaster General's Office) to R. E. France (Ministry of Supply), 4 April 1952, EG 1/38, TNA.
[59] G. P. Humphreys-Davies to Acting High Commissioner, Canberra, No. 690 Secret, 3 Sept. 1952, and minute by W. Harpham (FO), 5 Nov. 1952, FO 371/99742, TNA. See also National Archives of Australia, '1952 Cabinet Records', http://www.naa.gov.au/collection/explore/cabinet/notebooks/events-issues-1952.aspx.
[60] CANAM 385 Cabinet Office to BJSM (Washington), 29 April 1952, EG 1/38, TNA.
[61] 'Free World: Sources of Uranium 1952/58', Top Secret, enc. in E. J. S. Clarke to Paymaster General, 28 May 1952, EG 1/38, TNA.
[62] G. P. Humphreys-Davies (Treasury) to Sir Roger Makins (Foreign Office), Top Secret, 21 July 1952, EG 1/38, TNA.
[63] Note of meeting in Canberra House, 5 Oct. 1953, EG 1/71, TNA.
[64] Makins to Sir John Cockcroft, 14 July 1952, and R. E. France to W. Harpham (FO), 22 Dec. 1952, FO 371/ 99742, TNA. It was Oliphant who revealed this offer to Sir John Cockcroft (Director of the Atomic Energy Research Establishment, Harwell): see Cockcroft to Makins, 16 June 1952, ibid. As with Britain's own nuclear project, Australia's growing interest in civil nuclear energy was intimately linked to the country's discreet aspirations to acquire nuclear weapons: see Reynolds, 'Rethinking the Joint Project'.
[65] C. F. Davidson to Lt.-Gen. Sir Frederick Morgan (Controller of Atomic Energy, Ministry of Supply), 30 May 1952, AB 16/707, TNA.
[66] Cherwell to Lyttelton, 25 July 1952, EG 1/38, TNA.
[67] Paul, *Nuclear Rivals*, 189. Cherwell remained concerned about Washington's capacity to thwart British ambitions for a close partnership with Australia over uranium supplies, fearing that Canberra might be induced to make a 'private deal' with the US: CC 30(53), 21 April 1953, CAB 195/11, TNA.
[68] Quoted in Cawte, *Atomic Australia*, 41.
[69] Note for file by R. A. Thompson, 16 July 1952, AB 16/306, TNA.
[70] Report by J. G. Bower (DAE, Ministry of Supply) on Northern Rhodesia, 18 July 1952, AB 16/306, TNA.
[71] The key consideration, as the cabinet secretary's record confirms, was anxiety to prevent the growth of South African influence in central Africa, and a desire to proceed quickly, while Sir Godfrey Huggins, the Southern Rhodesian prime minister and driving force behind federation, could still succeed: CC 7(51), 15 Nov. 1951, CAB 195/10, TNA.
[72] CC 60(52), 17 June 1952, CAB 195/10, TNA.

[73] Jesse C. Johnson (Director of Raw Materials, USAEC) to J. G. Bower, 4 Aug. 1952, AB 16/306, TNA.
[74] R. A. Thompson to P. J. Eaton (Washington), 8 Aug. 1952, AB 16/306, TNA.
[75] CDA minutes, 12 Nov. 1952, AB 16/306, TNA.
[76] E. J. S. Clarke (United Kingdom Atomic Energy Authority) to M .I. Michaels (LPO), 11 Nov. 1954, EG 1/119, TNA. Whitehall's Strategic Minerals Committee had already agreed that the Ministry of Supply should arrange to buy Northern Rhodesia's uranium, ensuring British control of the territory's output: see Stockwell, 'African Prospects', 89, n77, citing SMC 27th minutes, 8 Sept. 1952, section IV, AB 16/1279, TNA.
[77] R. A. Thompson to P. J. Eaton (British Embassy, Washington), 15 Sept. 1952, AB 16/306, TNA; memo by Pierson Dixon, 'Uranium requirements in 1953', 26 Feb. 1953, EG 1/38, TNA; F.C. How to Cherwell, 25 Nov. 1953, EG 1/119, TNA.
[78] Stockwell, 'African Prospects', 85–88.
[79] Draft cabinet paper by Lord President of the Council, 'Atomic Energy – Commonwealth Co-operation', n.d. but late 1953, EG 1/71, TNA. See also Paul, *Nuclear Rivals*, 182–83.
[80] E. J. S. Clarke (Paymaster General's Office) to N. Pritchard (Commonwealth Relations Office), 2 Nov. 1953, EG 1/71, TNA.
[81] Baylis, 'Exchanging Nuclear Secrets', 36. The softening of Washington's attitude was prompted partly by recent advances in Soviet weapons technology. Full Anglo-US co-operation would have to await Macmillan's July 1958 agreement with Eisenhower, which effectively nullified the McMahon Act: Ball, 'Military Nuclear Relations', 441.
[82] Cherwell to F.C. How, 27 Oct. 1953, EG 1/119, TNA.
[83] Pierson Dixon (Foreign Office) to Sir Roger Makins (British Embassy, Washington), 21 Nov. 1953, EG 1/71, TNA. Equally, London's desire to deflect US involvement in central Africa remained strong: 'We are anxious not to give our friends the slightest encouragement to interest themselves in this part of the world ... we are hoping to develop any sources of uranium there ... without American help'. See EG 1/71, P. F. G. Twinn (Division of Atomic Energy) to P. J. Eaton (British Embassy, Washington), 8 Jan. 1954, EG 1/71, TNA.
[84] Shaw (UKAEA) to P. J. Eaton (Washington), 16 August 1954, AB 16/306, TNA; E. J. S. Clarke (UKAEA) to M. I. Michaels (Lord President's Office), 11 Nov. 1954, EG 1/119, TNA.
[85] 'Future Supplies of Uranium', AE(M)(54)5, 19 July 1954, EG 1/71, TNA.

References

Arnold, Lorna. 'A Letter from Oxford: The History of Nuclear History in Britain'. *Minerva* 38 (2000): 201–19.
Ashworth, William. *The History of the British Coal Industry, Vol. 5, The Nationalised Industry 1946–1982*. Oxford: Oxford University Press, 1986.
Ball, S. J. 'Military Nuclear Relations between the United States and Great Britain under the Terms of the McMahon Act, 1946–1958'. *Historical Journal* 38 (1995): 439–54.
Bamberg, James. *History of British Petroleum, Vol. 3, British Petroleum and Global Oil, 1950–1975: The Challenge of Nationalism*. Cambridge: Cambridge University Press, 2000.
Baylis, John. *Ambiguity and Deterrence: British Nuclear Strategy, 1945–1964*. Oxford: Clarendon Press, 1995.
———. 'Exchanging Nuclear Secrets: Laying the Foundations of the Anglo-American Nuclear Relationship'. *Diplomatic History* 25, no. 1 (2001): 33–61.
Best, Geoffrey. *Churchill: A Study in Greatness*. Harmondsworth: Penguin, 2002.
Butler, L. J. *Copper Empire: Mining and the Colonial State in Northern Rhodesia, c.1930–64*. Basingstoke: Palgrave Macmillan, 2007.
Cawte, Alice. *Atomic Australia 1944–1990*. Sydney: University of New South Wales Press, 1992.

Eckes, Alfred E., Jr. *The United States and the Global Struggle for Minerals*. Austin, TX, and London: University of Texas Press, 1979.
Edgerton, David. *Warfare State: Britain, 1920–1970*. Cambridge: Cambridge University Press, 2005.
Gowing, Margaret. *Britain and Atomic Energy, 1939–1945*. London: Macmillan, 1964.
Gowing, Margaret with Lorna Arnold. *Independence and Deterrence: Britain and Atomic Energy, 1945–1952*, Vol. 1, *Policy Making*; Vol. 2, *Policy Execution*. London: Macmillan, 1974.
Gupta, Partha Sarathi. *Imperialism and the British Labour Movement 1914–1964*. London: Macmillan, 1975.
Helmreich, Jonathan E. *Gathering Rare Ores: The Diplomacy of Uranium Acquisition, 1943–1954*. Princeton, NJ: Princeton University Press, 1986.
Holland, R. F. 'The Imperial Factor in British Strategies from Attlee to Macmillan, 1945–63'. In *Perspectives on Imperialism and Decolonization: Essays in Honour of A. F. Madden*, edited by R.F. Holland and G. Rizvi London: Frank Cass, 1984.
Holland, R. F. *The Pursuit of Greatness: Britain and the World Role*. London: Fontana, 1991.
Hyam, Ronald. 'The Geopolitical Origins of the Central African Federation: Britain, Rhodesia and South Africa, 1948–1953'. *Historical Journal* 30 (1987): 145–72.
———. 'Africa and the Labour Government, 1945–1951'. In *Theory and Practice in the History of European Overseas Expansion: Essays in Honour of R.E. Robinson*, edited by London: Frank Cass, 1988.
———. *The Labour Government and the End of Empire 1945–1951. British Documents on the End of Empire Series A*. Vol. 2. London: HMSO, 1992.
Kelly, Saul. 'No Ordinary Foreign Office Official: Sir Roger Makins and Anglo-American Atomic Relations 1945–55'. *Contemporary British History* 14, no. 4 (2000): 107–24.
Murphy, Philip, ed. *Central Africa Part I: Closer Association 1945–1958. British Documents on the End of Empire*. London: The Stationery Office, 2005.
———. '"Government by Blackmail": The Origins of the Central African Federation Reconsidered'. In *The British Empire in the 1950s: Retreat or Revival?*, edited by Martin Lynn. Basingstoke: Palgrave Macmillan, 2006.
Paul, Septimus H. *Nuclear Rivals: Anglo-American Atomic Relations 1941–1952*. Columbus, OH: Ohio State University Press, 2000.
Reynolds, Wayne. 'Rethinking the Joint Project: Australia's Bid for Nuclear Weapons, 1945–1960'. *The Historical Journal* 41, no. 3 (1998): 853–73.
Stockwell, Sarah. 'African Prospects: Mining the Empire for Britain in the 1950s'. In *The British Empire in the 1950s: Retreat or Revival?*, edited by Martin Lynn. Basingstoke: Palgrave Macmillan, 2006.
UKAEA Historian's Office. *Atomic Energy in Britain 1939–1978*. 4th ed. Harwell: Atomic Energy Research Establishment, 1979.

Overseas Mission, Voluntary Service and Aid to Africa: Max Warren, the Church Missionary Society and Kenya, 1945–63

John Stuart

In October 1953 a headquarters official of the Church Missionary Society (CMS) summed up the challenges faced by missions in colonial Africa, and particularly in Kenya. Bernard Nicholls was the CMS information officer, broadly responsible for what would now be termed media affairs. Nicholls wrote:

> To-day Conservatives, Liberals, Labour and Communists, and innumerable associations and pressure groups, including the whole phalanx of international agencies, vie with each other for the reputation of being the biggest and best champions of the interests and true welfare of the under-privileged peoples. Many people's livelihoods and much [sic] vested interests are concerned in this struggle.

His comments were addressed to the CMS Africa secretary, Canon Cecil Bewes, who was investigating abuses of authority by security forces in Kenya. 'I am finding it increasingly irritating', Nicholls went on with reference to that Labour MP of most pronounced anti-imperialist views, 'to have it thrown at me that the only champions of the Africans in Kenya are Fenner Brockway and his friends'.[1] Unique in certain important respects the situation in Kenya in 1953 was in other ways emblematic of broader changes in Africa since the end of the Second World War. Nationalism was growing and the continent was indeed the subject of increasing attention, in Britain and around the world. Politicians such as Brockway openly espoused the nationalist cause in ways that missionaries at this time were loath to do. Meanwhile 'international agencies' with links to governments and to the United Nations were becoming involved in regions where missions had until recently been almost the sole western provider to Africans of education and medical care.[2] In this context, thought Nicholls, it was vital that missions remember their obligation not merely to evangelise but also to support human rights and liberties.[3] This was especially the case in Kenya: since October 1952 a 'state of emergency' had been in force and Africans in their tens of thousands had been detained without trial in conditions of great hardship.

As Stephen Howe has recently noted, it ought to be possible to trace the effects of Mau Mau and its suppression on British public life rather as one might a barium meal in an x-ray.[4] Yet the effects appear to have been remarkably limited. Is this because outside Westminster and London Mau Mau failed to resonate in Britain? This article suggests otherwise. Mau Mau and its suppression did indeed resonate in Britain and also in other countries outside Africa but in sometimes oblique ways. In order to trace some of these effects we must look beyond the bilateral relationship between colony and metropole to the broader imperial and international context. The attention to which Kenya was subjected in the 1950s and after by governments, by religious organisations and by international aid and relief agencies was strongly indicative of and influential upon broader changes in western engagement with Africa as a whole.

Arguably no part of late colonial Africa has been more studied than Kenya.[5] Recently the work of David Anderson and of Caroline Elkins has attracted a great deal of interest and controversy. Elkins is extremely critical of Protestant missionaries' failure to challenge abuses of authority. Anderson, conversely, presents a more nuanced account of their actions, noting the sporadically successful efforts of individual missionaries to obtain redress of African grievances. Missionary responses both to Mau Mau and to colonial misrule were complex and ambiguous. And, while missions of many different denominations and nationalities worked in Kenya, this article focuses mainly on the CMS and on Canon Max Warren, its general secretary from 1942 to 1963. The CMS had a long history of mission work in east Africa. Warren (1904–77) was a major figure who is overdue critical re-evaluation, not merely for his role in mission but also for his place in post-war English (and especially Anglican) public life.[6] In addition to focusing on Kenya the article considers Warren's deep interest in mission and in voluntary service from Britain. It also looks at his role in the founding of Oversea Service, a British lay Christian initiative whose origins owed much to events in Kenya. According to Andrew Porter, Warren was convinced that 'the precondition of Christianity's future in the colonial world was an end to the formal and informal empires of the "old" churches and missionary bodies'.[7] What occurred in Kenya during the 1950s, however, gave Warren cause to fear that empire and mission in Africa might both give way to a new order in which international aid agencies exerted preponderant influence over African churches, and over African national states.

I

In the immediate aftermath of the Second World War and largely under Warren's direction the CMS began a retrenchment programme, officially described as 'realignment'.[8] This was only partially successful. Warren encountered stubborn resistance to his plans, especially from missionaries in Kenya jealous of what they regarded as their special, historic role in the expansion of Christianity in Africa. In consequence, relations between headquarters and Kenyan missions were characterised by prickliness. There were also further complications, not unique to Kenya. These included the presence of a white settler minority and an uneasy relationship between missions and local church dioceses. Having originated and developed as a voluntary association separate from the Church of England the evangelical CMS was suspicious of episcopal authority. But during the 1950s the diocese of Mombasa (coterminous with the colony of Kenya), particularly in the shape of its most influential cleric, Leonard Beecher, would exert a strong influence on CMS mission affairs. Yet Warren was not concerned merely with mission *in* Africa he was also extremely interested in mission *from* Britain and the west. The theology of mission was to him an immensely important matter. Warren believed the voluntary missionary organisation to be an essential component of the world church. Overseas mission, he reasoned, could not cease even with the devolution of ecclesiastical authority to indigenous churches (and indigenous church leaders) in Asia and Africa.[9]

Committed as he was to the indigenisation of the church in Africa, Warren was equally committed to overseas voluntary Christian service. Like many church and mission leaders in Britain during and after the war he worried about the omnicompetent tendencies of the state, not least in terms of the threat posed to individual spirituality.[10] Conversely he was impressed by William Beveridge's 1948 espousal of voluntarism, in his book *Voluntary Action*.[11] Warren perceived overseas mission service as an important means by which individuals and society in Britain as well as overseas could be spiritually enriched. Of course state interventionism (notably in the form of the welfare state) was by no means confined to Britain, as legislation for colonial welfare and development in 1940 and 1945 demonstrated all too clearly. Government funding (typically in the form of grants-in-aid) might benefit missions, but it might also impose upon them obligations both onerous and restricting. Despite this missions continued to place great importance on the provision of African education. But they encountered difficulty in recruiting suitably qualified Christian teachers. In 1946 British Protestant missions agreed to create a new employment category: the missionary associate. The typical associate would be a qualified teaching professional and an active Christian, contracted to work for a specific period, of three to five years. Rates of pay would be commensurate with those of others already undertaking the same duties but there would also be a completion-of-contract bonus.[12] What was Warren's attitude to this initiative? Even though he was a vigorous advocate of mission as lifetime vocation, he supported the idea of the missionary associate, believing it would give fresh encouragement to Christian laypeople thinking of working in the service of the church.[13] The scheme was in any case intended as a stop-gap, to meet the short-term needs of the missions and to assuage concern on two fronts: about 'dilution' of the missionary endeavour and about the bonus payment, with its preferential implications.[14]

The missionary associate scheme represented a limited mission response to contemporary difficulties; it failed to meet the continuing African demand for education. By the late 1940s the fierceness both of that demand and also of criticism for the missions' failure to meet it had begun to exert an unnerving effect on missionaries in Kenya and especially in Nairobi, by now the colony's undisputed centre of militant African politics.[15] The views of Rev. Martin Capon of the CMS were more reactionary than most but not entirely untypical; in May 1949 Capon urged that the missions work more closely with government to combat 'agitators' among the Kikuyu and to help 'produce the core of Christian citizens which alone can be an answer to any communist threat and the foundation for a continuance of the British way of life in Kenya'.[16] Missionary expectations had been raised by the publication in 1948 of a report by the Colonial Office's Advisory Committee on Education in the Colonies entitled *Education for Citizenship in Africa*. This envisaged missions as instrumental in the continuing provision of both primary and secondary education to African children. The British government was committed to colonial education and welfare, as part of ten-year development plans to be followed by governments in the colonies.[17] The response of those governments was varied, with that of Kenya being at first notably inadequate and ill planned.[18] This exacerbated local church and mission frustration. It influenced the findings of an official committee formed in January 1949 to inquire into African education.

At the time of his appointment by the government of Kenya to chair this committee, Leonard Beecher was an archdeacon, in effect an assistant bishop, and arguably one of the best-connected and best-informed Europeans in Kenya. He had come to the colony as a CMS missionary in 1927 already knowledgeable about the place and its people; he was affianced to Gladys Leakey, Kenyan-born daughter of CMS missionaries Canon Harry and Mary Leakey and sister of archaeologist Louis Leakey. Following marriage and ordination Beecher acquired a host of new responsibilities, among them nominated representative for African interests on Kenya's Legislative Council. He was pragmatic, compassionate and very high-minded. He knew Kenya and its peoples and was seldom slow to assert himself in this respect. He exerted a strong influence on the findings of the committee. Its report ('The Beecher Report') acknowledged that African education had indeed expanded since the war, but in an uncoordinated and unplanned fashion. The committee urged greater emphasis now on 'moral' Christian teaching in schools. This was deemed vital in order to remedy 'a breakdown in moral standards in

African society in recent years .... The aim must be to produce at all levels of African society morally sound, economically valuable citizens'.[19] The government in Nairobi accepted the report's recommendations.[20]

The report provoked a strongly critical reaction from Africans. They justifiably perceived it as biased against those independent schools that had developed as a reaction against missions during the 1920s.[21] Adverse African opinion was but one of several challenges that Beecher faced in his efforts to implement the proposals; he also had to contend with Warren's displeasure. Warren disputed the committee's findings, arguing that the CMS could not supply teachers and inspectors in the numbers required.[22] Protracted argument ensued between diocese and mission headquarters in which diocesan officials contemplated a recruitment drive of their own. Sensing potential for enormous confusion Warren yielded and in April 1951 committed the CMS to a fresh search for education staff.[23] The effort was extended to missions of other denominations and in January 1952 a small but significant development occurred: government in London allocated colonial welfare and development funds to set up an employment agency, the Overseas Appointments Bureau, to place teachers in mission-run and other Christian schools overseas.[24] Although it would place only twenty teachers in its first year of operation, the setting up of the bureau indicated that the recruiting of British Christians for educational work overseas would not remain the preserve of the missions. Six months before the declaration of a 'state of emergency' in Kenya Christian organisations in Britain were preparing to contribute to the expansion of African education provision in the colony.

II

'Do not think of us as a crowd of amateur politicians; we are concerned in these things because as ministers to both black and white we feel we have certain civic responsibilities as well as spiritual ones.'[25] This was Beecher's statement of intent, made to visiting Conservative secretary of state for colonies Oliver Lyttelton ten days after the imposition of 'emergency' conditions. With Bishop of Mombasa Reginald Crabbe about to retire Beecher was now in effect acting bishop. And at this time he had the support of other church leaders including the moderator of the Church of Scotland in east Africa, the Rev. David Steel. Beecher was determined that churches and missions should seize the opportunity to help make Christian citizens of the Kikuyu as a means of contributing to the defeat of Mau Mau. Christian theology, as John Casson has noted, would play a vital role.[26] But it would be adapted to local conditions. Anglican priest Obadiah Kariuki and missionaries based at Kahuhia and Weithaga devised a 'cleansing' ceremony, through which a participant might renounce the Mau Mau oath and seek purification 'through the blood of Christ [their] saviour who died on the Cross'.[27] Beecher also requested assistance from the CMS and from the Church of England in the form of funds and a proposed evangelistic 'task force' to combat the effects of Mau Mau oathing and to support Christian revival among the Kikuyu.[28] The CMS complied willingly. A public appeal raised £7,000, which was forwarded to Beecher for distribution to churches in the affected areas.

In April 1953 Beecher was enthroned as Bishop of Mombasa. That same month the governor of Kenya, Sir Evelyn Baring, estimated that 80,000 Africans were in detention and prison camps.[29] The authorities began to consider methods of 'rehabilitation', by which Mau Mau sympathisers could be persuaded to renounce the oath. Rehabilitation became part of a broader official strategy that also involved forced villagisation and land consolidation. As originally formulated, rehabilitation was to have a strongly 'moral', educative emphasis. Tom Askwith, Kenya's commissioner for community development, saw it in such terms, and regarded church participation as essential.[30] In February 1954 Askwith was co-opted onto a committee of the Christian Council of Kenya that had been formed to expedite the churches' participation in the new enterprise.[31] But the task was enormous, and far beyond the scope of existing resources. In March 1954 Beecher began a three-month visit to England. He lobbied politicians and campaigned widely for funds and staffing to support the rehabilitation effort. Kenya, he informed one audience, was at a turning point: 'it would never be the same country again'; the churches, he argued, must seize their opportunity.[32]

Beecher was far from alone in thinking this way. The worsening situation in Kenya was by now attracting the attention of a wide range of organisations in Britain, both secular and religious. Among these were the Oxford Committee for Famine Relief (later OXFAM), the Save the Children Fund and the Society of Friends. The interest of certain other groups, even with religious connections, was from Beecher's perspective far less welcome. Founder of Christian Action Canon John Collins announced in January 1954 plans for a public appeal for detainees' dependants.[33] The Africa Bureau's Rev. Michael Scott also spoke publicly on the situation in Kenya and in South Africa, where the Bantu Education Act had recently come into effect. Collins and Scott were too closely identified with the Left in Britain and with radical causes in Africa to be anything other than a source of unease to Beecher. Their expressions of concern stimulated him to greater efforts. In May 1954 he helped arrange a meeting at Friends House on London's Euston Road. There Quakers, representatives of churches and missions and of the Oxford Committee discussed the feasibility of an international, interdenominational appeal to support both rehabilitation and the dependants of detainees.

Among those present at the meeting was the CMS missionary the Rev. Stanley ('Sam') Morrison, who was about to take up the vacant secretaryship of the Christian Council of Kenya. Morrison was 60 years old. Decades of working with the CMS in Egypt had acquainted him well not merely with the intricacies of the relationship between missions and imperial authority but also of that between missions and local diocese.[34] Importantly, Morrison had experience in another sphere of activity: a large-scale humanitarian relief programme. In September 1951 CMS Egypt had seconded him to Gaza to work for an extended period with Arab refugees, homeless and destitute since the Arab-Israeli War of 1948. He adapted quickly to the peculiar demands of an international relief effort in which religious and secular agencies worked in sometimes uncomfortable proximity to each other and to official authority.[35] Morrison acquired expertise and influential personal contacts. His most important contact was Janet Lacey, the formidable secretary of the Inter-Church Aid and Refugee Service of the British Council of Churches (Inter-Church Aid, or ICA).

In Kenya the church and mission contribution to rehabilitation was being hampered by scarcity of resources and by the inefficiencies of the colonial administration. The entrusting of rehabilitation to the Moral Rearmament Movement at Athi River detention camp south east of Nairobi was not proving successful.[36] Morrison arrived in Kenya in June 1954 determined to transform the situation as a whole. He was committed to the policy of rehabilitation.[37] And his ambition was boundless: 'We shall probably have to look to the USA rather than to the UK for the major proportion of the money we shall require', he matter-of-factly informed Bewes, in London.[38] Morrison was not being unrealistic. Americans had learned about developments in Kenya through newsmagazines such as *Time* and *Newsweek* and also through a 1954 article in the mass-circulation *Reader's Digest*.[39] From another personal contact, the Geneva-based Scottish clergyman Robert Mackie of the Inter-Church Aid and Refugee Service of the World Council of Churches, Morrison received a pledge that the plight of the Christian Kikuyu would be brought to the attention of the second assembly of the World Council, to be held at Evanston, Illinois, in August. There British church and mission delegates and Lacey thrashed out plans for a public appeal that would be interdenominational and international in scope, to be co-ordinated by ICA and administered by the Christian Council of Kenya.[40] (Beecher made the plans known at the Anglican Congress, also held in August 1954, at Minneapolis.) Lacey was no less ambitious than Morrison: she decided that the target amount should be a not inconsiderable £50,000. But months of planning lay ahead.

III

Bewes had meanwhile continued to make discreet representations to the Colonial Office on the subject of abuses of authority in Kenya, but to little effect. During 1953, however, developments occurred within the Colonial Office that would indirectly influence ideas about Christian work overseas. Senior civil servants were perturbed by what they perceived as a turn for the worse in relations between Africans and Europeans in Kenya. As nationalist agitation grew British workers in other colonies (especially those on government service) might increasingly become the object of hostility. At this time civil servants and mission officials alike saw great potential in the study of 'race relations' and in government policies to promote racial 'partnership' and 'multiracialism' in east and central Africa. In January 1950 the British Council of Churches set up a Race Relations Group. In April 1951 what would subsequently become the Institute of Race Relations was formed at the Royal Institute of International Affairs, in London. Missionaries were interested in these developments. So too was the deputy under-secretary of state at the Colonial Office, Sir Charles Jeffries. In consultation with colleagues Jeffries conceived the notion that new recruits to the Colonial Service (the civil service for the colonies) might benefit from additional voluntary training, to prepare them for the new political and racial complexities that they would face.[41] A devout Anglican, Jeffries was a supporter of overseas mission and a vice-president of the Society for the Propagation of the Gospel.

Who better than the missions, he surmised, to advise government? In February 1953 he contacted Archbishop of Canterbury Geoffrey Fisher.[42]

Fisher was worried about Kenya. He liked Jeffries' idea. So did Warren. Six months earlier Warren had attended a conference of the International Missionary Council in Willingen, Germany. This had discussed among many other issues lay involvement in mission, about which Warren felt strongly. He had recently been contacted by an Edinburgh-based doctor just returned from Pakistan. His name was Harry Holland, and his father had for more than four decades run a renowned CMS eye hospital at Quetta. Holland was seeking a new vocation, perhaps as a priest. But he was also keen, as a result of his family's experience, to devise means of inculcating in Britons going overseas to work a sense of Christian responsibility and citizenship.[43] He had in mind a programme of residential training courses, aimed at government and at British businesses with overseas interests.[44] Warren encouraged him. Jeffries became an enthusiastic advocate. With their help and through assiduous lobbying on his own part Holland convinced sceptical business and commercial representatives that their firms should participate in training courses intended to enhance new employees' knowledge and awareness of life in Britain's overseas territories and other foreign countries. He eventually secured agreement from a number of firms including Barclays Bank DCO (Dominions and Colonial Office), Booker Brothers, British Petroleum, Cable & Wireless, Imperial Chemical Industries and Shell Oil. With funds obtained from the Cadbury Trust Holland set up Oversea Service, under the joint auspices of the Conference of British Missionary Societies and the British Council of Churches. Its slogan was 'Training for Responsible Partnership Abroad'.

Holland negotiated the use of two venues: the under-used (and unloved) Imperial Institute in South Kensington, London, and, through contacts in the Young Men's Christian Association, Dunford House in West Sussex, birthplace of Richard Cobden. He intended that the new organisation should become financially viable within three years. He expected that in excess of 50 per cent of income during this period would come from fees charged to participating government departments and businesses, with the remainder being provided by philanthropic bodies such as the Cadbury Trust and the Nuffield Foundation (notwithstanding Jeffries' influence he had little expectation of direct assistance from government). Thereafter the aim was complete reliance upon fee income. In the event 115 people participated in the first set of courses and this gave Holland grounds for optimism about the future.[45]

Each six-day course focused on a geographic area, such as east, west or central Africa, or India, or Pakistan, or Latin America. Holland employed lecturers with experience of these places. Guest speakers also featured; they included colonial governor Sir Charles Arden-Clarke, social anthropologist Kenneth Kirkwood and development advisor Arthur Gaitskell. Themes ranged from the workings of colonial administration to the role of industry overseas to personal health care in the tropics. Kenya figured heavily, with lectures on topics such as 'Nationalism and Race' and 'Mau Mau – Cause and Effect'. At least one lecture on each course had a religious emphasis, and was usually given by a missionary (and more occasionally by a visiting African, such as the Rev. Obadiah Kariuki). Holland requested that these speakers link Christianity with themes such as 'community service' and 'citizenship'. He was particularly concerned that participants on the courses should be able to distinguish between 'western' and 'Christian' ideas.[46]

For Holland Britons going overseas were unofficial ambassadors of their home country; but they were also unofficial ambassadors of the church. He believed that the courses would appeal mainly to British Christians keen to know more about their country of destination yet also willing to make the work of the church better known in that country. 'The layman's witness overseas (and in this country)', he argued, 'is not merely incidental to the Christian Gospel. It is unique. Without it "official" Christian presence of the Gospel is essentially incomplete, because it is not incarnate.'[47] But Holland's optimism was misplaced. In its first three years Oversea Service attracted only 405 participants onto its courses. Holland attributed this to shortcomings in British society and lamented the 'baffling strength of that familiar obstacle to the Church's work in this country – indifference'.[48] He acknowledged that, in order to survive, the organisation would have to broaden its appeal and lessen its overtly Christian focus. This was a disappointment to him, as it was also to Warren who had envisaged the work of Oversea Service as complementing that of the missions. Yet Oversea Service, as we shall see below, would adapt and survive but only with the loss of the 'Christian' aspect of its identity. As Holland struggled through the latter half of 1954 to keep his operation going, plans for the Kenya Appeal proceeded apace under the joint direction of Morrison in Nairobi and Lacey in London.

IV

Warren had also been at Evanston in August 1954 when plans for the appeal were discussed. Since then he had become increasingly uneasy about the appeal's lack of reference to Christian mission. Another, related problem now also bore heavily upon his thinking about Kenya. This was the implications for mission of Beecher's failure to convince government of the need to tackle abuses of authority by the security forces. Christian leaders in Kenya had by this time issued sundry public statements on the subject, to negligible effect. To Beecher such statements were almost a matter of form, and of no real significance. He cooperated in them to maintain unity with church and mission leaders of other denominations, preferring to exercise influence through personal communication with Baring. By January 1955 Beecher's tactics and government inaction had become an irritant not only to Warren in London, but also to David Steel in Nairobi. In a broadcast sermon Steel lambasted the authorities, likening security methods to those of a pogrom or of King Herod.[49] Warren was hugely impressed and decided that CMS headquarters should follow suit. A fortnight later it published a pamphlet condemning abuses and hinting that Baring be sacked.[50] All this created a great stir, in the short term. Beecher felt momentarily betrayed. But the fuss soon died down. On 17 February ICA launched the Kenya Appeal, for funds and for offers of Christian service in Kenya. It overshadowed entirely all the recent protests.

The success of the appeal stimulated Lacey to launch a second fund-raising effort in 1956. These initiatives helped transform the fortunes of the Christian Council and of other Christian agencies in Kenya. Success owed a great deal to the interdenominational and international character of the appeals. Missions had previously relied heavily upon denominational giving and on grants from government. The appeals opened up new sources of income; funds were received from Christian organisations in many parts of the world outside the UK, including North America, Australasia and Europe.[51] In Britain secular philanthropic organisations donated funds. The appeal was the subject of 'The Week's Good Cause' on the BBC, bringing in £8,000. Some funds came from unexpected sources. New Conservative secretary of state for colonies Alan Lennox-Boyd was more emollient than his notoriously brusque predecessor Lyttelton and threw his professional and personal weight behind the appeal, pledging Colonial Office and Crown Agents assistance in the recruitment of Christian workers for Kenya and obtaining £16,000 in donations from friends and business contacts in the City of London.[52] Two-fifths of the total funds raised went to churches and missions, the remainder to other organisations including the Salvation Army and the Society of Friends. This funding made possible greater church involvement in social welfare especially in urban centres such as Nairobi. It also made possible the recruitment of large numbers of overseas workers for an increasingly varied range of positions.

Even by February 1955 Kenya had begun to exert an increasingly strong pull on voluntary Christian workers of many nationalities and backgrounds. In Wellington, New Zealand, 23-year-old Jocelyn Murray was inspired to travel to take up a post as a teacher for the CMS at Kahuhia. She remained in Kenya until 1967. Eileen Fletcher travelled from England with four other Quaker volunteers, to participate in rehabilitation work. Later, from the United States, came Marion Forrester, to undertake a study of Kenya's economic development potential.[53] Ordained workers such as the English clergyman Andrew Hake had specialist expertise of use in an urban Kenyan environment.[54] Morrison died suddenly in July 1956, but the Christian Council (later the National Christian Council) was already exerting an important influence on social policy in Kenya.[55]

This was not a development to which Warren was easily reconciled. Workers going out to Kenya on two- or three-year contracts with the Christian Council, he thought, could hardly be expected (as could long-service missionaries) to contribute meaningfully to the life of the church.[56] Some mission officials perceived the council as 'sponsoring secular activity under Christian auspices' rather than 'giving the cup of water in Christ's name'.[57] For a time there was ill-feeling between the missions and ICA. Warren also found troubling Morrison's reluctance to criticise the security forces.[58] Eileen Fletcher's efforts to bring to public attention the maltreatment of detainees and the use of violence in rehabilitation brought rebuke from Morrison. He regarded her involvement with Brockway (who publicised Fletcher's allegations) as misguided, if not treacherous. As Lacey saw it, Fletcher had '"a chip on her shoulder"'.[59] In June 1956, at a London conference organised by the Africa Bureau, the Kenyan trade unionist Tom Mboya launched a swingeing attack on rehabilitation.[60] Warren concurred with Mboya's interpretation of events. He confided to Bewes:

> The really alarming thing about Kenya is that all the people out there are ... obsessed with rehabilitation under the pathetic illusion that Africa and the world are going to stand still while Kenya goes in for rehabilitation for the next twenty years. It is this frame of mind rather than anything else that is so terrifying.[61]

Indeed, rehabilitation had by now acquired a punitive aspect not envisaged by its Christian supporters. In 1959 guards at Hola detention camp killed eleven detainees. Bewes, who served on an official enquiry into conditions in the camps, privately concluded that 'Hola was just another incident – other things were smoothed over in 1957 and 1958'.[62]

There were many things that troubled Warren about Kenya. Not least was the way in which mission appeared by the late 1950s to have been subsumed into the provision of overseas aid and relief to African peoples. Warren saw this development as harmful to mission. What need would there be for missionaries if the west's engagement with Africa emphasised aid and development rather than spirituality? As well as this possibility he found repugnant the bureaucratic (and, as he saw it, impersonal) nature of ICA, with its myriad, complex links to the World Council of Churches. A decade earlier he had instigated in the CMS a policy of 'realignment', to reform a bloated and sclerotic institutional structure. His intention then had been in part to focus more strongly on recruiting and training missionaries in the expectation that within two decades missions would have finally ceded ecclesiastical authority to indigenous churches. But would missions then be succeeded by bloated, bureaucratic western aid agencies? Writing in 1958 the historian Hugh Tinker pondered the impact of such agencies on indigenous societies. He argued for a slimmed-down aid service that respected local conditions, suggesting that western technicians might in future live in conditions 'partially reminiscent of the life of a settlement officer in the old Indian Civil Service or of a pioneer Christian missionary'.[63] He was not optimistic of the prospect. Five years earlier, having forwarded to Beecher substantial sums of money for diocesan use, Warren cautioned against frittering these away 'in introducing European personnel and providing them with cars'.[64] Tinker's idea was for aid to be offered (rather than merely given) as a kind of public and personal service. This chimed closely with Warren's idea of overseas mission. But that idea was by now subject to increasing pressure.

V

By the late 1950s the western idea of overseas mission was proving more and more difficulty to justify. It was being subjected to criticism from within missions as well as from without. Warren might well exhort colleagues to 'understand much that is said about foreign missions being a form of cultural or even spiritual imperialism, as being a survivor of the colonial era. We shall be gravely mistaken if we do not take these accusations seriously.'[65] But that did not stop the accusations, to which missionaries from Britain were most susceptible because of their perceived links with empire. Yet African criticism of missions did not prove damaging to the extent that Warren feared. By the end of the decade some limited ecclesiastical devolution had already taken place. Dioceses (including that of Mombasa) were exerting greater control over mission. Missions cooperated with aid agencies under the coordination of organisations such as the Christian Council of Kenya, and this proved beneficial rather than detrimental to their interests. In the longer term, however, American evangelical missions rather than those of British origin would exert greater influence upon Kenya.[66]

In Britain overseas mission service still retained some appeal at the beginning of the 1960s. That it did so was largely due to changes in the nature of mission as vocation. No longer could missions reasonably expect candidates to undertake a lifetime commitment. There was an increasing emphasis upon lay service.[67] And British Christians might now choose to work with overseas aid agencies rather than with missions. In this respect Lacey continued to exert an influence not confined to Kenya. ICA helped broaden British public engagement with Africa, Asia and other parts of the world. In 1959 Lacey offered financial assistance to the Oversea Service organisation, whose future seemed uncertain. This enabled it to set up a subsidiary to act as a recruitment agency for ICA.[68] Lacey was determined that Oversea Service should succeed, even if this meant it having an identity 'only vaguely Christian'.[69] Oversea Service, Lacey would argue to representatives of British business and industry was *not* 'a sort of missionary breeding-ground'.[70] In 1960 government finally decided that the organisation could indeed fulfil an important role in the training of overseas aid, development and commercial workers, whether Christian or not.[71] Oversea Service became the Oversea Service College and later Farnham Castle, a company committed to 'intercultural' training for business and government. Reflecting in 1964 on what Oversea Service had by then become, Warren acknowledged its failure to stimulate Christian lay service overseas.[72] Harry Holland had already concluded as much. Earlier that year he had returned to Pakistan to take up medical work once more. In 1966 he would be ordained priest in the diocese of Lahore.

In May 1957 Lacey organised the first Christian Aid Week. It was a sign of things to come: ICA would be renamed 'Christian Aid' in 1964. In September 1957 Lacey participated in a meeting in London attended by representatives of more than forty religious and voluntary organisations. Its aim was to discuss how young people from Britain might 'give periods of voluntary service in the economically under-developed areas' of the world.[73] The idea was the brainchild of Alec Dickson and his wife Mora, and Lacey supported it.[74] The origins of VSO (Voluntary Service Overseas), the organisation that emerged from these and subsequent discussions in 1958, owed something to Christian ideas but its ethos was not avowedly Christian. Had it been, VSO would hardly have prospered. But VSO caught the public mood and also the attention of government, which in 1961 made £10,000 available to it from colonial welfare and development funds.[75] The VSO idea undoubtedly influenced the 1961 decision by US president John Kennedy to fund the creation of the Peace Corps. British missionaries looked askance at these developments. Warren was prepared to admit that the Peace

Corps might prove of some use but not as much use as trained doctors, nurses and teachers. 'The real need of...overseas communities', he complained, 'cannot be met by tourists, however well-intentioned.'[76] Missions, he suggested, still had an important role to play, in places such as Kenya. But so too by 1960 and the ending of 'emergency' conditions had VSO, which that year sent seven volunteers to the colony. Two were assigned to the Christian Council, one to the Young Women's Christian Organisation. Baring's successor reported that volunteers 'must be prepared to work within the framework of the African Church'.[77] The nature of that framework was changing, gradually. In August 1960 Fisher travelled to Dar es Salaam, to inaugurate the new Anglican ecclesiastical province of east Africa, an ostensibly indigenous church structure with a European, Leonard Beecher, as its primate. The new province was symbolically important for Anglicans: Tanzania would not achieve political independence until December 1961. By the time of Kenya's independence two years later, international aid and development agencies were already playing an important role in the country's economy and society.

In 1949 an internal commission reported on the likelihood of the CMS becoming a provider of overseas aid. It concluded that the society would be 'wasting its time. Its message of salvation cannot be conveyed in these ways.'[78] Max Warren's ideas for Christian mission and voluntary service drew in part on the history of the CMS, which in 1949 was celebrating a century and a half of overseas evangelistic endeavour. But those ideas owed more to Warren's belief that the CMS, suitably adapted to postwar conditions, could continue to convey a 'message of salvation' in terms equally understandable to voluntary Christian workers from Britain and indigenous peoples in Asia and Africa. Yet church and mission participation in schemes of rehabilitation in Kenya demonstrated how ambiguous and confusing that message might become. Government encouraged missions; conversely, it proved as impervious to church and mission criticism as to that of Fenner Brockway. As Galia Sabar has noted, Anglican missions and church in Kenya failed to provide Africans with political leadership during the 1950s, but they did at least help to provide means through which Africans might better their lives, materially and spiritually.[79] For the CMS in Kenya that meant coming to terms with the implications for mission not only of African nationalism and Mau Mau but also of the west's and western churches' commitment to aid and development in Africa.

There is no doubting the effect of Mau Mau and its suppression on Kenya. What of the effect on Britain? This article has suggested that the impact of events in Kenya on British society though oblique was far from insignificant. Religious organisations did much to stimulate public interest in Kenyan affairs. Of course that interest needs to be seen in the context of other contemporary overseas events – notably in South Africa – that also attracted British public attention.[80] Disaggregating the interest of British Christians from that of the British public at large is by no means a straightforward task. Nevertheless it appears likely that the development of interdenominational church-based (rather than mission-based) agencies such as Christian Aid did have the effect of broadening the nature of British engagement with Africa (as well as with other parts of the world). That is a subject that requires further study, in terms of post-war British Christianity and of post-war Britain as a whole.[81] Ultimately what Meredith Veldman has argued in relation to British Christians and nuclear disarmament might also apply to British Christians and late colonial Africa: the Christian witness flourished not inside but outside institutional Christianity.[82]

Notes

[1] B. D. Nicholls to Canon T. F. C. Bewes, 20 Oct. 1953, Church Missionary Society Papers at the University of Birmingham (CMS), A5/6/4.
[2] Missions were aided by American philanthropic institutions such as Carnegie Corporation and the Phelps-Stokes Fund.
[3] See also Nicholls to Bewes, 7 Jan. 1953, CMS, A5/6/2.
[4] Howe, 'When (if ever) did Empire End?', 225.
[5] Recent published work includes: Lewis, *Empire State-Building*; Odhiambo and Lonsdale, eds. *Mau Mau and Nationhood*; Lonsdale, 'Kikuyu Christianities'; Peterson, *Creative Writing*; Anderson, *Histories of the Hanged*; Elkins, *Britain's Gulag*.
[6] The only book-length biography is Dillistone, *Into all the World*.
[7] Porter, 'War, Colonialism and the British Experience', 287.
[8] On the CMS prior to these developments, see Hewitt, *Problems of Success*.
[9] The most recent detailed examination of Warren's theology is Kings, *Christianity Connected*.
[10] Grimley, *Citizenship, Community and the Church of England*, 203–22.
[11] Canon M. A. C. Warren to Rev. C. O. Rhodes, 10 Jan. 1948, CMS, G/AC5.
[12] Rev. H. D. Hooper to C. W. M. Cox, 24 Dec. 1946, 'Recruitment of Teachers' file, Conference of British Missionary Society Papers at School of Oriental and African Studies, London (CBMS), 254.
[13] Warren to C. W. Williams, 30 Sept. 1946, CMS, AFg AM13.
[14] Hooper to C. L. Cook, 6 Nov. 1946; Canon H. M. Grace, circular, 4 Feb. 1947, ibid.
[15] Anderson, *Histories of the Hanged*, 35–41.
[16] Rev. M. G. Capon, report, May 1949, CMS, G/EW/5/7i.
[17] Havinden and Meredith, *Colonialism and Development*, 252–58.
[18] Lewis, *Empire State-Building*, 298–340.
[19] Kenya Colony and Protectorate, *African Education in Kenya*, 55, 57.
[20] Sheffield, *Education in Kenya*, 41–44.
[21] Peterson, *Creative Writing*, 193–95.
[22] Warren to Rt Rev. R. P. Crabbe, 27 Feb. 1951, CMS, A5e1.
[23] Warren to Rev. P. G. Bostock, 11 April 1951, ibid.
[24] C. G. Gibbs to L. B. Greaves, 17 Jan. 1952, The National Archives, London (TNA), CO 859/447. The bureau was an offshoot of the Institute of Christian Education, founded in 1935.
[25] Official report of meeting, Government House, Nairobi, 31 October 1952, TNA, CO 822/460.
[26] Casson, 'Missionaries, Mau Mau and the Christian Frontier', 210–12.
[27] 'Restoration to Church Membership after Taking the Mau Mau Oath', memo encl. with W. H. Carey to Bewes, 27 Nov. 1952, CMS, A5/6/1.
[28] Very Rev. L. J. Beecher to Most Rev. G. F. Fisher, 11 Nov. 1952, Fisher Papers at Lambeth Palace Library, London (FP), 102; Beecher, memo, 'The Church's Response to the Challenge of Mau Mau', 6 Feb. 1953, FP,127.
[29] Sir E. Baring to O. Lyttelton, 4 April 1953, TNA, CO 822/440.
[30] T. G. Askwith, memo, encl. with Askwith to W. H. Chinn, 13 Jan. 1954, TNA, CO 822/794.
[31] Christian Council of Kenya executive committee minutes, 25 Feb. 1954, CBMS, 274.
[32] CBMS Africa Committee minutes, 30 April 1954, CBMS, 235.
[33] Nicholls, memo, 22 Jan. 1954, CMS, A5/6/5.
[34] Rhodes, 'The Anglican Church in Egypt', 70–72.

[35] International Missionary Council, *A Report of a Conference on Arab Refugee Problems*.
[36] Boobyer, 'Moral Re-armament', 223–27.
[37] Rev. S.A. Morrison, memo, 'What does Rehabilitation mean?', 5 June 1954, CMS, A5/6/5.
[38] Morrison to Bewes, 26 June 1954, ibid.
[39] High, 'The Mau Mau's Unexpected Enemy'.
[40] L. B. Greaves to J. Lacey, 4 August 1954, 'Kenya Appeal' file, CBMS, 577.
[41] On Colonial Service training, see Kirk-Greene, *On Crown Service*, 42–48.
[42] Sir C. Jeffries to Fisher, 9 Feb. 1953, TNA, CO 859/248.
[43] Warren to Rev. S. H. Dixon, 18 Dec. 1952, 'Appointment of Dr Holland' file, CBMS, 32.
[44] Rev. R. D. Say, memo, 'The Christian Responsibility of Men and Women Going Overseas', TNA, CO 859/248.
[45] Of the participants, sixty-three were attached to the Colonial Service or the Crown Agents, thirty-two were involved in business or banking (the ratio of women to men is not recorded). Holland encouraged the wives of male participants to attend, and twenty did so in the first year.
[46] Holland, 'Oversea Service', 188–91.
[47] Ibid.
[48] Harry Holland, report on Oversea Service to British Council of Churches, n.d. but *c*. April 1955, CBMS, 571.
[49] Steel, text of sermon, 9 Jan. 1955.
[50] CMS, *Kenya – Time for Action!*
[51] Lacey to Bostock, 28 Jan. 1957, Bodleian Library of Commonwealth and African Studies at Rhodes House, Oxford (BLCAS), MSS. Micr. Afr. 642 CCK/R/1/3/3/214–17.
[52] O. Paynton to Lord Kilmaine, 2 Oct. 1956, Christian Aid papers at School of Oriental and African Studies, London, CA/A/2/5. The contributors included Barclays Bank, Lloyds Bank, Barings Bank, Imperial Chemical Industries and Union Castle Line.
[53] Forrester, *Kenya Today*.
[54] Hake, *African Metropolis*.
[55] Lonsdale, Booth-Clibborn and Hake, 'Emerging Pattern', 267–84.
[56] Warren, 'Nationalism as an International Asset', 388–89.
[57] Goodall, 'The Limits of Co-operation', 452–54.
[58] Morrison, memo, 'Kenya Survey and the Christian Council of Kenya', Sept. 1954, CMS, A5/6/5.
[59] Lacey to P. D. Sturge, 27 June 1956, CMS, A5/6/3.
[60] T. J. Mboya, address, from Africa Bureau, 'Report of Conference on Kenya', 12 May 1956, BLCAS, MSS. Afr. S. 1681/289/2.
[61] Warren to Bewes, n.d., but June 1956, CMS, AFg O1.
[62] Bewes, diary entry, 5 July 1959, CMS, A5/6/11.
[63] Tinker, 'The Name and Nature of Foreign Aid', 50.
[64] Warren to Beecher, 24 Sept. 1953, CMS, A5/6/1.
[65] Max Warren, 'The Present Situation in the Christian Mission and the Problem of the Theology of Missions', paper for Canadian Council of Churches, 17 Oct. 1958, CBMS, 30.
[66] Hearn, 'The "Invisible" NGO'.
[67] Löffler, *The Layman Abroad*.
[68] This was the Overseas Appointments Information and Advisory Service, which continued in existence only until 1965.
[69] Rev. R. K. Orchard to Rev. N. Goodall, 15 March 1957, File 1, CBMS (1961–70), 109.
[70] Lacey to Rev. J. E. L. Newbigin, 17 Nov. 1959, File 1, CBMS, (1961–70), 107.
[71] Dept. of Technical Co-Operation, memo. 'Oversea Service', n.d. but *c*. Dec. 1961, TNA, OD8/4.
[72] Warren to J. K. Thompson, 31 Dec. 1964, File 1, CBMS (1961–70), 107.
[73] 'Report of the Steering Committee', n.d., on meeting held at Caxton Hall, London, 16 Sept. 1957, '1958' file, CBMS, 572.
[74] Bird, *Never the Same Again*, 15-40.

[75] Sir A. Cohen, minute, 19 July 1961, TNA, CO 859/1446.
[76] Warren to Rev. R. M. Bennett, 21 April 1961, CBMS (1961–70), 107.
[77] Sir P. Renison to C. Y. Carstairs, 24 Aug. 1960, TNA, CO 859/1445.
[78] CMS, 'Report of the Commission on the Realignment of the Foreign Work of the Society', Oct. 1949, CMS, G/C 2/3.
[79] Sabar, *Church, State and Society in Kenya*, 51–52.
[80] See, for example, Herbstein, *White Lies*.
[81] See, for example, Brown, *The Death of Christian Britain*; Prochaska, *Christianity and Social Service in Britain*; Garnett et al., eds. *Redefining Christian Britain*.
[82] Veldman, *Fantasy, the Bomb, and the Greening of Britain*, 159–60.

References

Anderson, David. *Histories of the Hanged: Britain's Dirty War in Kenya and the End of the Empire*. London: Weidenfeld & Nicolson, 2005.

Bird, Dick. *Never the Same Again: A History of VSO*. Cambridge: Lutterworth, 1998.

Boobyer, Philip. 'Moral Re-armament in Africa in the Era of Decolonization'. In *Missions, Nationalism, and the End of Empire*, edited by Brian Stanley. Grand Rapids, MI, and Cambridge: Eerdmans, 2005.

Brown, Callum. G. *The Death of Christian Britain: Understanding Secularisation, 1800–2000*. London: Routledge, 2001.

Casson, John. 'Missionaries, Mau Mau and the Christian Frontier'. In *Missions and Missionaries*, edited by Pieter N. Holtrop and Hugh McLeod. Woodbridge: Boydell, 2000.

Church Missionary Society. *Kenya – Time for Action!* London: CMS, 1955.

Colonial Office and Advisory Committee on Education in the Colonies. *Education for Citizenship in Africa*, Col. No. 216. London: His Majesty's Stationery Office, 1948.

Dillistone, F. W. *Into all the World: A Biography of Max Warren*. London: Hodder & Stoughton, 1980.

Elkins, Caroline. *Britain's Gulag: The Brutal End of Empire in Kenya*. London: Cape, 2005.

Forrester, Marion W. *Kenya Today: Social Prerequisites for Economic Development*. The Hague: Mouton, 1962.

Garnett, Jane, Matthew Grimley, Alana Harris, William Whyte, and Sarah Williams, eds. *Redefining Christian Britain: Post-1945 Perspectives*. London: SCM Press, 2007.

Goodall, Norman. 'The Limits of Co-operation'. *International Review of Missions* 44, no. 176 (1955): 447–54.

Grimley, Matthew. *Citizenship, Community and the Church of England: Liberal Anglican Theories of the State between the Wars*. Oxford: Oxford University Press, 2004.

Hake, Andrew. *African Metropolis: Nairobi's Self-Help City*. London: Chatto & Windus, 1977.

Havinden, Michael, and David Meredith. *Colonialism and Development: Britain and its Tropical Colonies, 1850–1960*. London: Routledge, 1993.

Hearn, Julie. 'The "Invisible" NGO: US Evangelical Missions in Kenya'. *Journal of Religion in Africa* 32, no. 1 (2002): 32–60.

Herbstein, Denis. *White Lies: Canon Collins and the Secret War against Apartheid*. Oxford: James Currey, 2004.

Hewitt, Gordon. *The Problems of Success: A History of the Church Missionary Society, 1910–42*, Vol. 1. London: SCM Press, 1971.

High, Stanley. 'The Mau Mau's Unexpected Enemy'. *Reader's Digest* 64, no. 385 (1954): 57–59.

Holland, H. B. T. 'Oversea Service: An Experiment in Lay Responsibility'. *International Review of Missions* 44, no. 174 (1955): 187–92.

Howe, Stephen. 'When (if ever) did Empire End? "Internal Decolonisation" in British Culture since the 1950s'. In *The British Empire in the 1950s: Retreat or Revival?*, edited by Martin Lynn. Basingstoke and New York: Palgrave, 2006.

International Missionary Council and Department of Inter-Church Aid and Service to Refugees of the World Council of Churches. 'A Report of a Conference on Arab Refugee Problems, Beirut, Lebanon, May 4–8, 1951. Geneva: International Missionary Council and World Council of Churches, 1951.

Kenya Colony and Protectorate. *African Education in Kenya*. Nairobi: Government Printer, 1949.

Kings, Graham. *Christianity Connected: Hindus, Muslims and the World in the Letters of Max Warren and Roger Hooker*. Zoetermeer: Boekencentrum, 2002.

Kirk-Greene, Anthony. *On Crown Service: A History of HM Colonial and Overseas Civil Services, 1837–1997*. London: I. B. Tauris, 1999.

Lewis, Joanna. *Empire State-Building: War and Welfare in Kenya, 1925–52*. Oxford: James Currey, 2000.

Löffler, Paul. *The Layman Abroad in the Mission of the Church: A Decade of Discussion and Experiment*. London: Edinburgh House Press, 1962.

Lonsdale, John. 'Kikuyu Christianities: A History of Intimate Diversity'. In *Christianity and the African Imagination: Essays in Honour of Adrian Hastings*, edited by David Maxwell, with Ingrid Lawrie. Leiden: Brill, 2002.

Lonsdale, John, Stanley Booth-Clibborn and Andrew Hake. 'The Emerging Pattern of Church and State Co-operation in Kenya', In *Christianity in Independent Africa*, edited by Edward Fasholé-Luke, Richard Gray, Adrian Hastings and Godwin Tasie. London: Rex Collings, 1978.

Odhiambo, E. S Atieno and John Lonsdale. *Mau Mau and Nationhood: Arms, Authority and Narration*. Oxford: James Currey, 2003.

Peterson, Derek R. *Creative Writing: Translation, Bookkeeping, and the Work of Imagination in Colonial Kenya*. Portsmouth, NH: Heinemann, 2004.

Porter, Andrew N. 'War, Colonialism and the British Experience: The Redefinition of Christian Missionary Policy, 1938–52'. *Kirchliche Zeitgeschichte* 5, no. 2 (1992): 269–88.

Prochaska, Frank. *Christianity and Social Service in Britain: The Disinherited Spirit*. Oxford: Oxford University Press, 2006.

Rhodes, Rev. Matthew. 'The Anglican Church in Egypt, 1936–56, and its Relationship with British Imperialism', PhD diss., 2005. University of Birmingham.

Sabar, Galia. *Church, State and Society in Kenya: From Mediation to Opposition, 1963–93*. London: Frank Cass, 2002.

Sheffield and R. James. *Education in Kenya: An Historical Study*. New York and London: Teachers College Press, 1973.

Steel, Rev. David. 'Text of sermon, 9 Jan. 1955'. *St Andrew's Journal*, (Nairobi) Feb. 1955:, 11–19.

Tinker, Hugh. 'The Name and Nature of Foreign Aid'. *International Affairs* 35, no. 1 (1959): 43–52.

Veldman, Meredith. *Fantasy, the Bomb and the Greening of Britain*. Cambridge: Cambridge University Press, 1994.

Warren, Max. 'Nationalism as an International Asset'. *International Review of Missions* 44, no. 176 (1955): 385–93.

'Splendidly Leading the Way'? Archbishop Fisher and Decolonisation in British Colonial Africa

Sarah Stockwell

Recent years have seen historians of missions and empire turning their attention to the later twentieth century, a period in which Andrew Porter's characterisation of the relationship of Protestant missionary societies to empire in earlier years as 'deeply ambiguous' holds at least equally true.[1] Porter pioneered research on missions at the end of empire, arguing that in the African context they were slow to anticipate and adjust to new conditions.[2] More recently he has reminded us of the importance of distinct theological and ecclesiastical traditions in shaping different missionary societies' responses to the end of colonial rule.[3] Despite the developing literature on missions and the end of empire, however, the Anglican church in *Britain* remains a shadowy presence in the history of decolonisation, consigned, not unnaturally, to supporting roles in missionary studies, or glimpsed fleetingly in regional studies whose primary focus lies elsewhere.[4]

The extraordinary dynamism of missions has ensured that attention has hitherto focused on this aspect of Christianity overseas rather than the church leadership at home. Moreover in the domestic as much as an imperial context there has recently been a tendency to eschew institutional history in favour of studies of the social history of religion, in reaction against an ecclesiastical history perceived as too narrowly focused on the institutions of the church, and to reflect a secularisation paradigm in which those institutions appear marginal. The role of religion in later modern British politics has been significantly underplayed, while the large literature on politics and religion in post-colonial societies has reinforced a sense that religion remains more relevant in politics overseas than in Britain.[5]

Yet the fragmentary accounts we have point, intriguingly, to a domestic Anglican church hierarchy engaged in a variety of ways in the processes by which Britain divested itself of empire. As Caroline Elkins remarks, at one key moment emerging news of abuses by security forces in Kenya first provoked criticism 'not from the Labour opposition but from the Anglican Church', albeit from clerics conscious of the need to maintain a working relationship with the Kenyan colonial state.[6] Robert Holland notes that in parliamentary debates following the deportation of Archbishop Makarios from Cyprus in 1956, 'curiously' the government's 'real difficulty' occurred in the Lords rather than the Commons, a consequence of Archbishop Fisher's intervention.[7] As these examples indicate, the domestic Anglican church arguably merits more attention in histories of decolonisation. This article represents the first fruits of an investigation of this theme. It will focus on Geoffrey Fisher, archbishop of Canterbury from 1945 to 1961, illuminating the very real part which Fisher played in imperial policy-making at the end of empire and illustrating the ways in which he advanced his own 'decolonisation' project.

Focusing on Fisher as a representative of the domestic Anglican hierarchy begs the question of how far Fisher's interventions can be distinguished from those of the Anglican missionary societies. By 1945 150 years of missionary activity and the creation of an overseas Anglican episcopate had transformed the Church of England into the worldwide Anglican communion. Overseas bishoprics once under the direct control of Canterbury had evolved into regional provinces headed by their own archbishops, united by theology and through their connections to the see of Canterbury. Since 1867 these Anglican bishops had met every ten years at informal gatherings at Lambeth; Fisher himself presided over two Lambeth conferences held in 1948 and 1958. Anglican churches in the old 'dominions', the former settler colonies, and the West Indies were already constituted into independent provinces, and in India the church had been self-governing since 1927. However, Anglican dioceses in the Indian Ocean and in Africa, with the exception of those belonging to the South African province, remained as 'Overseas Bishops of the Canterbury Jurisdiction' with the archbishop of Canterbury also consequently responsible for the selection of the colonial bishops in these areas.[8]

As archbishop of Canterbury, however, Fisher was also at the centre of networks connecting the church at home with overseas missions, especially the Anglican Universities' Mission to Central Africa (UMCA) and the Church Missionary Society (CMS), with whose principal officers Gerald Broomfield (general secretary UMCA, 1937–61) and Max Warren (the politically astute general secretary of the CMS, 1942–63) Fisher liaised closely.[9] When Fisher spoke or acted on colonial affairs, he did so in ways that more often than not were informed by information fed along missionary channels; in turn Fisher was a metropolitan voice for their concerns, especially in his capacity as chair of the British Council of Churches (established in 1942 by the principal non-Roman Catholic British churches) which through its watching brief on social and international affairs, John Stuart argues, became one of the principal organisations through which missionary representations on issues of race in the empire and elsewhere were articulated.[10]

It must nevertheless be remembered that the Anglican church did not see itself as just another voluntary agency or pressure group. Possessing a privileged institutional relationship with the state, it sought to provide leadership for the Christian conscience of both state and nation – even while acknowledging that the nation included significant numbers of non-Anglicans (although it took good note of the decline of non-conformity in the early twentieth century).[11] Fisher's centrality in this relationship was most obvious when occupying his seat in the House of Lords to participate in the British body politic and the Westminster apparatus of imperial policy-making, but correspondents from both home and abroad also frequently sought his intervention as head of the national church in colonial questions whether practical, political or moral. Moreover, Fisher exercised what one might describe as an informal supervisory role over ex-colonial bishops often retaining close ties with their former dioceses, some coming to the fore of loose lobby groupings in Britain interested in colonial issues, who sometimes spoke out in ways which Fisher believed necessitated his intervention.

I

Geoffrey Francis Fisher, born 1887, was elevated to the see of Canterbury in January 1945 following the death of William Temple.[12] His archiepiscopate – lasting until 1961 when, aged 74, he took the unusual step of resigning – coincided with much the most important years of British decolonisation. Born into an upper middle-class clerical family, Fisher brought to the role varied experiences. He had spent twenty-one years in public-school teaching, first as a master at Marlborough and then from 1914 to 1932 as headmaster of Repton. Like many of his class, Fisher's familial and professional activities furnished him with points of contact with empire – with the worlds of both missionary activity and the colonial state. Of Fisher's seven siblings who survived childhood, one, Katie, worked as a medical missionary for the CMS in Palestine; a second, Herbert, became a colonial civil servant; and a third, Leonard, became first bishop of Lebombo and later bishop of Natal. These family connections were reinforced in a second generation: the eldest of Fisher's six sons served as General Staff Officer I to General Slim in Burma.[13]

It is difficult to pin down the part personal connections had in securing Fisher's interest in colonial questions, but they appear to have reinforced in various contingent ways the involvement that resulted from institutional connections overseas. Fisher showed a particular interest in east and central Africa, travelling to the region several times. That these visits sometimes afforded the opportunity to meet family seems to have been an inducement to travel when he was invariably juggling domestic British and other commitments. Family and personal contacts also provided a network of informants above and beyond those associated with the church on whose experiences Fisher could draw. This enabled him to make empathetic personal connections with the concerns of individuals of all political persuasions, as he did with a female correspondent in referring to the experience of his niece, the head of Limuru school, during the Mau Mau emergency,[14] or in central Africa, where he met up with old Reptonians in the white settler community.

Fisher devoted a striking proportion of time to colonial political rather than domestic questions. Indeed colonial issues in some years predominated among those subjects on which he spoke in the Lords. Part of Fisher's involvement with empire as head of the Anglican church might be described as adding to the 'ornamental' aspects of empire and decolonisation, entailing goodwill visits to different communities, taking a close interest in royalty and its Commonwealth tours and peripheral involvement in celebrations of independence (he preached at a service in Ibadan on the occasion of Nigeria's independence and helped to arrange one at London's St Martin-in-the-Fields to mark that of the Gold Coast).[15] But the case made here for more attention to be paid to Fisher rests on two different, though related areas of his activity: first, that he propelled forward the devolution of authority in those places still under Lambeth's jurisdiction, overseeing the creation of new provinces within the overseas Anglican church in what could be said to constitute the church's own 'transfers of power'; and, second, the degree to which he intervened in colonial political questions, lobbying the Colonial Office and liaising with colonial politicians and administrators.

In these various activities Fisher, like Harold Macmillan and the post-war colonial secretaries, was assisted by the availability of air travel; as Purcell in his rather hagiographic biography put it, '[technological developments] gave the opportunity; he seized it'.[16] It is clear nevertheless that some colonial locations were of less immediate relevance – and some of less interest – to Fisher, whether because they were areas in which the Anglican church had already devolved authority or because Fisher had apparently less appetite for the political issues which arose in them. Both factors seem to apply, for example, in the case of British Guiana, part of a West Indian Anglican province established in 1883.[17] When in 1953 the British government responded to the election of the socialist People's Progressive Party by declaring the elections invalid and imposing martial law, Fisher was loath to intervene, resisting the archbishop of the West Indies' suggestion that he speak about the territory in the Lords.[18] At other times his intense engagement with one colony squeezed out consideration of others, as he was to admit was the case with Kenya in the early 1950s when interest in the colony was superseded by his close involvement with the affairs of the Kabaka in Uganda, or when during the critical period following the declaration of emergencies in central Africa in spring 1959 Fisher was away in the Far East.[19]

Political issues significant for the church and Fisher did not of course present themselves uniformly across the colonial empire. It is a commonplace that Britain's empires were many and diverse, and particular issues presented themselves in different places even within one region. For example, in Malta the primacy of Catholic political interests raised concerns about the security of religious freedom for Anglicans and non-Catholic Christians,[20] whereas in Cyprus it was the 'long and close ties of friendship' between the Church of England and the Orthodox churches of Greece and Cyprus that made it incumbent on Fisher to take a close interest in the conflict between the majority Greek and minority Turkish communities,[21] especially following the British government's deportation of the Orthodox Archbishop Makarios for alleged association with *EOKA* insurgents campaigning for *Enosis* with Greece. As already indicated, Fisher became a close observer of events in Cyprus in the 1950s, intervening in parliamentary debates and behind the scenes in attempts to persuade the Conservative government to abandon its insistence that all terrorist activity must cease before it negotiated with Makarios, while simultaneously urging Makarios to help end violence.[22] In March 1956 he proposed that Lord Radcliffe be appointed as constitutional commissioner, a suggestion adopted later that year.[23]

II

It was perhaps prophetic that in the days before his enthronement as archbishop, Fisher spent a few days in quiet retreat working on the proof of an overseas diocesan constitution,[24] for Fisher was to devote a significant proportion of his time as primate to devolving structures of authority and to constitution-writing in an African context. The latter, while addressed in Edward Carpenter's biography, is touched on only briefly in the general histories of the Anglican church.[25] Yet it deserves to be brought into sharper prominence for it yields interesting points of comparison between the ways in which the church sought to adapt its structure to changing political circumstances in the colonial empire and the adjustments made not only by the state but other British institutions operating in the colonies, such as businesses.

Significant developments occurred under Fisher: an African diocesan bishop was appointed in 1951 and by the end of 1960 there were seven in total.[26] Autonomous provinces were established in west Africa in 1951, in central Africa in 1955 and in east Africa in 1960, together with a separate province of Uganda in 1961, in a series of ceremonies, over which Fisher presided, that followed a form first devised for west Africa (the first occasion on which an archbishop personally attended the inauguration of a new Anglican province).[27] By the time Fisher resigned, the Anglican church had effectively 'transferred power' in tropical Africa.

In 1945 there were good reasons to move in this direction. As we have already noted, with his accession to Canterbury, Fisher assumed direct responsibility for African overseas dioceses except those in southern Africa. Moreover, by 1950 no African had been appointed as a diocesan bishop since Samuel Crowther in 1864, and, although the churches in Africa had long relied upon the activities of lay African catechists, there had hitherto been comparatively little commitment to the development of an African clergy independent of European missionary supervision and the related issue of local theological training. Europeans continued to fill senior clerical posts.[28] Although the Anglican church was not unique in these respects (for example, both the Baptist Missionary Society in the Congo and the Methodist church were slower to localise)[29] it did lag behind the Roman Catholic Church, which appointed its first African bishop in 1939, followed by a further twenty-one between 1951 and 1958, and established Catholic hierarchies in British west Africa in 1950, south Africa in 1951 and east Africa in 1953,[30] processes Fisher monitored and which probably reinforced his own commitment to rapid devolution.[31]

Fisher was not alone in appreciating the case for change. Max Warren especially was conscious from the Second World War of the need to transfer authority from missions to local churches,[32] and discussions about the establishment of African provinces predated Fisher's appointment as archbishop. Within the apparatus of the Church of England there was a special committee that handled constitutions of overseas dioceses and provinces, although it was only some time after Fisher's appointment that he became aware of it.[33] Yet Fisher's hand in encouraging, overseeing and managing devolution is clear. He personally worked through draft provincial constitutions, his interest extending to the choice of vestments and liturgy at inauguration ceremonies. Warren acknowledged Fisher's role in 'initiating' provincial development, anticipating that 'it will come to be recognised that the single most far-sighted piece of statesmanship during his archiepiscopate, was his steady and deliberate diminution of the metropolitan authority of the Archbishop of Canterbury'.[34]

Fisher's close involvement in devolution undoubtedly reflected his own interests and administrative talents (on the domestic front his primacy was notable for reform of canon law).[35] But in encouraging and bringing to fruition Anglican devolution, Fisher acted in ways that were also informed by his perspective as primate. For example, he appears to have wanted to rationalise the position whereby an increasingly busy post-war archbishop was required to engage with the particularities of African dioceses of which he remained metropolitan. Almost invariably courteous and generous with his time, Fisher could nevertheless be impatient of the more mundane business of mission and overseas church.[36] Moreover, in west Africa Fisher's commitment to provincial development was encouraged by his reluctance to face inevitably complex negotiations should proposals being mooted in the Niger Diocese in the late 1940s for a possible union of Nigerian churches along the lines of that in South India (whose relations with the Anglican communion remained unresolved) be acted upon.[37] That the development of provinces might help boost the local standing of the Anglican church was a further incentive in those places like Uganda where senior Anglicans worried about the degree to which Anglicanism risked being undermined by too close an association in local perception with an unpopular colonial regime.[38]

Fisher, like Warren and, perhaps to a lesser degree, Broomfield, was also acutely conscious of the need to cut the church's cloth according to the political climate. Commenting on the formation of the Ugandan province, Fisher, borrowing the current metropolitan political discourse, wrote that 'though for many reasons one could wish that developments of a provincial kind could have waited perhaps for another decade, the risks of moving too slowly are far greater and worse than the risks of moving too fast'.[39] One of these 'risks' was that identified by Warren: the 'grave danger' to the church from the fact that the growing ranks of highly educated African intelligentsia far outstripped the numbers of clergy.[40] Sometimes Fisher, Warren and Broomfield's wish for more African appointments ran ahead of local opinion, among both some European personnel and some African Christians. 'Your lordship we ask you to forget all about politics', petitioned the Toro Christians in July 1959, 'and try hard to get us a European bishop.'[41]

Just as Fisher's worries about proceeding 'too fast' while other imperatives pointed to the logic of moving more slowly echo official discourse, in discussions concerning the creation of the African provinces the distinctive priorities and contexts of religious and secular organisations did not preclude striking parallels with the transfers of secular power. One concerns the difficulty of negotiating conflicting local jealousies. Andrew Porter has demonstrated how the Anglo-Catholic UMCA, whose activities had centred on the five east and central African dioceses of Nyasaland, Zanzibar, Northern Rhodesia, Masasi and south-west Tanganyika, were anxious lest the creation of an East African province play to the strengths of the more evangelical CMS.[42] Other examples concern more overtly political issues.[43] When it came to the establishment of a separate Ugandan province, Fisher had to tread carefully in relation to fears among non-Bugandans that they might be dominated within the province by the Bugandan Christians.[44] Other political sensitivities arose not as a result of competition among African Christian communities, but from imperial and colonial policy. Hence among important considerations in East Africa was the political impossibility of including Uganda within an East African province given local concern that this might presage the much-reviled prospect of an East African federation. Federation was similarly something of a minefield in relation to central Africa. As momentum gathered behind the scheme for political federation in the region the church was aware that it made the case for provincial organisation more urgent; at the same time, when it looked like the federation might not materialise, Fisher was left with the dilemma that not to proceed with the creation of a central African province might suggest that church policy was dictated by the imperial political scheme.[45]

Fisher's handling of the dioceses of the smaller island territories also evokes parallels with imperial policy-making. Like British governments dealing with the 'problem' of the smaller colonial territories, Fisher worried about the relation of the island dioceses to the new provinces. In the case of Madagascar and Mauritius, Fisher proposed their inclusion within the East African Province, although the suggestion was opposed by the local bishops. The bishop of Mauritius favoured the creation of an Indian Ocean Province, an approach Fisher feared would create a province without a centre. In what can retrospectively appear a rather unseemly dash to divest himself of the responsibility for remote island dioceses, Fisher was anxious lest the difficult task of dealing with distant diocesan matters be rendered more so once the English diocesan had been replaced with a local incumbent (as the bishop of Madagascar proposed).[46]

Like some corporate strategies developed in response to colonial political change that emphasised the cosmetic value of a few (initially nominal) local appointments to company boards,[47] the business on which Fisher had embarked was partly concerned with appearances, at least until there was an African clergy deemed fully capable of taking on the leadership of the church. This assessment parallels Adrian Hastings' judgement that the 'real effect' of the creation of Catholic hierarchies remained 'rather slight' as long as the new dioceses remained subject to curial congregation of *Propaganda Fide*.[48] In the Anglican instance, Fisher was clearly aware of this. On the eve of the creation of the Ugandan province he warned the bishop of Uganda, its future archbishop, that he would need 'some really first class European seconds in command as Archdeacons, Diocesan Secretaries and the like' and that he and his fellow bishops required 'really competent Englishman to see the province on to its feet'; advice that was potentially difficult to follow in view of declining numbers of European personnel.[49] Fisher sought also to ensure that the creation of the new provinces did not entail a complete abandonment of Canterbury's authority. He framed the Ugandan provincial constitution so that, rather than having the authority to 'forbid' any unwelcome resolution of its Provincial Assembly and House of Bishops, the archbishop would have all resolutions referred to him for 'advice'; a formulation he believed left him in a 'much stronger position' and less likely to offend local 'amour propre'.[50]

Just as Fisher was conscious of the need to advance the African role within the church, so he was acutely aware of the importance of appearances both in the UK and locally, a view perhaps informed by a wider concern that he was sometimes misquoted in the press, although his most bruising such encounter was to come later, following Fisher's controversial invitation to Cypriot Archbishop Makarios to attend the 1958 Lambeth Conference.[51] In February 1956 Fisher reproached the editor of *The Times* for reports of the services attended by the Queen during her visit to Nigeria which mentioned only an English bishop and not the two African bishops who had preached: this obscured how the 'Church in Nigeria, as elsewhere' was 'taking a valiant part in leading the development of this great country in Godly and peaceful ways'.[52] More generally, Fisher was keen to emphasise the moral lead he presented the church as taking, 'splendidly leading the way', as he put it, speaking in east Africa in 1961. 'Why', he asked then, 'is there such a contrast between the godly and peaceful evolution of the Churches in parts of Africa after the example of the Apostolic Churches and the political evolution through hostile argument and disagreement?'[53]

III

Thus far it is tempting to depict Fisher as a religious equivalent of the decolonising Conservative secretary of state for the colonies, Iain Macleod, or, perhaps more aptly, as a Harold Macmillan of the church. Personally convinced of the necessity of moving with a 'wind of change' in Africa, he sometimes initiated and at other times enabled and encouraged others to act in ways that resulted in the church pursuing what can legitimately be described as its own 'decolonisation' project even while acknowledging the limits to the 'independence' achieved. Intriguingly, and in ways that call to mind Macleod's eye to the historical record in describing his own role in accelerating constitutional change in east and central Africa,[54] Fisher too sought to project a vision of his own authority over Anglican devolution. He objected, for instance, to a draft article prepared by the bishop of Lagos narrating the origins of the West African province that it took insufficient account of Lambeth's contribution since 1944, including a complete revision of a draft constitution.[55] His office ensured that no such mistake could be made in the case of the East African province: in this case a draft press release referred to the 'movement towards ecclesiastical as well as political self-government', a result of the 'personal initiative' of the archbishop.[56]

Fisher as 'decoloniser' corresponds to the view which emerges –in so far as he figures at all – in existing histories of decolonisation as a result of his involvement in various issues relating to post-war imperial policy and decolonisation, notably his intervention in debates over Cyprus and Suez. In such matters Fisher often criticised the Conservative governments' handling of particular aspects of colonial policy in specific locations in ways clearly informed by morality and perhaps, more tendentiously, by his role in representing the 'nation's conscience'. But, attractive as it is to view Fisher through such an analytical framework, his involvement in colonial affairs was more ambiguous than this, reflecting not only the Church of England's very distinct position between state and nation but also Fisher's individual understanding of the way the state could be trusted to exercise its responsibilities. Indeed Fisher's personality and style, familiar from his management of the domestic church, produced very particular approaches to issues which defy easy generalisation. We now turn to a couple of examples from his involvement in Africa: Uganda and Kenya. While others have explored in depth the role of the mission societies and the Anglican church in these areas after the Second World War (especially, in the case of Uganda, Kevin Ward and Caroline Howell), they are revisited here for the light they shed on Fisher's own approach.[57]

Few parts of British colonial Africa received more attention from Fisher than Uganda, and, more specifically, the Christian kingdom of Buganda, whose special status within the Ugandan colonial state was established in 1900 by an agreement under which Britain recognised the traditional monarch, the Kabaka, as ruler of the province. From the late nineteenth century, when the early success of CMS missionaries contributed significantly to the negotiation of the agreement and formation of the Ugandan protectorate, Anglicanism in Buganda had effectively enjoyed the status of an established church, one over which Fisher, until the formation of the Ugandan province, remained metropolitan. In 1953 tensions between the British colonial administration in Uganda led by Andrew Cohen, appointed governor in 1952, and the Bugandan hereditary leader, the Kabaka Mutesa II, came to a head after Cohen's proposed reforms raised the issue both of the Bugandan kingdom's future place within the state of Uganda and also of the Kabaka's relationship to the assembly of

Bagandan notables, the Lukiiko, which in line with developments in Uganda as a whole Cohen sought to democratise. As the clash between the Kabaka and Cohen escalated, with Mutesa seeking an independent Bugandan state and the British authorities concerned that he might mobilise support among Uganda's other traditional rulers, a state of emergency was declared, and the Kabaka deported to Britain in November 1953.[58]

The Church of England was plunged into the middle of the crisis. Fisher already had an established if uneasy relationship with Mutesa, having sought to act as moral guide when the latter embarked upon an affair with his wife's sister. Fisher had a poor opinion of Mutesa (he described him as 'charming' and 'pleasant' but 'a poor little person who sees the right course and has not the strength to follow it'),[59] but there were fears that for the church, and for Fisher, not to act in opposition to the deportation might have adverse consequences for the Anglican church, with Warren concerned lest the Roman Catholic Church, presently consigned to a subordinate role within Buganda, make capital out of the crisis.[60] As Howell and Ward both argue, the church's historically close association with the British colonial administration bound it in popular imagination to what had now become an immensely unpopular regime, and it was wrongly suspected by some locally that Leslie Brown, recently appointed as bishop of Uganda (which diocese encompassed Buganda), was complicit in the deportation, a charge which gained force when Brown's predecessor, now back in Britain, weighed in with vociferous support for the Bugandan case.[61]

Perhaps because the church was here caught between a rock and a hard place, Fisher presented himself as an honest broker between both the British government and the Kabaka and delegation of Bagandans that arrived in London after the deportation to campaign for Mutesa's restoration, while also acting as a (self-appointed) quasi adviser to the latter. Fisher's efforts concentrated behind the scenes where he sought to ensure an audience for the delegation with the Conservative secretary of state, Oliver Lyttelton, at the Colonial Office.[62] Fisher was simultaneously shaping the delegation's case, encouraging them to lay aside grievances associated with the precipitate and undignified manner of the Kabaka's deportation, not least because he believed Mutesa's recent marital conduct had weakened his moral authority, and instead to focus on getting reassurance from HMG that Uganda would progress to independence as an African rather than a multiracial state[63] (a line that corresponded with emerging concerns in the Colonial Office, shared by Cohen, that a recent declaration by Lyttelton might be misinterpreted as envisaging a multiracial rather than an African state).[64] Once reconsideration of the constitutional issues resumed with the dispatch of an independent commission under Sir Keith Hancock to Uganda in spring 1954, Fisher returned to the question of the Kabaka's restoration, suggesting to Lyttelton's successor, Alan Lennox-Boyd, that this would 'could work a real miracle throughout Africa and regain (as nothing else could possibly do) our initiative in leading Africa through its growing pains. Our friends would be our friends again. Our enemies would be nonplussed. Nothing would be lost.'[65]

Mutesa eventually returned to Uganda in October 1955 following the Lukiiko's acceptance of Hancock's constitutional proposals. Fisher continued to monitor Ugandan affairs, but was concerned more with the Kabaka's personal conduct than political issues until Uganda's swift progression to independence urgently raised the future place of Buganda within an independent Uganda as the Bagandan elite refused to accept direct elections to the legislature.

Fisher's place in these later negotiations provides further illustration of the duality of his position, with the archbishop at once frustrated by the refusal of the Kabaka's ministers to co-operate in elections while also troubled by a growing conviction that, however obstinate the Bagandans, 'justice was on their side' and hence by what he felt to be the church's historic moral obligation to them. By late October 1960 he wondered to Macleod whether 'I can detach myself any longer'.[66] Perhaps it was because Fisher remained uncertain as to how to proceed that his intervention fell between two stools. In November 1960 he drafted a six-page letter to the Bugandan chief minister, the Katikiro, encouraging him to act constructively, but also proposing that the Bugandan government put a 'question' to the Colonial Office, asking it to confirm that it would preserve in future constitutional arrangements the 'special royal prerogative and position' that now belongs to the Kabaka.[67] But the letter was never sent. Instead, after consultation with the Colonial Office, a much shorter letter omitted the proposed 'question' and focused instead on the Bagandans' boycott of the elections. 'My dear Brother [the Katikiro]', he wrote 'it is that kind of standing aloof that destroys all hope. It is not statesmanship, it is not politics; to be frank it is like the sulking child.'[68] Simultaneously, Fisher continued to petition Macleod urging the legitimacy of the Bugandan case while also intervening with the Kabaka on behalf of Lord Munster, chair of a commission considering relations between the central government and the four kingdoms including Buganda.[69] When Macleod accepted that there was indeed in the Kabaka's case a 'hard core of justice', but insisted that pragmatism and the imperative of avoiding the 'chaos we have seen in the Congo' had to prevail, Fisher directed his energies to persuading the Kabaka and his ministers to cooperate and accept the British government's good faith.[70] When the Munster report offered Buganda federal status, the Buganda government agreed to participate in elections alongside Milton Obote's Uganda People's Congress Democratic Party, which drew support from Catholics outside Buganda;[71] by then Fisher had resigned as archbishop.

If Fisher's involvement in Bugandan affairs exposes his willingness to engage, and not uncontroversially so, in colonial political affairs, while at the same time working with the British government, the case of Kenya reveals more acutely the ambiguities of his position. As Stuart shows, the colony's troubled history in the 1950s presented a variety of dilemmas for its missionary and church communities, concerns that were articulated principally by a group of churchmen and in the UK especially by Max Warren. For Fisher, however, it was typically one particular problem among these that was most troubling rather than the plethora of issues associated with mission: the question of the morality of state policy, in this case raised by evidence of state-sponsored violence. Fisher's response was intriguing. It undoubtedly reflected in part the concerns of the local churchmen whom Stuart and Elkins both argue were watching the colonial state,[72] but who were ultimately unwilling to rock the boat too much, conscious that their own position in the colony depended on the goodwill of the British administration, but it also demonstrated Fisher's own personal trust in British ministers and officials and the efficacy of colonial government.

By early 1953 senior figures in the Anglican church were in no doubt about the extent of Kenyan police and security force brutality. In January Warren and Fisher had arranged for Canon Bewes, the Africa secretary of the CMS, to visit the colony both as a goodwill mission and to gather information. Bewes' report contained ample allegations of brutality to and torture of Mau Mau detainees, including castration, the amputation of fingertips and rape, associated especially with the Police Force and the Kenyan Police Reserve.[73] Increasingly, Christian leaders in Kenya also became concerned about the way state policies impacted adversely on a Christian model of African family life, with married African women being 'swept up' without warning, separated from their children and interned in camps.[74]

Bewes' report was potentially highly damaging. As others have noted, it brought some of the earliest evidence of state violence and presented the church as, at this initial stage, to the fore of concerned voices in Britain.[75] Fisher was personally exercised by the accounts, and pursued the issue with the Colonial Office, securing an audience for Bewes with Lyttelton. But, significantly, he was also fully complicit in efforts to keep the criticisms within limits, accepting a memorandum signed by Bewes after this meeting in which Bewes declared that he had no evidence that 'could be produced in a court of law' and had received assurances from the governor that action would be taken in relation to those alleged cases he had reported. Perhaps as a result, when Bewes spoke at a cross-party meeting of MPs, he agreed to a request by the secretary of the Commonwealth Parliamentary Association that he would keep off the subject of police guards as this 'would embarrass the Government'.[76] For his part, Fisher, while behind the scenes continuing to maintain pressure on the British government, in public sought to dispel stories unfavourable to the British administration. So it was, for example, in September 1953, that Fisher replied to a letter from an Oxfordshire resident expressing concern at press reports of British authorities maltreatment of black Kenyans in the *Daily Worker* to the effect that:

> I do not know what the Editor of the *Daily Worker* has done, but his right course would be himself, privately, to approach the authorities and seek to strengthen their hands in tackling any such practices, if they exist, of which they would certainly disapprove. That is a far more useful and responsible thing to do than to publish a letter of this sort in his columns.[77]

Fisher's stance reassured an initially hostile Oliver Lyttelton, who in one meeting, Fisher recorded, 'began by being very offhand and uncommunicative until I convinced him that we were there to help'. Lyttelton, Fisher wrote, 'at once changed his attitude and became very understanding, very ready to help, and extremely anxious that everything possible should be done to cope with irregularities and scandals in Kenya.' Underlying Fisher's approach was a sense of pragmatism (evident elsewhere in his response to the American nuclear bombing of Hiroshima and Nagasaki and in his participation in British political debates about the death penalty). Mau Mau, he observed, was 'a civil war' and 'evil things are done', but he doubted whether anything would be gained by taking any public action beyond letting it be known, if necessary, that the Church and Church leaders have impressed upon the authorities the fact that scandals do exist, and are satisfied that the authorities are doing everything possible to restrain the forces under their command.[78]

This pragmatism was accompanied by what was, at least initially, genuine confidence in imperial and colonial government. Whatever his exasperation with Lyttelton (it was 'astonishing', Fisher recorded, 'how Lyttelton again and again does the stupid and wrong thing, and therefore spoils his own best endeavours'),[79] Fisher appears to have believed the assurances of British ministers and officials that once aware of the situation they would seek to rectify it. Hence, while there were 'frightful misbehaviours of one kind and another', he was 'perfectly sure' that the Kenyan governor, Evelyn Baring (who, Fisher noted in this context, was 'a very keen and devoted Christian'), and other authorities were 'doing their utmost to cope with them'.[80]

As time passed and events eroded his initial confidence, Fisher became more sceptical. In February 1955 writing to Arthur Phillips of the CMS Africa Committee, Fisher noted that, although he did not 'minimize the difficulties of the Governor', Baring had in the past 'certainly promised more than could be fulfilled' and it was consequently 'most necessary to keep him up to the mark this time'.[81] By then Fisher had found more of a voice as the 'nation's conscience' and had become more openly critical in debates in the Lords, observing on one occasion that, while the government had noticed two years before that 'many horrible things were being done by the forces of law and order', its efforts to eradicate abuses had been relatively unsuccessful. He then proceeded to make what was in many ways the remarkable suggestion that the British government establish rehabilitation centres for those within the 'forces of law and order' similar to those established for Mau Mau detainees in order to facilitate the 'restoration of trust all round and liberation from fear'.[82]

As in Uganda and Cyprus, Fisher's interventions strayed from questions of morality to the exclusively political. In October 1957, lamenting the breakdown of the Kenyan constitutional talks, Fisher complained to Baring that 'what distresses me is that it looks as if once again the Government is going to ruin everything by saying no ... to a detached person like myself it seems perfectly obvious that the ... vast African majority is under-represented'.[83]

Fisher was not always a critic of imperial policy: he could be an advocate of it. He spent some time deliberating the pros and cons of the proposed Central African Federation, characteristically absorbing information and advice received from churchmen in the field, until, no doubt influenced by what he was learning, he joined missionaries in the region[84] in supporting the project, writing to the bishop of Southern Rhodesia in November 1952 that he was 'more and more convinced that the Federation is the best hope for African and European', while cautioning that the church must none the less not identify too closely with the case either for or against – a position which had been urged on Fisher by the bishop of Northern Rhodesia.[85] Fisher, with his network of contacts, was a valuable potential ally for the British government in their pursuit of the federal scheme, and, at the request of the secretary of state for commonwealth relations, he agreed to intercede with the Africa Bureau in relation to what was rumoured to be its planned protest against the Conservative plans, subsequently assuring the minister that he had done his best to secure 'what one might call a fair hearing for the Federation proposals'.[86]

The Central African Federation shows Fisher attempting to intercede not just with black African politicians but white, in intermittent correspondence with Roy Welensky. In September 1961 a draft letter (which may not have been sent) urged Welensky to meet the Northern Rhodesian politician Kenneth Kaunda and to inform Macleod that he would accept disputed constitutional points to ensure that the Northern Rhodesian constitution could be given the best possible start; Fisher argued, whether from some lingering personal attachment to the Federation or because it was best to couch an appeal to Welensky in these terms, that this gave 'you the only remaining chance of keeping the Federation in hopeful and fruitful existence'.[87]

IV

Fisher was thus closely involved with a variety of African colonial issues during his archiepiscopate. His relations with the Colonial Office were inevitably coloured by personal appraisals of both secretaries of state and their policies. While often frustrated by Lyttelton and Lennox-Boyd, he found himself in much closer sympathy with Macleod. Although officials and ministers at the Colonial Office clearly sometimes regarded Fisher as a nuisance or politically naïve,[88] when preparing to step down as colonial secretary Macleod thanked Fisher 'for the close interest' he had taken in African affairs and the help he had given him while secretary of state.[89]

There remains the question of with what consequence this was so. On a number of occasions Fisher acted because he was conscious of possible repercussions for the church if he did not, but whether his political interventions produced political results is difficult to establish. In relation to Uganda, the Bagandans seem to have believed Fisher's intervention persuaded Lyttelton to see them in 1954 following the Kabaka's deportation;[90] nevertheless, it is hard to isolate the role of the church, and more specifically, of Fisher, in resolving this particular crisis, as illustrated by the different conclusions reached by Ward and Howell in their discussions, with the latter sceptical about the influence of the church on the Colonial Office.[91] Arguably more significant was Fisher's influence on the Bagandan delegation, and, later, with the government of Buganda. Certainly, looking back on his own place in the Ugandan negotiations of 1960–1, Fisher reflected: 'I do not think I did any harm. I think I did a little to soften them [the Kabaka and his Ministers] ... I made them a little more ready than they were before to look at the proposals of the Munster Commission, when they came, with a less jaundiced eye.'[92]

Throughout all this, Fisher's distinct preference for discretion is evident. One illustration of this is the degree to which Fisher distinguished his own approach from that of contemporary clerics like Michael Scott (from 1952 honorary director of the Africa Bureau), Canon John Collins of St Paul's and Trevor Huddleston, former cleric in South Africa, campaigning on race issues. On a number of different occasions Fisher cited Collins (whom he thought 'lack[ed] wisdom and judgement to an astonishing degree') as illustration of how not to behave: chastising Walter Carey, former bishop of Bloemfontein, then living in Kenya, for inflammatory comments in the press, he insisted on the need 'to keep ourselves from "Collinisation"'.[93] Fisher thus divorced himself from what he decried as open politicking by 'enthusiasts in this country for Africa' which he believed might encourage African resistance and so, presumably, render more difficult Britain's management of African colonial politics.[94]

Ironically for a man who could on occasion flare up and speak out in ways which fuelled controversy, Fisher's dislike of 'Collinisation' was underpinned by a liking for unity, consensus and common sense. In the Lords Fisher's comments and speeches aimed to smooth over party-political differences that, in relation to colonial policy, were becoming more acute by the later 1950s. Indeed, during a debate on the report of the Kenyan Constitutional Conference in March 1960, Fisher commented that could such consensus between the government and opposition 'apply to the whole discussion in every part of Africa it would be a great service to the cause of Africa and to ourselves'.[95] In similar vein in May 1959 – at the height of party political dispute over Africa – Fisher suggested to the bishop of Mashonaland that if only British parties could come to a 'common mind' it 'would do more than anything else to help you out in Central Africa'.[96] Earlier he had expressed relief that with his absence from the Britain he would be unable to speak in the debate about central Africa as, with 'everybody shouting', the 'voice of reason and reconciliation can hardly be heard'.[97] He thus came to offer a different question to that which dominated the later years of British decolonisation: the best way forward in central Africa was not just deliberating between 'too fast and too slow', but, 'for everybody to ask: "What has been done wrong, by commission or omission, and where does the fault on my side lie"—and never mind about the fault on the other side'.[98] Fisher's approach also derived from an innate optimism about many of those whom he encountered. Comments made in October 1958 about Welensky are revealing: 'I have a belief in him', and think 'perhaps it helps to keep him on the right path if one shows interest'.[99]

While Fisher himself speculated in relation to Uganda that I 'did no harm', the question remains of whether in his personal inclination to eschew open controversy Fisher did enough. To his critics he was complacent on race issues, espousing an overly benign view of white settler societies. Fisher's handling of race questions certainly attracted criticism from Collins and Huddleston. He was led into a series of heated exchanges with the former after he observed when discussing Nyasaland that 'All men are equal within the love of God but not within the sight of God', in which Fisher berated the canon for 'stupidly' thinking 'that I was in some kind of way arguing for a white supremacy in Africa ... [when] it was trust and confidence between all that I was preaching'.[100] Huddleston criticised Fisher for what he saw as his gradualist approach to reform: he was 'in spirit, a headmaster' who 'does not easily take any questioning of established authority, his own or anyone else's'.[101]

This judgement chimed with criticisms of Fisher in the domestic sphere, where the archbishop was seen as excluding radicals from appointments and maintaining a 'monochrome' episcopate.[102]

V

These examples illustrate the ambiguity of Fisher's contribution. He oversaw the church's own African 'transfers of power', absorbing and referring to a British political discourse, as well as being motivated, more pragmatically, by a concern to reduce Canterbury's direct responsibilities for the African dioceses. He engaged extensively with a variety of colonial political questions in ways that not only drew on information channelled via missionary as well as diocesan structures, but that also reflected the particularities of his own personality and his position as head of the established church. In relation to imperial and colonial policy, Fisher appeared caught between two, sometimes contradictory, impulses: deference to state authority, on the one hand, and, on the other, Fisher's own sense of morality and Christian public conscience. By the mid-1950s, as evidence continued to emerge of the state's failure to deal with abuses by the security forces in Kenya and of examples of colonial repression elsewhere, the balance between these conflicting dynamics shifted and Fisher seems more openly to have embraced the role of 'nation's conscience', a position he then assumed less equivocally still during the Suez crisis, when British actions not only ran counter to Fisher's own firm commitment to the United Nations, but also fuelled his ongoing anxieties about the British government and use of force.

For all Fisher's natural inclination to defer to authority and his dislike of open conflict, colonial Africa in the 1950s became one source among several others on the domestic front of friction between Fisher as primate of the Church of England and the British state (tensions that were to take on sharper dimensions over Cyprus and Makarios in 1958). Here we have, then, another example (arguably one underexplored in recent imperial historiography) of a metropolitan impact of the colonial empire. Moreover, although Fisher's extensive involvement in colonial affairs (and there has been space in this essay to comment only on a couple of examples) does not lend itself to easy generalisation, it does highlight two further points. The first is that, while we must be wary of treating religious institutions within the same analytical framework as political or other secular organisations, there are intriguing parallels between the disengagement the church undertook and that of the British imperial state and other organisations operating in the colonies. Second, whatever the lasting significance of Fisher's interventions in colonial political questions, they serve as another illustration of the extent to which a variety of British individuals, agencies and institutions engaged with the process of British decolonisation.

Notes

[1] Porter, *Religion*, 13. For an introduction to some of the research on missions and decolonisation, see, Stanley, *Missions*; Maxwell, 'Decolonization'. See Stuart, 'Race', as one example of research on this theme.
[2] Porter, 'War, Colonialism and the British Experience'.
[3] Porter, 'Universities Mission'.
[4] It is impossible here to cite all the work in which it makes an appearance, but there is especially useful discussion in Stuart, 'Race'; Howell, 'Church and State'; Ward, 'Church of Uganda'.
[5] See, e.g., Gifford, *African Christianity*; *Christian Churches*.
[6] Elkins, *Britain's Gulag*, 280.
[7] Holland, *Britain and the Revolt in Cyprus*, 123.
[8] For more on these processes see, Sachs, *Transformation of Anglicanism*, 192–7, 201–05, 299–300.
[9] On Warren, see Stuart in this volume.
[10] Stuart, 'Race', 14, 59, 63.
[11] See Burns, 'Authority of the Church', 198–99. Grimley, *Citizenship*; Green, 'Survival and Autonomy'; Williamson, 'Doctrinal Politics'.
[12] Of the three biographies – Carpenter, *Archbishop Fisher*; Purcell, *Fisher*; Hein, *Geoffrey Fisher* – the first by Carpenter is the most substantial and also devotes the most space to Fisher and colonial Africa, but it addresses different agendas from those considered in this article and is also (because written before Fisher's papers were catalogued) entirely unfootnoted.
[13] Purcell, *Fisher*, 20, 27–30, 58.
[14] Fisher to Mrs Eaden, 11 Feb. 1960, Fisher Papers, Lambeth Palace Library, Fisher 246, f. 77.
[15] At St Peter's Church, Ibadan, 27 Sept. 1960. See Fisher 250, ff. 62–117.
[16] Purcell, *Fisher*, 22.
[17] Jacob, *Making of the Anglican Church*, 301.
[18] See Fisher 269, f. 142; Fisher 119, ff. 180–87.
[19] Fisher to Bishop of Mashonaland, 27 May 1959, Fisher 225, f. 132.
[20] For example, Fisher, 19 Feb. 1959, *Parliamentary Debates*, Lords, vol. 214, cols. 393–95, 408, 419.
[21] Fisher, 11 April 1957, Lords, 202, cols. 1260–63.
[22] Fisher, 25 July 1956, Lords, 199, cols. 221–25, 25 July 1956.
[23] As referred to in debate 25 July 1956. Ibid.
[24] Warren, *Crowded Canvas*, 166.
[25] Neill, *Anglicanism*, provides a brief overview, useful for contextualising the post-war changes. Sachs, *Transformation*, and Jacob, *Making of the Anglican Church*, are largely concerned with the earlier period, while Welsby, *History of the Church of England*, also only touches upon the subject.
[26] Jacob, *Making of the Anglican Church*, 270.
[27] Purcell, *Fisher*, 225.
[28] Ibid., 266–67.
[29] Stanley, *History of the Baptist Missionary Society*, 366–68; for Methodists, see Beetham, *Christianity*, 25–26.
[30] Hastings, *History of African Christianity*, 112–13.
[31] See, e.g., cutting from *East African Standard* reporting the creation of an East African Catholic hierarchy, in Fisher 133, f. 67.
[32] See, e.g., Clark, 'CMS and Mission in Britain', 326.
[33] Purcell, *Fisher*, 125.
[34] Warren, *Crowded Canvas*, 169–70.
[35] Webster, 'Fisher'.
[36] See e.g., correspondence over future of Mengo Hospital, Uganda, 1958, Fisher 201, ff. 217–45; See also Purcell, *Fisher*, 125.
[37] Fisher to Bishop of Lagos, 25 June 1949, Fisher 60, ff. 370–79, esp. f. 371.

[38] As the Bishop of Uganda noted: Bishop of Uganda to Fisher, 3 Dec. 1953, Fisher 133, f. 87.
[39] Fisher to Bishop of Upper Nile, 16 May 1960, Fisher 253, ff. 110–11.
[40] Memo on Theological Training Courses in the Dioceses of Uganda and the Upper Nile, sent by Warren to Fisher, 27 July 1953, Fisher 133, ff.145–48.
[41] Letter to Fisher 24 July 1959, Fisher 231, f. 145; see also, Bishop of Uganda to Fisher, 3 Feb. 1951, Fisher 93, ff. 38–40.
[42] Porter, 'Universities Mission', 84, 100–01.
[43] Bishop of Uganda to Fisher, 8 April 1957, Fisher 194, f. 8.
[44] Bishop of Uganda to Fisher, 28 Aug. 1959, Fisher 231, f. 107.
[45] See, e.g., Fisher 82, ff. 233–34, 249–51; Fisher 95, ff. 250–51, 306, 311.
[46] Fisher to Bishop of Mombasa, 1 Feb. 1960, Fisher 240, ff. 304–09; Bishop of Mombasa to Fisher 9 Feb 1960, Fisher 249, ff. 197–200; Fisher to Bishop of Mauritius 15 June 1960, f. 217; Bishop of Madagascar to Fisher 18 Oct. 1960, Fisher 248, ff. 158–63.
[47] I am struck by these having come to this having worked on business strategies for decolonisation. Stockwell, *Business*.
[48] Hastings, *History of African Christianity*, 112.
[49] Fisher to the Bishop of Uganda, 5 Aug. 1959, Fisher 231, ff. 104–05.
[50] Fisher to Ken Sharpe (Diocesan Secretary, Diocese Upper Nile), 17 May 1960, Fisher 253, ff. 113–15.
[51] Purcell, *Fisher*, 251–57.
[52] Fisher to Haley (editor), 13 Feb. 1956, Fisher 182, f. 25.
[53] Fisher speaking on visit to East Africa 1961 and sermon at inauguration of Uganda Province, 16 April 1961, Fisher 269, ff. 4–5, 56–63.
[54] See Shepherd, *Macleod*, 151.
[55] Draft article and Fisher to Stopford, 10 Feb. 1951, Fisher 93, ff. 133–39, 144.
[56] Draft press release on Fisher's visit to East Africa, Fisher 241, ff. 19–21. One might speculate, however, whether in the East African case this was tactical and designed to detach the initiative from the politics of the UMCA and the CMS.
[57] Ward, 'Church of Uganda'; Howell, 'Church and State'.
[58] Low, *Buganda*, 106–12.
[59] Fisher to Stuart, 17 Aug. 1951, Fisher 93, f. 74; Fisher to Bishop of Uganda, 6 July 1953, Fisher 133, ff. 77–78.
[60] Bishop of Uganda to Fisher, 3 Dec. 1953, Fisher 133, f. 87; Warren to Fisher, 6 May 1954, Fisher 150, ff. 207–08.
[61] Ward, 'Church of Uganda', 413, 415, 429; Howell, 'Church and State', 210.
[62] Fisher to Lyttelton, 6 Jan 1954 and Fisher to Lyttelton, 15 Feb. 1954, Fisher 150, ff. 20–21, 122.
[63] Fisher to Kabaka, 22 Dec. 1953, Fisher 133, ff. 121–22; see also Fisher 150, ff. 89–91.
[64] Sir A. Cohen to Sir T. Lloyd 12 Jan 1954, CO 822/892, no 8, reproduced in Goldsworthy, *Conservative Government*, II, doc. 295.
[65] Fisher to Lennox-Boyd, 23 Oct. 1954, Fisher 150, ff. 269–72.
[66] Fisher to Macleod, 28 Oct. 1960, Fisher 257, ff. 194–95; Fisher to Macleod, 24 Feb. 1961, Fisher 268, ff. 190–93.
[67] Draft letter 15 Nov.1960, ibid, ff. 209–15.
[68] Fisher to Katikiro, 22 Nov. 1960, ibid, ff. 222–23.
[69] See correspondence between Fisher, Munster and Macleod, ibid., 190–93, 197–98, 231–32, 241–43.
[70] Macleod to Fisher, 16 March 1961, ibid, ff. 199–202.
[71] Darwin, *Britain and Decolonisation*, 260.
[72] Elkins, *Britain's Gulag*, 299; Stuart, 'Race', 195, 203–04.
[73] Bishop of Mombasa to Fisher 4 Dec. 1953, Fisher 127, ff. 259–69.
[74] 'Memo from the Church Leaders to HE the Governor of Kenya', undated but Jan. 1955, Fisher 158, f. 57.

[75] Elkins, *Britain's Gulag*, 91–92; Anderson, *Histories*, 309–10.
[76] Bewes to Fisher, 12 Feb. 1953 and Bewes to Fisher, 25 Feb. 1953, Fisher 127, ff. 209, 219–20.
[77] Fisher to Miss Hobart-Hampden, 15 Sept 1953, Fisher 127, f. 232.
[78] Fisher to Bishop of Chichester, 25 Nov. 1953, ibid., f. 255. On Hiroshima and Nagasaki, see Carpenter, *Archbishop Fisher*, 373–77; for the death penalty, Hein, *Geoffrey Fisher*, 85.
[79] Memo on conversation with Bishop of Mombasa, 2 April 1954, Fisher 159, ff. 310–15.
[80] Fisher to Bishop of Chichester, 25 Nov. 1953, Fisher 127, f. 255.
[81] Fisher to Philips, 10 Feb. 1955, Fisher 158, f. 65.
[82] Fisher, 10 Feb, 1955, Lords, 190, cols, 1143–48.
[83] Fisher to Baring, 19 Oct. 1957, Fisher 189, ff. 84–85.
[84] On missionary reactions to the CAF, see Stuart, 'Race' and 'Scottish Missionaries'.
[85] 4 Nov. 1952; see also letter from Bishop of Northern Rhodesia, 11 Oct. 1952, Fisher 95, ff. 302, 255–57.
[86] Fisher to Swinton, 12 March 1953, Fisher 95, f. 243.
[87] Notes for a letter to Welensky, Sept 1961, Fisher 278, ff. 156–57.
[88] See, e.g., correspondence from Macleod and Renison to Fisher, 24 April and 8 May 1961 concerning Fisher's attempt to expedite Kenyatta's release, Fisher 265, ff. 61–63.
[89] Macleod to Fisher, 9 Oct. 1961, Fisher 278, f. 141.
[90] A. Kalule Sempa to Fisher, 22 March 1954, Fisher 150, f. 181.
[91] Howell, 'Church and State', 207–09.
[92] Fisher to MacLeod, 22 April 1961, Fisher 268, f. 231.
[93] Fisher to Carey, 8 April 1953, Fisher 120, f. 79.
[94] Fisher to Kenneth Slack, 29 Jan 1958, Fisher 200, f. 292.
[95] Fisher, 28 March 1960, Lords, 222, cols. 342–47, 351.
[96] Fisher to Bishop of Mashonaland, 27 May 1959, Fisher 225, f. 132.
[97] Fisher to Archbishop of York, 21 March 1959, Fisher 215, f. 130.
[98] Fisher, 7 March 1961, Lords, 229, col. 378.
[99] Fisher to Archbishop Central Africa, 3 Oct. 1958, Fisher 200, f. 338.
[100] Fisher to Collins, 3 Nov. 1955, Fisher 154, ff. 345–46. For Collins's account, see Collins, *Faith Under Fire*, 218–21.
[101] Ibid., 219.
[102] Webster, 'Fisher'.

References

Anderson, David. *Histories of the Hanged: Britain's Dirty War in Kenya and the End of Empire*. London: Weidenfeld & Nicolson, 2005.
Beetham, T. A. *Christianity and the New Africa*. London: Pall Mall Press, 1967.
Burns, Arthur. 'The Authority of the Church'. In *Liberty and Authority in Victorian Britain*, edited by P. Mandler. Oxford: Oxford University Press, 2006.
Carpenter, Edward. *Archbishop Fisher: His Life and Times*. Norwich: The Canterbury Press, 1991.
Clark, John. 'CMS and Mission in Britain: The Evolution of a Policy'. In *The Church Mission Society and World Christianity 1799–1999*, edited by K. Ward and B. Stanley. Grand Rapids, MI and Richmond: Eerdmans, 2001.
Collins, Canon L. John. *Faith under Fire*. London: Leslie Frewin, 1966.
Darwin, John. *Britain and Decolonisation: The Retreat from Empire in the Post-War World*. Basingstoke: Macmillan, 1988.
Elkins, Caroline. *Britain's Gulag: The Brutal End of Empire in Kenya*. London: Cape, 2005.
Gifford, Paul , ed. *Christian Churches and the Democratisation of Africa*. Leiden: Brill, 1995.
———. *African Christianity: Its Public Role*. London: Hurst, 1998.

Goldsworthy, David. *British Documents on the End of Empire: Series A*, Vol. 3, *The Conservative Government and the End of Empire 1951–1957*. London: The Stationery Office, 2000.

Green, Simon. 'Survival and Autonomy: On the Strange Fortunes and Peculiar Legacy of Ecclesiastical Establishment in the Modern British State, c. 1920 to the Present Day'. In *The Boundaries of the State in Modern Britain*, edited by S.S.D. Green and R. Whiting. Cambridge: Cambridge University Press, 1996.

Grimley, Matthew. *Citizenship, Community and the Church of England: Liberal Anglican Theories of the State between the Wars*. Oxford: Oxford University Press, 2006.

Hastings, Adrian. *A History of African Christianity 1950–1975*. Cambridge: Cambridge University Press, 1979.

Hein, David. *Geoffrey Fisher. Archbishop of Canterbury 1945–1961*. Princeton, NJ: Princeton Theological Monograph Series, 2007.

Holland, Robert. *Britain and the Revolt in Cyprus*. Oxford: Oxford University Press, 1998.

Howell, Caroline. 'Church and State in Crisis: The Deposition of the Kabaka of Buganda, 1953–1955'. In *Missions, Nationalism and the End of Empire*, edited by B. Stanley. Grand Rapids, MI and Cambridge: Eerdmans, 2003.

Jacob, William M. *The Making of the Anglican Church Worldwide*. London: SPCK, 1997.

Low, Donald. *Buganda in Modern History*. London: Weidenfeld & Nicolson, 1971.

Maxwell, David. 'Decolonization'. In *Missions and Empire*, edited by N. Etherington. Oxford: Oxford University Press, 2005.

Neill, Stephen. *Anglicanism*. 4th edited. Oxford: Oxford University Press, 1977.

Porter, Andrew. 'War, Colonialism and the British Experience: The Redefinition of Christian Missionary Policy, 1938–1952'. *Kirkliches Zeitgeschichte* 5, no. 2 (1992): 269–88.

———. 'The Universities Mission to Central Africa: Anglo-Catholicism and the Twentieth-Century Colonial Encounter'. In *Missions, Nationalism and the End of Empire*, edited by B. Stanley. Grand Rapids, MI and Cambridge: Eerdmans, 2003.

———. *Religion versus Empire: British Protestant Missionaries and Overseas Expansion, 1700–1914*. Manchester: Manchester University Press, 2004.

Purcell, William. *Fisher of Lambeth: A Portrait from Life*. London: Hodder & Stoughton, 1969.

Sachs, William L. *The Transformation of Anglicanism: From State Church to Global Communion*. Cambridge: Cambridge University Press, 1993.

Shepherd, Robert. *Iain Macleod*. London: Pimlico, 1994.

Stanley, Brian. *The History of the Baptist Missionary Society, 1792–1992*. Edinburgh: T. & T. Clark, 1992.

———, ed. *Missions, Nationalism and the End of Empire*. Grand Rapids, MI and Cambridge: Eerdmans, 2003.

Stockwell, Sarah. *The Business of Decolonisation: British Business Strategies in the Gold Coast*. Oxford: Oxford University Press, 2000.

Stuart, John. 'Race Politics and Evangelisation: British Protestant Missionaries and African Colonial Affairs, 1940–1963, PhD diss., University of London, 2003.

———. 'Scottish Missionaries and the End of Empire: The Case of Nyasaland'. *Historical Research* 76 (2003): 411–30.

Ward, Kevin. 'The Church of Uganda and the Exile of Kabaka Mutesa II, 1953–55'. *Journal of Religion in Africa* 28, no. 4 (1998): 411–49.

Warren, Max. *This Crowded Canvas: Some Experiences of a Life-Time*. London: Hodder & Stoughton, 1974.

Webster, Alan. 'Fisher, Geoffrey Francis, Baron Fisher of Lambeth (1887–1972)'. In *Oxford Dictionary of National Biography*. Oxford: Oxford University Press, 2004. Available at www.oxford.dnb.com [accessed 11 June 2008].

Welsby, Paul. *A History of the Church of England 1945–1980*. Oxford: Oxford University Press, 1984.

Williamson, Philip. 'The Doctrinal Politics of Stanley Baldwin'. In *Public and Private Doctrine: Essays in British History Presented to Maurice Cowling*, edited by M. Bentley. Cambridge: Cambridge University Press, 1993.

Index

Page numbers in *Italics* represent Tables

Aborigines' Protection Society 25
Accra: riots 152
Act of Union 31
Adams, John 7, 15, 16
Adams, Revd J.E. 101
Aden 76
Advice to Afghans: (Ahmad) 82
Advisory Committee on the Welfare of Colonial Peoples 147
Afghan embassy: London 77
Afghan War: Second 80
Afghanistan: boundary with British India 78; stability 77
Afghanistan North-West frontier 75, 78, 89
Africa 125; appointment of bishops 203; British policy 135; church 184; colonies 30; conditions 33; criticism of missions 193; custom 135; educated elites 23; education 183, 184; enslaved 12; Freemasonry 131; historians 133; historical studies 131; ideology 137; Kings and Chiefs 137; legal systems 135; medical care 183; misunderstood 132; origin 24; pay 97; radicals in 30; Roman Catholic Church 204; scholars 136; scramble for 43; self-supporting church 101; southern colonies 25; students in Britain 148; sympathy for 132; voluntary associations 131; west 25, 31
African Association 31
African Bureau 211
African Church 194
African-British writers 27
Afridi 79, 83; uprising 85
Afrikaner influence 166
Agbebi, Pastor Mojola 101
Aggrey House 145
Ahmad, Rafiüddin 82; *Advice to Afghans* 82; *Inducement for a Holy War* 82; *Rectification of the Faith* 82
aid agencies 193
Akan 139; bureaucracy 134; historiography 135; law 138; society 136
Akan Laws and Customs: (Danquah) 139

Akbar, Mullah Sayed 80
Akim Abuakwa Handbook: (Danquah) 139
Alexander I, Tsar 44
All Blacks rugby tour 119
amakholwa 32
America: emigration to 16; north 6; nuclear planning 166; rivalry with Britain 176; uranium consumption 171; uranium needs 169, 173; uranium supplies 166; uranium as top military priority 170
American Ambassador: in London 15
American bishops: consecration 13
American Board of Commissioners for Foreign Missions 68, 94
American Methodist Episcopal Church: Lucknow 99
American Presbyterian Church: Hoshiarpur 102
American Revolution: supporters of 10
Amery, Leopold 113
Ancient Law: (Maine) 139
Anderson, David 183
Anderson, Rufus 93-4
Anglican Church 61
Anglican Church Missionary Society 61
Anglican Congress 188
Anglican Universities' Mission to Central Africa 201
Anglicanism: in Buganda 207; Uganda 204
Anglicans 6; American 12, 13; New England 10
Anglo-Corsican Union 42
Anglo-Egyptian relationship 43
Anglo-Hellenic relationship 43, 52
Anglo-Indians 58
Anti-Slavery Society 146
Anzac Corps 111
Appiah, Joseph 156
Archbishop of Canterbury 13; authority of 204
Arhin, Professor Kwame 139
Arians 15
Arminians 15
Asante 133; bureaucratization 133
Ashanti: law 138
Asia: church 184
Asian Christians 105

Asquith, Sir Cyril 147
Association of British Malaya 153
Athens: Ministry of Education 51
Athi River detention camp 188
Atlas of Overseas British Expansion 2
Atlee, Clement 167
atom bomb test: Soviet Union 179
atomic energy 172
Atomic Energy Authority 176
Atomic Energy Division 169
Atta, Nana Sir Ofori 137
Auckland University 121
Australia 111; nuclear testing 172; uranium 172, 173, 175
Austria 44

Baganda 134
Bajaur 79
Bajauris 77
Baker, Maurice 156
Balkan crises 46
Balkan states 52
Baluchistan 78; railway 77
Bankole-Bright, Herbert 145
Bantu Education Act 187
Baptist Missionary Society 61; in the Congo 204
Baptists 6, 17; English 7; New England 7, 16
Batang Kali 153
Battle of Messines (1917) 110
Battle of the Nile 42
Baylis, Rev. Frederick 95
Beecher, Leonard 185, 192; Bishop of Mombasa 187; evangelical task force 186
The Beecher Report 185
Belfast Ropeworks 124
Belgian Congo 168
Belgium 110
Benares 68-9
Bengal 58
Bengali Christians 67
Bennett, Richard 123
Berlin Congress (1878) 52
Beveridge, William: *Voluntary Action* 184
Bevin, Ernest 167
Bewes, Canon Cecil 183, 210
Bibliography of Imperial: Colonial and Commonwealth History 1
Bishop of London 6, 12
bishops: English 13
Bismarck, Count 46
Black Britons 26, 28
black list: colonial students 153
Blantyre Mission 97
Boers 26; South Africa 83
Bradburn, Rev. Charles 67
Bristol: making of 132

Britain: colonial mining 175; colonial scholars 145; defence policy 165; degrees from 158; as home 27; nuclear weapons 171; rivalry with America 176; values 30
British African American Methodist 27
British Army 28
British Christians 6
British Communist Party 151
The British Council 155, 156, 157
British Council of Churches 201; Race Relations Group 188
British Dissenters 9
British Documents on the End of Empire 1
British Guiana 202
British identity 24, 28, 29
British Imperial Policy and Decolonization 3
British India 25; boundary with Afghanistan 78
British Nationality and Status of Aliens Act (1914) 34
The British Negro (Williams) 31
British West African Dependencies 31
Brockway, Fenner 183
Broken Hill: Rhodesia 169
Brown, Bishop Leslie 208
Brown, Callum 58
Buganda 207; Fisher, Archbishop Geoffrey 208; government of 212
Bunerwals 79

Cadbury Trust 189
Cairo 45; financial control 47
Calvinism 58
Calvinists 15
Cambridge Illustrated History of the British Empire 2
Cambridge Seven 67
Canada 12, 14, 58, 123, 125; uranium 170, 172
Canning, George 52
Canterbury: see of 200
Cape 32
cape Colony 31, 61
Cappe, Newcome 11
Caribbean: British 61; colonies 24; RAF volunteers 147
Carpenter, Edward 203
Casely-Hayford, Augustus 131, 135, 138; *Gold Coast Native Institutions* 136, 137, 139
Catholic: Africa 204; Church 61; enemies 10; majority 14; minority in Northern Ireland 117
Cavagnari, Major Sir Louis 76
Central African Federation 212; origins 176
Chamberlain, General Neville 88
Cheshunt 65
children 66
China: Christianity 94; church 100; Protestant Church 94

China Centenary Missionary Conference (1907) 95
China Inland Mission 64, 100
Chitral 78, 79, 82
chivalry 31
Christia 53
Christian: British 6, 60; conscience 214; family 63; Kenyan leaders 190; workers for Kenya 191
Christian Aid Week: Lacey, Janet 193
Christian Council: Kenya 187, 188
Christian Manifesto 94
church 4; constitutional development 96; and gender 59; native form 96; pay of workers 96
Church of England 6, 61; in America 12
The Church in the Mission Field 94
Church Missionary Society 94, 183, 190, 201; retrenchment programme 184
church policy: imperial policy link 205
Church of Scotland 7, 10, 15, 62; Popular Party 8, 17
Church, Sir Richard 53
Churchill, Winston 43, 49, 52, 80, 87, 166; nuclear policy of 174
class 57
clergy: training 99
Co-ordinating Council for Colonial Students' Affairs 150
Coates, Joseph Gordon 112, 117, 121, 126; on Maori and Pakeha 122; visit to Belfast 121; visit to Derry 121
Codrington, Admiral Sir Edward 44
Cold War 150, 170, 171
College of New Jersey: Princeton 7
colonial: colleges 8; nationalism 30; policy in 1950s 166; scholars in Britain 145; uranium policy 173; welfare legislation 184
Colonial Geological Service 174
Colonial Office 147, 154, 202; hostels 155; policies 151; welfare regime 155
colonial students: accommodation problems 149, 155; anti-colonialism 151; black list 153; communism 152; experiences 149; figures 148; monitoring by security services 150; political advancement 152; political engagement 151; political significance of 154; racial discrimination 155; trafficking 154; West Indian protest 155
colonialism: hostility to 132
colonies: and British business 189; higher education in 145; universities 145, 147
colour 23
Combined Development Agency 167; Mindola 174; secret deals for uranium 170; uranium contracts 171; uranium territory 167
Combined Development Trust 166

Comboni, Daniel 94
Commission II 94, 95; discipline 104; literature and theology 105; membership 104; questionnaire 100; training and employment of workers 104; warnings 103
Commonwealth: uranium expoloration 168-9; uranium sources 167
Commonwealth of Nations 26, 123
Commonwealth Relations Office 149
communists 150; influence of 152; propaganda 153
Company of Merchants 135
Congo: Belgian 168; uranium 172; uranium oxide in 168
Congregationalists 6, 9
Congress of Peoples Against Imperialism 151
consecration: of American bishops 13
Constantine I of Greece 49
Constantine II of Greece: exile 49
Constantinople 47, 81
copper 167
Corfu 44, 48; Town 46
Cosgrave, Premier William 123
Craig, Sir James 112, 123
Craigavon, Viscount 112, 113-14, 118, 123; in Christchurch 115; Greymouth speech 115; at Masterton 116; New Zealand tour 117; at Timaru 115; at Wellington Town Hall 116
Craigavon, Viscountess 113, 124
creole population: Freetown 24
Crete 44, 48, 81
Crimean War 28
The Crown 29
Currie, Donald 4
Curzon, Lord 89
Cyprus 50, 53, 207; Max Fisher 203; occupation of 46

Danish-Greek house 48
Danquah, Dr J.B. 139; *Akim Abuakwa Handbook* 139; *Akan Laws and Customs* 139
Davidson, C.F. 169
Deane, Major H.A. 82
Declaration of Independence 7
decolonisation 45, 165, 214; history of 200
defence policy: British 165
Delhi 102, 105
Derry: siege of 116
deterrence: Cold War policy 171
devolution: Fisher, Archbishop Geoffrey 204, 207
Dinuzulu, King 33
Dir 82
Dissenting denominations 7
divine providence 11
Don Pacifio affair 48

Dow, Lorenzo 17
Duff, Alexander 62, 70
Durand line 78; demarcation 82; problems with 86
Durand, Sir H. Mortimer 77, 78, 84

East Africa House 157
East African federation: minefield of 205
East African Students' Federation 156
East India Company 12, 61, 80
East and West Friendship Council 157
Edinburgh Commission 104
education: and Empire 145; English curriculum 29; feminine-centred 63; missionaries 62; promotion of 144
Education for Citizenship in Africa 185
Egypt 45, 49; 1882 campaign 51
Eisenhower, President D.D. 175
electricity: atomic energy 172
Elgin, Lord 79, 84
Elkins, Caroline 183
Elton, Geoffrey 132-3
emancipation 24
emigration: to America 16
Empire: and education 145
English East India Company 68
English language 27, 29
English law 24, 32
Enlai, Zhou 94
Episcopal Church of the United States 13-14
Etherington, Norman *Missions and Empire* 60
Ethiopianism 101
European Imperialism (Porter) 3, 4
European masterfulness 105
European Union 53
evangelicalism 17, 62, 66

fakir: mad 80; sartor 80
family: Christian 63
father 64; role of 59
federation 174; Rhodesia and Nyasaland 176
femininity: expectations of 57
Finlay, George 44, 52-3
First World War 66; memorials 110; Ulster and Irish in 111
Fisher, Archbishop Geoffrey: advocate of Imperial policy 211; on African issues 212; African travels 202; appointment of African bishops 203; bishop of Uganda 200; Buganda 208, 209; Christian conscience 214; colonial issues 202; constitution writing 203; criticism of colonial policy 207; criticism of Imperial policy 211; decolonisation 200, 206, 207; devolution 204, 207; early life 201; family 201; in Far East 203; interest in Cyprus 203; and Kabaka in Uganda 203; Kenyan brutality 210; Nyasaland 213; pragmatism of 200; promoting Africa 206; scepticism of 211; Uganda 213
Forbes, Prime Minister George W. 117, 124, 125, 126
Foreign Office: International Relations 153
Formosa 97, 100
fourth-self 106
France 52
Francis, Martin 70
Free Church 65
Freemasonry: history in west Africa 131
Freetown: creole population 24

Gallipoli 111, 112
Gandamak: Treaty of (1879) 76
Gandhi, M.K. 33
Gellner, Ernest 140
gender: and church 59
General Synod of Ulster 7
Gentlemanly Capitalism 4
George I, King: assassination 48, 49
George II, King of the Hellenes 43, 49
George, Lloyd 52
Germain, Lord G. 9
Ghana 134, 139
Gibbs, Sir Philip 111
Gibraltar 42
Gibson, Rev. Dr J. Campbell 95, 103, 106
Gladstone, William 53
Glasgow and Edinburgh Missionary Societies 61
Glücksberg dynasty 48
Godley, Sir Alexander 111
gold 167
Gold Coast 26, 134; anthropology 138; self-government 176; Students' Union 156; Supreme Court 137; upheaval in 152
Gold Coast Native Institutions: (Casely-Hayford) 136
goldbugs 3
Gordon, William 11
Graham, John 69
Granville, Lord 50
Great Awakening 7
Greater Britain 25
Greco-Turkish war 81
Greece: church 45; dependency of 43; foreign debt 46; rebellion against Ottoman rule 44
Greek state: establishment of 44
Greek-Cypriots 51
Grey, Sir Edward 43
Grimshaw, Patricia 68
Gupta, Professor Partha 166
Gurkhas 68

Habeous Corpus Act 26

Hackney 65
Hadda Mulla 80, 84, 87
haka 119
Hamilton, Lord George 79, 85
Hans Crescent Hostel 155, 157
Harding, Field-Marshall Sir John 51
Harrow 158
Hartland, E. Sidney 136
Harvard 7, 12, 145
Hellenic navy 48
Herat 77
Hertzog, Prime Minister J.B.M. 123
Highbury 65
higher education: in colonies 145
Hindu Kush 78
HMS Cambrian 47
HMS Madagascar 44
Hodgkin, Thomas 132
Holdich, Colonel 83
Holland, Harry 189
Hollis, Thomas 7
Holy Orthodox Russia 52
homo-eroticism 58
homo-social clubs 69
Horne, George 9
Hoshiarpur: American Presbyterian Church 102
hostels: Colonial Office 155; Hans Crescent Hostel 155, 157
human rights: and missions 183
humanitarians 25

The Imperial Horizons of British Protestant Missions 2
Imperial policy: advocacy by Fisher 211; church policy link 205; Fisher criticism 211
Independents 6
India 61, 62, 70, 106, 158; Christians 105; church 102; Mahomedan 80; Muslims 80; poverty 102; universities 145
Indian Mutiny (1857) 80
Inducement for a Holy War: (Ahmad) 82
Inglis, Charles 14
Institute of Historical Research 2
Institute of Race Relations 188
Inter-Church Aid 187
International Control Commission 47
International Missionary Counicl 189
International Relations: Foreign Office 153
International Students' House 156
International Union of Students 150
Ionian islands 44, 45, 46, 53
Ionian Protectorate 45, 46
Iraq 45
Ireland 26; national identity 112
Irish Catholics 111
Irish Free State 5
Irish News 116-17, 122

Irish Peace Tower 110
Islam 81; King of 82; menace of 80

Jacobites 14
Jamaica 25, 32; soldiers from 28
Japanese church 100
jihad 80, 88
Johnson, Wallace 34
Jones, Creech 151
Journal of Imperial and Commonwealth History 1

Kabaka: deportation 208
Kabul 76, 81
Kabul court 77
Kafirs of Kafiristan 77
Kafiristan 82
Kaggwa, Sir Apollo 137
Kakar, Hasan Kawim 88
Kalimpong 69
Kandahar 77
Kapodistrias, John 44
Katikiro 209
Kaunda, Kenneth 212
Kenya 30, 154; Christian Council 187, 188; Christian leaders 190; Christian workers for 191; Europeans in 185; independence 194; killings in camps 192; missions 184; missions in 182; nationalist agitation 188; police brutality 210; rehabilitation 192; volunteers 191
Kenya Appeal 190
Kenyatta, Jomo 154
Keswick Convention 69
Khan, Dost Mohammed 76
Khan, Ghulam Haidar 79, 83, 87
Khan of Nawagai 87
Khan, Yakub 76
Khyber Pass: Afridis 79; closed 86
Kikuyu 185, 186
King of England's Soldiers 28
King of Islam 82
King's College 2, 145
Kirkland, Rev. S. 12
Kitchener, Lord 47
Kiwi Imperialists 125
Knibb, William 27
Korea: Presbyterian Church 101
Korean War 170
Kumase: royal court 133
Kunar valley 85
Kurram valley 76
Kwadwo, Asantehene Osei 133

Lacey, Janet 187, 188, 191; Christian Aid Week 193; Kenya Appeal 190; Oversea Service 193

Lagos 158; bishop of 207; Native Baptist Church 101
Lambeth conferences 200
law: Akan 138; Ashanti 138; customary 137; native 136
Law, Sir Edward 47
League of Coloured Peoples 32, 35, 157
Leakey family 185
Lee, William 10
liberators: of slaves 24
Libermann, François 94
Lim, Hong Bee 152-3, 154
Lindsey, Theophilus 15
Lingtung: Presbyterian Church of England 95
Liverpool: making of 132; missionary conference (1860) 93
Lockhart, General Sir William 86
London Greek Committee 46
London Missionary Society 61, 64, 99
London University College 145
Longueval 111
Love, Robert 30
Lucknow: American Methodist Episcopal Church 99
Lutheran Church: Madras 103
Lynn, Martin 3
Lyttelton, Oliver 173, 210-11
Lytton, Lord 80

Macaharia, Rawson M. 154
Macaulay's Education Minute 25
Macedonia 50
McMahon Act 166, 173
Macmillian, Harold 166, 202
Macpherson, Sir John 151
mad fakir 80
Madagascar 205
Madras 102; Lutheran Church 103
Maine, Sir Henry: *Ancient Law* 139
Maitland, Sir Thomas 44
Makarios, Archbishop: deportation 200
Malakand agency 82
Malakand Field Force 87
Malakand Pass 79
Malaya 145-6; state of emergency in 152; students in Britain 148
Malaya Hall 157
Malayan Bulletin 153
Malayan Forum 152
Malayan Monitor 153
Malayan Students' Union 152, 156
Malone, Lieutenant-Colonel William 111
Malta 44
Mamunds 79, 87
Manchester University 145
Manding 139
Manhattan Project 166, 172

manliness 57; British 58
Mansfield Judgment (1772) 24, 27
Manual of Military Law 34
Manye, Charlotte 33
Maori 119, 122
marriage: mixed 149
Marshall, Sir James 137
masculine: constructions 56; identity 58
masculinity 60
Massey, W.F. 112, 113, 121, 125; big chief 119; exhibitions of Ulsteria 118; memorial in Northern Ireland 114; Ulster Visit **120**; visit to Northern Ireland 117
Masshonaland 213
Mau Mau 35, 183, 194, 202; defeat of 186; detainees 211; sympathisers 187; torture of 210
Mauritius 205
Mavrocordatos, Alexander 49
Mayo, Lord 80
The Mediterranean 42
Mediterranean strategy 52
Melbourne University 145
Memorandum of Obligation (1880) 76
Mesen 110
Messines 110
Methodist: Church of Japan 99; revival 8
Methodists 16, 17; American 14, 15
MI5 150, 153, 154; and West African Students Union 151
Middle Eastern policy 80
middle-class 57
Mindola: Combined Development Agency 174; uranium plant 174
Ministry of Education: Athens 51
Minorca 42
missionaries: American 6; applications 65; criticism of 183; dominance of 105; education 62; female 59, 70; fiscal transgressions 68; honour 68; insecurities 66; making of a male 63; male 59; money 66; orphanages 62; preaching 62; refuges 62; salaries 14; salary 69; sexuality 68; work 61-2
missionary associate: teachers 185
missions: African criticism 186, 193; children 64; education and medical care 183; family 66; funds 99; and human rights 183; Kenya 184; policy failure 104; spiritual imperialism 192; as a vocation 185; Warren view on 184
Missions and Empire (Etherington) 60
mixed marriage 149
mixed-race 58
Moffat family 64
Mohawks 12
Mohmand tribe 79
Mohmands 79, 85

Molema, Modiri 33
Monroe, Walter Stanley 121, 122
Moody, Harold 32, 35
Moral Rearmament Movement 188
Morant Bay rising 25
Moravian Brotherhood 61
Morgann, Maurice 26
Morrision, Rev. Stanley 187, 188, 191; Kenya Appeal 190
Morrison family 64
mortality figures 64
Moule, Handley 70
Mount Lycabettus 50
Mountbatten, Philip 49
Mqhayi, Samuel 31
Munster, Lord 156, 209
Muslims 53; outrage 76; rulers 76
Mutesa II, Kabaka 207, 208

Napoleon 43
Natal 31, 32, 103
National Congress of British West Africa 31
national identity: Irish and Ulstermen 112
national service 165
National Union of Students 150
Native Americans 6, 8; missions to 12
Native Baptist Church: Lagos 101
Native Life in South Africa (Plaatje) 33
Native United Political Associations: Transvaal 32
NATO: nuclear capability 166
Navarino 44
Nazerali, Abdul 156
New England: Anglicans 10; Baptists 7, 16; Puritans 6
New Zealand: Anzacs 111; economy 118; Irish migrants in 125; Memorial Park 110; national identity 111; and Northern Ireland 114; royal visits to 112
Nicholls, Bernard 182
Nicholson, Arthur: incident 50
Nicholson, Harold 50
Nicosia 51
Nigeria 62, 145, 146, 151, 158; church 206; independence 202; northern 76; union of churches 204; uranium 168, 173
Nigerian Students' Union 156
Nile: Battle of the 42
Nisbet, Charles 17
Nkrumah, Kwame 151
Nkwenkwe, Nontheta 34
Northern Ireland: Boundary Agreement (1925) 123; Catholic minority 117; economy 118; and New Zealand 114; relations with Irish Free State 114
Norwegian Missionary Society 68
Nova Scotia 14; bishop of 14

nuclear: civil programme 172; deterrent 165; power programme 172; testing in Australia 172; weapons for British 171
Nuffield Foundation 189
Nyasaland 97, 166; and Fisher 213
Nyasland: federation with Rhodesia 176

Observations on the Importance of the American Revolution and the Means of Making it a Benefit to the World (Price) 15
Onyinah, S.A. 156
Orakzais 79, 85
O'Regan, P.J. *The Triumph of Tyranny* 117
The Origins of the South African War: Joseph Chamberlain and the Diplomacy of Imperialism: (1859-99) (Porter) 3
Orissa 102
orphanages 62
Otago University 145
Otto, King of Hellenes 44, 48
Ottoman loan 53
Ottoman rule 48; Greek rebellion against 44
Over-Seas League 157
Oversea Service 189; founding of 183; Lacey, Janet 193
Overseas Appointment Bureau 186
Overseas Bishops of the Canterbury Jurisdiction 200
Oxford Committee for Famine Relief (OXFAM) 187
Oxford Dictionary of National Biography 2
The Oxford History of the British Empire 1, 2, 42, 60
Oyewole, M.A. 156

Pakeha 122
Palmerston, Viscount 48
Pan-African Conference: (1900) 31; Fifth 151
Pan-African Congress (1921) 33
Paris Peace Conference (1919) 50, 51
Passendale 111
passport: British 26
Pax Britannica 42
pay: Africa 97; Asia 97; church workers 96-8; Rajpur 97; rates of 105
Peace Corps 193
peri-professional 56
persecution 99
Peshawar 82
Peshwar 85
Philadelphia Convention 14
Piraeus 48
Plaatje, Sol *Native Life in South Africa* 33
politics: role of religion in 200
Popular Party of the Church of Scotland 8, 17
Porter, Andrew 70, 105-6, 199, 205; early career 1; Empire and education 144; *European*

Imperialism 3, 4; missionaries 3; *The Origins of the South African War: Joseph Chamberlain and the Diplomacy of Imperialism; (1859-99)* 3; protestant mission movement 60; *Religion versus Empire? British Protestant Missionaries and Overseas Expansion (1700-1914)* 3; *Victorian Shipping; Business and Imperial Policy* 4; on Warren 184
preachers: missionaries 62; supply 65
pregnancy: before marriage 68
Presbyterian Church 61; Korea 101
Presbyterian Church of England: Lingtung 95
Presbyterians 6, 9, 58; English 7; from Ulster 7; Scottish 15
Price, Richard, *Observations on the Importance of the American Revolution* 15
Priestley, Joseph 7
Princeton 16, 145
Protestant Church: in Communist China 94
Protestants 30; history of 5; relations between British and American 11
Public Debt Commission 47
Punjab 89
Punjab mission 102

Quakers 8, 9, 16, 187

race 23
Race Relations Group: British Council of Churches 188
racial: difference 23; discrimination 34; discrimination legislation 31; equality 24; essentialism 104
racialism: at university 146
Radium Hill 167, 172
Rahman Khan, Amir Abdur 75, 88; accession 76; first campaigns 77
Rahman, Tunku Abdul 145-6
The Raj Quartet (Scott) 146
Rajpur: pay 97
Randall, Thomas 9
Rational Dissent 10
Rational Dissenters 7, 15, 17; British 16
Rattray, Robert S. 134, 137, 138, 139
Razak, Abdul 152
Rectification of the Faith (Rafiüddin) 82
refuges: missionaries 62
regime change 76
rehabilitation: Kenya 192
religion 23; role in politics 200
Religion versus Empire? British Protestant Missionaries and Overseas Expansion (1700-1914) (Porter) 3
religious: vocation 64; voluntary activities 65
Rhode Island College 16
Rhodesia: Broken Hill 169; federation with Nyasaland 176; Northern and Southern 166; uranium for Britain 175; uranium disappointments 169; uranium potential 168
Robertson, Sir George 79
Roman Catholic *see* Catholic
Roosevelt, President F.D. 166
Royal Hellenic Forces 49
Royal Historical Society 2
Royal Navy 28, 47
Royal Ulster Constabulary 118
Rum Jungle 167, 172, 176
runaway slaves 24
Russia 44, 52, 76; invasion 88

St Kitts 31
salaries *see* pay
Salisbury, Lord 77, 80, 81
Salonica 47
Sarbah, John Mensah 135, 136, 137, 138
sartor fakir 80
Saunders, Brigadier Stephen: assassination of 43
Save the Children Fund 187
Scholes, Theophilus 34
Scotland 7
Scots 57; missions 57-8
Scott, Paul *The Raj Quartet* 146
The Scottish Society 12
Scullin, Prime Minister James 123
Seabury, Samuel 13
Seacole, Mary 28
Secker, Archbishop T. 6, 7, 8, 11
Second Afghan War 80
Second Great Awakening 17
Second World War: students 146
security services 150
self-support 100; Japan 100; priority 104; Uganda 101
self-theologising 106
Serbia 46, 51
Seven Years War 8, 25
sexual impropriety 67
sexuality 60; regulation of 58
Shabkadr: fort 79, 84
Shanghai Centenary Conference 103
Shantou 101, 106
Shanxi province 100
Sicily 44
Siege of Derry (1689) 116
Sierra Leone 27, 32, 61, 145
Sillitoe, Sir Percy 153
sipah salar 79, 83, 84, 87
Six Nations 6, 12
slave trade 16, 24, 25, 26, 27
Slessor, Mary 62
Society of Friends 187
Society of Peoples of African Origin 34

Society for the Propagation of the Gospel 6, 188
Socinians 15
Sog, Tiyo 30
Solanke, Ladpido 145
Somaliland 76
Somme 110, 112
Sorensen, Reginald 156
South Africa 28, 29, 31, 101, 123, 125; uranium 170, 171; war 31
Southern Baptist Convention 101
Soviet Union: atom bomb test 179
sports 30
Stanley, Oliver 147
Steel, Sir Christopher 170
Stephen, James 135
Stockwell, Sarah 167
Storks, Sir Henry 45
Studdert-Kennedy, Gerald 67
Student Volunteer Movement 69
Sudan 76
Suez 43, 207
Sukuna, Sir Lala 137
Sunday School 65
Swat 79, 80, 82
Swatis 79, 83
Sydney University 145

Tamil: Christian 102
teachers: missionary associate 185
Teacher's League 28
Telegu 103: Christians 102
Test and Corporation Acts 9
theology 3
Thompson, Dudley 156
three-self: ideal 93; strategy 95
three-self church: building 104
Toro Christians 205
Tosh, John 68
trafficking: colonial students 154
Training for Responsible Partnership Abroad 189
Transvaal 101; Native United Political Associations 32
Treaty of Vereeniging 32
Trevelyan, Mary 156
Trevor Reese Prize in Imperial and Commonwealth History 2-3
Trikoupes, Charilaos 49
Trinidad 157
Trinitarian 15
The Triumph of Tyranny (O'Regan) 117
Turkey 44, 46; entry to EU 54

Uganda: 1960 negotiations 212; Anglicanism 204; church devolution 206; and Fisher 213; independence 209; Mutesa's return 208; self-support 101; uranium 168
Ulster 7; Division 112; national identity 112; New 116
Ulster Union Council 123
Ulster Unionists 125
Union Jack 28, 51; as a political symbol 30
Unitarians 15
United Church of Christ: Japan 100
United Nations 183
Universalists 125
universities: across the Empire 145; India 145; racialism in 146
Universities Defence Group 2
uranium: Australia 172, 173, 175; Canada 170, 172; Combined Development Agency 170, 171; commonwealth sources 167; Congo 172; consumption in America 171; exploration in Commonwealth 168; Nigeria 168, 173; plant at Mindola 174; potential in Rhodesia 168; prospecting 167; rush 167; sources of 166; South Africa 170, 171; supplies and America 166, 170; Uganda 168

V Beach Landings 112
Valera, Eamon de 123
Venizelos, Prime Minister Eleutherios 43, 47, 49, 51
Venn, Henry 93-4, 106
Vereeniging: Treaty of 32
Victoria League 145, 157
Victoria, Queen 48
Victorian Shipping: Business and Imperial Policy (Porter) 4
Victorian society 70
Vischer, Hanns 145
vocation: mission as a 185; religious 64
voluntarism 184
voluntary: religious activities 65
Voluntary Action (Beveridge) 184
voluntary associations: Africa 131
Voluntary Service Overseas (VSO): origins 193
volunteers: Kenya 191

Wales 17
Warburton, Sir Robert 81
Ward, Sir Joseph 113, 117
Warren Baptist Association 11
Warren, Canon Max 183, 190, 192, 194, 201, 209; on missions 184; Porter on 184
Wellington, Duke of 44, 45
Wesley, Charles 68
Wesley, John 15, 18
Wesleyan Methodist Missionary Society 64
West African National Secretariat 151
West African Parliamentary Committee 147

West African Students' Union 145, 147, 156: and MI5 151
West Indian Students' Union 155, 156
West Indies 31; British 30, 32, 34; emancipation of slaves 27; student body in Britain 148; university colleges 147
Western Front 126
Weston, Major General Aylmer Hunter 112
White, Sir George 81
Whitehead, Bishop Alfred 102
Wilks, Ivor 133
Williams, Henry Sylvester 31; *The British Negro* 31
Williams, Prime Minister Eric: student 149
Windscale 172
Witherspoon, John 7, 16, 17

women: lives of 19th century 63; new 58; role of 59, 63
Workers' Educational Association 157
World Council of Churches 94
World Federation of Democratic Youth 150
World Missionary Conference: race 106
World Missionary Conference (1910) 94
World Peace Congress (1949) 150

Yale 145
Yaozong, Wu 94
YMCA 157
Yoruba 139
YWCA 157

Zulu 134, 139